Contemporary Research Methods and Data Analytics in the News Industry

William J. Gibbs
Duquesne University, USA

Joseph McKendrick
Independent Analyst and Columnist, USA

A volume in the Advances in Media, Entertainment, and the Arts (AMEA) Book Series

Information Science REFERENCE
An Imprint of IGI Global

Managing Director: Lindsay Johnston
Managing Editor: Austin DeMarco
Director of Intellectual Property & Contracts: Jan Travers
Acquisitions Editor: Kayla Wolfe
Development Editor: Brandon Carbaugh
Cover Design: Jason Mull

Published in the United States of America by
Information Science Reference (an imprint of IGI Global)
701 E. Chocolate Avenue
Hershey PA, USA 17033
Tel: 717-533-8845
Fax: 717-533-8661
E-mail: cust@igi-global.com
Web site: http://www.igi-global.com

Library of Congress Cataloging-in-Publication Data

Contemporary research methods and data analytics in the news industry / William J. Gibbs and Joseph McKendrick, editors.
pages cm
Includes bibliographical references and index.
ISBN 978-1-4666-8580-2 (hardcover) -- ISBN 978-1-4666-8581-9 (ebook) 1. Journalism--Research. 2. Data mining. I. Gibbs, William J., editor. II. McKendrick, Joseph, editor.
PN4784.R38C66 2015
070.4'3--dc23

2015012016

This book is published in the IGI Global book series Advances in Media, Entertainment, and the Arts (AMEA) (ISSN: Pending; eISSN: pending)

British Cataloguing in Publication Data
A Cataloguing in Publication record for this book is available from the British Library.

Advances in Media, Entertainment, and the Arts (AMEA) Book Series

Giuseppe Amoruso
Politecnico di Milano, Italy

ISSN: Pending
EISSN: pending

MISSION

Throughout time, technical and artistic cultures have integrated creative expression and innovation into industrial and craft processes. Art, entertainment and the media have provided means for societal self-expression and for economic and technical growth through creative processes.

The **Advances in Media, Entertainment, and the Arts (AMEA)** book series aims to explore current academic research in the field of artistic and design methodologies, applied arts, music, film, television, and news industries, as well as popular culture. Encompassing titles which focus on the latest research surrounding different design areas, services and strategies for communication and social innovation, cultural heritage, digital and print media, journalism, data visualization, gaming, design representation, television and film, as well as both the fine applied and performing arts, the AMEA book series is ideally suited for researchers, students, cultural theorists, and media professionals.

COVERAGE

- New Media Art
- Print Media
- Digital Heritage
- Communication Design
- Drawing
- Computer aided design and 3D Modelling
- Data Visualization
- Film & Television
- Music & Performing Arts
- Fine Arts

IGI Global is currently accepting manuscripts for publication within this series. To submit a proposal for a volume in this series, please contact our Acquisition Editors at Acquisitions@igi-global.com or visit: http://www.igi-global.com/publish/.

The Advances in Media, Entertainment, and the Arts (AMEA) Book Series (ISSN Pending) is published by IGI Global, 701 E. Chocolate Avenue, Hershey, PA 17033-1240, USA, www.igi-global.com. This series is composed of titles available for purchase individually; each title is edited to be contextually exclusive from any other title within the series. For pricing and ordering information please visit http://www.igi-global.com/book-series/advances-media-entertainment-arts/102257. Postmaster: Send all address changes to above address.

Titles in this Series

For a list of additional titles in this series, please visit: www.igi-global.com

Handbook of Research on Digital Media and Creative Technologies
Dew Harrison (University of Wolverhampton, UK)
Information Science Reference • copyright 2015 • 554pp • H/C (ISBN: 9781466682054) • US $310.00 (our price)

Handbook of Research on the Impact of Culture and Society on the Entertainment Industry
R. Gulay Ozturk (İstanbul Commerce University, Turkey)
Information Science Reference • copyright 2014 • 737pp • H/C (ISBN: 9781466661905) • US $345.00 (our price)

Table of Contents

Detailed Table of Contents

Media organizations deliver news services online employing various design techniques and technologies to make services useful, usable, and effective for news consumers. How people use news services, their perceptions of them, and how their design impacts the user experience (UX) is an important area of study. In this chapter, the authors examine service design, UX, and related research methodologies and their importance for online news. Additionally, they report on a study that examined how the type of news provider (TV versus newspaper) and associated services affected user behavior and perception of the user experience. Participants perceived news websites differently based on the type of news provider and their interactions with services differed based on type of provider. The findings have implication for the UX research, specifically UX related to online news.

This chapter describes the results of a study that compared a strongly market-oriented newsroom and a less market-oriented newsroom in terms of how they used web analytics in news work. Using ethnographic methods, the study finds that web analytics influenced editorial decisions in both newsrooms. However, the two newsrooms differed in the extent to which they used analytics and in their reasons for doing so. These differences are examined using the framework of market theory in news construction.

Things are changing dramatically within the publishing industry. However, news media itself isn't on the wane, as many pundits are stating. In this chapter, the author explores how the business model for media organizations is shifting away from print, and away from the "gateway" approach to journalism and content development, in which a few select articles are presented to audience by editors, writers and reporters. In its place, the new digital media model is creating a plethora of content from many different sources, oftentimes first-hand accounts, original sources, or commentary. In the process, rather than resulting in a dearth of news content, audiences have access to an often dizzying, overwhelming and potentially contradictory content. This is creating potentially new roles for news and publishing organizations, serving as sources of validation and aggregation of content. At the same time, the rise of digital media is providing consumers a far wider range of choices pushing media organizations to provide content more tailored to their audiences.

Section 2
Harnessing the Power of Data

This chapter examines the effects that Web 2.0 technologies have had on traditional news organizations and how those organizations have been forced to adapt their content style, speed of production, and distribution models. It specifically focuses on real-time analytics and how news organizations can utilize new opportunities presented by social media platforms and web usage mining to analyze their audience, the competition, and popular opinions. The chapter will explain in detail how a news organization can compile data from social media and web usage, gain insights from that data, and act upon those insights. To further examine real-time analytics, the chapter presents real examples from BostInno, an online news source, where real-time analytics affected content and distribution. To conclude, the authors will reflect on the impact real-time analytics has on the news industry and how it might affect it in the near future.

User data has become the foundation of many businesses. The ability to increase the breadth and depth of user data to analyze trends is now the roadmap for information companies – providing direction for new business, content strategy, print to digital shifts and overall retention and engagement. In this chapter, the author will explore user identity and the three key core data buckets – Profile, Activity, and Behavioral – that define how to decipher audience members and their 'user records.' The chapter will specifically showcase how user identity shapes editorial strategy, marketing messaging and drives revenue. It will look at the impact specific technologies are having on what data can be captured as well as the complexities around data capture in general – standardization, preservation, storage, relational data opportunities and data optimization.

Mining the natural language text of news content has great potential for academic researchers seeking to understand and visualize patterns and relationships buried within everyday news coverage and content. Mining news can help researchers across many disciplines understand the impact of news, biases in news coverage, and language usage. It can also help them detect unknown patterns in news coverage. However, researchers must understand the challenges of using news text for text-mining-based research. Many challenges are inherent in the news form, including the complexity of the news environment; changing patterns of news consumption and distribution; growing use of social media; and the use of visual and audio information. Additional challenges relate to determining if the news content is available in a digital format, access and license restriction on use of the news text, and how complete and completely searchable the news text really is. This chapter explores these challenges and the impact they may have on how researchers gain access to news text, and methodologies used.

Billions of social media users communicate via Web and mobile platforms. A variety of measurement tools may be used to advance research methodologies in the study of computer-mediated communication (CMC). Social networking sites (SNS), such as Twitter, allow researchers to conduct exploratory data scraping and create visual mapping of possible relationships between social network accounts. The nature of the visualization depends upon the number of accounts within the social network, the amount of communication activity, the direction of specific communication, the amplification of messages across the network and other factors. A major challenge of this research method is disclosure and verification of individuals operating online identities. Additionally, most free research tools fail to disclose algorithms for generating scores and ranks. The purpose of this chapter is to explain how individual position, or centrality, is one reflection among many in the measurement of social network influence.

In this chapter, context for understanding the phenomenon of "big data" and disruptive innovation is introduced relative to current changes affecting the future of the journalism industry. Perspective is provided on market forces and emerging technologies that now shape the demand for data journalism. Current best practices and strategies to analyze, scrape, personalize, visualize and map data are presented. Trends and resources to access data and effectively analyze information are outlined for journalists to use when researching and reporting online. Three contemporary case studies explore the day-to-day operations and decision-making processes of media organizations struggling to remain profitable; adapt to changing consumer demands and try to serve a new demographic that is increasingly global, wireless, mobile and socially networked.

This chapter outlines the trend toward research within news organizations based upon big data and the increasing emphasis of growth-oriented companies on promoting a positive and passionate User Experience (UX). It discusses the implications of digital research techniques developed by successful technology and consumer merchandising organizations, and links the 24/7 nature of digital research methodologies to the development of more user-responsive and successful news organizations. A journalistic organization that wants to grow in the digital age must revamp its operations to take advantage of the continuous big data research cycle. This means creating a feedback loop from the organization to the information consumer and back, viewing journalism as content to be shaped to the UX through constant modification and change based on growing sets of user behavior and preference data.

Preface

THE DATA IS THE MESSAGE!

The medium is the message. This is merely to say that the personal and social consequences of any medium - that is, of any extension of ourselves - result from the new scale that is introduced into our affairs by each extension of ourselves, or by any new technology. – Marshall McLuhan, 1964

When Marshall McLuhan wrote these words in his ground-breaking book, *Understanding Media: The Extensions of Man,* he posited that the medium through which content is delivered is as impactful on the social discourse as the content itself. In 1964, he was referring to the rise of television, as well as other forms of "media," even electricity and electric light bulbs, which reshapes messages and human association. McLuhan's words are just as applicable with the rise of today's online media. Digital media certainly represents powerful "extensions of ourselves" as well as powerful new influencers of human behavior.

There has never been a better time to be in the publishing business, or to be an editorial manager or professional. Print-based media has been rapidly receding, but it is being rapidly replaced by an explosion of digital media sites and services.

Many publications have been struggling in their efforts to move from print-based offerings to digital offerings. Monetizing digital venues to achieve the types of revenues once seen in the print world has been a challenge. Many editorial operations have been pared to the bone, or ceased print altogether.

The hometown newspaper of both co-editors of this book, *The Philadelphia Inquirer,* illustrates the pain of this transition. Up until 2011, the Pulitzer Prize-winning newspaper occupied a prominent, 18-story building near the center of the city. In late 2011, the newspaper, under new ownership, consolidated all its operations on a single floor of a nearby converted office building.

While it's painful to watch the newsroom of a highly respected newspaper shrink, it's important to note that this isn't the end of the story. The news and publishing business has been through many technology-instigated transitions before, starting with the proliferation of the printing press. With each wave, as McLuhan alluded to, the news media has extended our understanding and connectivity to each other, and the world around us. The same holds true for digital media. It could be argued, for example, that the proliferation of digital technologies is creating more journalists than ever before, as quick and easy access to global communications media has brought about "citizen journalists," who come from every walk of life.

At the same time, professional journalists themselves are reorienting their skills and capabilities to employ technology to better understand and engage with their audiences. Social media platforms – Facebook and Twitter being the leading examples – have become tools that have greatly expanded the abilities of journalists to reach newsmakers, verify facts, discover new leads, and interact with their audiences.

Opportunities across the publishing sector are multiplying, and there is a great deal of convergence taking place with other forms of media, including television broadcasting and social media. The interesting development seen with television broadcasting is the increasing overlap between electronic media and newspapers. Both media are converging on the web, taking very similar forms. TV news networks such as CNN and CBS are posting videos of their programs online, of course, but with it, are text-based narratives of their stories.

While TV networks post more written content, newspapers are increasingly getting involved in video presentations. Peruse the websites of *USA Today* or *The Wall Street Journal*, and you will find videos along with the text narrative. The bottom line is there is very little difference, if any at all, between the sites of TV networks and newspapers.

The gap between traditional print publishers and social media or information technology vendors is another area of interesting convergence. Print publishers are increasingly developing tools and platforms that serve to disseminate information to their targeted audiences. They are focused on building interactive communities of common interests, much in the manner of social media platforms such as Facebook or Twitter. A professional information publisher no longer simply churns out journals for its audiences; rather, it serves as an online information source.

For example, Penton, among the publishers profiled in this book, had acquired a digital media platform provider, effectively doubling its presence in the tech sector (Mickey, 2015). Not too long ago, Penton (formerly known as Penton Media), was known as a trade magazine publisher. The company announced its rebranding as an "information services business" in late 2014 (Mickey, 2014).

With such repurposing comes new types of opportunities for editorial professionals and managers who are willing to capitalize on the intersection of their informational-gathering and judgment skills with data-driven development. Across all types of media companies – from newspapers to television networks to professional B2B (Business-to-Business) publishers – a pronounced shift is underway.

The way content is delivered to audiences is changing dramatically as well. It wasn't too long ago that selecting editorial content was a very subjective process. That is, the writer and the editor made decisions about what to publish based on their personal experiences, and yes, personal biases. This is what determined the subject matter that appeared in documents.

In this book, we assembled the views of experts, and practitioners across the media industry and academia. The book is divided into three sections, reflecting the convergence of providing information and managing what is called "big data:"

1. Why editorial content is changing now, and what's driving the changes;
2. The definitions and applications of big data; and
3. The future of news and information gathering.

It's clear that technology has changed the way information is gathered, vetted, interpreted and disseminated. It's important to see this shift as a major shift in the business and information-delivery model. Initially, as publishers moved their content online, it simply was a digital replication of the same material appearing in print. (Some in the technology industry sarcastically referred to this type of content as "shovelware.") As time went on, though, many publishers began to recognize that online material had its own dynamic, and to some degree, even different sets of readers. Increasingly, online offerings began to diverge from what was appearing in print. Publishers recognized that the online world offered opportunities for rich interactions with their audiences, enabling two-way interactions with the posting of comments. Even editing became a possible crowdsourced activity, with the community of engaged readers alerting publishers to typos, grammatical errors, and even issues with the logic of articles appearing online.

Along with reader engagement, the online world began delivering an even more potent tool for publishers: data. As audiences interacted with digital interfaces, they left "digital exhaust" trails of their content preferences, the order in which they read pieces, whether or not they moved onto other works on the site or left altogether, and even the length of time spent reading the pieces.

There are several common themes that emerge within the points discussed by the authors participating in this book, impacting the jobs and roles of key parties involved in the creation and dissemination of content and the business model that supports this dissemination:

- *The practice of journalism is changing, away from selecting stories based on inherent biases to more data-driven processes.* The ability to gather data on the preferences and habits of readers is helping to shape the way content decisions are made. This information is increasingly becoming more readily available, due to the increased use of media organizations' own online channels, as well as social networks, which are highly open sources of data.
- *There's a convergence occurring between editorial content and advertising/marketing -- both rely on the same data-driven processes.* One of the tenets of journalism, especially in general newsrooms, is that there is a "wall" separating editorial from advertising. Data-driven content and new media are diminishing this wall -- for example, the business side of media concerned with generating traffic at their sites. To some degree, selling subscriptions has always been a factor in journalism, as editors have always had an eye toward what will captivate or draw the most readers, be they paying subscribers or targets of advertisers' campaigns. The question now, with traffic being measured to gauge interest in topics and how they are transferring to online adverting, is how much this may be affecting the "purity" and biases of content providers.
- *The big data trend is shaping both "traditional" general newsrooms and more specialized B2B media publishers.* The trend toward data-driven editorial isn't just being seen in newsrooms – it's seen among other types of content publishers as well. B2B media publishers, who engage with a more focused audience, are not only turning to data analytics to drive their content decisions, but in the process, changing the nature of their business models as well. No longer are these companies printing and distributing professional journals and books, but they have evolved into information hubs, and even technology companies to some degree. There is also a greater granularity to content, which is enabling audiences to select and assemble content on a subscription basis. Digital interfaces and the user experience (UX) have become a critical element in these offerings as well, as publishers seek to employ technology platforms to enable deeper experiences for information consumers. This new evolving channel is built on participation from consumers, and even dialogue with thought leaders within their professional or industry segments.
- *Journalists, editors and content providers on the editorial side and marketers and executives on the marketing side need to become more familiar with big data and its implications.* "Big data" can be defined as the four "Vs" – the rise of data in large volumes, at high velocity, in great varieties, and of significant value. There are tools and solutions – developed and refined in the marketing industry -- that now help capture, parse and measure these data. This should be part of every editorial decision.

ORGANIZATION OF THE BOOK

The book looks at these opportunities to reshape editorial professions and operations, as well as challenges presented, in multiple ways. The book is organized into 14 chapters. A brief description of each of the chapters follows:

Chapter 1 describes the early experiences of publishing organizations embracing the new online medium in the early days of the mid-1990s. Mike Dillon, Associate Professor of Journalism and Multimedia Arts at Duquesne University, asks how journalists and publishing organizations venturing online in this era planned and acted as they did in the areas of functionality, utility, design, marketing, anticipation of future trends and assessment of the online audience. Dillon provides an analysis of the salutatories journalists wrote for their inaugural online editions, noting how they tell a story not of what was happening, or what eventually happened, but of what people believed (or hoped) would happen based on what they believed was happening.

Chapter 2 details how the rise of big data as a device for gathering, writing and disseminating news is giving rise to a new area of expertise: "computational journalism." Lady Dhyana Ziegler, Garth C. Reeves Eminent Scholar, Chair of Journalism at Florida A&M University, explains how computational journalism combines journalism, computer science, and social science research. She points out that the standards of the profession cannot be lowered in a big data world, but serve as an enhancement of the overall news products.

Chapter 3 covers how the emergence of digital media and publishing – and the empowerment of end-users -- has resulted in a pressing need for rich, front-end experiences. This requires greater design thinking in the creation of content delivery products. William Gibbs, Associate Professor at Duquesne University and co-editor of this book and Ronan Bernas, Professor at the Department of Psychology of Eastern Illinois University, explain service and user experience (UX), in which the customer or user is central to building better services and systems critical to today's and tomorrow's digital media organization. Service and UX design precepts can prove valuable to news organizations as they continue to build and refine innovative interfaces to online news services. Gibbs and Bernas also report on the results of a study that examines instrumental (e.g., task efficiency, effectiveness, usability) and non-instrumental (e.g., like, trust, aesthetics) qualities of news interfaces for both newspaper sites and television sites.

Chapter 4 discusses how closely data or content should be deciphered, and its impact on editorial decisions. Patrick Ferrucci, Assistant Professor in the Department of Journalism, College of Media, Communication and Information at the University of Colorado-Boulder, and Edson C. Tandoc Jr., Assistant Professor at the Wee Kim Wee School of Communication and Information at Nanyang Technological University, compare a strongly market-oriented newsroom and a weakly market-oriented newsroom in terms of how they used web analytics in news work. Using ethnographic methods, the study finds that web analytics influenced editorial decisions in both newsrooms. However, the two newsrooms differed in the extent to which they used analytics and in their reasons for doing so.

Chapter 5 explains why the news media itself isn't on the wane, as many pundits are stating, but are evolving rapidly into new roles, tasked with new missions as sources of validation and aggregation of content. Joseph McKendrick, independent consultant, contributor to leading national business publications, and co-editor of this book, observes the rise of digital media is providing consumers a far wider range of choices pushing media organizations to provide content more tailored to their audiences.

Chapter 6 analyzes the tremendous impact of Web 2.0 technologies – social, mobile, cloud and big data -- on traditional news organizations, and how those organizations have been forced to adapt their content style, speed of production, and distribution models. Kyle Gibson, Web Analyst with BostInno, and Greg Gomer, Senior Vice President of BostInno, provide a profile on how BostInno, an online news source, has employed real-time analytics to shape their content and distribution.

Chapter 7 discusses how the ability to increase the breadth and depth of user data to analyze trends has become the roadmap for information services companies. Tricia Syed, Vice President of User Marketing and Marketing Analytics with Penton, describes strategies for the news business, content strategy, print to digital shifts and overall retention and engagement. Syed also showcases how user identity shapes editorial strategy, marketing messaging and drives revenue.

Chapter 8 describes how the natural language text of news content has great potential to provide understanding and visualization of patterns and relationships buried within everyday news coverage and content. Debora Cheney, Associate Director for Public Services and Librarian at the University at Albany, State University of New York, explains that text mining has the potential to help academic researchers across many disciplines understand the impact of news, to help understand biases in news coverage, and language usage.

Chapter 9 is a comprehensive overview of the variety of methodological approaches from which today's content providers and product teams can choose – based on either qualitative or quantitative research. Judith Durgin Pilla, an independent research analyst, and Louis Pilla, a publishing executive, review the various techniques available to digital media planners, providing descriptions of several qualitative and quantitative research approaches that are frequently used to inform publishing business decisions.

Chapter 10 discusses how data research plays a crucial role in understanding and improving the content consumer experience. Gregg Bernstein, Manager of Customer Research for MailChimp, and Laurissa Wolfram-Hvass, Researcher with MailChimp, provide a case study describing MailChimp's data collection, analysis, and communication methodologies.

Chapter 11 describes how social media has emerged as a powerful distribution method which changes the dynamic of media organizations' relationships with their audiences. Robert J. Baron, Assistant Professor of Communication at Austin Peay State University, suggests a method of rhetorical analysis that focuses less attention on the content of news productions and more attention on analyzing how audience members might make use of the news.

Chapter 12 reveals how the data coming out of social media also provides a wealth of information on content consumer trends. As explained by Jeremy Harris Lipschultz, Researcher and Professor, UNO Social Media Lab and School of Communication with the University of Nebraska at Omaha, a variety of measurement tools may be used to advance research methodologies in the study of computer-mediated communication. Social networking sites such as Twitter enable researchers to conduct exploratory data scraping and create visual mapping of possible relationships between social network accounts.

Chapter 13 highlights the importance of understanding the disruptive innovation of big data and how it is affecting the future of the journalism industry. Gordon J. Murray, Associate Professor of Journalism and Mass Communication at Kent State University provides perspective on market forces and emerging technologies that now shape the demand for data journalism.

Chapter 14 reviews one of the most essential components in today's digital media -- the user experience (UX). Stuart Schwartz, Professor of Communication Studies at Liberty University, calls for a "positive and passionate" UX. In addition, a journalistic organization that wants to grow in the digital age must revamp its operations to take advantage of the continuous big data research cycle, to create a continuous feedback loop.

Ultimately, digital media and data analytics are opening up new approaches to editorial delivery that have not even been considered. The previous methodologies of content development and delivery cannot simply be layered over online venues. As McLuhan (1964) stated in his seminal work, *Understanding Media: The Extensions of Man:* "For the 'message' of any medium or technology is the change of scale or pace or pattern that it introduces into human affairs. The railway did not introduce movement or transportation or wheel or road into human society, but it accelerated and enlarged the scale of previous human functions, creating totally new kinds of cities and new kinds of work and leisure. This happened whether the railway functioned in a tropical or a northern environment, and is quite independent of the freight or content of the railway medium. The airplane, on the other hand, by accelerating the rate of transportation, tends to dissolve the railway form of city, politics, and association, quite independently of what the airplane is used for." (p. 8)

Technology is a constant through the ongoing development of news media and publishing, but the current phase – in which organizations are discovering the richness of data now being captured – is changing the way information is delivered in an unprecedented fashion. We hope this book will help guide the way.

William J. Gibbs
Duquesne University, USA

Joseph E. McKendrick
Independent Consultant, USA

REFERENCES

McLuhan, M. (1964). *Understanding media: The extensions of man*. Cambridge, MA: MIT Press.

Mickey, B. (2014, November 11). Penton rebrands itself as information services business: Events, marketing services and digital are biggest revenue-makers. *Folio*. Retrieved January 23, 2015 http://www.foliomag.com/2014/penton-rebrands-itself-information-services-business/

Mickey, B. (2015, January 20). Penton scales tech portfolio with iNET acquisition, deal gives penton instant traction in tech market. *Folio*. Retrieved January 23, 2015 from http://www.foliomag.com/2015/penton-scales-tech-portfolio-inet-acquisition/

Introduction

THE MAKING OF THE DIGITAL PROVOCATEUR: HOW DATA, INTERACTION, AND DESIGN DRIVE TODAY'S AND TOMORROW'S CONTENT DECISIONS

For anyone living in the United States in the 1960s, the evening news was a defining moment toward the end of the day. Family members dutifully congregated by the television to watch and listen to luminaries such as Walter Cronkite, Harry Reasoner, and David Brinkley speak about important events in places that often seemed far away and foreign. The anchorman's presence and auditory imparted the seriousness and importance of world affairs, implying that everyone, even young children, should devote undivided attention. During commercial breaks and after the programs, people discussed the news. In families, children listened or questioned, "What is Vietnam?", "Who is JFK?," or "What do we mean by civil rights?" Many of those conversations and the questioning carried on for days, and ultimately had a profound impact on national policies. The most striking example of the impact of broadcast television news on the national psyche was CBS anchor Walter Cronkite's editorial following the communists' February 1968 Tet Offensive in Vietnam, in which he opined that a U.S. victory may be out of reach in Vietnam, and that a negotiated peace may be the only resolution to the conflict (Folkenflik, 2009). With the war and many other issues broadcasted over the evening news, people took positions, they extrapolated, expressed their views and ideas, and challenged others' views. For many people, the nightly news experience was communal, thought providing, engaging, controversial, and it engendered much discussion.

In times past, to access this world of news luminaries, one turned or pushed a switch on the television, chose a broadcast station from a limited number of channels (in many cases there were only three), and occasionally adjusted the "rabbit ears" antenna on top of the television to enhance reception. Aside from intermittent antenna adjustments, viewers' physical interactions with the television were discontinuous. People sat back, watched, and listened as news organizations delivered information on the events of the day to them. While television technologies seemed unwieldy and archaic by today's standards, what transpired in living rooms, restaurants, shops, and meeting places around the world was often a unique and captivating experience that, at times, carried over to the days subsequent to a news broadcasts. And yet, aside from what existed in public memory and dialogue, the broadcast itself was intangible and ephemeral. The news organization provided a service and people watch and listened, with little information exchanged or interaction taking place between the two.

Characteristics of these early media delivery forms (i.e., television, radio, newspapers, magazines, journals) embody and influence how online news is delivered to people and how people use and interact with today's media technologies. In the following section, the authors examine attributes of delivery media formats, specifically the amalgamation or separation of news and medium, and the relevance of human interaction both with the medium and the news organization. In the authors' view, an initial overview of these factors is important because they are foundational to and have implications for digital news media, user experience, and the study of big data and analytics.

BACKGROUND

In the 1960s, the television was a relatively new delivery format for the average news consumer. Television (and radio) sets were content neutral; they could receive an entertainment as well as news broadcast, for instance. News organizations were not involved in their design, which was left to product designers and engineers whose primary professional interest was not news. Television and radio were electrical devices with electromechanical parts with which people had to interface to get news. There were electromechanical controls – such as volume knobs – that enabled people to get news and control its attributes. Unlike newspapers, the physical properties of television and radio made for the partitioning of the news and the physical medium used to deliver it. To get news, people had to adjust to a new layer of complexity and learned how to operate the controls.

Despite the separation, someone who owned a television or radio starting in the 1950 and 1960s could look inside to see and feel the dials and other physical components, and if nothing else to make a mental connection between what controls looked like and how they functioned. This made it easier to understand how the controls worked. In years to come, news organizations would find this separation between news and medium even greater as they developed digital interfaces and new skeuomorphic modes of interaction, references to an earlier medium used as a metaphor (Gross, Bardzell, & Bardzell, 2014), so people could access, control, and traverse news in virtual spaces.

With digital interfaces, no such tangible connection exists between what controls look like and how they physically operate. Users' access to news depends more on how well the software or designer represents the functionality of the delivery medium at the interface. In fact, because that same physical connection does not exist in digital interfaces, designers use concepts from previous familiar media to help people understand how to operate the interface. For instance, most people who use news websites are familiar with the video *Play* icon (large arrow pointing to the right) or an audio speaker icon to control sound volume. These icons have no real connection to how the digital interface actually works behind the scenes. Touching the *Play* icon on a digital interface, for example, does not start a magnetic tape moving in a rightward direction. However, because people are familiar with them or have learned about them from older technologies, interface designers use these concepts (e.g., large arrow point rightward) to help people to more easily understand the interface and how it works, which ultimately encourages people to return to a website.

This has significant implications for the work investment needed to design news interfaces (and positive user experiences) so that people understand them and their functionality. In some cases today, entire departments with teams of individuals are responsible for building digital interface controls so that news consumers can access the news and have a positive user experience.

As was the case with early television and radio, newspapers, magazines and journals brought news and information to people, delivered to homes, or purchased at newsstands. The periodical afforded a highly individualized experience, unlike television or radio that provided both individual and group experiences. The paper was a tangible material onto which a printer printed words and images. People interacted with it physically and there was more continuous physical interaction with it compared to a television or radio. The newspaper, magazine or journal was malleable, portable, and disposable. The news and content was inseparable from the physical paper on which it was printed and there was a direct connection between what a reader did with the paper and how it impacted the paper. When the reader folded the paper, he or she could see and feel the direct result of his or her actions on the newspaper. Moreover, the newspaper, as the title suggests, was a medium devoted to news. People used it for the primary purpose of getting the latest information on events within their communities, states, nations, or across the world. It was rarely used for assorted purposes such as the reading of a biography or works of fiction.

The conception of newspapers, magazines or journals encompasses the paper material and the printed word. These publications were not content neutral. Moreover, periodicals had been following an established design formula for hundreds of years, with relatively minor modifications, so people thought little about how the design of the publications themselves impacted how easy or difficult it was to get news and information. With newspapers, major stories were printed with large-typeface heads "above the fold," so they would be prominently displayed to catch the attention of readers. Magazines and tabloids highlighted major features prominently on their cover pages. People knew how to get information from the printed paper, as it was a familiar medium. And yet, while there may have been more direct and continuous interaction with periodicals (people touch them more than they did a television or radio), there was in this experience little exchanged or interaction taking place between publishing organizations and consumers.

Due to digital technologies, the Internet, and mobile connectivity, major changes are taking place today regarding how people get news. People interact more with various types of devices to get news and information. During these interactions, the content and physical medium are detached and mediated by a digital (virtual) interface, which often adds complexity to interactions and challenges to creating positive user experiences. A digital device is content neutral, as are television and radio. However, interaction is more regular and continuous - people touch it more for longer periods of time, not unlike a newspaper. Those points of contact (the interaction) at the interface and the technical capacity to record them have significant implications for journalists, user experience designers, editorial professionals and publishers seeking to interact with and better serve audiences by employing big data and analytics. They open up innumerable opportunities for ongoing interaction between publishing organizations and information consumers.

INTERACTION, BIG DATA, AND ANALYTICS

At a most fundamental level, technological advancement has incited more people than ever before to pick up and engage with technology. Their engagement with digital devices is more frequent and sustained over longer periods of time – more people are touching, speaking to, moving, looking at, clicking, gesturing, and interacting with digital technologies. At the same time, technologies now have the capacity to chronicle interaction events aggregated as data that can be studied. Streams of interaction data, despite how voluminous, can be amassed and analyzed regardless of the mode of interaction, the duration, frequency, or geographic location in which the interaction event occurred. As Chen, Chiang, and Storey (2012) indicate, at the beginning of the twenty-first century, Internet and web technologies (Web 1.0-type systems) presented unparalleled possibilities for data collection and measurement as businesses and organizations began interacting with customers one-to-one online. They further point out that user-generated content aggregated with Web 2.0-type systems (e.g., social media) made possible the compilation, measurement, and analysis of additional, novel types of data associated with textual information and less structured content and these data hold valuable insights into customer opinions and behavior; therefore aiding researchers in attending to and understanding the views and habits of their target audiences. This is important because due to the growth of digital technologies, mobile connectivity, the escalating effects of social media, and the overall increased usage of technology makes for a more informed and discerning consumer (Pain & Lively, 2013). If organizations ignore consumers' opinions and behaviors, consumers will seek comparable good and services elsewhere.

WHAT IS BIG DATA AND ANALYTICS?

The Internet has made information throughout the world and associated media accessible to any person on the planet with the touch of a button. Twenty-four hours a day, seven days a week, human connectivity through mobile and desktop devices is unparalleled. Unlike any other period in human history, people have the information of the world instantly accessible to them. Exponential growth of Internet, technology-enabled connectivity, and increased accessibility to information engender new opportunities for observing human behavior, data collection, and measurement (Google, 2014).

Sensor-equipped devices, mobile technologies, the *Internet of Things*, "the vast repository that we call the Web, user-generated content, social media, data generated and consumed on mobile platforms, and data from enterprise systems" (Goes, 2014, p. iv) allow for monitoring human behavior, location, emotion, and temporal patterns, among other things. Analyst, researchers, businesses, and organizations can now inquire about, explain and potentially predict human behavior patterns and trends using data compiled from sensor-equipped devices and the *Internet of Things* (Goes, 2014). As Chen, Chiang, and Storey (2012, p.1168) indicate,

Other sensor-based Internet-enabled devices equipped with radio-frequency identification RFID, barcodes, and radio tags (the "Internet of Things") are opening up exciting new steams of innovative applications. The ability of such mobile and Internet-enabled devices to support highly mobile, location-aware, person-centered, and context-relevant operations and transactions will continue to offer unique research challenges and opportunities throughout the 2010s. Mobile interface, visualization, and HCI (human–computer interaction) design are also promising research areas. Although the coming of the Web 3.0 (mobile and sensor-based) era seems certain, the underlying mobile analytics and location and context-aware techniques for collecting, processing, analyzing and visualizing such large scale and fluid mobile and sensor data are still unknown.

Ninety percent of the world's data today have been produced in the last two years from sources such as sensors used to collect and model weather conditions, social media, digital media, online purchases, and Global Positioning Signals (GPS) (IBM, 2014a). The sheer volume of data is a key factor instigating the title *Big Data*. There is a transformation in the scale of data and scope of the possible sources as well as means for managing those sources (Taylor, Schroeder, & Meyer, 2014). According to Goes (2014, p. vii), "Big data is about massive amounts of observational data, of different types, supporting different types of decisions and decision time frames."

Big data or the high volume data streams (often in real-time) being collected today are distinctive because of the following four "V"s (see Chen, Chiang, & Storey, 2012; Waller & Fawcett, 2013; Goes, 2014; Taylor, Schroeder, & Meyer, 2014): (a) the *volume* or scale of data – volume can mean more data and/or data are captured in more detail, or it can also be the large amounts of sentiment data that accumulate from social media, or opinion commentaries (Waller & Fawcett, 2013); (b) the *velocity* or real-time or almost real-time analysis of data that can be achieved, the big data world is moving toward real-time or close to real-time decision making (Goes, 2014, p. vii); (c) *variety* of data – data are being collected with various technologies (e.g., sensor-equipped devices, mobile devices) and from a variety of sources, (e.g., social media, tweets, identification, emotion detection, eye tracking, etc.); and (d) *veracity* or ensuring the quality of data because often the quality of captured data vary and analysis depends on the accuracy of source data. Some contend that another "V" should be *value*, that having access to large amounts of data is not useful unless they can be used to add value to the organization.

Einav and Levin (2014) point out three important characteristics of big data. First, data sources are frequently real-time accessible, which is advantageous for making observations about present conditions or predicting the present, commonly known as *nowcasting*. A second characteristic is data volume, as mentioned earlier. Among other things, large data sets help "...resolves the statistical problem of limited observations and makes analysis more powerful and potentially more accurate, while their granularity increases their power in terms of understanding individual actions" (Taylor, Schroeder, & Meyer, 2014, p. 2). Third, because the breadth of data sources and information has expanded, data are less structured. Now researchers have the capability to identify, observe, and measure an almost limitless collection of distinct behavioral attributes. Additionally, data sources enable the collection of data relating to certain attributes of human behavior (e.g., social relations, sentiment, geo-location, etc.) that were previously problematical to observe.

Analytics is or should be linked to decision making (Goes, 2014) based on the data collected. It is a domain of study that has materialized as a dynamic research area (Chen, Chiang, & Storey, 2012) that offers business and organizations opportunities for continual improvement using the aforementioned large data sets. Digital analytics employs sophisticated methodologies to these large and distinct data (big data) sets; some of those methods include predictive analytics, data mining, text mining, web analytics integrated statistics, opinion mining, social network analysis, spatial-temporal analysis, visualization, and summarization tools (Zhang, Chitkushev & Brusic, 2014). Kaushik (2010, p. 5) defines digital analytics as encompassing the following three elements:

(1) the analysis of qualitative and quantitative data from your website and the competition, (2) to drive a continual improvement of the online experience that your customers, and potential customers have, (3) which translates into your desired outcomes (online and offline).

Because of the ubiquity of digital technologies, people in today's society continuously interact with digital interfaces that mediate the exchange between human action and computing. At these points of contact or interfaces large amounts of data can and are being collected and these data (and related analytics) are shaping, among other things, publishing, news services, the news interfaces, the user experience, how news is gather and received, who participates in news making and news distribution.

THE NEXT MEDIA FRONTIER: DETECTING, RECORDING HUMAN-TECHNOLOGY INTERACTIONS

Consider how far along digital media has come, with technology widely and readily available today, to interact with audiences, in real-time, and understand and accommodate their informational requirements. Data streaming in from websites and devices provide a comprehensive picture of when, where and how audience members are consuming information. At the same time, consumers may be contributing responses and feedback in a passive way that does not require active engagement, if they choose not to do so.

The data now available from news and information consumers can determine what parts of a screen are getting the most attention, and even electronically detect the reader's interest in the topics being delivered. The technology exists that can provide instantaneous services and feedback as consumers move through the day. As renowned science author Arthur C. Clarke once wrote, "Any sufficiently advanced technology is indistinguishable from magic." This is certainly the case with the new generation of media technologies that is emerging, enabling consumers to receive, on their screens in front of them, the exact information they need, tailored to their reading habits and even to their moods. Bearing in mind Clarke's statement, it would have been incomprehensible (magic) for most news consumers in the 1960s to imagine many of today's innovations (existing or emerging) that have implications for big data collection. To provide a measure of historical context, the authors examine a few relevant examples that might have been perceived as miraculous just 50 years ago.

Few people in the 1960s could have envisioned that one day the screen they were watching might have electrical sensors connected to it that monitor eye movements, determining the locations on the screen where viewers' fixated to process visual information or their saccades, the brief periods between eye fixations when perception is attenuated (Palmer, 1999). The data from these sensors could tell news organizations and advertisers what viewers found interesting, what caught their visual attention and, perhaps more importantly, what they did not see. Additionally, the sensors could help determine if viewers left the room during commercials, how much time they fixated on the screen, where they fixated the most, was the time spent gazing at the screen continuous or discontinuous, and the visual scan paths or the ways their eye traversed the screen. As people watched a broadcast on the presidential elections, for example, a switch on the device might enable people in living rooms nationwide to engage in conversation. The audio from these conversations or text they typed on a keyboard could be analyzed on the fly, to determine sentiment. Geographical maps with overlays (heat-maps) enable viewers to ascertain the tenor of discussions as well as the locations of contentious conversations so they could avoid them or join in.

This technology can be applied to the periodical space as well. For most news consumers in the 1960s, it would have been inconceivable to think that when they brought a newspaper or magazine at the newsstand, the publication could record their location, the time of day as well as their reading habits based on the hundred other times they brought periodicals. The publication would know by the location and time of day that the consumer is traveling to the office by public transportation – to most consumers just 50 years ago, that would certainly be magic. Consequently, the publication presents itself in a smaller viewport so the reader does not have to make adjustments to prevent from interfering with people in adjacent seats. The publication also knows that on the way to work, the news consumer reads major news stories of the day and the financial news and so it displays those sections in its viewport. Most news consumers could not have imagined these things in the 1960s. Continuing this example a bit further, when the consumer travels home, he or she likes to read the world news and comics. Because the publication knows the consumer's location and the direction he or she is traveling, world news stories and comics display or are readily accessible on the viewport. On the way home, the consumer touches a travel advertisement on the display and then begins reading it and several other travel advertisements. As he or she exits the transportation terminal, related travel advertisements display on electronic billboards in the terminal. The publication detects that the individual may not have finished reading a particular news story. When he or she returns home and re-opens the newspaper or magazine, the point at which he or she left off is prominently displayed in the viewport. Alternatively, if he or she turns on the television or radio that story is listed as an option so he or she may continue learning about a particular topic or news event.

Fifty years ago, the news consumer could not envision that if he or she felt passionate about particular topics, he or she could write comments about them using the interface. Those comments get added to millions of other comments from people worldwide, enabling the individual to understand these topics from unique and varying vantage points and cultural perspectives. The commentary can be depicted graphically in maps and charts showing, among other things, the tenor of conversations, who is central in debates, the group formations, group splintering, homogeneity, and activity. Because people are discussing and exchanging information on topics, they extend the life of many stories. Accordingly, people have recording devices that enable them to record events in high-quality multimedia that can be shared with others and with publishing organizations. Thus, people, in conjunction with media organizations, actively engage in spreading news and content worldwide.

Finally, in concluding this example, imagine what consumers in the 1960s would have thought if the publication (device) came equipped with electrodermal response sensors to measure reactions. It can ascertain when the person is excited or upset, and thus may change background color and type size, the amount of content displayed, or it may simplify the interface to better suit the person's state. If the device can determine that the person is in an anxious state, it might display or include in the interface advertisements for relaxing vacations or techniques to relieve tension. The device might also display a reminder screen so the individual can remember to schedule an appointment with a physician – and perhaps, if the individual prefers, this stream of electrodermal response data can be sent to his or her physician for monitoring.

The aforementioned applications may sound futuristic – they were certainly futuristic (*magic*) to news consumers 50 years ago – but most actually exist today because of advances in technology that facilitated developments in areas such as graphical user interfaces (GUI), personal computing, networking and information sciences, Web, and mobile technologies. From a human-technology interaction perspective, people's increased and continued interaction with digital technologies and the technical capacity to chronicle those interaction events are requisite in the evolution of what is known today as big data and analytics. They also change many facets of the news and publishing industries and the ways information consumers interact and engage with them.

THE MESSAGE IS THE PLATFORM

For decades, the media – regardless if it was print or electronic – was primarily a one-way interaction. News and information was collected, selected, edited, packaged up and delivered to consumers, and consideration of its ultimate value to audiences, or exactly how it was being received, was only given on a high-level basis (see Figure 1). The acceptance and selection of content was only loosely tied to overall subscription sales of periodicals or journals. As long as these sales were profitable, it was generally assumed that audiences' needs were being met.

Up to even a few years ago, this one-way delivery of content was always regarded as the go-forward model of publishing. The interactivity of television and radio was limited to consumers selecting a station, and either remaining with that station, or tuning to another. Content adoption was based on the selection of samples, collected and reported to networks by specialized third-party firms such as A.C. Nielsen. This was also the primary form of feedback on consumer content preferences available to networks.

For print publications such as newspapers, magazines and journals, feedback on consumer content preferences was even more generalized. Subscription and newsstand sales on daily, weekly or month-to-month basis gave editors and journalists a very general picture of how well their material was being accepted. Publishers also conduct market research surveys and focus groups to develop a better picture of their audiences.

Even when the future of media was considered, it usually followed the traditional one-way delivery model. For example, a number of futurists predicted that newspapers would ultimately be delivered in the form of some type of electronic facsimile device to homes (Novak, 2013). There were predictions that content would be tailored to users' preferences, but in a very broad sense. It was also assumed that traditional existing media outlets would be the providers of this information.

With the capability to chronicle human behavior (interactions), news and publishing organizations began investing in real-time data and associated analytics to better understand consumer behavior and to assess their own effectiveness. Nobody foresaw the rise of big digital, content-sharing platforms that would serve as disruptive news and information platforms. Social media sites such as Facebook, Twitter, Yahoo! and Google are playing prominent roles in information delivery, often serving as alternatives to traditional media – effectively competing for readership numbers as well as advertising dollars.

A survey of 5,173 adults conducted by The Pew Research Center in collaboration with the John S. and James L. Knight Foundation found that about half of both Facebook and Twitter users get news on those sites, while one-fifth of YouTube use the site for that purpose (Holcomb, Gottfried, & Mitchell, 2013). It is also reported that Facebook delivers almost a quarter of all digital advertising views in the U.S., and Google takes in almost half the dollars spent on online ads through its search advertising (Grueskin, Seave, & Graves, 2011).

The value of social media platforms is not lost on traditional media companies. Many are leveraging social media sites to amplify their content, or to better interact with their audiences. Media organizations, for example, are setting up "fan pages" on Facebook, along with Twitter feeds, in which they encourage readers to share links. Media organizations also include social sharing tools on their websites, including Facebook, LinkedIn, Twitter, Digg and Reddit.

Online platform providers continue to seek ways to play more prominent roles in the media markets. At the time of the first authorship of this book, Snapchat, the mobile-based instantaneous video sharing service, announced that it was partnering with media companies such as CNN, ESPN, Vive and Warner Music to "skim" selections of their multimedia content and sell ads against the videos, photos and articles, and share the revenue with the publishers (Kafka, 2015).

The advantage that many of these new platforms provide is greater transparency and enhanced analytic capabilities for media organizations to employ. Readership demographics, preferences, and content trends are easily trackable through these platforms, which offer open web application programming interfaces (APIs), which provide windows to audiences.

Figure 1. Traditional news services, providing news to consumers

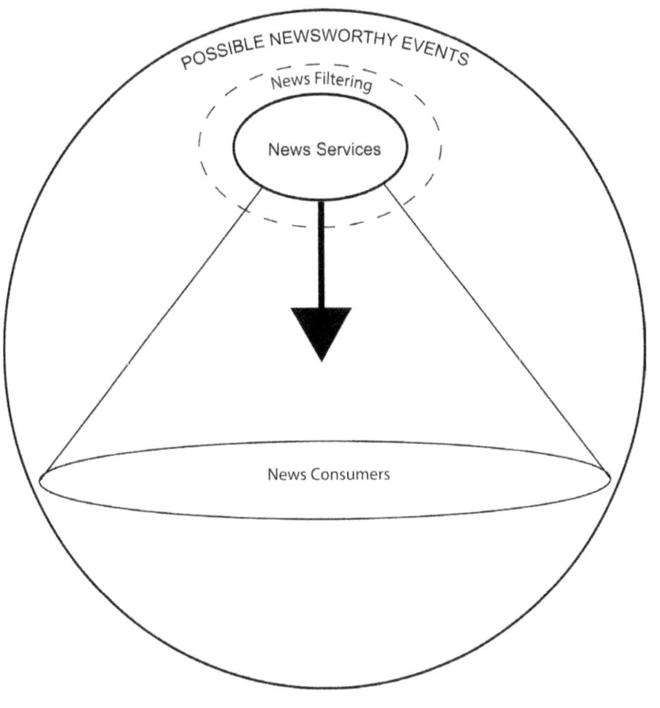

The impact of the entrée of these new platforms is a dramatic shift in the way content and information is collected, produced and delivered. Content is now selected and shared among consumers (see Figure 2). In the process, consumers leave "digital exhaust" – data on the articles they select, how much of it they read, how long and how many times they re-read it, their location, and even what type of device they used to access the article. Their choices and preferences are instantly communicated to publishers, editors, journalists, and other content providers to help assess their responses.

THE RISE OF THE NEW MEDIA PROFESSIONAL

Powerful forces are converging and changing the way people consume information around them. More people are doing more things (interacting) with digital technologies, and increasingly, technologies are equipped to keep track of these interactions as data, representing human behavior and opinion. This has given rise to what is often referred to as "big data" – the availability of terabytes, petabytes, and exabytes of information in all forms – is enabling news consumers and professionals to dig into trends occurring across the globe, as well is their own backyards – to gain deeper insights and even make predictions on the future course of developments. The world is increasingly mesmerized by the growing array of social networking services available from the web. Global online communities with hundreds of millions of participants have emerged through sites such as Facebook, Twitter and LinkedIn. The "traditional" means of gathering news information – print media, broadcast radio and television – is rapidly being subsumed and disintermediated by new channels enabled by the web. No longer is information filtered by a few gatekeepers within centralized media sources.

Figure 2. News consumer is more central in news services

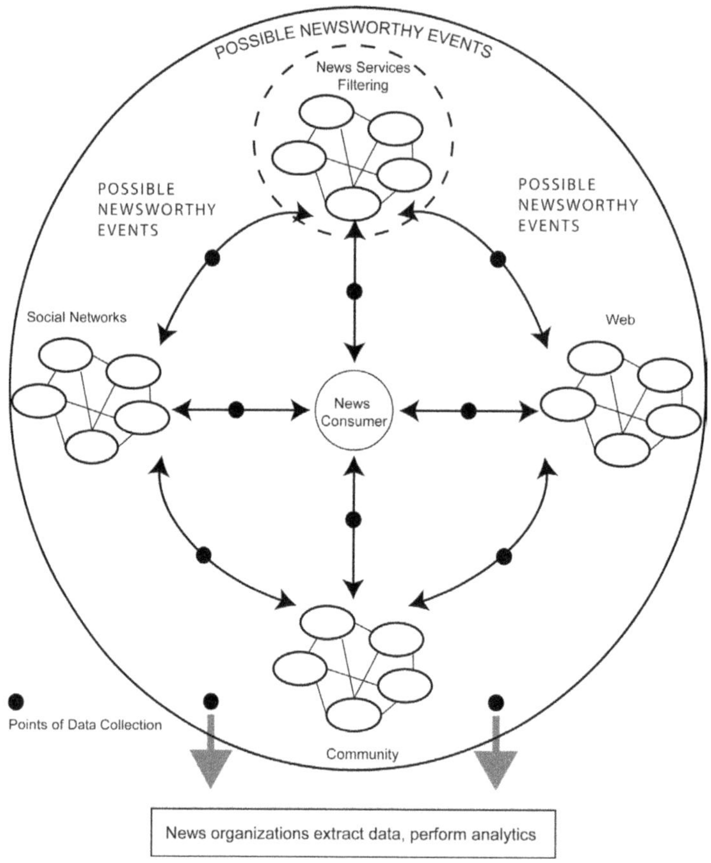

News consumers are more empowered and have greater control, than ever before in selecting news services, contributing to the news, and promulgating news stories.

The enablers of this significant shift, digital technologies that support human interaction, the Internet, web, and mobile connectivity, have become primary vehicles in shaping today news services. The choices people make during interactions are instantly available to cadres of entities (journalists, editors, content providers, researchers, etc.) that can evaluate them and be responsive to the consumer needs.

This also opens up new kinds of roles for journalists, editorial professionals, and publishers. Today's media professional is more than a purveyor of information and gatekeeper of information, he or she also needs to function partially as a data scientist, partially as curators of highly interactive and growing online communities, and full-time as critical thinkers who understand the value of questioning and revisiting the information they receive or uncover.

At the same time, there is greater demand than ever for the classic editorial skills that provide balance, vetting and critical thinking to content being delivered across digital channels. As anyone familiar with the Internet can attest, this network of networks is rife with inaccurate statements, rumors and unsubstantiated information. A paper published at the *MIT Communications Forum* quotes Thomas Cekay, who served as editor at *The Chicago Tribune*, who observed that traditional editorial roles – determining if readers need to see information, and if the information is intelligently presented – will increase in importance in the digital age. Information that is offered up by major media outlets still needs to meet certain criteria: its magnitude; its unexpectedness (which always makes it interesting); sociocultural values; continuity from previous content; and cultural proximity or relevance (Harper, 1998).

To a large extent, data-driven news and content still abide by these thresholds of what constitutes material of interest to audiences. The availability of data across many venues and activities opens up vistas for today's media professionals. Data itself provides the raw material for news and informational reporting. Helping audiences to make sense of the petabytes worth of data now flowing through the public domain requires a high level of "storytelling," in which data is analyzed and interpreted in ways that connect with audiences (Harper, 1998). To some degree, this requirement is the same that is found with the emerging category of data scientist, who is also charged with a storytelling role based on analysis and conclusions drawn from data sets. A description provided on the IBM website captures the nature of the data scientist role (IBM, 2014b, para. 3):

The data scientist role has been described as "part analyst, part artist. Anjul Bhambhri, vice president of big data products at IBM, says, "A data scientist is somebody who is inquisitive, who can stare at data and spot trends. It's almost like a Renaissance individual who really wants to learn and bring change to an organization."

Media professionals fit the mold as "Renaissance" individuals – capable of seeing the greater trends, of seeing incongruities or inadequacies in various situations, of being able to connect to their audiences. This data scientist-like storytelling role not only serves in being able to deliver data-driven content to audiences, but also for internal purposes – uncovering and evaluating data that provides insights on how deeply the content they publish is being absorbed by audiences.

The data increasingly are getting more detailed. At first, data from websites provided rudimentary feedback, such as the number of page views a particular article was receiving, and whether readers were responding to links to additional content, as well as advertising, on those pages. Now, tools and technologies are available to gain much deeper insights, reviewing audience members' digital exhaust to provide real-time insights as to how readers are interacting with content.

It would be remiss not to mention the potential implications of automated article preparation, or what is affectionately referred to as "robot journalism" (Miller, 2015). The Associated Press is now employing algorithms that pull data from various press releases, including earnings reports, and formats the data into a readable news article. According to Miller, "the AP implemented the system six months ago and now publishes 3,000 such stories every quarter — and that number is poised to grow." The AP reports were first closely monitored by human journalists before they were released to publication, but now, many are being released with minimal human intervention.

In an article in *New York*, Roose describes the typical process of generating an automated earnings report, and the various data feeds that make it possible. In this case, AP was employing software called Wordsmith from Automated Insights, to produce and publish the Alcoa earnings report:

When Alcoa's earnings report hit the wire that day, the data was instantly compiled by a firm called Zacks Investment Research and passed through the AP's proprietary algorithm, which pulled out key numbers and phrases and matched them against other contextual information. In milliseconds, the software produced a full story written in AP style, indistinguishable from one made with human hands. In short order, the story appeared on many AP member sites, including NPR, Hawaii News Now, and KAIT8. (Roose, 2014, para. 3)

Robot journalism has already been employed for the last few years in another data-intensive area of reporting, and that is sports reporting (Schonfeld, 2010). Such articles are produced in a matter of seconds, at minimal cost to the publishing organization. There are a range of potential publishing applications in which automated journalism will play an increasing role, including corporate financial statements, sales reports, and scientific findings. Automated report-writing algorithms may have a place in situations where audience sizes are too small to justify paying for the services of a human author. As explained by Kristian Hammond, co-founder and chief technology officer at Narrative Science, which developed authoring technology, in an interview with *Marketwatch*: "The place where it's most powerful is where we have an audience of one," he said. "Those stories tend not to be written by people, but they can be written by a machine" (Bemis, 2012).

While at first blush the specter of automated journalism appears to be a threat to the job security of journalists and editorial professionals, the technology may actually enhance and enrich the profession as it develops. Automated journalism has its limits, as it cannot interpret data and information within varying contexts, apply critical thinking, or be able to reach out to newsmakers or subject matter experts capable of providing perspective on what is being presented to audiences. Notably as well, algorithms cannot interact in a thoughtful and engaging way with consumers on social networks.

As Roose put it:

… these robots, as sophisticated as they are, can't approach the full creativity of a human writer. … My colleagues' jobs (and mine, knock wood) are too complex for today's artificial intelligence to handle; they require human skills like picking up the phone, piecing together data points from multiple sources, and drawing original, evidence-based conclusions. The stories that today's robots can write are, frankly, the kinds of stories that humans hate writing anyway. (Roose, 2014, para. 8)

It will still be up to humans – journalists, editorial professionals and publishing executives – to apply the critical thinking that is essential to develop meaningful and engaging content for their audiences. These professionals still need to function as the "window" to events and information that may be inaccessible to audience members. Journalists and editorial professionals still need to connect and channel the thoughts of newsmakers and subject matter experts, while asking the hard questions that need to be asked.

CONCLUSION

Network connectivity, increased and ongoing human interaction with digital interfaces (devices), and the technical capacity to chronicle those interactions have been instrumental factors in the production of large amounts of data (big data) that news and publishing organizations can use to better understand consumer behavior and ultimately enhance services and the user experience. Increasingly, more sophisticated analysis, tied to tracking technologies and analytic tools, give news organizations an even more in-depth view of their audiences. Through these new channels, consumers are also communicating directly, in both verbal and non-verbal ways, back to publishers, editors, journalists and other content creators.

William J. Gibbs
Duquesne University, USA

Joseph E. McKendrick
Independent Consultant, USA

REFERENCES

Bemis, T. (2012, August 31). Start-up turns data into plain english. *Marketwatch.* Retrieved January 29, 2015 from http://www.marketwatch.com/story/start-up-turns-data-into-plain-english-2012-08-31

Chen, H., Chiang, R. H. L., & Storey, V. C. (2012). Business intelligence and analytics: From big data to big impact. *Management Information Systems Quarterly*, *36*(4), 1165–1188.

Clarke, A. (1962). Sir Arthur's quotations (attributed to Clarke in Hazards of Prophecy: The Failure of Imagination). *The Arthur C. Clarke Foundation.* Retrieved February 1, 2015 from http://www.clarkefoundation.org/sample-page/sir-arthurs-quotations/

Einav, L., & Levin, J. (2014). The data revolution and economic analysis. *Innovation Policy and the Economy*, *14*(1), 1–24. doi:10.1086/674019

Folkenflik, D. (2009, July 17). Walter Cronkite, The nation's narrator, dies at 92. *NPR.* Retrieved January 31, 2015 from http://www.npr.org/templates/story/story.php?storyId=106775685

Goes, P. B. (2014). Big data and is research. *Management Information Systems Quarterly*, *38*(3), iii–viii.

Google. (2014). *The importance of digital analytics.* Retrieved October 16, 2014, from https://analyticsacademy.withgoogle.com/course01/unit?unit=2&lesson=1

Gross, S., Bardzell, J., & Bardzell, S. (2014). Skeu the evolution: Skeuomorphs, style, and the material of tangible interactions. In *Proceedings of the 8th International Conference on Tangible, Embedded and Embodied Interaction* (pp. 53-60). ACM. DOI= doi:10.1145/2540930.2540969

Grueskin, B., Seave, A., & Graves, L. (2011, May 10). *The story so far: What we know about the business of digital journalism.* Columbia Journalism School, Tow Center for Digital Journalism. Retrieved November 12, 2014 from http://www.journalism.columbia.edu/news/448

Harper, C. (1998). *Journalism in a digital age.* MIT Communications Forum. Retrieved November 12, 2014 from http://web.mit.edu/comm-forum/papers/harper.html

Holcomb, J., Gottfried, J., & Mitchell, A. (2013). *News use across social media platforms.* Pew Research Foundation: Journalism & Media. Retrieved from http://www.journalism.org/2013/11/14/news-use-across-social-media-platforms/

IBM. (2014a). *Big data at the speed of business*. Retrieved Mar. 10, 2014 from http://www-01.ibm.com/software/data/bigdata/what-is-big-data.html

IBM. (2014b). *What is a data scientist?* Retrieved November 12, 2014 from http://www-01.ibm.com/software/data/infosphere/data-scientist/

Kafka, P. (2015). Snapchat's content play comes into focus: 'Discover' debuts Tuesday. *CNBC/Recode*. Retrieved January 27, 2015 from http://www.cnbc.com/id/102372575

Kaushik, A. (2010). *Web analytics 2.0: The art of online accountability & science of customer centricity*. Indianapolis, IN: Wiley.

Miller, R. (2015). AP's 'robot journalists' are writing their own stories now. *The Verge*. Retrieved January 29, 2015 from http://www.theverge.com/2015/1/29/7939067/ap-journalism-automation-robots-financial-reporting

Novak, M. (2013, March 18). *The newspaper of tomorrow: 11 predictions from yesteryear: eNewspapers were being developed as far back as the 1930s*. Smithosonian.com. Retrieved November 12, 2014 from http://www.smithsonianmag.com/history/the-newspaper-of-tomorrow-11-predictions-from-yesteryear-3327057/

Pain, F., & Lively, S. (2013). Human science and user experience. *Bell Labs Technical Journal*, *17*(4), 1–4. doi:10.1002/bltj.21570

Palmer, S. E. (1999). *Vision science: Photons to phenomenology*. Cambridge, MA: The MIT Press.

Roose, K. (2014). Robots are invading the news business, and it's great for journalists. *New York*. Retrieved January 29, 2015 from http://nymag.com/daily/intelligencer/2014/07/why-robot-journalism-is-great-for-journalists.html

Schonfeld, E. (2010, November 12). Automated news comes to sports coverage via statsheet. *TechCrunch*. Retrieved January 29, 2015 from http://techcrunch.com/2010/11/12/automated-news-sports-statsheet/

Taylor, L., Schroeder, R., & Meyer, E. (2014). Emerging practices and perspectives on big data analysis in economics: Bigger and better or more of the same? *Big Data & Society*, *1*(2), 1–10. doi:10.1177/2053951714536877

Waller, M. A., & Fawcett, S. E. (2013). Data science, predictive analytics, and big data: A revolution that will transform supply chain design and management. *Journal of Business Logistics*, *34*(2), 77–84. doi:10.1111/jbl.12010

Zhang, G. L., Sun, J., Chitkushev, L., & Brusic, V. (2014). Big data analytics in immunology: A knowledge-based approach. *BioMed Research International. Article ID*, *437987*. doi:10.1155/2014/437987

KEY TERMS AND DEFINITIONS

Analytics: The analyses of both qualitative and quantitative data gather from sources such as server logs, data and text mining for the purpose of understanding trends and enhancing customer experiences.

Automated Journalism: The employment of algorithms to translate data and information into a human-readable article format.

Big Data: Large amounts of observational data, of different types, that are collected as user interact with computing devices. Often these data are collected in real-time.

Content-Sharing Platforms: Popular computing environments that allow people to exchange information in various media forms (text, video and audio, images) and to interact with other people worldwide in real-time.

Data Streams: Data that are collected in real-time. Technologies today enable researchers to record users' interaction/behavior as they are happening.

Interface: A medium through which a human interacts with a system or machine.

Internet of Things: Refers to the connectedness of devices, platforms, and services from which vast stores of data from the Web, user-generated content, and social media can be obtained.

User Experience (UX): A user experience occurs when a person interacts with a system. It is influenced by internal characteristics of the user, attributes of the system's design such as usability and functionality, and the context of use.

Section 1

Computational Journalism:
Entering the New World

Chapter 1
When Journalism Met the Internet:
Old Media and New Media Greet the Online Public

Mike Dillon
Duquesne University, USA

ABSTRACT

American news organizations have long been criticized for failing to anticipate, appreciate and exploit the Internet as it became a fact of daily life in the mid-1990s. This chapter explores and analyzes the lack of planning that stymied the development of journalism on the Web and cast doubt on the viability of traditional public-service journalism with its enduring values of accuracy, fairness and advocacy. Specifically, the essay documents and analyzes the online debuts of two venerable "old media" news outlets (The New York Times and The Los Angeles Times) and two "new media" Web news outlets (Salon and Slate) in the mid-1990s by exploring the claims they made about their aims, purposes and expectations as they introduced themselves to the public via their salutatory editorials. It is a cautionary tale for a digital world that reconfigures itself in ever-quickening cycles.

INTRODUCTION

The Internet became a fact of everyday life in the mid-to-late 1990s (Manjoo, 2009). By 1996, about 13% of Americans were online, and spent about 30 minutes per day surfing the Web; by 2000, the number of Internet users had more than tripled and penetration had reached 44%. By 2014, penetration reached 87% (Internet World Stats, 2014).

DOI: 10.4018/978-1-4666-8580-2.ch001

The Internet's impact on traditional news media outlets was quickly, and painfully, felt in the mid-to-late 1990s. Many newspapers and magazines created online versions without giving careful thought to aesthetics, function, audience or – most disastrously – revenue. Some stepped into the digital realm assuming that familiar and predictable models of economic support would manifest naturally. Others took a build-it-and-they-will-come approach.

Meanwhile, Internet service providers, Web portals and aggregators, such as AOL, Netscape, Yahoo and (eventually) Google, presented users with a Whitman's Sampler of news, information, entertainment and trivia from a wide and rapidly expanding array of sources and services that undercut every facet and feature of the traditional news business – information, speed, and display and classified advertising. Aggregating gave regional or specialized publications entrée to new audiences, but reduced all members of the aggregate – including the flagships of American journalism – to the status of supporting players in an epic ISP-directed narrative of the day's events.

"Old media," i.e. traditional newspapers and magazines, continued to conceive of and market themselves as destinations designed for specific kinds of visitors (people interested in journalism and advertising), but Web portals functioned like airports, serving as points of departure to an almost infinite number of destinations. Thus, just about any kind of advertiser could be confident that his or her message would find interested parties at Web portals. Between 1999 and 2009, as advertising revenues at newspapers slumped, annual online advertising revenues increased from just under $5 billion to nearly $25 billion (Kirchhoff, 2011).

Newspapers stumbled onto the Web with crude avatars of their print products. It was as if in the 1930s, as highways expanded, the Pennsylvania Railroad rushed into production a steam-powered, cast-iron automobile that looked just like a locomotive. Meanwhile, "new media" enterprises, such as Microsoft-sponsored *Slate*, reached into the world of tradition and cast celebrity cable journalist Michael Kinsley in the role of digital shaman whose reputation in the world of print and broadcasting would serve as a foundation for a new, Web-based journalism.

According to Chyi & Lasora (2007), newspapers had widely proliferated this model:

By 1996, most major metropolitan newspapers had rolled out websites, but seemingly with little thought to new opportunities – and problems – inherent in the new technology, and little more than wishful thinking when it came to a revenue model. By 2003, more than 1,500 U.S. newspapers had launched websites. (p. 177)

Whether tethered to established newspapers or magazines, or created out of thin air, Web products that promised the "feel," credibility, ethos and style of traditional professional journalism by and large did not capture the public's attention, or at least not enough of its attention to compel it to seek out and pay for online news, information, commentary and entertainment from established newspapers. It's also possible their indifference had deeper roots – i.e., they hadn't been terribly interested in the old media products they'd been buying for years but simply acting out of habit or lack of choice – until they were offered new options via the web (Barnhurst & Nerone, 2001).

BACKGROUND

American news organizations have long been criticized for a lack of planning, for not more effectively anticipating, appreciating and exploiting the Internet. Journalists such as ProPublica Editor Richard Tofel (2012) assert that this lack of planning stymied the development of online journalism and cast doubt on the viability of enduring journalistic values such as accuracy, fairness and advocacy. The diminishment of these values, in turn, endangered democracy itself (Jones, 2009).

Looking back from the perspective of 2010, *Newsweek* (which after a long decline, became an online adjunct of the Web-based *Daily Beast*) concluded that

...newspapers are getting wiped out in part because they didn't realize they were in the information business; they thought their business was about putting ink onto paper and then physically distributing those stacks of paper with fleets of trucks and delivery people. Papers were slow to move to the Web. For a while they just sort of shuffled around, hoping it would go away. Even when they did launch websites, many did so reluctantly, almost grudgingly. (Lyons, 2010)

The uncertainty, tentativeness and anxiety with which traditional news organizations reacted to the online environment is unsurprising and understandable given the rapidity with which the Internet permeated American – and global – culture. According to Rogers (2003), "The Internet has spread more rapidly than any other technological innovation in the history of humankind (p. xix)."

In trying to react to rapid change, some newspapers formed partnerships with ISPs (as *The New York Times* did with AOL), invested in an architecture (doomed, as it turns out) of micropayments, and counted on existing copyright laws to protect their product. The powerful synergies propelling the Internet, however, quickly swept these strategies aside.

JOURNALISM AND THE WEB: FLAWED ASSUMPTIONS, MISSED OPPORTUNITIES

In his essay, "Newspapers and Thinking the Unthinkable," Shirky (2009) argues that newspaper publishers were not taken completely unaware by the Internet but underestimated its potential and were unimaginative in their preparations for its ascent as audiences' prime medium of communication:

Revolutions create a curious inversion of perception. In ordinary times, people who do no more than describe the world around them are seen as pragmatists, while those who imagine fabulous alternative futures are viewed as radicals. The last couple of decades haven't been ordinary, however. Inside the papers, the pragmatists were the ones simply looking out the window and noticing that the real world increasingly resembled the unthinkable scenario. These people were treated as if they were barking mad. Meanwhile the people spinning visions of popular walled gardens and enthusiastic micropayment adoption, visions unsupported by reality, were regarded not as charlatans but saviors.

Nonetheless, successful or not – and they were not – news organizations that created online news sites in the 1990s *did* make plans. The explanations and justifications they offered for those plans as they introduced their new online products reveal their assumptions about their audience, the role of journalism in American society, the uses of new technology, and revenue models. With few exceptions the assumptions and predictions old and new media organizations made about journalism on the Internet would prove to be disastrously deficient and shortsighted.

How their plans panned out, however, is not the focus of this paper, which instead attempts to answer a different question: Why did journalists venturing online in the mid-1990s plan and act as they did in the areas of functionality, utility, design, marketing, anticipation of future trends and assessment of the online audience? The most compelling answers to that question are provided by the journalists themselves, in the form of "salutatories "they wrote to introduce their inaugural online editions to prospective audiences.

The salutatory is an old tradition in journalism. People and organizations have founded newspapers, magazines, cable networks, websites and blogs for a wide range of reasons. In addition to whatever financial or ideological motives they reveal, the salutary editorials that heralded the appearance of new offerings since the first days of the Republic have made rather bold assertions about their authors' visions and values: *This is the way journalism should be done! These are the ideas that matter! This is what people need and want! Listen up!*

Salutatories are valuable not because they can be proved prescient or foolish in hindsight, but because they are an expression of epistemology – a speculation of the future based not just on the circumstances of the historical moment in which they are written, but also on perceptions, interpretations and assumptions about change in the past, as well as the nature of change itself.

Taking salutatories on their own terms, in the context of their own time, reanimates a rhetorical situation by examining "those contexts in which speakers or writers create rhetorical discourse" (Bitzer, 1995, p.301). They tell a story not of what was happening, or what eventually happened, but of what people believed (or hoped) would happen based on their perceptions of the environment in which they were operating. As Walter Lippmann (1922) pointed out in *Public Opinion*, published in an age when technology was increasing the might of both the sword and the pen:

> *. . . . . . whatever we believe to be a true picture, we treat it as if it were the environment itself . . . what each man does is based not on direct and certain knowledge, but on pictures made by himself or given to him. If his atlas tells him the world is flat he will not sail near what he believes to be the edge of our planet for fear of falling off. (p.4)*

The online debuts of venerable "legacy" news outlets (*The New York Times* and *The Los Angeles Times*) and new media news outlets (*Salon* and *Slate*) demonstrate how a flawed reading of the environment, as well as a failure to draw sensible lessons from the past, fueled flawed expectations and predictions about the future of journalism – on the Internet and in general.

The debuts of online versions of *The New York Times* and *The Los Angeles Times* were chosen as old media case studies because they propose vivid and distinct approaches to providing online journalism. *Slate* and *Salon,* meanwhile, represent prominent and well-financed new media ventures that combined the functions of traditional magazines and newspapers, in addition to new features unique to the digital sphere, attracted significant attention, and achieved instant, if short-lived, popularity. In addition, all four websites debuted within a 13-month period, between

November 1995 (*Salon*) and December 1996 (*The Los Angeles Times*) – the dawn of the age of journalism on the "Information Superhighway," as boosters were fond of calling the Internet.

In method and narrative form, history proceeds from hindsight. The arc and final act of the story are known; memoirs and letters shed light on motives that principal actors succeeded in concealing from their contemporaries, or even themselves; the endeavors that so-called rugged individuals imagined they were carrying out in perilous isolation are shown to have emerged from broad social patterns. And yet, whatever we might be able to demonstrate after the fact about motives, or powerful social currents that were inchoate to the people navigating them, the experience, reality and *weltanschauung* of those people as they acted in history are worth considering on their own merits.

Novice reporters learn that the primary measure of a story's value is the "so what" test. Throughout the history of American journalism, publishers, editors, producers – and now aggregators, bloggers and social media creators – have anticipated the same question from audiences they hoped to reach: So what?

They've responded with a wide variety of answers, promising everything from a revolution in class relations (Joseph Pulitzer's New York *World*, 1883), to a revolution in morals (Hugh Hefner's *Playboy*, 1954), to an assertion of basic humanity in the face of slavery (Lloyd Garrison's *Liberator*, 1833), to a flippant promise to pay no attention whatsoever to "the old lady in Dubuque" (Harold Ross's *New Yorker*, 1925), to a cheerful vow to furnish advertiser-friendly information with undemanding brevity (The Gannett Corporation's *USA Today*, 1982). So, too, late 20th Century journalists venturing online projected a vision of the place of journalism in a digital American culture and promised a new approach to journalism they were confident would resonate with the online publics they sought to captivate.

ISSUES, CONTROVERSIES, PROBLEMS

A variety of factors shaped the rapid expansion of the Web, increasing content, platforms and audiences/users. First, broadband capacity and usage expanded (De Argaez). As Internet usage increased, sales of computers rose; as a result, the per-unit cost of PCs, which in 1996 typically sold for $2,500, decreased rapidly (Polsson, 2012). Blogs, websites with specialized content, and video sites captivated audiences by offering a mélange of approaches and styles to reporting and telling stories about the world. The number and reach of these sites grew exponentially and were embraced by ecstatic investors. According to Lewis (1996-b), despite losses of $600,000 in 1995, Yahoo's initial public offering in April, 1996, took off "like a rocket ship," with an initial valuation of nearly $1 billion. On the initial day of trading, shares opened at $13 and reached $43 within a few hours.

The introduction of cheap desktops and dial-up Internet service during the 1990s is often described as a "revolution," but it was a revolution that tended to anarchy, without a grand or coherent cause propelling it, nor a consensual vision of what the revolution might accomplish. Instead, whether they ventured online eagerly or with trepidation, news and information providers offered wildly diverse perspectives on how the Internet would affect the content, and commerce, of journalism.

Established and new high-tech companies exploited emerging connective technologies, focusing their energies on designing portals (Netscape, Microsoft Explorer, Yahoo, AOL) that allowed access to an unwieldy set of Web destinations, or producing machines (PCs), or software (MS Office) that helped users utilize those portals.

The development of the destinations to which these portals transported users, however, was haphazard and unsystematic. For instance, after an astounding initial success, MySpace lost favor with users and was overtaken and made irrelevant by Facebook, in part because MySpace had no page design parameters and users proceeded to build a psychedelic Tower of Babel of different fonts, colors and templates. After paying $580 million to acquire MySpace in 2005, News Corp unloaded it in 2011 for $35 million (Horne, 2011).

New ventures created exclusively to do business on the Internet were hit-or-miss. Some sites possessed the traction for long-term relevance and even financial success while others could not capture the attention of a fast-grazing public. No matter how farfetched the business plan, investors were eager to shovel money into Internet startups in a variety of fields. For instance, "Webvan" proposed to deliver sundries ordered online within 30 minutes – with no delivery charge. The venture burned through nearly $400 million in two years and went bankrupt in 2001 (German). Even Disney's sure touch could not create online alchemy: its go.com portal was here and gone in three years and forced Disney to take a write-down of nearly $1 billion.

In a sense, the early days of the Internet resembled the emergence of radio seven decades earlier. Like radio, the Internet represented a connective technology that offered a relatively cheap and uncomplicated vehicle for people to participate as both receivers *and* senders. Frequency limitations and signal interference led to federal license requirements for radio broadcasters and ended an early period of democratic, if chaotic, participation in radio. No such scarcity justified government intrusion on the Web, however.

How did new news media and old news media publishers introduce themselves to a new public environment, the online public forum, in the mid-1990s? Echoing salutatories throughout American journalism history, they announced their debuts on the digital stage with aplomb and optimism, but their framing of the Internet as a medium of news and comment took distinctly varied forms.

Traditional news outlets were slow to see the threat the Internet posed to their utility and profitability and even slower to identify opportunities to effectively exploit the new medium. Like everyone with something to sell or something to say, they seemed to know only that it was necessary to establish an online presence as quickly as possible.

According to Peterson (1996), while newspapers took tentative steps to collaborate in the areas of advertising, distribution, they dithered on the issues central to online viability. The failure to assess both threat and promise, the failure to formulate a workable financial model for what amounted to an entirely new – and competing – version of their editorial product, and the inability to coordinate their efforts to establish standards, combined to catalyze an astonishingly swift decline in perceived and actual value for an institution whose flagship members, such as *The New York Times*, *The Los Angeles Times* and *The Washington Post*, traced their roots to the nineteenth century and which, less than two decades earlier, in the age of Watergate, enjoyed unprecedented social prestige, pop culture cachet, political influence and profitability.

These old media outlets described the Internet as an exciting new vehicle to deliver traditional news to the public. The content, form and standards of traditional journalism would be maintained. When the *Washington Post* made its online debut on June 19, 1996, Publisher Donald Graham declared that, "People look to *The Washington Post* for the most authoritative and complete coverage of government and politics as well as for our investigative reporting, foreign news and our lively style features."

Traditional news outlets, confident in their own influence and power, declared that their content, acquired at great expense, would also be protected: The *Los Angeles Times* initial user agreement (1996) sternly warned users: "You may not modify, publish, transmit, transfer, sell, reproduce, create derivative work from, distribute, repost, perform, display, or any in anyway commercially exploit any of the Content . . ."

Editors made a nod to the ways in which Web-based news might indeed offer new forms of content, but these ideas were vague and tentative. Their salutatories, for all their bravado and good cheer, contained a tone of wistfulness that indicated traditional journalists would be perfectly satisfied to do business as usual if not for the fact that the Web was undeniably now a part of the media landscape and must be dealt with somehow. To be fair, though, they were navigating with crude maps. Data analytics began to emerge as a sophisticated tool to discern audience tastes and preferences in the late 1990s, after news organizations initial surge to the digital environment. The term "big data" and its early proponents such as John Mashey, the chief scientist at Silicon Graphics, did not begin to gain cachet outside of the tech sector until the early 2000s (Lohr, 2013). Newspapers struggling to translate journalism into a new environment cannot be fully faulted for lagging behind companies whose sole focus was on technological efficiency.

The salutatories of *Salon*, *Slate*, *The New York Times* and *The Los Angeles Times* illuminate the assumptions that propelled journalism on to the Internet in the 1990s and sowed the seeds of its ongoing struggles in the new electronic environment. While news sites have evolved and journalists have become more sophisticated in their creation of content and understanding of audiences, one gets but one chance to make a first impression.

SALON

What Is SALON?

SALON is an interactive magazine of books, arts and ideas. Inside SALON you'll find not only authors, artists and thinkers, but a kinetic community of readers and kindred spirits eager to thrash out cultural issues.

We are inspired by the creative potential of the Internet, but unlike many other websites, SALON is not a techno-cult. As refugees from the atrophying world of newspapers and magazines, our primary allegiance is to written communication, to the power of the word. We think of digital technology as an exciting means to an end, but not the end itself. – From the Salon salutatory, November 12, 1995.

New media news outlets such as *Salon* bid a rude good riddance to the obsolete world of print and promised a bold new journalism – democratic, interactive, instantaneous and perpetually in motion. It was also still married to "the power of the word" in a medium designed to transcend the word.

Salon (1995) sneered at the "atrophying world of newspapers and magazines." These were dead forms and *Salon's* editors were delighted to dance on their graves. "American journalism has become a pitiful giant, ensnarled by commercial formulas and political tribalisms. Where once its voice shook mountains, it now squeaks cautiously and banally." *Salon* boasted it embodied a powerful (if syntactically awkward) new voice, amplified in importance and influence by the new digital technologies: "The Net allows publishers to burst these bonds, to howl again."

While *Salon* promised "militant centrism" and made confidently clairvoyant assertions about journalism's new role, it also assumed that the ideal reader – as the publisher imagined him or her – would remain *exactly* the same: interested, attentive, concerned, engaged, sober, reasonable, and respectful of fair play. In contrast to its storm-the-Bastille call to digital arms, *Salon's* instruction in the decorum it expected of visitors who wished to participate in interactive democracy (as defined, hosted and refereed by *Salon*), sounded rather like an English butler reluctantly inviting the downstairs staff to tea: "We request that you use your real name when participating in a discussion. This makes for a responsible exchange. We also make a plea for common courtesy. Slander and boorishness don't encourage an enlightening meeting of the minds."

Salon instituted a fee structure, but few readers cared to pay the toll. By the early 2000s it was nearing bankruptcy and eviction from its San Francisco offices . . . and pleading for donations. It survived, barely, but by 2008 the militant tone had faded and *Salon* was humbly describing itself as a purveyor of "social content [and a] curated blog network." At this writing it persists, but as a whisper, not a howl, another bit of backchannel flotsam in a churning digital river that long ago passed it by.

SLATE

Welcome to SLATE

By Michael Kinsley -- Posted Tuesday, June 25, 1996, at 3:30 AM ET

An introduction and apologia.

The name? It means nothing, or practically nothing. We chose it as an empty vessel into which we can pour meaning. We hope SLATE will come to mean good original journalism in this new medium. Beyond that, who knows? Good magazines are exercises in serendipity . . .

SLATE is basically a weekly: Most articles will appear for a week. But there will be something new to read almost every day. Some elements will change constantly. Other elements will appear and be removed throughout the week. Every article will indicate when it was "posted" and when it will be "composted." – From the Slate salutatory, June 25, 1996.

Slate debuted as an online-only product and in that sense can be classed as a new media news outlet. It was, however, bankrolled by Microsoft, which by the mid-1990s qualified as a warhorse in the software business, and fronted by Michael Kinsley, a 45-year-old former *New Republic* editor and a panel member on CNN's *Crossfire* program.

Kinsley's address to readers assured them, by invoking the Old Testament-era metaphor of "the empty vessel," that new media *Slate* was a great blank to be filled in by a talented editorial team with deep roots in print. Kinsley spoke to readers in a chatty, we're-all-in-this-together tone of voice, but quickly established that *Slate* was in business to attract followers *and* profits. His explanation of *Slate*'s financial model, alas, could well have served as the motto of Internet journalism for nearly two decades to come: "For the reader – you – there is good news . . . our billing system isn't ready yet."

Nonetheless, *Slate* intended to, and eventually did, charge $19.95 per year. That subscription fee, readers were assured, was far less than the cost of printed magazines (at least at newsstand prices) and was essential to ensuring quality journalism.

Depending on advertisers would not be healthy even if it were possible. Indeed, one of Slate's main goals is to demonstrate, if we can, that the economies of cyberspace make it easier for our kind of journalism to pay for itself. If the Web can make serious journalism more easily self-supporting, that is a great gift from technology to democracy. (Kinsley, 1996)

Slate also promised an early form of aggregation – intelligence from other news publications in advance of their press runs: "'In Other Magazines' uses the covers and contents of *Time*, *Newsweek*, etc., as a handy measure of what the culture considers important. (We aim to have these magazines in *SLATE* even before they reach the newsstands or your mailbox)." Under the heading "So What's In It?" *Slate*, like many of its online brethren, offered the readers a very limited "new experience" that would remain largely under the control of professional gatekeepers.

Hedging its bets on hypertext, *Slate* explained that readers who clicked on the "Consider Your Options" tab could download the entire magazine, reformat it to look like a traditional magazine, and then print the entire issue (A pre-printed mail subscription to *Slate* could be had for $29.95, far less, presumably, than the cost of ink for one's printer to print it oneself).

Some of *Slate's* "innovations" recalled the medium-is-the-message mentality of early film actualities of dancing horses and sound recordings of barking dogs, reflecting an age-old assumption that simply offering a familiar experience through a novel medium was enough to draw – and keep – an audience: "Every issue will have a poem, read aloud by the author, with text." *Slate* also promised to post downloadable video and audio of political ads that political consultant Robert Shrum would deconstruct.

Slate assured readers who might feel disoriented or anxious by the rate of mid-1990s digital change that it could depend on *Slate* to protect and preserve the informational proprieties to which they were accustomed. *Slate* vowed it would soon have the freewheeling, audacious and often ill-mannered Internet under control.

Finally, we intend to take a fairly skeptical stance toward the romance and rapidly escalating vanity of cyberspace. We do not start out with the smug assumption that the Internet changes the nature of human thought, or that all the restraints that society imposes on individuals in 'real life' must melt away in cyberia. There is a deadening conformity in the hipness of cyberspace culture in which we don't intend to participate. Part of our mission at SLATE will be trying to bring cyberspace down to earth. Should be fun.

Fun it may have been, but profitable it was not. While *Slate* drew distinguished contributors and was recognized for journalistic excellence, it dropped its subscription plan in 1999; it is now owned by The Washington Post Co.

The Los Angeles Times

Welcome to The Los Angeles Times Website

It is a pleasure to share with you the resources of our fine newspaper and our knowledge, guidance and experience of Southern California. By looking for our home page, you have indicated that you are curious, someone who wants to discover, someone who appreciates information that is timely, well-written, useful or just plain interesting . . . It is our hope that what you find in our pages is an invitation. We want your participation as we evolve with additional information about how we see the world from Southern California, about how we can provide sources, data and personal observations that can make our time together richer and most useful.

We think the newspaper itself provides a variety of classy reports from near and from far away. We think we can help link you to other Southern California sites that we find helpful. We think we can give you the basic Internet tools to make your time at the computer worthwhile. Our name stands for credible, accurate and timely information. We hope you agree we deliver. – From The Los Angeles Times salutatory (Schwadron, 1996)

Beyond platitudes and vague promises of enriched content, old media companies struggled to explain to readers how their online versions would work and what advantages they offered.

Los Angeles Times Deputy Managing Editor Terry Schwadron's stiffly solicitous inaugural message to online readers flattered them for their good taste in seeking out the *Times* on the Web and told them they could expect pretty much what they already got in the print editions (except for free, a fact he omitted). In any case, Schwadron assumed people truly interested in "credible, accurate and timely information" would continue to buy and read the print edition, and he encouraged them to do so.

Enthusiastic early adopters of the new digital media of the sort Schwadron was addressing, however, were disdainful of hierarchy and assumptions of professional privilege and prestige, and were drawn to the Internet as an alternative to top-down, take-it-or-leave-it content, an attitude established news outlets either missed or chose to ignore. Instead, in promoting their online products, they repeatedly stressed the idea that the journalists would "provide," "guide" and "monitor" users' online experience.

Schwadron's promise to keep users abreast as the *Times* evolved, as the *Times* "saw the world," and as the *Times* selected and chose to "provide" information, assumed that the traditional gatekeeper approach to journalism would continue to define and regulate the relationship between journalists and citizens on the Web. (*The Washington Post* also conceived "interactivity" in hierarchical terms, creating a "Web Exploration Society . . . that encourages visitors to the site to explore the online universe through guided, themed Web Safaris.")

The interface *The Los Angeles Times* constructed to help readers navigate its site appeared to have been designed for small children or elders who could not set the blinking clock on their VCRs. It completely missed the point that in the early days of Internet availability, users were typically affluent young professionals undaunted by technology and relatively unencumbered by old media habits . . . or loyalties. Atkin and Jeffres (1998) applied diffusion theory to Internet user demographics and concluded that early Internet users represented "a young, educated adopter profile," who were likely to have been early computer adopters a few years earlier (p. 475). This was not the same relatively homogeneous mass that made up newspaper circulation in 1996.

To this savvy cohort, *The L.A. Times* (1995) offered "Hunter," a Golden *Retriever* who spoke to readers (under an adorable photo) in the first person-canine: "HI! My name's Hunter, and I'd like to welcome you to the website of *The Los Angeles Times*. The Web people here asked me to introduce the site because I know its nooks and crannies. I spend all day fetching stories to match members' interests, so I know my way around better than almost anyone. (Come visit me after you've read this!) If this is your first time here, you may not realize the depth and breadth this site has – it makes my paws hurt just thinking about all the places to go."

Again, in a medium built to foster self-designed, decentralized, user-selected pathways to information, *The Times* promised users a controlled experience with a faintly Soviet-style appellation: "Think of us as Information Central. We're to help you through every step of your Internet experience." Hunter signed off with a Winnie the Pooh-inspired "TTFN" (ta-ta for now).

While sophisticated customer relationship management (CRM) and enterprise resource planning (ERP) programs would not be widely diffused and adopted until the late 1990s, *The Los Angeles Times* and other media companies – particularly those covering the dot.com revolution – did not need sophisticated analytics to tell them their approach to the new web audience was woefully misguided; they needed only to read their own news reports.

The New York Times

The New York Times Introduces a Website

The New York Times begins publishing on the World Wide Web today, offering readers around the world immediate access to most of the newspaper's contents . . . The electronic newspaper is part of a strategy to extend the readership of The Times *and to create opportunities for the company in the electronic media industry, said Martin Nisenholtz, president of* The New York Times *Electronic Media Company. – From the salutatory of the online iteration of* The New York Times *(1996)*

After making select content available online to AOL members since 1994, *The New York Times* online edition debuted on January 22, 1996 with a very specific, and limited, mission: "Offering readers around the world immediate access to most of the daily newspaper's contents . . . including the newspaper's crossword puzzle" (the very first feature it successfully hid behind a pay wall).

The *Times* created a separate corporate division to run its site, which would offer free access, "initially at least . . . and generate revenue from advertising." The story introducing the service quoted Publisher Arthur Sulzberger, who somewhat contradictorily vowed to seize the possibilities of the Internet but also asserted that *The Times*' online objectives would not stray far from its print traditions.

Like other old media outlets, Sulzberger assumed readers in the new digital universe would want and accept a hierarchical experience – with *The Times* acting as filter and agenda-setter:

Our site is to take full advantage of the evolving capabilities offered by the Internet. We see our role on the Web as being similar to our traditional print role – to act as a thoughtful, unbiased filter and to provide our customers with information they need and can trust.

The story's kicker quoted the optimistic president of a consultancy that lent counsel to interactive ventures: "*The New York Times* name will get people to look at the product once, or maybe twice," he predicted. "The market is booming for newspapers on the World Wide Web."

Actually, it wasn't. Nor was it booming for online-only sites that offered users traditional journalistic content, even when those sites represented a new approach to creating and delivering that content. Joint online efforts such as PoliticsNow.com, a partnership of ABC News, *The Washington Post*, *Newsweek*, *The Los Angeles Times* and *The National Journal*, launched in advance of the pivotal 1996 elections and described as "a deep-dish digital buffet of campaign news, chat and games," failed to attract advertisers or visitors. PoliticsNow.com went offline in March 1997 and was revived, briefly, as "Cloakroom" by *The National Journal* (Allen, 1997).

CONCLUSION

Whether they represented old media or new media, journalists who ventured onto the Web in the mid-1990s were explorers in a new and, initially, sparsely populated landscape. Only 20 million Americans – a mere seven percent – were online in 1996, and dialup service offered a slow and severely circumscribed experience; just connecting to the Web through a modem could take up to a minute and there was not enough channel capacity for much more than text and images.

No one knew how large the audience would become or what effect broadband and wireless access would soon have on Web content, interactivity and mobility. But a lack of certainty does not preclude an assessment of probability. Despite fuzzy acknowledgements that the Web would "evolve," old *and* new media outlets showed little foresight or realization that the dialup internet was a crude prototype that would quickly be refined, made faster, more versatile, and easier to use – a development anyone with even a layman's knowledge of older communication technologies like radio, television and recorded music, could have predicted.

New and old media news outlets also misjudged their audiences, though audience metrics were available from ISPs and data provided by cookies from the sites themselves. Neilson would soon be monitoring and measuring the audience as well. Absent in most old and new media online salutatories is a clear idea of who the online audience really was.

Rather than framing an appeal that offered unique features to new potential audiences – young, mobile consumers who were not subscribing to newspapers in great numbers even before the dawn of the Internet – news outlets such as *The Los Angeles. Times* seemed to assume they were addressing the exact same people who already bought, and would continue to subscribe to, the newspaper. There seemed to be no insight that online function should dictate online form; newspapers simply digitized print conventions in the areas of graphic design, story selection and presentation. In addition, even news organizations that managed to reach the end of the digital rainbow found that there was no pot of gold waiting for them. Online advertising is diffused across hundreds of thousands of websites, not a few thousand traditional and online media companies focused primarily on news. As ad revenues from print plunged in the 1990s, the uptick in internet-generated revenue was miniscule, and hardly enough to offset losses.

Hindsight proves this was a disastrous strategy based on a short-sighted reading of the emerging online market. By 1999, about 40% of people aged 18-34 read newspapers, a figure that would decline by 25% by 2011. By contrast, in 1999 about 70% of older citizens (aged 55 and up) subscribed to newspapers, although the size of the cohort would also drop dramatically (Edmonds, Guskin & Rosensteiel, 2012).

Clearly, the assumptions news organizations made about the present led them to stumble into the future. However, no one set out to fail. A key assumption of both old and new media journalists was that journalists should embed traditional values and methods into a new platform.

The preservation of these traditional values remains a prime objective for online journalists committed to the public service functions of journalism. According to ProPublica's Tofel (2012),

We should care not about newspapers themselves but about the highest level of quality journalism that they have represented for a century or so. The future of that kind of journalism will depend largely on our ability to create new institutions, and adapt old ones, so that we can respond to technological change with business creativity, entrepreneurial determination, self-confidence, and common sense.

But, as Jay Rosen (1999) has pointed out:

The press cannot speak to the same country twice. Nor can it claim its common paths to news are the only ones imaginable . . . To cover news is to judge what is newsworthy; such estimates of worth involve ideas about politics and power, images of democracy, views of culture, and of the individual, all of which are subject to change as conditions remake themselves. In these ways and others, journalism requires imagination.

Those conditions changed radically in the mid-1990s with rise of the Internet, which has thus far transformed virtually every form of news, entertainment, politics and social interaction. While journalists could not be expected to see into the future, the salutatories that heralded their entrance to the online world of information of ideas demonstrated a distinct lack of imagination and a stubborn desire to transport the past into the future instead of assessing and reacting to the realities of the present.

REFERENCES

Allen, M. (1996). In time for campaign '96, a new political website. *The New York Times*. Retrieved March 12, 2012, from http://www.nytimes.com/1996/06/10/business/in-time-for-campaign-96-a-new-political-web-site.html

Atkin, D. J., Jeffres, L. W., & Neuendorf, K. A. (1998). Understanding internet adoption as telecommunications behavior. *Journal of Broadcasting & Electronic Media*, *42*(4), 475–490. doi:10.1080/08838159809364463

Barnhurst, K., & Nerone, J. (2001). *The form of news: A history*. New York: Guilford Press.

Bitzer, L. F. (1995). The Rhetorical Situation. In W. A. Covino & D. A. Jolliffe (Eds.), *Rhetoric: Concepts, definitions, boundaries* (pp. 300–310). Boston: Allyn and Bacon.

Business Wire. (1996, June). Washingtonpost.com launches on world wide web. Retrieved December 11, 2011, from http://www.thefreelibrary.com/washingtonpost.com+Launches+on+World+Wide+Web.-a018406746

Chyi, I. H., & Lasora, D. (2006). The market relationship between online and print newspapers: The case of Austin, Texas. In X. Li (Ed.), *Internet news: The making of a mainstream medium* (pp. 177–192). Mahwah, NJ: Lawrence Erlbaum Associates.

De Argaez, E. (2003). *Broadband usage USA*. Retrieved March 1, 2012, from http://www.internetworldstats.com/articles/art030.htm

Edmonds, R., Guskin, E., & Rosensteil, T. (2012). Newspapers: By the numbers. The state of the news media 2012. *Pew Research Center's Project for Excellence in Journalism*. Retrieved March 1, 2012, from http://stateofthemedia.org/2012/newspapers-building-digital-revenues-proves-painfully-slow/newspapers-by-the-numbers/

German, K. (n.d.). Top 10 dot-com flops. *CNET*. Retrieved March 1, 2012, from http://www.cnet.com/1990-11136_1-6278387-html

Horne, L. (2011). Sean parker: myspace could have been facebook. *P.C. Magazine*. Retrieved September 12, 2014, from http://www.pcmag.com/article2/0,2817,2387799,00.asp

Jones, A. (2009). *Losing the News: The Future of News That Feeds Democracy*. New York: Oxford University Press.

Kinsley, M. (1996). *Welcome to Slate*. Retrieved August 25, 2010, from http://www.slate.com/articles/news_and_politics/readme/1996/06/welcome_to_slate.html

Kirchhoff, S. M. (2011). Advertising industry in the digital age (CRS Report R40908). *Congressional Research Service*.

Lewis, P. (1996). The New York Times Introduces a Web Site. *The New York Times*. Retrieved March 13, 2012, from http://www.nytimes.com/1996/01/22/business/the-new-york-times-introduces-a-web-site.html?scp=2&sq=The%20New%20York%20Times%20Introduces%20a%20New%20Web%20Site&st=cse

Lewis, P. H. (1996a, April 13). Yahoo. Gets a Big Welcome on Wall Street. *The New York Times.* Retrieved January 1, 2012, from http://www.nytimes.com/1996/04/13/business/yahoo-gets-big-welcome-on-wall-street.html?scp=2&sq=yahoo&st=nyt

Lippman, W. (1922). *Public Opinion.* New York: Harcourt Brace.

Lohr, S. (2013, February 1). The Origins of 'Big Data:' An Etymological Detective Story. *The New York Times.* Retrieved September 15, 2014, from http://bits.blogs.nytimes.com/2013/02/01/the-origins-of-big-data-an-etymological-detective-story/?_r=0

Los Angeles Times (1995). *Hi!* Retrieved January 15, 2011, from http://web.archive.org/web/19961221161651/http://www.latimes.com/HOME/HELP/WEBSITE/welcome.htm

Lyons, D. A. (2010, November). Decade of Destruction. *Newsweek.* Retrieved February 24, 2012, from http://2010.newsweek.com/essay/a-decade-of-destruction.html

Manjoo, F. (2009). The Internet of 1996 is almost unrecognizable compared with what we have today. *Slate.* Retrieved November 10, 2011, from http://www.slate.com/articles/technology/technology/2009/02/jurassic_web.html

Peterson, I. (1996, September 23). Newspapers increasingly cooperate in the face of growing competition for ads. *The New York Times.* Retrieved October 12, 2011, from http://www.nytimes.com/1996/09/23/business/newspapers-increasingly-cooperate-in-the-face-of-growing-competition-for-ads.html

Polsson, K. (2012). *Chronology of Personal Computers.* Retrieved March 1, 2012, from http://www.islandnet.com/~kpolsson/comphist/

Rogers, E. (2003). *Diffusion of innovations.* New York: Free Press.

Rosen, J. (1999). *What are journalists for?* New Haven: Yale University Press.

Schwadron, T. (1996). Welcome to the Los Angeles Time Web Site. *Los Angeles Times.* Retrieved December 11, 2011, from http://web.archive.org/web/19961223123414/http://www.latimes.com/HOME/HELP/WEBSITE/message.htm

Shirky, C. (2008). Newspapers and thinking the unthinkable. *Edge.com.* Retrieved February 13, 2012, from http://edge.org/conversation/newspapers-and-thinking-the-unthinkable

Stats, I. W. Usage and Population Statistics. (2014). *United States of America: Internet usage and broadband usage report.* Retrieved September 14, 2014, from http://www.internetworldstats.com/am/us.htm

Tofel, R. J. (2012). *Why American newspapers gave away the future.* Venice, CA: Now and Then Reader.

Agreement, U. (1996, December). The Los Angeles Times. Retrieved March 3, 2012, from https://web.archive.org/web/19970217092615/http://www.latimes.com/HOME/HELP/WEBSITE/member_agreement.htm

What is Salon? (n.d.). *Salon.com.* Retrieved December 17, 2010, from http://web.archive.org/web/20000903031050/http://salon.com/12nov1995/bookfront/editorial.html

KEY TERMS AND DEFINITIONS

Aggregators: Web sites that offer news and information for a variety of distinct news websites.

New Media: News organizations created exclusively for the Internet.

Old Media: Traditional, print-based news organizations that created online iterations.

Revenue Model: Organizational and financial mechanisms to generate revenue and profit.

Rhetorical Situation: Those contexts in which speakers or writers create rhetorical discourse.

Salutatory: An editorial in which debut print and web publications introduce themselves and explain themselves to the public.

Chapter 2
Computational Journalism: Shaping the Future of News in a Big Data World

Lady Dhyana Ziegler
Florida A&M University, USA

ABSTRACT

In this chapter, the use and application of big data in the news gathering process is discussed. The author explains how the combination of journalism, computer science, and social research introduces a new paradigm to the news industry and academic programs. The chapter explains how the impact of computational journalism on the news product and the use of big data analytics are applied to assess trends and habits of human interaction in all aspects of news coverage. The author purports that big data is essential to the news industry to make predictions and/or draw conclusions to produce a better news package. The author stresses the point that shaping news in a big data world challenges the foundation of journalistic principles and practices but the credibility and integrity of the news product must be maintained. The chapter introduces the Z Wheel communication process model as a new tool for shaping news in this big data environment.

INTRODUCTION

According to IBM, 90% of the data that exists in the world today is only two years old. It is also estimated that there is now 2.5 quintillion bytes of data in the world, up from only 800,000 petabytes in the year 2000. This number is expected to rise to 35 zettabytes by 2020. Much of the new data is being generated by social media. Twitter alone generates 7 terabytes (TB) daily, and Facebook generates 10 TB. It is also estimated that other businesses generate terabytes of data every hour of every day. Ultimately, these volumes are incalculable, since estimates of the amount of big data tend to be out of date as soon they are published (Zikopoulos, et. al., 2012).

DOI: 10.4018/978-1-4666-8580-2.ch002

Big data is defined as "the overwhelming volume of information produced by and about human activity, made possible by the growing ubiquity of mobile devices, tracking tools, always-on sensors, and cheap computing storage" (Lewis, Zamith, & Hermida, 2013, p. 34). So how do we keep up in a "big data" world and discuss its impact at such a rapid growth rate? Perhaps the answer lies in the question, and we have to keep swimming upstream and hope we survive. Nonetheless, big data is instrumental in predicting our future, ready or not. The problem is we are not ready for it. "In short, the term big data applies to information that can't be processed or analyzed using traditional processes or tools" (Zikopoulos et al., 2012, p. 3). This is the challenge for most corporations, the news industry, and educational institutions. Even the powerful search engine Google is grappling with the challenges of living in a big data world and generating effective measurement tools for predictions. Hal Varian, Google's chief economist admits as much: "we don't have any better ways to predict the future. What we're working on is predicting the present" (Mui, 2014, p. A5).

If corporations and powerful search engine platforms such as Google are trying to keep up, then the news industry and educational institutions have their work cut for them as it relates to teaching and training the next wave of journalists who will create and disseminate news, using big data as a tool. Yet, big data is already part of the news cycle. Social media, which relies on and disseminates big data, is increasingly becoming the central part of human interaction. Social media sites have replaced news wire services and other traditional means of researching and packaging news. As a result, news theories and communication process models of the past are almost non-existent in the world of "big data." Social media and citizen journalism are now major players in the shaping of news today. This is a major challenge with which the news industry and educational institutions are grappling, despite experiencing budget cuts, outdated equipment, and a lack of resources that are needed to function in this new environment.

There are also questions associated with the rise and reliance on big data. Does bigger make it better? How does it impact the field of journalism in relation to truth, ethics, overall news product, and the audience? What about the need for privacy, given the fact that so much data are collected on individuals and communities? How about protection from hackers, who seem to be able to crack any safety net that stores big data including personal finances, medical information, user habits, and other consumer information? This is the new world in which we live. There are some who point out that companies and institutions are relying too much on hard data, and thus may be blinded to other critical ways to gauge trends. "Some argue that what's really needed is an overhaul of how we measure – and judge – the world to include intangibles such as happiness, education and health" (Mui, 2014, p. A5). While this is a noteworthy suggestion, the issue is much more complex.

More data is not always better, said Jasper McMahon, co-founder of Now-Economics, which does not use social media or search trends in its calculations. You can be blinded by having access to masses and masses of data. But that exposes you to masses and masses of noise." (Mui, 2014, p. A5).

McMahon has a point but many do not have a choice and must engage with big data in their corporate, educational, or public service institutions. It's no easy task because the widespread embrace of big data can be overwhelming to many who are faced with having to sift through volumes of data in an effort to stay on the competitive edge and maximize effectiveness.

Journalists and educators will need to rise to these challenges to maintain their stance as interpreters of credible news that is transmitted to an audience. This chapter will discuss the challenges journalists and educators are facing and the skill sets needed to assess and shape the news in a big data environment.

BACKGROUND

The Emergence of Computational Journalism

Today's journalism requires a set of new skills that incorporates big data. Journalists need to understand computer-assisted reporting techniques and navigate the Internet. They must create and apply analytics and data visualization techniques to enhance their story telling. While some analytical techniques have long been used by journalists, social science techniques are now being added to explore certain phenomenon in the reporting of news stories and analysis of trends. In the past, social scientists were used as sources, but now reporters must adopt social science skills as well, and develop a broader understanding of research techniques. This new skill set can be called "computational journalism."

Computational journalism involves the application of software and technologies to the activities of journalism, and it draws from the fields of computer science, the social sciences, and media communications. New technologies may enhance the traditional aims of journalism, or may initiate greater interaction between journalists and information and communication technology specialists. The enhanced use of computing in news production is related in particular to three factors: larger government data sets becoming more widely available; the increasingly sophisticated and ubiquitous nature of software; and the developing digital economy (Flew et. al., 2010, p. 1).

This definition in itself indicates the new approaches to news gathering or reporting skills that are needed in this new digital environment. It goes further than basic computer knowledge. Computation journalism includes an understanding of analytics, algorithms, data sets, data visualization, and a more specialized approach to the gathering of information. According to technology journalist Leah Hoffmann (2013), "computation is really the only way to grapple with large data sets," (p.22). Learning these skills require a new approach to journalism education and shifts in gathering techniques for news organizations across the countries. Time Berners-Lee, founder of the World Wide Web, urges journalists to get comfortable with big data.

Data-driven journalism is the future. Journalists need to be data-savvy. It used to be that you would get stories by chatting to people in bars, and it still might be that you'll do it that way some times. But now it's also going to be about poring over data and equipping yourself with the tools to analyze it and picking out what's interesting (Gray. et. al., 2012, p. 2).

As stated earlier, this big data environment takes the interactivity of several entities: journalists, computer scientists, software developers, social scientists, educators, and other scholars -- to make this shift to generating digital news from big data. While computational journalism "provides greater opportunities for collaboration and co-creation between professional journalists, citizen journalists, and their readers" (Flem, et. al., 2010, P.6), there are several questions and challenges associated with this approach. Audiences have expectations of the final news product they receive; journalists have expertise in news gathering; and citizens bring a fresh approach to news. But where are the gatekeepers to ensure truth, quality, ethics, and credibility in the end product?

To some this shift may look like a good deal: Why not trade a few newspapers for what appears to be infinite access to information? But as news staff decline, so too does the public's ability to monitor power (Cohen, Hamilton, &Turner, 2011, p. 66).

Undoubtedly, the future of journalism is still unfolding and there is much to teach and learn as it evolves to the big data world. As is the case with the profession itself, journalism education will have to become a part of this change and include other disciplines to survive in this new world. It's also worth mentioning that this isn't the first time the profession has gone through dramatic change. Technology developments have reshaped journalism.

A half-century ago, photocopying machines quietly revolutionized accountability journalism. The ability to copy documents worked in tandem with new freedom-of-information laws to make possible more sophisticated investigations. The machines let whistleblowers share agency records (such as correspondence and memoranda, inspection forms, and audits). Previously, investigations would often depend on undercover reporting, an ethically dicey practice. But the copy machine turned reporters' attention to documents and with them, to a new level of ethical clarity and accuracy (Cohen, Hamilton, & Turner, 2011, p. 66).

Clearly, there will be more lessons learned in this big data environment that will set the stage for the future. There can be no denying that advances in computers, the Internet, interactive multimedia, and social media have created an exciting future for journalism. The old saying "a picture is worth a thousand words," has never had more meaning in this world of big data. Data visualization and graphics paint pictures of data that have enhanced how we view government information, economic, consumer trends and geographical data.

SOCIETAL IMPACT ON EMERGING TRENDS

The news industry has changed and will continue to change as budgets shrink and news staff struggle to shift their news gathering techniques in a big data world. But the question still remains, what will be the impact on news consumption? The decline of newspapers and a less reliance on the traditional news agencies and other gatekeepers have changed the game. And the impact of this is on the news product. Journalists and educators must understand how large-scale data collection, algorithmic analysis, computational practices, and the production of public knowledge interact. That is the challenge of now and the future.

Today, there are fewer reporters gathering original material than in a generation. By some reports, full-time newsroom employment has fallen by one-quarter over the past ten years. Bloggers, citizen journalists, and some non-profit news agencies have made up for only a small part of this loss. The growth in the online news organizations has been mostly in the role of aggregators, who read other blogs and news reports, and select, aggregate, edit, and comment on their findings. There is a real danger that the proud tradition of original, in-depth investigative reporting will fade away with the ailing traditional news media (Cohen, et. al., 2011, p.1).

There is no question the news media can and will evolve. But will it maintain its standards as things change?

Internet of Things

The next phase of technology infrastructure, called the Internet of Things, is on the horizon and expected to have a phenomenon impact on economic life in the future.

This new technology platform is beginning to connect everything to everyone. Today more than 11 billion sensors are attacked to natural resources, production lines, the electricity grid, logistics networks and recycling flows, and implanted in homes, offices, stores and vehicles, feeding big data in the Internet of Things. By 2020, it is projected that at least 50 billion sensors will connect to it (Rifkin, 2014, p. 2).

The Internet of Things is expected to have an enormous impact on the global economy by 2025, according to a General Electric study. The Internet of Things is about collaboration, universal access, and what is considered a shared economy, in which goods and services are exchanged outside of the traditional economic system, which results in a creation of social capital that is evolving outside of the capitalistic approach that has existed in society. People are already sharing car services and using social media sites and redistribution networks to share many goods and services. The Internet of Things is more concentrated on access as opposed to ownership which has far-reaching implications for the economy.

People can connect to the network and use big data, analytics and algorithms to accelerate efficiency and lower the marginal cost of producing and sharing a wide range of products and services to near zero, just as they now do with information goods (Rifkin, 2014, p. 3).

Journalists will increasingly find new avenues of data gathering as the Internet of Things becomes a greater part of the economy. Besides the implications for the economy, journalists will have to adjust data gathering techniques as this era of societal collaboration continues to evolve.

Social Engagement

Social media has changed the way audiences consume and share information. It has had a profound impact on the news industry and the way news is received and disseminated. One impact has been the reduction in the number of print newspapers. Some believe that even though traditional news media sites are online, they are too slow to break the news, compared with the almost real-time delivery of information on events via social media postings.

Aided by social media networking sites and smaller social media outlets, users are able to document the news as it happens in real time and reach a huge number of people. Furthermore, people reading the news posts of others are able to engage with the original poster by contributing their views on the topic while sharing it with others. Suddenly, online papers are no longer the favored place to get the news and instead (intentionally or unintentionally) turning to 'citizen journalists' for their news (Demers, 2014, p. 1).

Citizen Journalism

Aided by social media, citizen journalists – individuals outside the journalism profession and often contributing content on a voluntary basis -- are finding their way into traditional media. In many cases, they are hired by news organizations to serve as their eyes and ears in various markets. Additionally, while users posting their thoughts encounter both positive and negative interactions, but the feedback encourages more reaction and engagement, thus adding to the conversation -- regardless of the outcome.

There are both positive and negative issues associated with citizen journalism which is now at the center stage of user-generated news and dissemination. Information must be accurate, and often, it's difficult to verify initial reporting. One example is the information that appeared on the Reddit site after the bombing of the Boston Marathon in April 2013. The information posted on Reddit was incorrect and resulted in a manhunt for the wrong man. This is just one example of how inaccuracies can occur with citizen journalism, employing social media sites such as Facebook, and Twitter. This further underscores the fact that information must be checked and double checked – one of the sacred tenets of traditional journalism. Besides the need for accuracy in reporting, social media and ethics are occasionally finding themselves on a collision course. After all, social media, like the larger internet, "evolved without a moral framework" (Ziegler, 2014, p.1).

Crowdsourcing

These new initiatives are resulting in, much more collaboration between individuals, and a trend that will only continue to evolve into the future. It's a shift in the communication paradigm, and the voices shared in this technological environment demonstrate the true meaning of living in a democratic society as more people express their opinions through the use of social media and crowdsourcing. One effective example of crowdsourcing was demonstrated by *The Guardian* in the United Kingdom when they investigated the expense claims made by Members of Parliament in 2009. They released their data collection and the public could search these data by member. "A key benefit to *The Guardian* was that no other media entity was able or prepared to replicate the study, enhancing the reputation of *The Guardian* for investigative journalism" (Flew, et. al., 2010, p. 6).

WikiLeaks

Another example of crowdsourcing as a form of news reporting is WikiLeaks. "WikiLeaks is an international organization that publishes anonymously submitted document submissions and leaks otherwise unavailable to the public (Flew, et.al., 2010, p. 6). The site was launched in 2006 and has posted numerous confidential government documents including 75,000 on the War in Afghanistan and 300,000 on the War in Iraq. Other documents include illegal websites addresses, email accounts, and other types of sensitive information involving several countries. While the release of this information can be a national security nightmare for governments, WikiLeaks contends it only releases attributed documents and believes the worldwide community are more than capable of discussing and scrutinizing these data. Others, however, argue the release of these types of documents by WikiLeaks is irresponsible and morally unacceptable. The United States government has condemned WikiLeaks for disclosing classified information.

Clearly, crowdsourcing, as it relates to the release of unauthorized information by WikiLeaks, has far-reaching implications for the future. There are broad ethical and moral implications as it relates to safety, security, and privacy. In fact, the impact of WikiLeaks is still in motion.

Social Trends

Technology has changed the way researchers gather, view, and disseminate information, and this is impacting the perceived quality of news. A survey on the impact of social media on news conducted by ING among a sample of international journalists and public relations professionals found that journalists are widely engaging in social media posts, "despite having doubts about their reliability" (ING, 2014, p. 1). The study reveals that while journalists did not believe the news generated through social media was reliable, more than half of those in the survey were still using it to find out what people were talking about. In addition, 60% stated that they felt less restrained to share their ideas on social media than in traditional media and did not feel a need to apply journalistic principles, such as fact-checking. The journalists also stated they found the opinions of individual consumers more credible than those coming out of professional organizations. PR professional agree news is less reliable due to journalists not checking their facts (ING, 2014, p.1). The survey results further indicate that 45% of the journalists surveyed are putting out 60% to 100% of the news published as soon as possible without checking facts. In fact, only 20% surveyed check facts before publishing their stories (ING, 2014, p. 2). They feel they can correct it later. This is extremely troubling because, unfortunately, most people don't see the corrections. They will accept the first story they see on traditional and/or social media.

If social media is driving this trend of disseminating news without fact-checking and just correcting it later, it is a sad commentary for the field of journalism and the future of the industry. It represents a shift from truth, credibility, and integrity that are at the core of the profession as well as journalism education and training. There is a code of ethics by which journalists are supposed to abide. These basics, principles, and practices are at the cornerstone and foundation of the field of journalism that have existed for centuries.

The ING (2014) survey results indicate that the use of social media to generate news is expected to be a growing trend among journalists in the future. According to the responses, 73% are using tweets, videos, and other user-generated content in their stories, although 32% find these posts unreliable. Based on these data, the future will generate more questions than answers and even if there are answers, will they be reliable?

Along with the social engagement and information delivery of social media, it's also big business. Social media trends have emerged to such a level of importance that IBM, the world's largest computer company and supplier to large enterprises, built and markets a solution specifically to accelerate use of social networking. Cognos Consumer Insights (CCI) describes what people are saying, how topics are trending, and all sorts of data that affect a business and displays it into a rich visualization engine. CCI is a personal analytics solution that empowers analysts and business users to explore, analyze, visualize and share insights without compromising IT values (IBM Corporation, 2010). The news industry will also utilize these tools to generate news stories on business and consumer trends. While all of this information is important, it may still not be ready or verified to be shared with audiences, though it may be considered a great tool for product marketing.

SOLUTIONS AND RECOMMENDATIONS

Toward a New Paradigm

To succeed in a big data world, journalists will need data skills and analytics to assess "the volume and variety of data while it is still in motion and not at rest" (Zikopoulos, et.al., 2012, p. 9). However, traditional, established approaches cannot get lost in the shift to adaptation of a big data environment. In fact, there must be a blending of traditional journalism practices and new data skills to assess and deliver news to audiences today. News is still about storytelling and bringing important information to the public. It may require new approaches and processes to gather information but the goal of packaging information and delivering it to an audience remains the same. Therefore, it requires the blending of the old with the new. Computational journalism introduces new tools to journalists that can be utilized to gather and package the news of the minute, hour, or day. Delivering the news today and the future calls for an adjustment to new tools just as electric typewriters replaced manual ones and computers replaced those.

Several leading journalists agree that big data is reshaping the profession, and these opinions are voiced in the *Data Journalism Handbook*. Here are a few comments that appear in the introduction:

Around the globe, in fact, the bond between data and journalism is growing stronger. In an age of data journalism lies in the ability of its practitioners to provide context, clarity and, perhaps most important, find truth in the expanding amount of digital content in the world (Alex Howard, O'Reilly Media)...

Some stories can only be understood and explained through analyzing-and sometimes visualizing – the data (Cheryl Phillips, The Seattle Times)...I think it's important to stress the "journalism" or reporting aspect of 'data journalism'. The exercise should not be about just analyzing data or visualizing data for the sake of it, but to use it as a tool to get closer to the truth of what is going on in the world (Cynthia O'Murchu, Financial Times)...

Data journalism is bridging the gap between stat technicians and wordsmiths (David Anderton, freelance journalist)....

Good data journalism is hard, because good journalism is hard. It means figuring out how to get the data, how to understand it, and how to find the story (Chris Taggart, OpenCororates), (Gray, J. et. al., 2012, pp. 1-7).

These journalists' comments underscore the importance of blending traditional journalism practices with new data skills.

The Z Wheel

For decades, journalists operated under the Lasswell Model, a linear communication process model that describes communication from point to point. Who says what, in which channel, to whom and with what effect cannot be applied in a linear fashion in this technological savvy world that now exists. Journalists cannot apply the Lasswell Model to communication today because it no longer fits the paradigm shift to big data. It was simple to apply because one could easily identify the originator of the message but that is no longer true today. Additionally, the Lasswell Model did not take in account any feedback from audiences. Today, the news story can start with the audience especially with the addition of citizen journalists. Couple with these factors, there is constant feedback generated from a variety of sources, such as social media.

The Z Wheel (see Figure 1) is a circular communication process model that can be applied to the field of journalism in this big data environment where information is constantly in motion. The Z Wheel emphasizes practices and processes of news gathering from assessment to dissemination of the news content. It blends traditional journalism skills with new ones. It emphasizes the need for strong reporting skills, research, truth, and ethics at its core. The root of journalism principles and practices remain the same, and that is, to deliver news that is credible to an audience. It relies on the principles and practices of journalism that have existed for decades. The objective is to deliver a quality news product to an audience that is grounded in truth.

Figure 1. The Z Wheel, a circular communication process model

This will also require the ability to conduct adequate research. Mark Hansen, director of Columbia University's Brown Center for Media Innovation, says data "have something to say about how we live. But they aren't neutral, and neither are the algorithms we rely on to interpret them. The stories are often incomplete, uncertain, and open-ended" (Bell, 2012, p.3). The issue grows more acute when coupled with the fact that journalists often do not check facts and just want to get information out fast and make corrections later. Even in era with abundant data, there is still a need for skilled journalists that have strong reporting skills. "Without journalists thinking in data," Hansen states, "who will help us distinguish between good stories and bad?" (Bell, 2012, p.3). This has important implications for the credibility of news, as well as, accuracy, truth, research and ethics in reporting.

The pressure to speed up content production and delivery of news in order to beat out the competition can sometimes garner mistakes. The Z Wheel re-emphasizes practices and processes that should occur in the news-gathering environment. The impact of big data on ethics requires a special note because social media and the Internet which houses big data have evolved without a moral compass. Fairfield and Shtein (2014) explain the impact of big data on ethics:

Most of social science ethics focuses on rights and responsibilities toward the individual human participant. Big data as a technique does not accommodate this well. There can be millions of research subjects, yet none of them has given informed consent. The traditional focus of social science has been on physical, rather than information harms, and on not harming individuals, but big data impacts communities as much (or more) than individuals (p.39).

This has strong implications for various races, ethnic groups, cultures, etc. The privacy issues are enormous. The digital divide may even grow wider as a result of big data.

The other spokes on the Z Wheel indicate the need for big data skills and analytics but the assessment of that data is the key to credible news. "Newsrooms will rise and fall on the documentation of real-time information and the ability to gather and share it" (Bell, p. 1). Journalists will have to know what information is credible and how to use it in generating the news intelligence of the day since big data can now generate from so many spaces and places. There is a need to assess credible sources and double check facts. As the Z Wheel spins journalists don't always know where the information originated which is another big shift from the Lasswell model that is linear in nature. The circular Z Wheel does more than just describe who, what, which channel, to whom, and what is the effect of the communication process.

The Z Wheel serves as a check and balance of the practice of journalism in relations to the news process and big data in general. Therefore, journalists will have to be diligent in the practice of their craft. Other spokes on the Z Wheel display the need to deliver and package a quality product, response time, distribution, and interactivity because there is an expectation of feedback due to today's world of social media and user engagement. There will be constant feedback from the audience regardless if it is a message received through traditional mass media, social media, or other means on the Internet which are outlined on the outer Z Wheel. Feedback will be constant. Therefore, the reputation of a reporter or newsroom will rest in his or her ability to deliver credible news that is not at the expense of good journalism principles and practices.

The purpose of the Z Wheel is a reminder of journalism's responsibility. It serves as a guide that blends traditional journalism practices with the evolution of new skills that interact and intersect in this evolving technological environment. As the Z Wheel spins, the center circle always reminds us of the end goal, to deliver credible news to the audience.

FURTHER RESEARCH DIRECTIONS

The term "big data" describes the volume of information produced. It can be accessed on the Internet from mobile devices, and other computing systems. The technology will continue to evolve and big data will expand. Journalists and educators must continue to discuss the use and application of big data in classrooms and newsrooms. This phenomenon will require ongoing research. Anderson (2013) asserts that "if computational practices are the salvation of journalism, this salvation is certainly a double edge sword" (p. 1009). He believes the answers lie outside of journalism. Daniel (2010) says "the concept of computational journalism is not new, and builds upon computer assisted reporting, precision journalism or database journalism techniques" (p. 2). Nonetheless, journalism is still transitioning to computational journalism so more research is needed in the area to discuss the impact, practices, and processes. One thing is for sure. Big data will continue to take a center stage in the news process and checks and balances must be in place to ensure credibility of the news product. The Z Wheel circular communication process model can serve the industry well in that capacity.

As Google executives intimated, they are just trying to keep up with the present. Perhaps other futurists will have predictions similar to Philip Meyers to help guide us through the thicket of change but for now, various disciplines such as journalism, computer science, social science, business and other fields of study must keep their fingers on the pulse. The tools will continue to evolve and improve. Software will increase and the learning curve will be steep for some and easy for others who are growing up in this new world. The implication of the impact of "big data" on the news product must continue to be assessed and studied as well as user engagement. Audience feedback will continue to be a measuring stick; however, since there may not be an originator, the cycle of the feedback will have to be measured against its own impact. In short, future research will grow out of the evolution of big data and journalists, educators, and researchers will learn along the way. This is only the beginning of an exciting future. There will be a need for on-going research and analysis along the way to measure the impact of "big data" on shaping news.

CONCLUSION

The world has changed. Journalists and educators need to adjust to the challenges of big data and make a shift in the way news stories are generated, researched, and packaged in order to meet the needs of the audience. There is no doubt that change is inevitable and it's time to embrace new skills. Computational journalism has arisen to the forefront of this new environment as journalism and computer science merge together as a new skill set to engage in a big data world. It's considered by many to be a good marriage as long as there is mutual respect by both disciplines. Houston (2010) reminds us about the predictions of futurist Philip Meyers "for journalist to prepare themselves for the new journalism environment," (p. 50). He quotes from Philip Meyers' book *Precision Journalism:*

They are raising the ante of what it takes to be a journalist," pointing out that at one time a successful journalist needed only dedication, energy, and talent for writing. From the time his book first appeared in 1978, Meyer recognized the need for new skills for journalists: "The world has become so complicated, the growth of available information so explosive, that the journalists needs to be a filter, as well as a transmitter; an organizer and interpreter, as well as one who gathers and delivers facts...In short a journalist has to be a database manager, a data processor, and a data analyst, (p. 51).

Meyers' predictions have indeed come to pass, and journalists and educators have to embrace change. In doing that, journalism practices and principles cannot be forgotten in the transition. Clearly, there is a need to incorporate new skills in the delivery of the news products. The Internet, social media, and citizen journalists are dictating this shift. But trained journalists must maintain the insight, news judgment, and understanding of the true rules of what is quality and credible news. Journalism is still communicating a message and about telling stories. It is the interpretation of the intelligence of the day in the news cycle. It still requires research, credible sources, ethics, truth, and reporting skills to package credible and quality news that is clearly communicated to an audience. The Z Wheel is a circular process communication model to remind journalists and journalism educators of their responsibility to the profession.

There are many challenges associated with the ability of journalists to assess big data. However, trained journalists know how to deliver and shape the news. Those who are just trying to be timely and not checking facts to keep up with trends and social media are doing the field of journalism an injustice. It is still important to check and double-check the facts. Credibility and integrity have to be established out the gate. The standards of the profession cannot be lowered in a big data world. It should be an enhancement of the news product with all the data accessible for journalists to use.

Search engines and new technologies represent tools that can be used to generate and package news stories across digital platforms. Algorithms, data visualizations, mapping are tools that can be applied to provide a clearer understanding of the data to guide the reader but the journalists must still explain the meaning. Since all these data are available, the use and application of this information must be grounded in ethics. Remember, just because it's there doesn't mean one has a right to invade privacy and forget the journalism code of ethics. The Internet and social media evolved without a moral compass so journalists must still apply the rules of the profession. Journalism has an amazing future with its ability to tell a credible story across digital platforms. Journalists must take the responsibility seriously and stay true to the profession.

REFERENCES

Anderson, C. W. (2013). Towards a sociology of computational and algorithmic journalism. *New Media & Society*, *15*, 1005–1021.

Bell, E. (2012, September 5). Journalism by numbers. *Columbia Journalism Review*. Retrieved from http://www.cjr.org/cover_story/journalism_by_numbers.php?page=all

Cohen, S., Hamilton, J. T., & Turner, F. (2011). Computational journalism. *Communications of the ACM*, *54*(10), 66–71. doi:10.1145/2001269.2001288

Cohen, S., & Yang, L. J. & Yu, C. (2011). Computational journalism: A call to arms database researchers. In *CIDR' 11* (pp. 148-151). Asilomar, CA. Retrieved from http://db.cs.duke.edu/papers/cidr11-CohenLiEtAl-cjdb.pdf

Daniel, A. (2010, November). *The Guardian reportage of the UK MP expenses scandal: A case study of computational journalism*. Paper presented at a meeting of the Communications Policy & Research Forum. Sydney, Australia.

Demers, J. (2013, May 8). *How social media is supporting a fundamental shift in journalism*. Retrieved from http://www.huffingtonpost.com/jayson-demers/how-Social-media-suppo_b_3239076.html

Fairfield, J., & Shtein, H. (2014). Big problems: Emerging issues in the ethics of data science and journalism. *Journal of Mass Media Ethics*, *29*(1), 38–51. doi:10.1080/08900523.2014.863126

Flew, F., Daniel, A., & Spurgeon, C. L. (2010). The promise of computational journalism. In McCallum, K. (Ed.) *Media, Democracy and Change: In Refereed Proceedings of the Australian and New Zealand Communications Association Annual Conference*. (ACT, pp. 1-19). Canberra, Australia. doi:10.1080/17512786.2011.616655

Gray, J., Chambers, L., & Bounegru, L. (2012). *Data Journalism Handbook*. Sebastopol, CA: O'Reilly Media, Inc.

Hoffmann, L. (2013). Looking back at big data. *Communications of the ACM*, *56*(4), 21–23. doi:10.1145/2436256.2436263

Houston, B. (2010). The future of investigative journalism. *Daedalus*, *13*(2), 45–56. doi:10.1162/daed.2010.139.2.45

IBM Corporation, (2010). *Social media analytics solutions: Social solutions powered by IBM Cognos Consumer Insight*. Retrieved from https://www-950.ibm.com/events/wwe/grp/grp004.nsf/f7002a8c9f4c84708525737f006be109/801ebdf1a1a2a8d1852579fb0052bbea/$FILE/Ed Burek's Presentation.pdf

IBM Corporation, (2013).*Big data at the speed of business*. Retrieved from http://www-01.ibm.com/software/data/bigdata/what-is-big-data.html

IBM Corporation, *Big data and analytics-overview-United States*. Retrieved from http://www.ibm.com/big-data/us/en/big-data-and-analytics/

ING Group, (2014). *2014 study on impact of social media on news: more crowd checking, less fact checking*. Retrieved from http://www.ing.com/Newsroom/All-news/NW/2014-Study-impact-of-Social-Media-on-News-more-crowdchecking-less-factchecking.htm

Lewis, S. C., Zamith, R., & Hermida, A. (2013). Content Analysis in an Era of Big Data: A Hybrid Approach to Computational and Manual Methods. *Journal of Broadcasting & Electronic Media*, *57*(1), 34–52. doi:10.1080/08838151.2012.761702

Mui, Y. Q. (2014, June 4). Want to take economy's pulse? Try digging into Google, Twitter. *The Washington Post,* pp. A1, A5.

Rifkin, J. (2014, March 15). The rise of anti-capitalism. *The New York Times,* pp. 1-4.

Ziegler, D. (2014). *Ethics and social media: A collision course*. Retrieved from https://zpcrspectiveblog.wordpress.com/2014/05/29/ethics-and-social-media-a-collision-course/

Zikopoulos, P., Eaton, C., deRoos, D., Deutsch, T., & Lapis, G. (2010). *Understanding big data*. New York, N.Y.: McGraw Hill.

KEY TERMS AND DEFINITIONS

Algorithms: A step-by-step procedure or formula for solving problems. They are used for calculation, data processing, and automated reasoning.

Analytics: A methodology used to discover and communicate meaningful patterns in data.

Computational Journalism: The application of software and other technologies to the field of journalism that draws from the fields of computer science, the social sciences and media communications.

Crowdsourcing: The process of obtaining needed services and ideas or content by soliciting contributions from a large group of people, and especially from an online community, rather than from traditional employees or suppliers.

Data-Visualization: The modern equivalent of visual communication that uses information graphics, such as, tables and charts.

Lasswell Model: One of the earliest communications model developed by Harold Lasswell in 1948 that describes the communication process of who says what, in which channel, to whom, and with what effect. It is linear in nature.

Quintillion: The number that is represented as a one followed by 18 zeros.

Terabytes: It is a measure of computer storage capacity and is 2 to the 40th power or approximately a thousand billion bytes.

Wikileaks: An international, online, non-profit, journalistic organization which publishes secret information, news leaks, and classified media from anonymous sources.

Z Wheel: It is a circular communications process model that emphasizes the process and practices of journalism in a "big data" environment. It is a tool designed for journalists and journalism educators for use in the newsroom and classroom.

Zettabytes: It is a measure of the storage capacity and is 2 to the 70th power bytes or, in decimal, approximately a thousand exabytes or a million terabytes.

Chapter 3
Research Methods, Data, and Analytics:
Examining Service Design and User Experience in TV- and Newspaper-Oriented Digital News Interfaces

William J. Gibbs
Duquesne University, USA

Ronan S. Bernas
Eastern Illinois University, USA

ABSTRACT

Media organizations deliver news services online employing various design techniques and technologies to make services useful, usable, and effective for news consumers. How people use news services, their perceptions of them, and how their design impacts the user experience (UX) is an important area of study. In this chapter, the authors examine service design, UX, and related research methodologies and their importance for online news. Additionally, they report on a study that examined how the type of news provider (TV versus newspaper) and associated services affected user behavior and perception of the user experience. Participants perceived news websites differently based on the type of news provider and their interactions with services differed based on type of provider. The findings have implication for the UX research, specifically UX related to online news.

DOI: 10.4018/978-1-4666-8580-2.ch003

INTRODUCTION

As more people access news online, they interact with digital interfaces. Although a somewhat imprecise term (see Murray, 2012), an interface is the visible control mechanism operated by the user that sits between the system and the human or interactor (Murray, 2012, p.10). It is a medium through which a human interacts with a system or machine where reciprocal action and effect are shared between user and system in a specific context of use (Hartson & Pyla, 2012). It is designed to support the user's tasks so he can accomplish a goal. From motor vehicles, home appliances, the web, to mobile applications, interfaces are ubiquitous. For people who seek news online, the interface is their means of experiencing and learning about local, national and international events. It is the medium through which they engage with others about news and participate in news making. It is becoming the primary way many people become informed about the world. To them, the interaction experience supported, or in some cases afforded, by the interface comprises the system (and organization) that provides news services. Regardless of sophisticated "back-end" technologies or the breadth of possible services, the point of interaction at the interface is often the determinant for how users perceive and build trust in the system and ultimately the organization that sponsors it.

Information architecture, screen layout, functionality, system feedback, system affordances or the perceived or actual properties of an interface object that determine (intuitively tell the user) how the thing can be used (Norman, 2002; Heim, 2009) influence the interaction experience and, to a great degree, determine the extent to which it is positive or frustrating for users. All too often news interfaces and corresponding interactions are inconsistent. They change unexpectedly or they are visually or functionally complex. At the very least, such factors cause users to think about the interface, distracting them from the task they aim to accomplish. More significantly, they impede users' ability to get news, participate in news related experiences, or engage with the news services. It should be noted that for convenience the term online is used to convey networked devices that may include desktop, laptop, smartphone, tablets and other devices through which people get news over a network.

Creating interfaces that engender positive interaction experiences is a challenging endeavor. Much research in engineering, computer science, and the humanities is devoted to studying human–computer interaction (Thuring & Mahlke, 2007). Understanding the complexity of interactions occurring within today's interactive systems is an arduous scientific endeavor but one of much practical value (Chi, Pirolli, Chen, & Pitkow, 2001). By understanding user behaviors, developers can redesign interfaces to improve usability, more effectively accommodate user needs and tasks, help users achieve their goals more efficiently, and improve designs and services overall (Heer & Chi, 2002, p. 243; Chi, Pirolli, Chen, & Pitkow, 2001).

The potential for creating innovative and engaging interaction experiences relevant to news and information services is exciting but there are many challenges. Designing interfaces for desktop displays is no longer adequate. Computers have become far too ubiquitous. They are in appliances, offices, vehicles and even being worn by people. One of the fastest growing areas of ubiquitous person computing is mobile communications (Hartson & Pyla, 2012, p. 3). Estimated to reach 10 billion in 2020, mobile connected devices are changing many facets of society, from education to entertainment (Chen, Chiang & Storey, 2012). A survey of news use in the United States found that people actively follow news using multiple devices, with a majority (56%) using smartphones and 29% using tablets, which represents the vast majority of people who own these devices (American Press Institute, 2014). Another report found that people get news digitally with 82% of them using desktop or laptop computers and 54% using mobile devices (Mitchell & Page, 2014).

More and more people go online for news and interact with news services with a multitude of devices. These factors impact the experience one has with news. News organizations are faced with many challenges not the least of which is how to design news interfaces and engaging user experiences for an array of devices capable of displaying multiple media content on varying viewports sizes in disparate environments. These issues are further compounded by rapidly advancing technologies. In the following sections, the authors explore Service Design, User Experience Design (UXD) and related research methodologies to explicate the value of understanding customers or users and their behavior in the context of such challenges. Placing customers or users central in the design of news interfaces and experiences can play a pivotal role in positively shaping online news services.

BACKGROUND

Service Design

Service design is concerned with systematically applying design methodology and principles to the design of services (Bruce & Bessant, 2002; Holmlid & Evenson, 2008). It is a human-centered approach that concentrates on the customer experience and service quality encounter at the interface level (touchpoint). Service designers endeavor to produce services that are useful, useable, desirable, efficient and effective (Service Design Network).

While there is no single inclusive and universally used definition of what does and does not constitute a service (Sampson & Froehl, 2006), researchers (e.g., Pinhanez, 2007, 2008a, 2008b; Sampson & Froehl, 2006) have discussed basic service characteristics, several of which the authors view as relevant to online news: heterogeneity, simultaneity, perishability, customer-as-input, and coproduction. *Heterogeneity* refers to the extent that service consumers have a unique identity and needs. For instance, users of online news have idiosyncratic interests (politics, local news, world news, sports) and needs. This is especially true when news consumers actively participate in the news by uploading stories or contributing to news discussions. From a service design perspective, a designer must consider all possible instances of inputs at the interface level and how to handle specific cases, such as when a news story is presented in multiple media channels. *Simultaneity* and *perishability* refer to immediacy at which services are produced and consumed as well as the time-sensitive nature or capacity to produce services. *Coproduction* refers to requests for consumers to perform part of the production process, which often leads to greater affiliation with the organization and satisfaction. According to Parker and Heapy (2006, p. 15), "Learning to understand and map how people experience the point of delivery, the interface between a service and their lives, is essential for creating the conditions for co-production." Coproduction in terms of online news is important as citizens actively engage in news production. *Customer-as-input*, refers to the extent to which consumers/users have input to the production process. In terms of online news content, customer-as-input is becoming increasingly relevant as users comment on news stories and contribute to the news. Moreover, as technologies evolve and interfaces change, input from news consumers is essential to ensure a positive UX. It is less obvious how news organizations engage users at the interface level to shape the acquisition and distribution of news. Pinhanez (2007) used services theory to examine trends relevant to the design and development of online applications, such as multiple unrelated users using software distributed on servers, and users storing personal data on those machines. He delineates between online applications that have characteristics similar to traditional services based on two dimensions: 1) how much the user controls the means of production and 2) how much the user is an essential part of the input to the production process. While Pinhanez acknowledges problems with the classification, he categorized news sites as online information providers, not services because users are not essential to the production process. However, given recent trends in the news industry whereby users not only acquire but contribute newsworthy content and help spread or distribute news, the authors feel that online news falls into the categories of services. In addition, news providers define their websites (online presence) as services and, in fact, they meet the aforementioned service characteristics (Sampson & Froehl, 2006). Therefore, in terms of coproduction and customer-as-input, a substantial portion of the world's population now has the capability to produce media content (capturing images, words, video and audio with portable recording devices such as smartphones), instigating major changes in human communication behavior as well as information access and distribution. Communication devices enable people to be active in news gathering and dissemination and not solely news recipients. Additionally, network connectivity and digital media support two-way communication, allowing people to engage in mass conversations about the news (and other topics of interest). Such developments have engendered a proliferation of social media-type sites that deliver news more interactively, rather than being "filtered" and processed by editors. These online news features and services are unprecedented. It is more critical than ever that news organizations endeavor to understand customer needs and recognize the value of their input in defining new and evolving types of services. Online technologies afford many innovations in capturing customer data. Text analyses of social media, for example, may provide data on customer sentiment, among other things. These approaches as well as many others may prove to be useful in better understanding customers so that news service can be designed or refined.

Just as service design put emphasis on customer needs in the design of services, human-computer interaction (HCI) and user experience design (UXD) seek to understand human cognition and behavior to better design interactive systems. The following section provides an overview of the HCI field and UX. It highlights their importance to the design of online news services, and especially to the design of digital interfaces, the point through which many of today's news seekers get news.

Human-Computer Interaction, User Experience

The field of human-computer interaction (HCI) is concerned with humans using computer systems to accomplish their goals (Hartson & Pyla, 2012, p.11). Not unlike service design, methodologies and approaches used in HCI (e.g., user-centered design) focus on users and their ability to understand, interpret and use systems. A great deal of effort gets invested in conducting research to understand users so that systems can be designed to accommodate their needs. In recent years, Interaction Design (ID) has been used widely by some researchers as an umbrella term that includes characteristics of user experience design, interface design, user-centered design, product design, and interactive system design (Sharp, Rogers & Preece, 2012). "It captures many aspects of a system that have to be the subject of coordinated design decisions, including social and cultural elements as well as technical and visual components" (Murray, 2012, p. 11). A key distinction between HCI and ID is that ID pertains to any system of behavior, digital (computing) and non-digital whereas HCI is more narrowly focused on the study of interactive computing systems (digital) for human use. Usability endeavors to ensure that human or user interactions with the computing systems are effective, efficient, easily learned, and satisfying (Hartson & Pyla, 2012). In the past, research on human–computer interaction almost exclusively concentrated on aspects of usefulness and usability (Thuring & Mahlke, 2007). The practicality and usability of computing systems pervaded HCI research literature (Nielsen, 1993). Much research focused on behaviorally-oriented tasks as well as the instrumental aspects of systems (i.e., effectiveness, efficiency, learnability, and satisfaction) so that users could better attain work performance goals. Thus, in user research and analysis, task performance became a focal point along with techniques to study human behavior during system use, such as usability testing. This ultimately contributed to instrumentality or the instrumental value of systems becoming a major undertaking in the field (Hassenzahl & Tractinsky, 2006). However, as Rafaeli and Vilnai-Yavetz (2004) point out, the significance of instrumental qualities as measures to evaluate systems is incontrovertible but there are other factors germane to such evaluations including aesthetics and symbolism, the meanings or associations brought about by the artifact or system. A user's experience when using an interactive system encompasses emotions and perceptions of the system's instrumental and non-instrumental qualities (Thuring & Mahlke, 2007). The aesthetics of system design and users' emotional experiences when using a system influence perceptions of quality. Thuring and Mahlke (2007) proposed the Components of User Experience (CUE) model that differentiates instrumental qualities related to usefulness and usability (i.e., effectiveness, efficiency, learnability, and satisfaction) and non-instrumental qualities associated with appeal, aesthetics, and attractiveness. Instrumental and non-instrumental qualities are likely to influence the emotions experienced by users during interaction. They argue for a more encompassing perspective regarding how to evaluate systems that includes three elements: "(a) the perception of instrumental qualities, such as the controllability or the effectiveness of a system; (b) the perception of non-instrumental qualities, such as visual aesthetics or haptic quality; and (c) the user's emotional responses to system behavior" (p. 254). Thus, there is increasing recognition that while assessing instrumental qualities of systems is essential other factors also impact user interaction and experiences. For example, people often have a preferred news service. Different services may be equally usable, efficient, and effective but the preferred service may have time-honored or sentimental value because it has been in existence for 75 years. Consequently, measuring instrumental qualities in this case will not tell the researcher much about why people prefer the long-established news service.

Around the turn of the millennium, the apperception that interaction may be influenced by more than instrumental qualities engendered the emergence of User Experience (UX) research, a new paradigm for understanding and investigating the non-instrumental qualities of systems and the experience users have with them (Bargas-Avila & Hornbæk, 2011). A user experience occurs in the process of interacting with a system and it is influenced by: (a) the user's internal cognitive state (expectations, needs, motivation, etc.); (b) the attributes of the system's design (e.g., usability, functionality, etc.); and (c) the context in which the interaction occurs (Hassenzahl &Tractinsky, 2006; Thuring & Mahlke, 2007). In an experience of a product or interactive system, there is continuous interaction between the user's cognitive and sensory-motor-perceptual (i.e., visual, touch, auditory) processes (top-down) and system attributes and functionality (bottom-up) that "…influence the timing, rhythm, flow, and feel of the interaction" (Locher, Overbeeke & Wensveen, 2010, p.71). In defining UX, Hassenzahl and Tractinsky (2006) indicate,

UX takes a human perspective. It is interested in understanding the role of affect as an antecedent, a consequence and a mediator of technology use. In addition, it is rather focused on positive emotions. To prevent frustration and dissatisfaction had always been a core objective even of the most cognitively driven perspective on HCI. What is new in UX research is a focus on positive emotional outcomes such as joy, fun and pride. (p.93)

User Experience and the Design of Interfaces

Newspaper and television news organizations have long-established traditions for distributing news in their respective media (print or television). The inherent attributes of these media and their instrumental and non-instrumental qualities likely influence the UX and how people access and comprehend news as well as how news is reported. Television broadcasts provide a vastly different news gathering experience compared to newspapers. People choose a preferred news service and adapt their behavior to accommodate it. Why someone prefers one service over another often relates to the experience he had with it. Factors such as aesthetics and/or the emotions experienced (i.e., elements of UX) frequently come into play. In digital environments, system (interface) designers as well as users must contend with additional often confounding factors that impact the UX. The digital interfaces or the touch-points where people access news content are fundamentally different from those used in traditional newsprint and television. Online news congregates newspaper and television media. People can watch video on a newspaper-oriented website or read news articles on television-oriented site. When reading a printed newspaper or magazine, there is a familiar, natural pairing between the physical properties of the paper and its appearance, and the possibilities for how the paper can be used to get news, and the actions required to obtain and navigate news stories. The physical paper also provides indications of scale and amount of news. In a printed news magazine, the reader moves forward by physically touching the printed page to turn it. Concepts of page, collection of pages, and magazine are tangible to users and familiar. There is a physical connection with the paper and how to use it to get news. When news is digital, the user needs a virtual interface to interact with it. The digital interface lacks a physical connection to tangible objects. It may display objects that look like pages but they are only conceptual and lack physical properties. They exist so users may more easily conceptualize or form accurate mental models of how the system operates. "Mental models allow people to understand phenomena and to make inferences and predictions. This stored knowledge enables quicker interpretations of internal and external events, and faster, more precise and efficient responses" (Roth et al., 2013, p.229). Users form mental models of information spaces such as websites and consequently have expectations about how they should be designed, including the placement of information, visual elements, and navigation objects (Roth et al., 2013). Violation of these expectations or forcing users to reform mental models likely impedes their ability to use the system. It is therefore critical that the interface be designed to effectively provide users feedforward information about interaction possibilities (e.g., what can I do here, what is the purpose of this object, etc.) and feedback information after the user initiates some action. These forms of information help users understand and interpret the system and connect their actions with its functionality (Locher, Overbeeke & Wensveen, 2010). Without accurate system information provided by the interface, it is unlikely that users will be able to use it. For example, based on conventions and experience, website users are accustomed to words (labels) appearing at the top of a website as navigation. When using a mouse pointer and the pointer hovers over a label, it highlights indicating functionality. Clicking a label usually displays another page. Labels are meaningful and often grouped according to how a majority of users navigate. They constitute navigation, an essential means by which users get access to information. By using the site, users form a mental model about navigation. Positioning, functionality (highlighting, clicking, and navigation to new pages), color, and semantic information, among other things, help users understand phenomena surrounding navigation and to make inferences and predictions about how it works. Recently CNN revised its web interface as a responsive design. When the viewport is large (i.e., desktop), navigation labels are present at the top of the page. However, on small viewports (i.e., mobile) navigation gets hidden, replaced by a three-lined icon colloquially known as the hamburger icon. Users click the icon to see navigation. Unless users are already familiar with this convention, they are likely to be confused, questioning why navigation disappeared. They will probably be unable to immediately associate the hamburger icon with access to navigation, which can lead to a disconcerting UX. These types of issues become quite pronounced when users have limited time to make choices or when decisions at the interface are of critical importance. Because a user's experience with a system is influenced by a multitude of intervening factors such as user characteristics, systems aesthetics, and instrumental qualities (Thuring & Mahlke, 2007), the ability of the interface to effectively convey system information and aid users in forming (or adapting) accurate mental models is paramount.

The Evolving News Interfaces

The web and other networked-based services have become primary vehicles for news dissemination. As people access news, they use a multitude of computing devices with varying viewport sizes. The interaction experience is highly dynamic and characterized by a proliferation of media and functionality that surpasses what is found in either traditional newsprint or on television. It is unclear how such factors shape the way users attend to news information or the UX they have with it. Additionally, there is a preponderance of major TV and newspaper online news services, each with distinctive information architecture and visual layouts designed to underscore the news organization's television or newsprint traditions and reporting methods. For example, The New York Times, a newspaper-oriented site, reflects a newsprint layout that engenders reading. It presents a minimalistic design with headlines and article summaries dispersed throughout the page, not unlike a newspaper. Fox News, a TV-oriented site, features minimal text, concentrated listings of links, and dominant images, many with corresponding video play icons indicating video is available. In early 2015, the number of words on Fox News desktop site homepage, including navigation, was 2630 whereas the word count on the New York Times homepage was 5195. Because the New York Times features headlines and story summaries distributed throughout, and high density text, one might expect a user's visual attention to be more dispersed and browsing to be prolonged compared to a TV-oriented site like Fox News, which presents limited text and concentrated navigation links. In fact, in a survey conducted in the United States, 93% of respondents indicated that they recently used some kind of TV news source. Specifically, respondents most often used Fox News, CNN, and MSNBC, the three national network broadcast operations (American Press Institute, 2014). This suggests that people perceived TV-oriented and newspaper sites as different and they interact with them in different ways, which may have implications for the UX.

As new organizations discern industry trends, their interfaces change often (unexpectedly) and they have given greater prominence to personalized services (e.g., enabling people to discuss news stories or contribute to news), seemingly without regard to the needs of users, the UX, or the service quality they encounter at the interface. The extent to which interfaces support or impede users' access to news content, while organizations advance their newsprint or television traditions and keep pace with industry trends and technology is unknown. Correspondingly, an examination of the interfaces of TV and newspaper online news from a service and user experience design perspectives, suggests a mass production services model, wherein services are viewed as commodities and user and product are separate in production processes. For instance, whereas a service designer or UX designer would probe how engagement at the interface has a role in establishing relations with users, users of major news site will often encounter unexpected changes to the interface that dramatically affect, among other things, their loyalty to the site, and how they browse and access information. Some news services modify the interface and its functionality without notifying or consulting users, thus separating services (products) and users as well as restricting user input and potentially impeding the UX. As Parker and Heapy (2006, p. 28) noted, "We are more likely to remember something about the company brand from our interactions with the company than from looking at some element of a design work." Thus, it may be that users are more likely to remember the news organization by how the interface supports their interactions and affords a positive UX over how well the interface reflects technology trends or traditions in TV or newsprint. As technology advances rapidly, it is imperative to maintain stability and to recognize that users form mental models of how interfaces operate. Sudden or unexpected changes to the interface will likely conflict with existing models and pose a detriment to the UX. This is particularly germane to online news service interfaces because, in many cases, they serve as the sole enabler of relationships between news consumers and service providers.

Increasingly, researchers and practitioners recognize the need to design and develop usable interactive systems that also provide users a positive experience. At the same time, large numbers of people become informed about the world today by interacting with digital interfaces designed for news services. In many ways, the complexity and evolving nature of these interfaces pose impediments to users that inhibit accessibility to the news and discourage a positive UX. Research, data collection and analysis are critical to creating usable systems that support positive interaction experiences. In the following section, the authors discuss research approaches that aim to help investigators understand user behavior for the purpose of refining interfaces and the overall UX.

Research Methods and Data

In any system that requires human-machine interaction, the human poses the greatest complexity and is the probable source of system failure or mishap, which is the reason so much energy gets invested engineering the performance of the human component (Hartson & Pyla, 2012; Bailey, 1996). Designers, developers, and researchers who engage in work related to UX design, interface design, HCI, or interaction design more generally recognize that human behavior and cognition are key factors that should steer the design of a system and human performance is a measurable product of system use (Hartson & Pyla, 2012) and possibly a source of refining it. Not unlike service design, much of the work of practitioners and researchers in the field pertains to understanding human users, observing them, recording observations about their goals and tasks, data collection, analyses and using related findings to build or refine the system. As Rohrer (2014) notes, there are a variety of UX research methods available from lab-based usability studies to more recently developed online UX assessments. At the same time, practitioners and researchers are continually seeking new and improved data collection methods and metrics to measure human behavior. Pirolli, Chen, and Pitkow (2001) point out that the potential for user interaction data is enormous and thus it is essential to identify efficient and effective methods to analyze user intentions and behaviors as well as analyze and forecast usability. They advocate for more tools to investigate and improve predictive models, user interaction analyses, and measures of usability. Their work aimed at developing models capable of replicating the behaviors of hypothetical users on websites and developing methods to automate the calculation of usability measures (Pirolli, Chen, & Pitkow, 2001). Gibbs (2008) used several research metrics to identify information seeking behavior on websites including: (a) information seeking trails, (b) interaction variance, (c) Web pages recurrence, (d) URL frequency, (e) browse behavior identification, and (f) sequence analysis (for detailed analysis of browsing behavior). These measures afforded information about browsing directionality, complexity, and temporal order that served as means to better understand how users interacted with web interfaces.

Large Data Sets

In the early part of the 21st century, the Internet and the Web instigated unprecedented data collection and analytical research and development prospects from which an enormous amount of user and customer data can be congregated, organized and visualized using various text and web mining methods (Chen, Chiang & Storey, 2012). Web traffic and server log data, can provide researchers greater understanding of user behavior and how the design of systems can be improved to effectively support user needs and the overall experience (Wiggins, 2007). Many new data collection instruments such as online surveys and web-server logs record large amounts of data that are easily coded for quantitative analyses (Rohrer, 2014). For instance, Abedin and Sohrabi (2009) evaluated and improved website usability and link structure using web usage mining techniques. Web usage mining involves extracting data "generated by the user interactions with the web, typically representing as web server access logs, user profiles, user queries, and mouse-clicks" (Arotaritei & Mitra 2004, p. 6). Using interaction data obtained from a news oriented websites, Liang and Lai (2002) developed an approach for ascertaining user interests based on the time spent viewing objects. Among other things, their automated recording module tracked: (a) participant choice of news article, (b) time spent in reading news, (c) time spent in selecting a news article. They found their approach significantly outperformed the existing method for headline news titles that were previously determined by an editor.

A primary purpose of the above-mentioned approaches is to observe and understand behavior with the intent of improving systems for human use and to ultimately enhance the UX. In recent years, the Internet, Web, and mobile technologies allow researchers to collect large amounts of data, oftentimes at the moment interactions transpire. This has major implications for understanding human behavior when interacting with digital interfaces and how these data might help designers improve designs and experiences. In this regard, the next section presents a study that uses precepts of the CUE model and UX constructs to examine qualities of online news interfaces. Similar to the aforementioned methods, the study uses metrics that involved the collection of usage data such a click stream and aggregated data about web page visits and sequences to gain insights about user behavior and attitudes on news websites.

PERCEPTIONS AND USE OF TV- AND NEWSPAPER-ORIENTED INTERFACES

Purpose

New organizations adapt interfaces to reflect their TV or newsprint traditions. The designs of online news services often appear driven more by the expectations of service provider and technology advances than by user or consumer needs. This study examined if people evaluate non-instrumental qualities of online news interfaces differently based on the orientation (television or newsprint) of the service, and information-seeking task (direct vs. exploratory/open-ended). In addition, it investigated whether there were differences in browsing behavior (instrumental qualities) based on news orientation as well as the information-seeking task being performed. By understanding users' perceptions and behaviors on news interfaces in terms of service design and UX precepts, news providers can ultimately redesign online news to improve usability and UX, more effectively support user needs and tasks, help users achieve their goals more efficiently, and improve interface designs and services overall (Heer & Chi, 2002, p. 243; Chi, Pirolli, Chen, & Pitkow, 2001). The following questions were examined:

1. Do people evaluate news interfaces differently depending on the type of information-seeking task or goal being pursued (goal-directed vs. exploratory/open-ended) and the type of online news source (TV-oriented vs. newspaper-oriented news sites)?
2. Do information-seeking behaviors and practices in online news interfaces differ depending on the type of information-seeking task or goal being pursued (goal-directed vs. exploratory/open-ended) and the type of news source (TV-oriented vs. newspaper-oriented news sites)? If they do, what accounts for the differences?

Method

Participants

Fifty-five people participated in the study. Initially, thirty-two individuals participated in the study by locating information on news provider websites and evaluating the interfaces. A follow-up evaluation was administered approximately 3.5 years later and twenty-three people participated. All were experienced with obtaining news online. Most indicated that they read news online each day or several times daily.

Materials

Six popular online news services were selected for the study that had tradition in either television (e.g., CNN.com) or newsprint (e.g., New York Times). The TV-oriented services were: (1) CNN - cnn.com, (2) Fox News - foxnews.com, and (3) MSNBC – msnbc.com. The newsprint-oriented services were: (4) Pittsburgh Post-Gazette - post-gazette.com, (5) New York Times - nytimes.com, (6) USA Today - usatoday.com. The authors chose these services based on the following criteria: (a) type, the website could be classified as either television or newspaper; (b) popularity, the website characterized prevailing online news outlets from which many people obtain news; (c) the website presented interface screens of distinct categories of visual imagery and high information density and; (d) the authors felt that major characteristics of the websites (layout, link concentration) were indicative of many popular newspaper and TV-oriented sites.

Procedure

Participants used each of the six news websites. The entire session lasted for approximately one hour. The sequencing of the site presentations was counterbalanced to reduce order effects. Instrumental qualities included controllability, efficiency, or the effectiveness of a system. To try and capture indices of these qualities, the researchers observed behaviors of different information-seeking tasks. Participants were assigned to either a directed or non-directed group. Both groups viewed the same sites but the task assignment differed. For each of the six sites, the directed group was asked to locate two (top) news stories about an environmental issue and to browse to the end of the story. In addition, they had to find (a) when the story was last updated, (b) an author name, if one existed, and (c) an email link, to email the story to someone. Participants assigned to the non-directed group viewed the same six sites and they were asked to: (a) browse each of the sites freely, (b) locate stories of interest, and (c) browse to the end of each story.

The Internet, Web, and mobile connectivity combined with the technical capability to record voluminous and detailed aspects of human-technology interactions afford researchers unparalleled possibilities for data collection and measurement. Many researchers (e.g., see Abedin & Sohrabi, 2009; Ivory, Sinha & Hearst, 2001; Arotaritei & Mitra. 2004) use a variety of methods to try and understand human behavior at the interface level to enhance the interface and the overall UX. Some of these methods include tracking webpage visits, user search queries and clicks, traffic and temporal based analyses such as number of visitors to a page and times spent viewing a page. In this study during each task all on-screen events were tracked (logged). Video and audio of the participant using the interface were also recorded for later analysis. For analysis the collected data included:

- **Mouse Events:** All mouse clicks were recorded and tallied. This measure provided potential insight in the number of steps required by the user to reach the information target as well as the sequence of events that led to the target.
- **Time Browsing:** Amount of time participants spent on information-seeking tasks can provide insight about the efficiency with which a user reached the information target or the amount of time he takes before giving up.
- **Mouse Movement:** Number of pixels the cursor moved during a task provided information about user efficiency at browsing and their approach to information-seeking. It should be noted that users often move the mouse randomly around the screen for no information-seeking reasons. In this study, there were no incidences of this behavior. All mouse movement during information-seeking appeared related to the task.
- **Web Page Changes:** Number of pages visited to reach a target provided an information trail.

To obtain indices of non-instrumental qualities, participants completed a survey that rated each site using a 5-point Likert scale from 1 (Disliked) to 5 (Liked) on the following dimensions: a) screen layout; b) navigation; c) ease of finding information; d) completeness of information; e) overall site design; f) overall rating of site; and g) how much they liked the site. In addition, participants indicated whether or not they would use the site as a primary news source. Law, van Schaik and Roto (2013) reviewed 58 studies identifying 42 unique UX constructs. The authors believe the survey items (*Layout, Site Design and Overall Site rating, Like*, and *Use as a Primary Source*) used in this study reflect indices of UX constructs identified by Law, van Schaik and Roto (2013) including aesthetic/beauty, enjoyment, attractiveness, and satisfaction. Because online news interfaces change often, a follow-up survey, identical to the original, was administered approximately 3.5 years later.

Results

Individuals who participated in the study perceived themselves as experienced in online environments. Online is their medium of choice for obtaining news followed by television, and then newspapers. They access online news daily spending approximately 30 minutes or less each time they go online.

Participants obtain a majority (50%) of news online, 27% from television, and 21% from newspapers. Some respondents indicated that they receive 2% of their news from other sources. Participant familiarity ratings (*1 = very unfamiliar, 5 = very familiar*) of the Pittsburg Post Gazette, New York Times, and CNN were average (M = 3.00) whereas they rated their familiarity with Fox news, USA Today, and MSNBC as low (M = 2.00).

Research Question 1

Do people evaluate news interfaces differently depending on the type of information-seeking task or goal being pursued (goal-directed vs. exploratory/open-ended) and the type of online news source (TV-oriented vs. newspaper-oriented news sites)?

Using a 5-point Likert scale with 1 representing a low rating and 5 a high rating, participants rated each site on the following dimensions: a) screen layout; b) ease of navigation; c) ease of finding information; d) completeness of information; e) overall site design; f) overall rating of site; and g) how much they liked the site. In addition, they indicated whether or not they would use the site as a primary news source. Two survey evaluations were conducted.

The initial survey evaluation results are presented first followed by the results of the follow-up evaluation. For each of the seven dimensions, a two-way analysis of variance (ANOVA) for mixed factorial designs was conducted to examine if the dimension depended on the type of information-seeking task and the type of online news site. The type of information-seeking task was a between-subjects factor while the type of site was a within-subjects factor.

Screen Layout

In terms of participant evaluations of the screen layout, results show that only the main effect of type of news site was statistically significant, $F(1, 30) = 6.05$, $p = .02$, $\eta_p^2 = .17$. Screen layout ratings for TV-oriented news sites were significantly more positive ($M = 3.81$, $SD = .59$) than for newspaper-oriented sites ($M = 3.53$, $SD = .62$). See Table 1.

Ease of Navigation, Ease of Finding Information, and Completeness of Information

Participant evaluations of the three dimensions a) ease of navigation, b) ease of finding information, and c) completeness of information did not depend on the type of information-seeking task or type of news site. There were no statistically significant main and interaction effects.

Table 1. Participant rating of screen layout as a function of type of information-seeking task performed and type of online news site

	Open-Ended Information-Seeking Task	Goal-Directed Information-Seeking Task	Average
Newspaper-oriented Online Site	$M = 3.59$ $SD = .71$	$M = 3.47$ $SD = .52$	$M = 3.53$ $SD = .62$
TV-oriented Online Site	$M = 3.75$ $SD = .61$	$M = 3.89$ $SD = .57$	$M = 3.81$ $SD = .59$
Average	$M = 3.67$ $SD = .56$	$M = 3.68$ $SD = .45$	

Overall Site Design

Participant evaluations of overall site design depended on type of news site but not the type of information-seeking task (see Table 2). Results show that only the main effect of type of online news site was statistically significant, $F(1, 28) = 10.43, p = .003, \eta_p^2 = .27$. Overall site design ratings for TV-oriented news sites were significantly more positive ($M = 3.78, SD = .54$) than for newspaper-oriented sites ($M = 3.44, SD = .56$).

Overall Site Rating

Participant overall site ratings depended on the type of news site but not the type of information-seeking task (see Table 3). Only the main effect of type of news site was found to be statistically significant, $F(1, 29) = 5.31, p = .03, \eta_p^2 = .16$. TV-oriented news sites were given more positive overall site ratings ($M = 3.78, SD = .54$) than newspaper-oriented sites ($M = 3.54, SD = .50$).

How Did You Like the Site?

Participant rating of how much they liked a site did not depend on the type of information-seeking task or the type of news site. There were no statistically significant main and interaction effects.

Table 2. Overall site design rating as a function of type of information-seeking task performed and type of online news site

	Open-Ended Information-Seeking Task	**Goal-Directed Information-Seeking Task**	**Average**
Newspaper-oriented Online Site	$M = 3.49$ $SD = .63$	$M = 3.40$ $SD = .51$	$M = 3.44$ $SD = .56$
TV-oriented Online Site	$M = 3.83$ $SD = .48$	$M = 3.73$ $SD = .61$	$M = 3.78$ $SD = .54$
Average	$M = 3.66$ $SD = .46$	$M = 3.57$ $SD = .50$	

Table 3. Overall site rating as a function of type of information-seeking task performed and type of online news site

	Open-ended Information-Seeking Task	**Goal-Directed Information-Seeking Task**	**Average**
Newspaper-oriented Online Site	$M = 3.58$ $SD = .56$	$M = 3.49$ $SD = .43$	$M = 3.54$ $SD = .50$
TV-oriented Online Site	$M = 3.75$ $SD = .52$	$M = 3.80$ $SD = .53$	$M = 3.78$ $SD = .54$
Average	$M = 3.66$ $SD = .45$	$M = 3.64$ $SD = .40$	

Would You Use the Site as a Primary Online News Source?

For each of the sites, participants indicated whether they would use it as a primary online news source. A majority (26%) of votes went to CNN and The New York Times (23%) followed by MSNBC (18%), and the Pittsburgh Post Gazette (16%). USA Today (11%) and Fox News (6%) received the lowest percent of votes.

Written Commentary: Layout and Design

To further examine the findings related to layout and design, the authors reviewed the written comments provided by participants on the site surveys. They identified statements that noticeably reflected positive or negative perceptions about layout and design. For instance, the three statements below were provided by participants. The first two statements reflect a positive perception about layout and design while the third and fourth statements indicate a negative perception:

1. *Layout is simple and allows people to easily scroll through information quickly;*
2. *Layout and design is interesting in that it draws attention but does not overload senses;*
3. *Content heavy, colors are not exactly pleasing;*
4. *Way too cluttered, small print for headlines, the individual story link has larger print, sensationalized fluff should be pushed to bottom of page.*

Table 4 shows the percent of positive and negative statements about layout and design by site as well as the number of statements of this type made by participants. CNN and MSNBC had greater percentages of positive statements compared to the other sites. Fox News, Pittsburgh Post-Gazette, and USA Today had greater percentages of negative statements.

There was a significant difference in the proportion of positive and negative comments in TV-oriented vs. newspaper-oriented sites, $\chi^2(1) = 6.82$, $p = .009$, $V = .17$. There were at least twice more negative (69%) than positive (31%) comments for the newspaper-oriented sites. On the other hand, positive (48%) and negative (52%) comments were almost equally made for the TV-oriented sites.

Table 4. Positive and negative layout and design statements by site

	TV-Oriented Online Site			Newspaper-Oriented Online Site		
	CNN	**FOX**	**MSNBC**	**NYT**	**POST**	**USA**
Positive	62%	24%	54%	36%	21%	35%
Negative	38%	76%	46%	64%	79%	65%
# of Comments	48	45	50	47	38	43

Research Question 2

Do information-seeking behaviors and practices in online news interfaces differ depending on the type of information-seeking task or goal being pursued (goal-directed vs. exploratory/ open-ended) and the type of news source (TV-oriented vs. newspaper-oriented news sites)? If they do, what accounts for the differences?

Data were collected on the following dimensions to address whether browsing behaviors differed by information-seeking task and news site orientation: a) mouse events - all mouse clicks were recorded and tallied; b) time browsing - amount of time participants spent on information-seeking tasks; c) mouse movement - number of pixels the cursor moved during a task; and d) Web page changes - number of pages visited to reach target. For each of these dimensions, a two-way analysis of variance (ANOVA) for mixed factorial designs was conducted to examine if the dimension depended on the type of information-seeking task and the type of online news site. The type of information-seeking task was a between-subjects factor while the type of site was a within-subjects factor.

Mouse Events, Time Browsing, and Mouse Movements

The participant behaviors observed in the three dimensions of: a) mouse events; b) time browsing; and c) mouse movement did not depend on the type of information-seeking task and the type of news site. For each of these dimensions, none of the main and interaction effects were found to be statistically significant.

Web Page Changes

The number of times web pages changed depended on the type of news site but not the type of information-seeking task (see Table 5). Only the main effect of the type of news site was statistically significant, $F(1, 30) = 6.05$, $p = .02$, $\eta_p^2 = .66$. Web page changes happened more on TV-oriented news sites ($M = 18.19$, $SD = 15.17$) than on newspaper-oriented ones ($M = 13.46$, $SD = 6.73$).

Table 5. Number of times web pages changed as a function of type of information-seeking task performed and type of online news site

	Open-Ended Information-Seeking Task	Goal-Directed Information-Seeking Task	Average
Newspaper-oriented Online Site	$M = 12.98$ $SD = 6.06$	$M = 14.00$ $SD = 7.60$	$M = 13.46$ $SD = 6.73$
TV-oriented Online Site	$M = 16.20$ $SD = 10.92$	$M = 20.44$ $SD = 19.04$	$M = 18.19$ $SD = 15.17$
Average	$M = 14.59$ $SD = 7.93$	$M = 17.22$ $SD = 12.72$	

To examine the manner in which participants browsed, the authors identified two types of browsing events: a) browse-forward to a page not previously visited on the information seeking trail and b) browse-backward where an individual revisited a page on the trail. A two-way ANOVA for mixed factorial designs was conducted to examine if the number of times participants browsed forward depended on the information-seeking task and the type of news site. Only the main effect of the type of news site was statistically significant, $F(1, 29) = 6.32, p = .02, \eta^2 = .18$. Participants browsed forward more times on TV-oriented news sites ($M = 11.23, SD = 6.82$) than on newspaper-oriented sites ($M = 9.33, SD = 4.11$). Another two-way ANOVA was conducted to examine if the number of times participants browsed backward depended on the type of information-seeking task and the type of news site. Only the main effect of the type of news site was statistically significant, $F(1, 29) = 4.83, p = .04, \eta^2 = .14$. Participants browsed backward more times on TV-oriented news sites ($M = 6.28, SD = 6.40$) than on newspaper-oriented sites ($M = 4.08, SD = 2.91$).

Follow-Up Survey Evaluation

A follow up survey evaluation was administered approximately 3.5 years after the initial evaluation survey. Unlike the initial evaluation, the newspaper-oriented online news sites were rated more positively than the TV-oriented ones on the first seven dimensions listed in Table 6, but only the difference in information completeness was found to be statistically significant. The newspaper-oriented online news sites received significantly higher information completeness ratings ($M = 3.57, SD = .46$) than the TV-oriented sites ($M = 3.10, SD = .74$), $t(19) = 2.13, p = .02, d = .48$ (one-tailed). With regards to the last dimension in Table 6, on average, at least one of the newspaper-oriented sites was used as a primary online news source ($M = 1.00, SD = .79$) while the average use of the TV-oriented sites as a primary source was less than one ($M = 0.70, SD = .57$). This difference though was not statistically significant.

Table 6. Mean ratings of TV-oriented and newspaper-oriented online news sites

	TV-Oriented Online News Sites	Newspaper-Oriented Online News Sites
Screen Layout	$M = 3.33$ ($SD = .60$)	$M = 3.37$ ($SD = .58$)
Navigation	$M = 3.35$ ($SD = .62$)	$M = 3.45$ ($SD = .56$)
Ease of Finding Information	$M = 3.20$ ($SD = .60$)	$M = 3.45$ ($SD = .65$)
Information Completeness	$M = 3.10$ ($SD = .74$)	$M = 3.57$ ($SD = .46$) **
Site Design	$M = 3.28$ ($SD = .67$)	$M = 3.35$ ($SD = .57$)
Site Rating	$M = 3.02$ ($SD = .69$)	$M = 3.27$ ($SD = .47$)
Liking	$M = 2.98$ ($SD = .73$)	$M = 3.35$ ($SD = .51$)
Use as Primary Source	$M = 0.70$ ($SD = .57$)	$M = 1.00$ ($SD = .79$)

** $p < .05$

Discussion

Research Question 1

Do people evaluate news interfaces differently depending on the type of information-seeking task or goal being pursued (goal-directed vs. exploratory/open-ended) and the type of online news source (TV-oriented vs. newspaper-oriented news sites)?

Users of online news media perceived distinctions between newspaper and TV-oriented new sites. The findings indicate that people perceived sites differently based on orientation but not by the goal being pursued. Some ratings for non-instrumental qualities of news interfaces differed based on orientation. The initial evaluation revealed that TV-oriented sites were rated higher on screen layout, site design and overall site rating. However, this was not the case in the follow up evaluation whereby newspaper-oriented sites were rated higher for completeness of information and there were no other differences. The findings suggest that non-instrumental qualities of interfaces shape user perceptions and possibly the UX based on, to some extent, whether the site is TV or newspaper oriented. A possible explanation for this finding is the differences in the design and layout of the sites used in the study. It is plausible that at the interface level, the interaction provided to users was more accommodating on some sites (initially on TV sites), providing a more positive UX.

On the initial evaluation, when sites were ranked according to mean ratings in these areas, two TV-Oriented sites (CNN and MSNBC) and one newspaper oriented site (The New York Times) ranked highest whereas two newspapers (USA Today and Pittsburgh Post Gazette) and one TV-oriented site (Fox News) ranked lowest (see Table 7). It is noteworthy that those ranked highest had what might be characterized at the time as a minimalist layout and design compared to lower ranked sites. CNN and MSNBC provided minimal text and clusters of links that made it easy for users to navigate and to discern types of news stories. USA Today, Fox News, and the Pittsburgh Post-Gazette used prominent colors and images that occupied substantial portions of the interface. In the follow-up evaluation, however, USA Today ranked highest and MSNBC ranked lower in all categories. The interface design of USA Today and MSNBC changed significantly between the two evaluations, which the most recent ratings may reflect. Specifically, the MSNBC interface is now dominated by large images. In fact, several participants noted, "*Have to scroll down main page to see all major stories*; *really hated this website; too many photos; Make headings more consistent with other news websites; Photos too massive*."

It appeared that participants perceived the array of colors combined with scores of media elements (pictures, advertisements) as detractors of a site's news worthiness. While speculative, it suggests that minimalist designs on news sites provide a context in which users expect and may prefer to get news. Several participant comments seemed to support this claim. Regarding the abundance of colors and media elements, participants wrote the following: (a) *a lot of media elements, color, pics that take away from how newsworthy the site might be*; (b) *more videos and pictures than information, unnecessary advertising*; (c) *too much color distracts from news*; d) *a lot of information but I don't know where my eyes want to go*; (e) *didn't come to see the photos of the reporters, the faces are out-weighting text*; (f) *there are many videos and I just wanted to read something*.

Table 7. News sites ranked by mean ratings on layout, site design, and overall site rating

Initial Evaluation					
	Layout	**Site Design**	**Overall Site Rating**	**Like**	**Primary**
1 (Highest)	CNN	CNN	CNN	MSNBC	CNN
2	MSNBC	MSNBC	MSNBC	CNN	NYT
3	NYT	NYT	NYT	NYT	MSNBC
4	USA Today	USA Today	USA Today	Post	Post
5	Fox	Fox	Fox	USA Today	USA Today
6 (Lowest)	Post	Post	Post	Fox	Fox
Follow-Up Evaluation					
	Layout	**Site Design**	**Overall Site Rating**	**Like**	**Primary**
1 (Highest)	USA Today	USA Today	USA Today	USA Today	USA Today
2	CNN	CNN	CNN	CNN	CNN
3	NYT	NYT	NYT	NYT	NYT
4	Fox	Fox	Fox	Fox	Post
5	MSNBC	MSNBC	Post	Post	MSNBC
6 (Lowest)	Post	Post	MSNBC	MSNBC	Fox

Primary News Source

For each of the sites, participants indicated whether they would use it as a primary online news source. It is plausible that when someone selects a news service as a primary source, he invests, among other things, trust in that service. Most noteworthy about this item are MSNBC and USA Today. In the follow-up evaluation, USA Today ranked high on this item but low on the initial evaluation. MSNBC ranked lower on the follow-up evaluation but high initially. Both interfaces went through significant redesigns. This finding is indicative of the potential influence a redesign of an interface can have on the UX. Participant comments such as, "*I really disliked this website and in the past it used to be one of my favorites*" seemingly support this claim. In addition, it indicates that user trusts in online news services may be impacted by changes in the interface causing users to go elsewhere for news.

Navigation, Finding Information, and Completeness of Information

On the initial evaluation, participant ratings of all sites in terms of navigation, finding information, and information completeness were comparably high. However, on the follow-up evaluation information completeness was rated higher for newspaper interfaces. The comparable ratings may be due to the interface conventions followed by news sites. Generally, the home page provides a navigational bar across the top; a convention found on many non-news sites. They have broad hierarchies with numerous descriptive links (included headings and images) organized vertically. Users are accustomed to these conventions and thus they may have perceived navigation as positive or at least consistent with what they are used to. It is plausible that because of this perception and the fact that navigational elements affect users' ability to find information, users rated both navigation and ease of finding information consistently across all sites.

Information completeness was rated higher for newspaper interfaces. It appears when browsing online news users may try to quickly get an overview of the information space. Sites such as the New York Times, depending on viewport size, provide users a fairly comprehensive view of the information on the site. With an initial glance, users can easily take in the visual landscape, type of stories, and categories of information. The interface segments information by whitespace and a light gray diving line. On a continuous white background, no contrasting blocks of content, other than images, interrupt the user's visual scan of the space. Conversely, a site such as MSNBC is dominated by large images, some of which are surrounded by a dark background color. Even when the viewport is large, users see limited information. It is probable that the size of images causes users to focus on one topic initially and thus they do not readily perceive the other information categories. Moreover, the size of the images, requires user to work (i.e., scroll) to see the information. They may therefore feel it lacks complete information.

Research Question 2

Do information-seeking behaviors and practices in online news interfaces differ depending on the type of information-seeking task or goal being pursued (goal-directed vs. exploratory/ open-ended) and the type of news source (TV-oriented vs. newspaper-oriented news sites)? If they do, what accounts for the differences?

Four measures were obtained to examine these questions: a) mouse-clicks; b) time spent on information-seeking tasks; c) number of Web pages visited to reach target; d) number of pixels the user moved the cursor during tasks. The findings indicate that information-seeking behaviors did not differ by the type of task or, except for Web page changes, type of online news source.

Information-Seeking Tasks

The fact that participants' information-seeking behavior did not differ by task (goal-directed vs. exploratory/open-ended) was unexpected because undirected behavior is often more complex than directed behavior (Byrne, John, Wehrle, & Crow, 1999; Cypher, 1986). Though not significant, however, there was a trend showing that directed participants made more mouse-clicks, spent more time, visited more pages, and had more mouse movements than the non-directed. It is possible that the nature of the tasks presented in the study and the controlled setting did not engender greater diversity of information-seeking. The differences observed may become significant with a greater number of participants, and if testing occurred over a longer period of time and under more natural conditions. Moreover, it may be that news sites elicit goal-directed types of behaviors rather than open-ended browsing. It appears that as one engages in information-seeking (goal-directed or exploratory/open-ended) there is a goal. Thus, it may not be the person's goal that delineates browsing behaviors but whether the information being sought in the pursuit of that goal is specific enough or not.

An interesting observation made about information-seeking tasks was that directed users spent the most time on CNN and Fox News and the least amount of time on The New York Times. Conversely, non-directed users spent the most amount of time on The New York Times and USA Today and the least amount of time on CNN. It is possible that for directed users The New York Times afforded efficient access to the target information and thus they found what they needed quickly. At the same time, The New York Times and USA Today, newspaper-oriented sites, afforded reading and thus non-directed participants spent the most time on them. This suggests interplay among type of site and information seeking tasks. However, the aforementioned differences were not significant. Further research is needed to examine them more fully.

Site Orientation: Web Page Changes

Web page changes, and correspondingly browse-forward and browse-backward events, occurred more on TV-oriented news sites than on newspaper sites. One plausible explanation for this finding is that the design of TV-oriented sites afforded exploration whereas newspaper sites afforded reading or more focused browsing. For example, the home pages of CNN, Fox News, and MSNBC consist of images, advertisements, and clusters of hyperlinks. Other than the main story, text information is limited. While foraging for information, users must rely on the short text descriptions in hyperlinks, which may inaccurately depict the information obtained by clicking the link. A user may click a link only to find that the information was not what he expected and then he may navigate elsewhere. On the other hand, The New York Times, USA Today, and the Pittsburgh Post Gazette provide textual information to supplement links to stories. The New York Times home page, for example, provides roughly 30 words under a link heading to describe a story. It is possible that the additional text adds descriptiveness allowing users to find information efficiently while, at the same time, it engenders focused browsing and less exportation. Alternatively, the amount of information on the page may simply slow users down making browsing less efficient and users less inclined to explore. Placing numerous links on a page will increase the search time to locate information (Catledge & Pitkow, 1995). However, the additional information did not appear to impede the search efficiency of directed users who spent the least amount of time on the New York Times.

CONCLUSION

In this chapter, the authors reviewed service design, UX design and pertinent research methodologies. In service and UX design, the customer or user is central to building better services and systems. Much work is invested in learning about people and how they think and behave and using this information to enhance services and systems. Service and UX design precepts can prove valuable to news organizations as they continue to build and refine innovative interfaces to online news services. In addition, the authors reported a study that examine instrumental (e.g., task efficiency, effectiveness, usability) and non-instrumental (e.g., like, trust, aesthetics) qualities of news interfaces. Perception of non-instrumental qualities of sites differed based on orientation but not by the goal being pursued.

At the interface level, key elements of news sites appear derived more from the expectations of service provider and technological advancement than by user needs and the UX. For instance, many TV and newspaper sites reflect their media traditions, seemingly irrespective of the impact the interface design has on interaction and UX. Moreover, industry trends often perpetuate changes to interfaces that users are expected to accommodate regardless of the impact on UX. One important outcome of the study relates to the initial and follow-up evaluations. TV-oriented sites were initially rated high but their ratings lowered on the follow-up evaluation. In the follow-up evaluation, newspaper-oriented sites were rated high on completeness of information. The authors suspect that these differences were due in large part to a redesign of the site interfaces. This underscores the importance of how changes in interfaces influence UX. While the authors do not know the development processes followed by the sites used in this study, the findings suggest that use of or greater adherence to service design and UX precepts would likely yield favorable ratings. Greater user engagement in refining services would engender more positive ratings as well as user experiences.

It is probable that minimalist designs positively impacted user perceptions. For news sites, readers appear to prefer less salient visual treatments and may feel that conspicuous treatments diminish the news worthiness of a site.

The observed behaviors (mouse-clicks, time on task, Web page changes, and mouse movements) of directed and non-directed users did not differ significantly. However, the values obtained for directed users for all these behaviors were higher than for non-directed users. One would expect greater differences between the information-seeking tasks but the controlled environment and short duration of tasks may have constrained such differences.

Based on the sites used in this study, the frequency of Web page changes is likely to be higher on TV-oriented sites than newspaper sites. The newspaper sites studied provided additional text information that may serve at least two functions: a) it helped inform users about linked news stories and thus they are better able to find sought after information; b) it may have helped users be more discerning. The additional information may be sufficient enough to inform a user that the story would not be of interest to him. Conversely, the TV-oriented sites studied provided short text links of limited information about the story. Users may click several links to unwanted stories, a process that is less efficient but promotes greater exploration.

REFERENCES

Abedin, B., & Sohrabi, B. (2009). Graph theory application and web page ranking for website link structure improvement. *Behaviour & Information Technology*, *28*(1), 63–72. doi:10.1080/01449290701840948

American Press Institute and Associated Press-NORC Center for Public Affairs Research. (2014). *The Personal News Cycle: How Americans choose to get their news*. American Press Institute, 17 Mar. 2014. Retrieved November 27, 2014, from http://www.americanpressinstitute.org/publications/reports/survey-research/personal-news-cycle/single-page/&gt

Arotariteia, D., & Mitrab, S. (2004). Web mining: A survey in the fuzzy framework. *Fuzzy Sets and Systems*, *148*(1), 5–19. doi:10.1016/j.fss.2004.03.003

Bailey, R. W. (1996). *Human performance engineering: Designing high quality professional user interfaces for computer products, Applications, and Systems* (3rd ed.). Upper Saddle River, NJ: Prentice Hall.

Bargas-Avila, J. A., & Hornbæk, K. (2011). Old wine in new bottles or novel challenges? A critical analysis of empirical studies of user experience. In *Proceedings of the CHI'11*. Vancouver, Canada: ACM.

Bruce, M., & Bessant, J. (2002). *Design in business: Strategic innovation through design*. Design Council.

Byrne, M. B., John, B. E., Wehrle, N. S., & Crow, D. C. (1999). The tangled web we wove: taxonomy of WWW use. In *Proceedings of ACM CHI 99 Conference on Human Factors in Computing Systems* (volume 1, pp. 544-551). New York: Addison Wesley. doi:10.1145/302979.303154

Catledge, L. D., & Pitkow, J. E. (1995). Characterizing browsing strategies in the world-wide web. *Computer Networks and ISDN Systems*, *26*(6), 1065–1073. doi:10.1016/0169-7552(95)00043-7

Chen, H., Chiang, R. H. L., & Storey, V. C. (2012). Business intelligence and analytics: From big data to big impact. *Management Information Systems Quarterly*, *36*(4), 1165–1188.

Chi, E. H., Pirolli, P., Chen, K., & Pitkow, J. (2001). Using information scent to model user information needs and actions and the Web. In *Proceedings of the SIGCHI Conference on Human Factors in Computing Systems* (CHI '01, pp. 490-497). New York, NY: ACM. doi:10.1145/365024.365325

Cypher, A. (1986). The structure of users' activities. In D. A. Norman & S. W. Draper (Eds.), *User Centered System Design* (pp. 243–263). Boca Raton, Florida: CPR Press.

Gibbs, W. J. (2008). Examining users on news provider web sites: A review of methodology. *Journal of Usability Studies*, *3*(3), 129–148.

Hartson, R., & Pyla, P. S. (2012). *The UX book: Process and guidelines for ensuring a quality user experience*. Waltham, MA: Morgan Kaufman.

Hassenzahl, M., & Tractinsky, N. (2006). User experience – a research agenda. *Behaviour & Information Technology*, *25*(2), 91–97. doi:10.1080/01449290500330331

Heer, J., & Chi, E. H. (2002). Separating the swarm: Categorization methods for user sessions on the Web. In *Proceedings of the SIGCHI conference on Human factors in computing systems: Changing our world, changing ourselves* (CHI '02, pp. 243 – 250). New York, NY: ACM.

Heim, S. (2008). *The Resonant Interface: HCI Foundation for Interaction Design*. Boston, MA: Pearson Education.

Holmlid, S., & Evenson, S. (2008). Bringing service design to service sciences, management and engineering. In B. Hefley & W. Murphy (Eds.), *Service science, management and engineering: Education for the 21st century* (pp. 341–345). Berlin: Springer Verlag. doi:10.1007/978-0-387-76578-5_50

Ivory, M. Y., Sinha, R. R., & Hearst, M. A. (2001). Empirically validated web page design metrics. In *Proceedings of the SIGCHI Conference on Human Factors in Computing Systems* (CHI '01, pp. 53-60). New York, NY: ACM. doi:10.1145/365024.365035

Law, E. L.-C., van Schaik, P., & Roto, V. (2013). Attitudes towards user experience (UX) measurement. *International Journal of Human-Computer Studies*, *72*(6), 526–541. doi:10.1016/j.ijhcs.2013.09.006

Liang, T., & Lai, H. (2002). Discovering user interests from web browsing behavior: An application to internet news services. In *Proceedings of the 35th Annual Hawaii international Conference on System Sciences* (Hicss'02, pp. 2718 - 2727). Washington, DC, USA: IEEE Computer Society. doi:10.1109/HICSS.2002.994214

Locher, P., Overbeeke, K., & Wensveen, S. (2010). Aesthetic Interaction: A Framework. *Design Issues*, *26*(2), 70–79. doi:10.1162/DESI_a_00017

Mitchell, A., & Page, D. (2014). Key indicators in media and news. Pew State of the News Media 2014, March 26, 2014, Retrieved October 16, 2014, from http://www.journalism.org/packages/state-of-the-news-media-2014/

Murray, J. H. (2012). *Inventing the medium: Principles of interaction design as a cultural practice*. Cambridge, Massachusetts: The MIT Press.

Nielsen, J. (1993). *Usability engineering*. San Diego, CA: Academic Press.

Norman, D. A. (2002). *The Design of Everyday Things*. New York: Basic Books.

Parker, S., & Heapy, J. (2006). *The Journey to the interface: How public service design can connect users to reform*. London: Demos Magdalen House.

Pinhanez, C. (2007). A services theory approach to online service applications. In Proceedings of IEEE Services Computing Conference, Application and Industry Track (SCC'07, pp. 395-402). Salt Lake City, Utah: IEEE Computer Society. doi:10.1109/SCC.2007.19

Pinhanez, C. (2008a). A service science perspective for interfaces of online service applications. In *Proceedings of the VIII Brazilian Symposium on Human Factors in Computing Systems* (IHC '08, pp. 11-20). Sociedade Brasileira de Computação, Porto Alegre, Brazil: ACM.

Pinhanez, C. (2008b). Service systems as customer-intensive systems and its implications for service science and engineering. In *Proceedings of the Proceedings of the 41st Annual Hawaii international Conference on System Sciences* (pp. 117-126).Washington, DC, USA: IEEE Computer Society.

Rafaeli, A., & Vilnai-Yavetz, I. (2004). Instrumentality, aesthetics and symbolism of physical artifacts as triggers of emotion. *Theoretical Issues in Ergonomics Science*, *5*(1), 91–112. doi:10.1080/1463922031000086735

Rohrer, C. (2014). *When to use which user-experience research methods.* Nielsen Norman Group, 12 Oct. 2014. Retrieved November 23, 2014, from http://www.nngroup.com/articles/which-ux-research-methods/

Roth, S. P., Tuch, A. N., Mekler, E. D., Bargas-Avila, J. A., & Opwis, K. (2013). Location matters, especially for non-salient features–An eye-tracking study on the effects of web object placement on different types of websites. *International Journal of Human-Computer Studies*, *71*(3), 228–235. doi:10.1016/j.ijhcs.2012.09.001

Sampson, S. E., & Froehle, C. M. (2006). Foundations and implications of a proposed unified services theory. *Production and Operations Management*, *15*(2), 329–343. doi:10.1111/j.1937-5956.2006.tb00248.x

Service Design Network. (n.d.). *What is service design?* Retrieved September 21, 2014, from http://www.service-design-network.org/intro/

Sharp, H., Rogers, Y., & Preece, J. (2012). *Interaction design: Beyond human-computer interaction.* Hoboken, New Jersey: John Wiley & Sons, Inc.

Thuring, M., & Mahlke, S. (2007). Usability, aesthetics and emotions in human–technology interaction. *International Journal of Psychology*, *42*(4), 253–264. doi:10.1080/00207590701396674

Wiggins, A. (2007). Data-Driven design: Using web analytics to validate heuristics. *Bulletin of the American Society for Information Science and Technology*, *33*(5), 20–24. doi:10.1002/bult.2007.1720330508

KEY TERMS AND DEFINITIONS

Human-Computer Interaction (HCI): Human-Computer Interaction is concerned with humans using interactive computing systems to accomplish their goals. It is a field of study focused on research, theory, and practice of computing systems for human use.

Instrumental Qualities of Systems: Characteristics of systems or products related to usefulness and usability (i.e., effectiveness, efficiency, learnability, and satisfaction).

Interaction Design (ID): Interaction Design pertains to research, theory, and design of interactions or the behavior of a system, digital and non-digital. ID is concerned with the system design so that when users interact with the system or product they understand how to use it and it supports what they are trying to accomplish. ID encompasses characteristics of user experience design, interface design, user-centered design, and product design.

Interface: A medium through which a human interacts with a system or machine. It is the control apparatus operated by the user that sits between the system and the human and is designed to support the user's tasks so he can accomplish a goal.

Non-Instrumental Qualities: Characteristics of systems or products that may influence the emotions experienced by users during interaction. Non-instrumental qualities include characteristics such as aesthetics, engagement, and joy.

Usability: Employing various methods and technologies, usability is the practice of studying systems and products for the purpose of making sure that user interaction with the system is effective, efficient, easily learned, and satisfying.

User Experience (UX): User experience is new way of understanding and investigating the non-instrumental qualities (e.g., aesthetics) of systems and the experience users have with them. A user experience occurs when a person interacts with a system. It is influenced by internal characteristics of the user, attributes of the system's design such as usability and functionality, and the context of use.

Chapter 4
A Tale of Two Newsrooms:
How Market Orientation Influences Web Analytics Use

Patrick Ferrucci
University of Colorado-Boulder, USA

Edson C. Tandoc Jr.
Nanyang Technological University, Singapore

ABSTRACT

This chapter describes the results of a study that compared a strongly market-oriented newsroom and a less market-oriented newsroom in terms of how they used web analytics in news work. Using ethnographic methods, the study finds that web analytics influenced editorial decisions in both newsrooms. However, the two newsrooms differed in the extent to which they used analytics and in their reasons for doing so. These differences are examined using the framework of market theory in news construction.

INTRODUCTION

In September 2009, software developer and market leader Adobe Systems Inc. announced it was buying the fast-growing, but still much smaller, company behind a five-year-old analytics program called Omniture (Corkery, 2009). The price tag puzzled a lot of market analysts: Why would Adobe spend a whopping $1.8 billion on such a young company? But after three years, Adobe seemed to be a satisfied buyer, renaming Omniture as Adobe Site Catalyst (Carey, 2012). Omniture is a software program that allows for collection and analysis of audience data over long periods of time (Johnson, 2009). In buying Omniture, Adobe entered the lucrative market of selling software solutions that optimize websites by enabling owners to collect information from their audiences. This information enables website owners to better understand online be-

DOI: 10.4018/978-1-4666-8580-2.ch004

havior. Soon, other software programs hit the market, such as Chartbeat and Visual Revenue, creating pricey programs specifically tailored for news organizations that allow tracking of audience metrics in real-time (Sonderman, 2011a, 2011b).

Newsrooms have embraced web analytics, a technological ally seen as a tool that can help the journalism industry grow back a rapidly shrinking audience-base for news. Information generated by web analytics are now being used to determine placement of stories (Lee, Lewis, & Powers, 2012), to decide which stories to do follow-ups on (Vu, 2013), to guide decisions on adding photos or graphics (Vu, 2013), and even to structure payment models for contributors (Fischer, 2014). These applications of web analytics in many newsrooms are arguably motivated by survival instinct—a need to increase traffic and generate more revenues (Lowrey & Woo, 2010; Vu, 2013), a motivation that does not sit well with the normative goals of journalism (Christians, Glasser, McQuail, Nordenstreng, & White, 2009). Indeed, critics are beginning to sound alarm bells on the potential impact of web analytics on the kind of journalism being produced (Fischer, 2014). But this motivation is also something not shared by all newsrooms, particularly those that operate under business models not dependent on advertising. Does the motivation for revenues, in essence a newsroom's market-orientation, affect how it uses web analytics?

Journalism has always been closely related to technology, and journalists have long been normalizing new communication technologies to fit existing norms and routines (Lasorsa, Lewis, & Holton, 2011; Singer, 2005). But the availability of new technologies does not directly impact news production, and the effects across organizations unfold in different ways, mediated by several factors, such as organizational structures (Boczkowski, 2004; 2005). This chapter is interested in exploring and understanding the impact of organizational structure, particularly market orientation, on the ways newsrooms use web analytics. The authors compare two newsrooms that both use web analytics, but come from the opposite sides of the continuum of market orientation.

BACKGROUND

Market Theory and News Production

An organization's market orientation describes how strongly it caters to customers' wants (Kohli & Jaworski, 1990). A traditional, for-profit company frequently strives for a strongly market-oriented approach, one that will maximize profit potential and produce goods or services that a prospective customer will seek out (Atuahene-Gima, 1996). However, for a news organization, there remains an inherent paradox between producing news and maximizing profit (McChesney, 2004), one that even iconic news publisher Joseph Pulitzer commented on in the early days of for-profit journalism (Schudson, 1978). Pulitzer remarked that the most difficult impediment for creating important journalism aimed at strengthening democracy came from a tension between the civic and economic interests of news companies. Journalism remains a business and a civic service, two different goals that commonly do not align (Kovach & Rosenstiel, 2007). The kind of content that drives profits may not also strengthen democracy (Habermas, 1989).

McManus (1994) crafted a theory combining classic elements of market theory with basic characteristics of news production. This theory argues that for-profit "rational news departments should compete with each other to offer the least expensive mix of content that protects the interests of sponsors and investors while garnering the largest audience advertisers will pay to reach" (p. 85). Fundamentally, McManus (1994) argued that since for-profit corporations run newspapers as businesses and not public services, newsrooms will compete with each other to generate the most profit from advertisers while also spending as little as possible producing news that its readers want.

Market theory suggests that when markets work appropriately, they possess certain features. Main and Baird (1981) stated that in a market economy, consumers decide quality; producers respond to consumers' needs and desires; a market self-corrects if it is not fulfilling those needs; consumers possess a freedom of choice; the market allocates society's resources efficiently; and producers possess a motivation to succeed and innovate. McManus (1994) argued that news organizations in the United States trade within four markets concurrently: the *market for audience*, in which firms compete for readers and viewers; the *stock market*, because most firms trade stock of their corporations and desire superior valuations; the *advertising market*, as most firms compete for advertising revenue; and a *market for sources*, as the firms compete for information to disseminate from sources. If these four markets operate efficiently and consistently, news outlets would produce high-quality and immensely interesting news products because of success in the market for audience; successful news outlets would increase stock prices and then make their product even stronger; news organizations would entice numerous advertisers lured through large consumer numbers and a quality product; and journalists would have a large amount of sources providing information who desire the most thorough dissemination of their information (McManus, 1992; 1994; Meyer, 1987). However, news organizations and news consumers would agree these desired outcomes so far elude both parties (Gans, 2004). The more market-oriented a news organization, the more likely it prioritizes the advertising, audience and the stock markets, while caring significantly less about the source market.

The Role of Market Orientation

Beam (1998) argued that regardless of goals, all news organizations are market-oriented. News organizations prioritized different objectives, but the need to cultivate and sustain an audience as well as generate operating capital precludes ignoring market goals entirely. Market orientation falls on a continuum, one that would label some organizations as weakly market- oriented, some as strongly, and some somewhere in the middle (Beam, 2001). As Beam (1998) points out,

> *For a news organization, market orientation is judged by how strongly a firm identifies a potential market opportunity, selects a group of customers that it wants to serve and develops a strategy for efficiently meeting the wants and needs of those customers. The central business assumption is that long-run success depends on a strong, organization-wide focus on customer wants and needs. (p. 2)*

Therefore, the difference between a strongly market-oriented news organization and a weakly market-oriented one lies in their priorities. Barnouw (1997) deduced this difference down to a single question: Does the organization consider news as a service or a product?

In the 1980s, the news industry saw an influx of market-oriented thought. Corporations pursuing pure profit began purchasing family owned news organizations—both print and broadcast—and priorities shifted (McManus, 1994). This shift resulted in an industry more focused on generating large financial gains, much of the time at the expense of quality journalism (McChesney, 1999). This focus continues today, with the vast majority of both print and broadcast media prioritizing profit (Kaye & Quinn, 2010; Klinenberg, 2007). This shift results in not just differing priorities but, inevitably, different content.

Beam (2003) explicitly studied how content produced by both weakly and strongly market-oriented print news organizations differed. He found that because market research showed readers wanted more feature news, strongly market-oriented papers published less about government and more about arts and entertainment, lifestyle, and sports. Pompilio (2009) found, based on a series of interviews, that journalists believed their organizations prioritized profit over news and this significantly and negatively affected job satisfaction. Cohen (2002) studied online journalism done in print newsrooms and found that "conflicts in commercial and journalistic values pose a problem every day in how newsrooms make decisions" (p. 542). Cohen (2002) also noted that the priorities of a strongly market-oriented organization undermine the norms, routines and ethics of journalists.

Market orientation can directly affect not only content, but also indirectly alter how journalists produce content (McChesney & Nichols, 2010). For example, the stronger the market orientation of an organization, the more likely it would adopt technologies as a means of separating and distinguishing itself from perceived competition (Beam, 2003). Kovach and Rosenstiel (2007) posited that these differences could result in the use of more market research from strongly market-oriented firms. Indeed, McManus (1994) found a heavy reliance on reader survey data for determining the wants of readers and viewers. This data influenced news decisions. Thus, one of the ways that strongly and weakly market-oriented newsrooms differ is the manner in which they utilize market research (i.e., Klinenberg, 2007; Kovach & Rosenstiel, 2007; McChesney & Nichols, 2010). In this chapter, the authors are interested in the impact of market orientation on the adoption of web analytics, which represent a new form of market research, something common in market-driven newsrooms (McManus, 1994).

Web Analytics

The term *web analytics* refers to the "collection and analysis of data relating to website visitors" (Miller, 2011, p. 107). Since the first commercial web analytics vendor launched in 1994, web analytics has become institutionalized, particularly for websites engaged in promotion and sales (Chaffey & Patron, 2012). Web analytics go beyond tracking the number of visitors, with businesses interested in finding out the reasons behind web traffic (Chaffey & Patron, 2012). Thus, web analytics help website owners "learn more about how people use a site and why" (Miller, 2011, p. 108). For news websites, this means being able to know not only how many people are on the site, but also what specific content people are reading, how much time they are spending on a specific story, and what platforms lead people to specific pages on the site (Napoli,

2011). These pieces of information refer to *web metrics*. Many newsrooms have embraced the technology of web analytics (e.g., Anderson, 2011; Lowrey & Woo, 2010; MacGregor, 2007; Vu, 2013) and journalists have been using web metrics in their editorial decisions (Lee, et al., 2012; MacGregor, 2007). Observations in a newsroom found that web traffic "exerted strong influence" on editors' news judgment (Anderson, 2011).

Tracking audience preferences isn't entirely new. Newspaper surveys and broadcast ratings were aimed at measuring what the audience wanted (Gans, 1979; Schlesinger, 1978). Phone calls to the newsroom and letters to the editor also provided avenues for audience feedback (Gans, 1979; Schlesinger, 1978). However, these traditional forms of audience research took time to put together, were based on volunteered information, and came from a subset and not the actual audience (Beam, 1995; Gans, 1979; Schlesinger, 1978). In contrast, the metrics that come from web analytics programs are collected unobtrusively and therefore are considered more accurate and more immediate measurements (MacGregor, 2007; Napoli, 2011).

But just like in the adoption of other technologies, the availability of web analytics does not result in uniform levels and patterns of adoption (Boczkowski, 2004; 2005). For example, bigger news organizations were found to be more likely to track web metrics more often than smaller companies (McKenzie, Lowrey, Hays, Chung, & Woo, 2011). The higher the degree of economic uncertainty editors feel, the more they engaged in monitoring of audience metrics (Lowrey & Woo, 2010). Editors who perceived the economic benefits of getting more readers were also found to be more willing to adjust editorial decisions, such as story selection and assignment of topics, based on web metrics (Vu, 2013). A pattern that emerges from these different studies is how the motivation to increase revenues seems to predict use of web analytics among newsrooms in the United States.

Not all newsrooms are the same, however. A study of editors at the Al Jazeera newsroom found that journalists recognized the importance of web analytics, but often ignored audience metrics in their editorial decisions (Usher, 2013). Al Jazeera is funded by its government, and the pressure to increase web traffic is absent, exerting no effect on how journalists in the newsroom use web analytics (Usher, 2013). These studies, despite the variations in what they found in terms of how journalists from different newsrooms use web analytics, agree on one crucial point: a news organization's market orientation affects many aspects of news work.

DIFFERENT NEWSROOMS, DIFFERENT ANALYTICS

Newsrooms have adopted web analytics and have integrated audience metrics into their news work in varying degrees (Anderson, 2011; Lowrey & Woo, 2010; MacGregor, 2007; Vu, 2013). But not all newsrooms are the same. In this chapter, the authors are focusing on the impact of market orientation on how journalists use web analytics in their work. A news organization's market orientation has been found to influence the different stages and facets of news construction. The extent of that influence, as the authors will demonstrate by comparing two newsrooms and their use of web analytics, is partly shaped by a news organization's degree of market orientation.

METHODOLOGY

This chapter is based on ethnographic methods conducted at two newsrooms in the United States. Paterson (2008) argued that only ethnographic methodologies "can come close to providing an adequate description of the culture and practice of media production, and the mindset of media producers" (p. 2). Singer (2008) wrote that we cannot truly understand a news organization without ethnography. The two authors separately conducted observations and interviews at each of the two newsrooms involved in this study. The authors planned an identical set of interview questions and sensitizing concepts for observation embedded in their respective research designs that allowed careful and comprehensive comparison of the two newsrooms in terms of their adoption of web analytics. The newsrooms selected both use web analytics, but differ in their market orientation, allowing the authors to engage in a comparison to understand the impact of market-orientation on news practice.

First Newsroom

The second author spent a total of 110 hours spread over 12 days at the first newsroom in March 2013. There, he was assigned to his own workstation, sitting three rows away from the managing editor, who oversees the digital operations, and just next to a few digital editors taking turns working on the homepage. The second author stayed at the newsroom from 8 a.m. to 6 p.m. every day, attending the daily budget meetings at 10 a.m. and 2 p.m. Employing an *observer-as- participant* stance, he was able to explicitly observe the editors and make notes. He also conducted respondent interviews with 15 editors to ask them about their web analytics use as well as about specific things he observed during the course of fieldwork. The first newsroom is a previously newspaper-only news organization in a competitive two-newspaper market in a large city in the Midwest. Its newspaper is among the 25 biggest in the United States in terms of circulation. The same is true for its website, which claims to have about 3 million unique monthly visitors. The newsroom is large—in the afternoons, when both digital and print editors are present, the number of people working in the newsroom can go as high as 100 individuals. In this chapter, the first newsroom is considered a strongly market-oriented newsroom.

Second Newsroom

The first author spent a total of about 360 hours in the field spread between January and April 2013. The editors at this second newsroom sit at a half-moon shaped workstation and the second author sat at a desk in this workstation. He sat in between two editors and within five feet of the other three editors. Also employing an *observer-as-participant* stance, he was able to observe the editors and take notes. The first author arrived in the newsroom at 9 a.m. daily and did not leave until 6 p.m., a time period that coincides with the entire working day for the news organization. He attended two daily news meetings and all other meetings during a given week. He was given complete access to the organization. He conducted long-form interviews with 17 editors and reporters at the newsroom. These interviews focused on a number of things, including web analytics. The second newsroom is a digitally native news nonprofit situated in one of the 20 largest media markets in the country, a relatively close but different city from where the first newsroom is based. The second newsroom's website receives roughly 70,000 unique visitors per month. The staff at the second newsroom includes 17 full-time journalists and roughly 10 part-time freelancers. The second newsroom is considered a weakly market-oriented newsroom.

Data Analysis

The authors both kept detailed field notes from their independent observations. They also had all interviews transcribed for data analysis. They shared their qualitative data with each other after they completed gathering data. Using a constant comparative approach (Glaser, 1965; Glaser & Strauss, 1967), they initially proceeded with independent open-coding. Practicing an iterative strategy that "alternates between emic, or emergent, readings of the data and an etic use of existing models, explanations, and theories" (Tracy, 2013, p. 184), the authors coded their field notes and transcripts based on emerging codes as well as based on the sensitizing concepts from the literature that guided the research.

Corbin and Strauss (1990) argued that the goal of constant comparison in grounded theory is not generalization but theoretical explanation, and as such what is required is representativeness of concepts, not of persons. Following the completion of open coding, the researchers discussed the codes they independently came up with in order to proceed with axial-coding. This is the stage where initial codes are organized into categories, making sure that theoretical saturation is achieved, that is, no new codes are emerging from the data, and that the categories discerned from the initial codes are fully developed (Saldaña, 2009; Tracy, 2013). In the process of engaging in axial coding, analytics memos were written. These memos specifically and fully explain the themes so that researchers can code data more effectively. Researchers then subsequently helped in the construction of themes around related categories, as reflected in the presentation and discussion of the results.

RESULTS

Three important areas of discussion about the use of web analytics in the two newsrooms observed emerged during the constant comparative analysis. The first section of this analysis documents how each of the two newsrooms tracked audience metrics. The second section outlines the ways in which the newsrooms incorporated web metrics into their news construction processes. Finally, the third section presents the motivations that will explain the patterns that emerged in the first two sections.

Tracking Metrics

The first newsroom uses two analytics programs to track audience metrics. First, the editors at the first newsroom use Omniture (Adobe Site Catalyst) to monitor and analyze long- term data. For example, the deputy managing editor referred to Omniture as a "big beast," which the newsroom uses to review web traffic across months. Omniture is able to compare, for example, total traffic this month with total traffic within the same period last year. Second, it also uses

Chartbeat to monitor day-to-day traffic. Chartbeat is able to report, in real-time, how many views each page gets, how many visitors are currently accessing the website, among others things. It also reports data from social media, such as how many retweets on Twitter a story receives. Both Omniture and Chartbeat are expensive third-party programs. Top-level editors have access to Omniture, which is also accessed by the company's advertising and marketing officers. Online editors all have access to Chartbeat. The managing editor, who is in-charge of the website's day-to-day operations, as well as the two digital editors who alternate with him in managing the homepage, would open Chartbeat as soon as they logged into their work stations. They look at it all the time. "It can be all-consuming," the deputy managing editor said. "I call it like the editorial crack, right?"

The second newsroom uses Google Analytics, a free analytics program which also provides information on online traffic in real-time. The second newsroom's Google Analytics account can be accessed by anyone, but in reality only the editor-in-chief, the presentation editor, and the general manager open the account. The general manager is the person in charge of the analytics. She said, we monitor "average weekly unique (visitors) and we look at how some weeks do better than others." So even if they upload stories most days in a week, the monitoring of metrics comes only on a week-by-week basis.

Metrics in News Construction

- **Budget Meetings:** The daily budget meetings at the first newsroom, when about 10 editors representing different sections of the newsroom plan and discuss the line-up of stories, start at 10 a.m. The managing editor usually presides over the meeting where stories for both the newspaper and website are discussed. The managing editor always keeps an eye for stories that will potentially draw traffic. For example, when an editor talked about a story a reporter was working on concerning newborn lambs in a farm, the managing editor said: "Anyone want to bet that will be the most popular feature in our website?" Traffic always comes up during the budget meetings, although the editors do not refer to specific numbers when talking about audience size. But attracting traffic is one of the considerations when editors discuss which stories to pursue as well as when they evaluate stories and plan for follow-ups. For example, one editor was talking about a video she had posted, when the managing editor cut her off and said: "Did you see my note on that? The video did very well."

The budget meetings at the second newsroom are also scheduled to start at 10 a.m. every day, but the editor-in-chief typically arrives late, delaying these meetings about 30 minutes on average. In these meetings, editors also devote a few minutes to already-published stories. This is when references to web traffic come up. For example, during one of the budget meetings, the editors talked about how adding a photo to the homepage usually results in more page views for the main story. The editor-in-chief said they should do this more often. The implication, during this conversation, was clear to other editors, and the newsroom responded by adding more photos during the next week than any other week observed. They would also discuss stories that surprised them based on traffic. For example, one meeting started with a discussion of the stories that were popular online the previous day. They focused on a speech story that became the most read story. The editor-in-chief did not expect the story would get good traffic, but the editors speculated it must be because Rush Limbaugh, a well-known radio personality in the United States, was mentioned in the speech.

- **Selecting Stories:** In the first newsroom, web analytics clearly played a role in editorial decisions. A digital editor said that web analytics could be used to know what stories attract traffic, so that more stories can be assigned about those topics. For example, during a budget meeting, an editor proposed a story about stopping the use of schools as voting spots during elections. Another editor said it was already an old issue. But the managing editor said: "It might generate some traffic." Popular stories also tend to be updated often by adding additional information or by adding photographs. They are also promoted in social media. A digital editor said she uses analytics in deciding how to play a story. "So you see that a lot of people are clicking on a story but not spending a lot of time on it. So you might want to see what other content you could add to make it a more engaging experience for the readers. So adding photo galleries, videos, as many things as you can." The managing editor also said one can use analytics to determine an important story that is not getting good traffic, so that one can update it, display it more prominently, or promote it in social media, to help the story get the traffic it deserves.

In the second newsroom, while editors discuss web traffic during budget meetings, they rarely refer to it when choosing stories to publish. For example, they discussed how the previously mentioned speech story became, rather unexpectedly, the most read story the previous day. But that did not result in a follow-up or even an update to the existing article. Normally, the editors would discuss the top stories, in terms of traffic, of the week or of the month, but it stops at analytics just being talked about. The editors, especially the editor-in-chief, also inferred audience behavior based on web analytics: If the site publishes more than 15 stories during a day, the public will overlook some. That is, if stories end up being placed very low on the homepage because more than 15 stories have to be crammed in, individual stories tend to get less traffic. So, when the news organization schedules more than 15 stories to be produced in a day, the editors will choose to hold some of the stories for another day. This decision—to narrow down stories into a particular quota for the day while holding off others for another day—is usually made based on which stories editors believe to be the most newsworthy.

- **Placement of Stories:** The digital editors at the first newsroom also used web analytics to decide which stories to put on which spot. The homepage has a limited number of spots for headlines and story blurbs. A photo, a headline, and a short blurb usually accompany the main story. Other stories carry a smaller photo and a shorter blurb. The rest of the stories displayed on the homepage carry just headlines. Thus, placement of stories matter in the limited space on the homepage, especially because, as one reporter who also works as a desk editor on weekends said, keeping the homepage fresh is important to keep visitors coming back to the site. One time, a digital editor at the first newsroom was routinely checking Chartbeat when he suddenly saw that an opinion piece published on the opinion page was getting a lot of traffic even if it was not being promoted on the homepage. So he put the opinion piece on the homepage and replaced a story that was no longer attracting much traffic.

The editors at the second newsroom also displayed keen awareness about the importance of the homepage. For example, they discussed how they should keep the number of stories per day to absolutely no more than 15. Generally, traditional editorial judgment determined which stories were displayed prominently. The organization also placed a large premium on the homepage. The editors chose a homepage that looked like a front page of a newspaper because this allowed them to exercise news judgment in deciding story placement. The story the editors deemed most newsworthy earned the top spot on the page. They did not choose the main story based on projected clicks. During a meeting concerning a potential merger with another nonprofit outlet, leaders broached the topic of which organizations' website to migrate to after the merge. Especially because the other website was set up differently, the editor-in-chief said: "We cannot use that website; it defeats everything we've been working toward. Our site now lets readers know what is and isn't the most important stories of the day."

- **Work Flow:** The first shift at the first newsroom starts at 6 a.m. A digital editor comes in early morning to start uploading wire stories and review how stories that were uploaded in the evening are performing. The morning shift is considered important, because many readers access the website on their mobile phones while on their morning commute to work and those who get to work before 8 a.m. access the website from their computer stations. Stories that were getting good traffic are moved to more prominent places in the homepage.

The same thing happens in the second newsroom. The goal is to publish some stories by 8 a.m. The editor-in-chief even announced during one of the afternoon meetings that she would try to be better at posting stories before 8 a.m. This adjustment to the online reading habits of their readers is not only based on what the editors believe, but more so based on the spike in traffic they see on Google Analytics in the mornings. The second newsroom rarely publishes stories in the middle of the day—unless there is breaking news—because they know web traffic is slow during particular hours in the afternoon. In one particular instance, the features editor even said that publishing a story at 4:30 p.m. on a Friday "does a disservice to the work" because at that time, going into the weekend, very few people visit the site.

Motivations for Using Analytics

The first newsroom, during the period observed, just experienced a spate of layoffs that caused a lot of uncertainty in the newsroom. The company had filed for bankruptcy some five years before, and a new owner had just taken over and brought in a new editor-in-chief, who prioritized a digital-first goal. The new editor-in-chief started his journalism career with the paper, but left many years before and worked with other news organizations, one of which was an online-only newsroom where he was exposed to web analytics. "I think that traditional newsrooms can learn from digital operations like (my previous newsroom), so I had that advantage when I came back to (this city) to bring a little of that." He found an ally with the company's longtime visuals editor whom he promoted to managing editor. "I put (the managing editor) in that position because he understands, he drives that vision through the newsroom, he really kind of built that web desk—that was his vision."

This awareness of the need to keep the company afloat amid financial uncertainty trickles down to other editors and reporters. On an almost regular basis, the editors get confronted by news of another laid off co-worker. "Since 2008, we've been having constant layoffs and it's never stopped," a long-time reporter said. "We think we can't lay off anybody else, then another person gets laid off." In interviews, many editors refer to traditional journalistic roles in their news work. A digital editor, for example, talked about keeping the public informed. The metro editor referred to the audience as "the people we have to inform, we have to educate." But he also acknowledged that in order to achieve that, journalists also have to make stories interesting for the audience. Thus, the editors find themselves having to balance their news judgment with the need to drive traffic, because these usually do not match. Sports and celebrity stories are the ones that usually attract traffic. The managing editor said: "We don't really want to tailor our editorial judgment or our news judgment specifically to get page views. But we have to be smart about what people are reading and not. And you know, some stories just don't have the importance we thought they have."

The discourse is far different at the second newsroom, where editors acknowledge the capabilities of web analytics, but use it for reasons different from the first newsroom. The second newsroom is composed of editors who had mostly come from a newspaper company in the city, and have therefore been socialized into traditional newsroom culture. But now they are running a news organization that is largely funded by private donors and grants. Positioning themselves as an alternative to the dominant newspaper in the city—the newspaper most of them had come from—the editors and their reporters are also aware that their audience size is not big. "Sometimes, I feel I'm working real hard and I'm writing good stuff and the people who are in the field that I'm writing about may read it and say that's good, but I don't feel we're reaching as wide an audience," a reporter at the second newsroom said. "And that can really be frustrating because you wonder if you're doing a good job."

The general manager said they monitor the number of unique users and page views—the same metrics that editors at the first newsroom monitor. "We look at some of that stuff from time to time and we pass it on to potential donors," the general manager said. But while they are sharing their analytics to funders, it appears that the discourse is absent in their day-to-day operations. The first time the general manager, who is the point-person for the newsroom's analytics, attended a budget meeting came weeks after observations for this study began. The editor-in-chief, who spoke during that meeting, described the goal of having the general manager attend by explaining: "We make decisions with what we're covering to reach more people if we were covering in different ways. That's not quite right—more we're trying to increase impact."

Impact to the community is paramount in the second newsroom, and it appears that they do not equate it with web traffic. "We're journalists, not marketers. It doesn't matter to us what that number is. What we're saying is this is important and you should be aware of it," the presentation editor said. The general manager recognizes "a lot of opportunity" in web analytics and displays familiarity with the kinds of information web analytics can provide—such as number of hits, location of visitors, bounce rate, and others. "But we weren't really responding to the information we got... We don't make assignments or switch resources around based on metrics and we don't make money off of page views." This comes from the acceptance that while the news organization runs smoothly through donations and grants, the website does not really attract a lot of traffic, at least when compared with traditional news websites. Traffic, then, is not the primary goal for the newsroom. The general manager said:

You know, there's this line I think that's scary in something we put a bunch of resources into and we think is really important and then only 200 people or something read it. What do we do with that? And if we're not willing to do something with that, then we should probably not look. But there is a lot of that that goes on, and if we're not going to dig in and if we're going to decide that doesn't inform our decision-making and we say we think this is important, and we don't care what the metrics say, then we don't care what the metrics say.

FUTURE RESEARCH DIRECTIONS

This chapter is not without limitations. First, it only compared two newsrooms. The selection of the newsrooms meet the goals of theoretical comparison, but as market orientation operates in a continuum, other nuances of web analytics use from newsrooms in different locations in the continuum are not captured in this study. Second, while interviews and observations allow holistic understanding of news practices, the chapter, as in other ethnographies, is limited by the extent of access the researchers were allowed. Fieldwork in the first newsroom was much shorter than time spent in the second newsroom. The authors carefully planned the study design to allow for a meaningful and comprehensive comparison. Thick descriptions and in-depth interviews in the first newsroom were particularly conducted to offset the limitations brought about by temporal limitations. But while the findings presented here demonstrate theoretical saturation, temporal limitations might have also affected the results.

In the future, researchers examining how web analytics affects news production processes should continuing studying the intriguing link between market-orientation and the adoption and usage of web analytics. McManus (1994), writing more than two decades ago, identified market and audience research as a key component of how newsrooms adopted market-driven ethos. In effect, web analytics are simply a new form of audience research, with programs providing journalists and other news organization workers with real-time data about readers, the same information surveys attempted to provide decades ago. McManus (1994) argued that non market-driven newsrooms would conduct far fewer, if any, audience-research endeavors. This chapter provides some interesting evidence to support the same conclusion concerning web analytics. More research examining this link is needed to confirm and gather more nuance.

CONCLUSION

This chapter compared a strongly market-oriented newsroom and a weakly market- oriented one in terms of how they used web analytics in news work. It's important to examine how web analytics influence news work, and different newsrooms use web analytics in different ways. Understanding the impact of analytics on news construction requires an investigation of factors that influence the degree to which journalists institutionalize technology to begin with. This chapter focused on the impact of market orientation on the extent to which newsrooms used web analytics.

The two newsrooms used web analytics in similar ways. The editors in both newsrooms talked about audience metrics during budget meetings, and information from web analytics influenced editorial decisions in selecting and displaying stories on the homepage. However, the two newsrooms differed in the *extent* to which they used analytics and in their *reasons* for doing so. The strongly market-oriented newsroom used analytics extensively while the weakly market-oriented newsroom used analytics less frequently, with only a few editors accessing their analytics usually once a week.

These patterns of use are also shaped by the different intentions the two newsrooms have for using web analytics. The goal in the strongly market-oriented newsroom is clear—use web analytics to grow traffic. To some extent, the same is true with the second newsroom, but the motivation to attract traffic is much weaker. The general manager, not an editor, maintained primary responsibility for monitoring analytics. The difference with this and the first newsroom is the general manager is not a journalist—she was not part of the newsroom. To some extent, the wall between editorial and business has not been torn down in the weakly market-oriented newsroom. More importantly, the second newsroom produces stories not based on expected traffic, but on news judgment.

This brings us back to market theory in news production (McManus, 1994). These differences in practices and intention in terms of web analytics stem from the effects of market orientation as manifested in the markets where these newsrooms compete or do not compete. The strongly market-oriented newsroom, confronted with financial uncertainty, requires profits. Thus, it needs to compete for more traffic (the market for audience), which will generate more advertisers (the market for advertising), which will hopefully raise their parent company's stock (the stock market) and lend it more legitimacy that will help get sources (the market for sources). In contrast, the weakly market-oriented newsroom operates through donations and grants. Therefore, while it still needs to maintain a profile to generate attention from potential funders, it does not compete in many of those markets and can therefore mostly eschew web analytics. It most definitely wants an audience, but it doesn't compete for a large one (the market for audience), nor does it compete for advertising money (the market for advertising).

This authors hope to contribute in the growing area of research into the impact of web analytics on news work. Though ethnographies of profit-oriented and government-funded online newsrooms have been conducted to examine their use of web analytics (see Anderson, 2011; Usher, 2013), this chapter carefully compares a strongly market-oriented and advertising-driven newsroom with a weakly market-oriented counterpart that relies on private funders. In doing so, it hopes to contribute not only to conceptualization of the contexts through which journalists should understand the impact of web analytics on news work, but also to their understanding of the impact of market orientation on news practices, especially in an age when the journalism field is in a frantic pursuit of business models that can either save traditional newsrooms or sustain digital ones.

REFERENCES

Anderson, C. W. (2011). Between creative and quantified audiences: Web metrics and changing patterns of newswork in local US newsrooms. *Journalism*, *12*(5), 550–566. doi:10.1177/1464884911402451

Atuahene-Gima, K. (1996). Market orientation and innovation. *Journal of Business Research*, *35*(2), 93–103. doi:10.1016/0148-2963(95)00051-8

Barnouw, E. (Ed.). (1997). *Conglomerates and the media*. New York, NY: New Press.

Beam, R. A. (1995). How newspapers use readership research. *Newspaper Research Journal*, *16*(2), 28–38.

Beam, R. A. (1998). What it means to be a market-oriented newspaper. *Newspaper Research Journal*, *19*(3), 2–20.

Beam, R. A. (2001). Does it Pay to be a Market-Oriented Daily Newspaper? *Journalism & Mass Communication Quarterly*, *78*(3), 466–483. doi:10.1177/107769900107800305

Beam, R. A. (2003). Content differences between daily newspapers with strong and weak market orientations. *Journalism & Mass Communication Quarterly*, *80*(2), 368–390. doi:10.1177/107769900308000209

Boczkowski, P. J. (2004). The processes of adopting multimedia and interactivity in three online newsrooms. *Journal of Communication*, *54*(2), 197–213. doi:10.1111/j.1460-2466.2004.tb02624.x

Boczkowski, P. J. (2005). *Digitizing the news: Innovation in online newspapers*. Cambridge, MA: MIT Press.

Carey, R. (2012). How to gracefully retire a brand name. *Search Engine Land*. Retrieved May 22, 2014, from http://searchengineland.com/how-to-gracefully-retire-a-brand-name-125611

Chaffey, D., & Patron, M. (2012). From web analytics to digital marketing optimization: Increasing the commercial value of digital analytics. *Journal of Direct. Data and Digital Marketing Practice*, *14*(1), 30–45. doi:10.1057/dddmp.2012.20

Christians, C. G., Glasser, T., McQuail, D., Nordenstreng, K., & White, R. A. (2009). *Normative theories of the media: Journalism in democratic societies*. Urbana, IL: University of Illinois Press.

Cohen, E. L. (2002). Online Journalism as Market-Driven Journalism. *Journal of Broadcasting & Electronic Media*, *46*(4), 532–548. doi:10.1207/s15506878jobem4604_3

Corkery, M. (2009). Adobe buys Omniture: What were they thinking? *The Wall Street Journal*. Retrieved May 22, 2014, from http://blogs.wsj.com/deals/2009/09/16/adobe-buys-omniture-what-were- they-thinking/

Fischer, M. C. (2014). The pay-per-visit debate: Is chasing viral traffic hurting journalism? *American Journalism Review*. Retrieved May 22, 2014, from http://ajr.org/2014/03/27/pay-per-visit- debate-chasing-viral-traffic-hurting-journalism/

Gans, H. J. (1979). *Deciding what's news*. New York, NY: Pantheon Books.

Gans, H. J. (2004). *Democracy and the News. New York, NY*. USA: Oxford University Press.

Glaser, B. G. (1965). The constant comparative method of qualitative analysis. *Social Problems*, *12*(4), 436–445. doi:10.2307/798843

Glaser, B. G., & Strauss, A. (1967). *The discovery of grounded theory: Strategies for qualitative research*. London, England: Weidenfeld and Nicolson.

Habermas, J. (1989). *The structural transformation of the public sphere: An inquiry into a category of bourgeois society*. Cambridge, MA: MIT Press.

Johnson, B. (2009). Experts puzzled over Adobe's surprise purchase of Omniture. *The Guardian*. Retrieved March 26, 2014, from http://www.theguardian.com/technology/2009/sep/16/adobe-mergers- acquisitions

Kaushik, A. (2010). *Web analytics 2.0: The art of online accountability and science of customer centricity*. Indianapolis, IN: Wiley Publishing, Inc.

Kaye, J., & Quinn, S. (2010). *Funding Journalism in the Digital Age: Business Models, Strategies, Issues and Trends*. New York, NY: Peter Lang.

Klinenberg, E. (2007). *Fighting for air: The battle to control America's media*. New York, NY: Metropolitan Books.

Kohli, A. K., & Jaworski, B. J. (1990). Market orientation: The construct, research propositions, and managerial implications. *Journal of Marketing*, *54*(2), 1–18. doi:10.2307/1251866

Kovach, B., & Rosenstiel, T. (2007). *The elements of journalism: What newspeople should know and the public should expect*. New York, NY: Three Rivers Press.

Lasorsa, D. L., Lewis, S. C., & Holton, A. E. (2011). Normalizing Twitter: Journalism practice in an emerging communication space. *Journalism Studies*, *13*(1), 19–36. doi:10.1080/146167 0X.2011.571825

Lee, A. M., Lewis, S. C., & Powers, M. (2012). Audience clicks and news placement: A study of time-lagged influence in online journalism. *Communication Research*, *41*(4), 505–530. doi:10.1177/0093650212467031

Lowrey, W., & Woo, C. W. (2010). The news organization in uncertain times: Business or institution? *Journalism & Mass Communication Quarterly*, *87*(1), 41–61. doi:10.1177/107769901008700103

MacGregor, P. (2007). Tracking the online audience. *Journalism Studies*, *8*(2), 280–298. doi:10.1080/14616700601148879

Main, R. S., & Baird, C. W. (1981). *Elements of microeconomics*. Eagan, MN: West Publishing Company.

McChesney, R. W. (1999). *Rich media, poor democracy: Communication politics in dubious times*. Urbana, IL: University of Illinois Press.

McChesney, R. W. (2004). *The problem of the media: U.S. communication politics in the twenty-first century*. New York, NY: Monthly Review Press.

McChesney, R. W., & Nichols, J. (2010). The death and life of American journalism: The media revolution that will begin the world again. Philadelphia, PA: 1st Nation Books.

McKenzie, C. T., Lowrey, W., Hays, H., Chung, J. Y., & Woo, C. W. (2011). Listening to news audiences: The impact of community structure and economic factors. *Mass Communication & Society*, *14*(3), 375–395. doi:10.1080/15205436.2010.491934

McManus, J. H. (1992). What kind of commodity is news? *Communication Research*, *19*(6), 787–805. doi:10.1177/009365092019006007

McManus, J. H. (1994). *Market-driven journalism: Let the citizen beware?* Thousand Oaks, CA: Sage Publications.

Meyer, P. (1987). *Ethical journalism: A guide for students, practitioners, and consumers*. New York, NY: Longman.

Miller, M. (2011). *The ultimate web marketing guide*. Indianapolis, IN: Pearson Education, Inc.

Napoli, P. (2011). *Audience evolution: New technologies and the transformation of media audiences*. New York, NY: Columbia University Press.

Paterson, C. (2008). Introduction: Why ethnography? In C. Paterson & D. Domingo (Eds.), *Making Online News* (Vol. 1). New York, NY: Peter Lang Publishing Inc.

Pompilio, N. (2009). A Porous Wall. *American Journalism Review*, *31*(3), 32–37.

Saldaña, J. (2009). *The coding manual for qualitative researchers*. Thousand Oaks, CA: Sage.

Schlesinger, P. (1978). *Putting 'reality' together*. Beverly Hills, CA: Sage.

Schudson, M. (1978). *Discovering the news: A social history of American newspapers*. New York, NY: Basic Books.

Singer, J. (2005). The political j-blogger. *Journalism*, *6*(2), 173–198. doi:10.1177/1464884905051009

Singer, J. (2008). Ethnography of newsroom convergence. In C. A. Paterson & D. Domingo (Eds.), *Making online news: The ethnography of new media production* (pp. 157–170). New York, NY: Peter Lang.

Sonderman, J. (2011a). New generation of Web analytics applies 'big data' to newsroom decisions. *Poynter*. Retrieved March 27, 2014, from http://www.poynter.org/latest-news/top- stories/143389/new-generation-of-web-analytics-applies-big-data-to-newsroom- decisions-visual-revenue-jumptime/

Sonderman, J. (2011b). Newsbeat debuts as robust, real-time Web analytics tool for news publishers. *Poynter*. Retrieved March 27, 2014, from http://www.poynter.org/latest-news/top-stories/140998/newsbeat-debuts-as-robust-real-time-web-analytics-tool-for-news- publishers/

Tracy, S. (2013). *Qualitative research methods: Collecting evidence, crafting analysis, communicating impact*. Malden, MA: Wiley-Blackwell.

Usher, N. (2013). Al Jazeera English Online: Understanding Web metrics and news production when a quantified audience is not a commodified audience. *Digital Journalism*, *1*(3), 335–351. doi:10.1080/21670811.2013.801690

Vu, H. T. (2013). The online audience as gatekeeper: The influence of reader metrics on news editorial selection. *Journalism*, 1–17. published online October 28, 2013

ADDITIONAL READING

Anderson, C. W. (2011). Between creative and quantified audiences: Web metrics and changing patterns of newswork in local US newsrooms. *Journalism*, *12*(5), 550–566. doi:10.1177/1464884911402451

Beam, R. A. (1998). What it means to be a market-oriented newspaper. *Newspaper Research Journal*, *19*(3), 2–20.

Beam, R. A. (2003). Content differences between daily newspapers with strong and weak market orientations. *Journalism & Mass Communication Quarterly*, *80*(2), 368–390. doi:10.1177/107769900308000209

Boczkowski, P. J. (2005). *Digitizing the news: Innovation in online newspapers*. Cambridge, MA: MIT Press.

Boczkowski, P. J. (2010). *News at work: Imitation in an age of information abundance*. Chicago, IL: University of Chicago Press. doi:10.7208/chicago/9780226062785.001.0001

Chaffey, D., & Patron, M. (2012). From web analytics to digital marketing optimization: Increasing the commercial value of digital analytics. *Journal of Direct. Data and Digital Marketing Practice*, *14*(1), 30–45. doi:10.1057/dddmp.2012.20

Cohen, E. L. (2002). Online Journalism as Market-Driven Journalism. *Journal of Broadcasting & Electronic Media*, *46*(4), 532–548. doi:10.1207/s15506878jobem4604_3

Ferrucci, P. (2013). *Poor media, rich democracy: How economics and technology affect construction of news processes*. Unpublished doctoral dissertation, University of Missouri, Columbia.

Kaushik, A. (2010). *Web analytics 2.0: The art of online accountability and science of customer centricity*. Indianapolis, IN: Wiley Publishing, Inc.

Kaye, J., & Quinn, S. (2010). *Funding Journalism in the Digital Age: Business Models, Strategies, Issues and Trends*. New York, NY: Peter Lang.

Kennedy, D. (2013). *The Wired City: Reimagining journalism and civic life in the post-newspaper age*. Amherst, MA: University of Massachusetts Press.

Lasorsa, D. L., Lewis, S. C., & Holton, A. E. (2011). Normalizing Twitter: Journalism practice in an emerging communication space. *Journalism Studies*, *13*(1), 19–36. doi:10.1080/1461670X.2011.571825

Lee, A. M., Lewis, S. C., & Powers, M. (2012). Audience clicks and news placement: A study of time-lagged influence in online journalism. *Communication Research*, *41*(4), 505–530. doi:10.1177/0093650212467031

MacGregor, P. (2007). Tracking the online audience. *Journalism Studies*, *8*(2), 280–298. doi:10.1080/14616700601148879

McChesney, R. W. (2004). *The problem of the media: U.S. communication politics in the twenty-first century*. New York, NY: Monthly Review Press.

McChesney, R. W. (2013). *Digital disconnect: How capitalism is turning the internet against democracy*. New York, NY: The New Press.

McManus, J. H. (1994). *Market-driven journalism: Let the citizen beware?* Thousand Oaks, CA: Sage Publications.

Napoli, P. (2011). *Audience evolution: New technologies and the transformation of media audiences*. New York, NY: Columbia University Press.

Nee, R. C. (2013). Creative Destruction: An exploratory study of how digitally native news nonprofits are innovating online journalism practices. *International Journal on Media Management*, *15*(1), 3–22. doi:10.1080/14241277.2012.732153

Singer, J. (2008). Ethnography of newsroom convergence. In C. A. Paterson & D. Domingo (Eds.), *Making online news: The ethnography of new media production* (pp. 157–170). New York, NY: Peter Lang.

Tandoc, E. C. (2013). *Web analytics, social media, and the journalistic doxa: The impact of audience feedback on the evolving gatekeeping process.* Unpublished doctoral dissertation, University of Missouri, Columbia.

Tandoc, E. C. (2014). Journalism is twerking? How web analytics is changing the process of gatekeeping. *New Media & Society*, *16*(4), 559–575. doi:10.1177/1461444814530541

Usher, N. (2013). Al Jazeera English Online: Understanding Web metrics and news production when a quantified audience is not a commodified audience. *Digital Journalism*, *1*(3), 335–351. doi:10.1080/21670811.2013.801690

Vu, H. T. (2013). The online audience as gatekeeper: The influence of reader metrics on news editorial selection. *Journalism*, 1–17. published online October 28, 2013

KEY TERMS AND DEFINITIONS

Ethnography: The study of a culture and its languages and behaviors.

Market Orientation: Describes how closely situated an organization is to market principles.

News Production: This describes the acts and processes of how news is produced by journalists and other agents.

Newsroom Comparison: A study that empirically compares different newsrooms.

Online Journalism: Journalism produced for the web and not print or broadcast.

Qualitative: A type of methodology aimed at understanding, through in-depth study, human behavior. This type of research tries to answer how and why.

Web Analytics: Measuring, gathering and analyzing data gained from examining web usage. This data can then be used as a tool for optimizing business processes.

Chapter 5
Data-Driven Information Consumption:
Heralding a New "Golden Age" of Journalism and Content Creation?

Joseph McKendrick
Independent Consultant, USA

ABSTRACT

Things are changing dramatically within the publishing industry. However, news media itself isn't on the wane, as many pundits are stating. In this chapter, the author explores how the business model for media organizations is shifting away from print, and away from the "gateway" approach to journalism and content development, in which a few select articles are presented to audience by editors, writers and reporters. In its place, the new digital media model is creating a plethora of content from many different sources, oftentimes first-hand accounts, original sources, or commentary. In the process, rather than resulting in a dearth of news content, audiences have access to an often dizzying, overwhelming and potentially contradictory content. This is creating potentially new roles for news and publishing organizations, serving as sources of validation and aggregation of content. At the same time, the rise of digital media is providing consumers a far wider range of choices pushing media organizations to provide content more tailored to their audiences.

INTRODUCTION

This chapter takes a broad view of changes shaping the publishing industry and the editorial and journalism profession. The author will examine the current state of traditional media, and how that is evolving, driven by digital platforms and new types of industry participants taking advantage of those platforms. The author will look at the ways data analytics is opening up new opportunities for news organizations.

DOI: 10.4018/978-1-4666-8580-2.ch005

WELCOME TO THE NEW AGE

Are we in the midst of a decline in the editorial and journalism profession, or are we actually entering a new golden era? Many observers have been arguing that we have and continue to experience the former; that is, the pillars of the profession are being swept away by the internet tide, that the business model that supported the hiring and paying of editors and journalists is being disrupted. In its place is a wide online assortment of services and community-based social sites, with an easily clickable, vast array of information –often first-hand accounts on social media or original sources posted on the web -- on a moment's notice.

Beneath all the doom and gloom however, there is a new movement afoot. That is, the editorial and journalism profession is arising in a new form, built on electronic capabilities, more responsive to readers, and driven by data on what audiences seek and prefer within their content. Behind this is the need for informed reporters capable of looking behind the misinformation and hysteria potentially created by the internet, capable of validating information being provided and shared on a particular issue or event.

Events such as the disappearance of Malaysian Airlines Flight 310 in March 2014, or the downing of Flight 210 over Ukraine in July 2014, resulted in wild, unsubstantiated rumors over the internet (Pepitone, 2014). As NBC News reported shortly after the disappearance of Malaysia Flight 310, Chinese social media (most of the passengers were Chinese citizens) was rife with rumors that the aircraft had been spotted making an emergency landing somewhere in China (Pepitone, 2014). As the Ebola virus ravaged parts of Africa and a traveler from an affected country was diagnosed and died of the disease in Texas, social media networks lit up with rumors and exaggerated accounts of the spread of the disease to North American shores (Luckerson, 2014).

The ultimate trusted authority on such events, in turns out, were editors and journalists reviewing and reporting the facts as they were known, through well-known news channels. While there is a wide and almost unlimited variety of sources of information now available through internet-based channels, few have the credibility that signals that due diligence was taken to ensure that the information was the most up-to-date and credible reporting available.

Is the "old" news delivery model – built on a few, established gatekeepers and editors checking and double-checking on reported information – threatened with extinction? Is this model being replaced by a more free-for-all mode of multiple delivery channels, in which audiences are expected to survey and assemble to draw their own conclusions? Looking at the numerous obituaries that have been surfacing on the state of today's news organizations, one can be forgiven for thinking so.

But from the ashes of the collapsed old news delivery model, a new phenomenon may be rising. There is evidence that contrary to the common accepted belief that the news business is on the wane, the editorial and journalism profession may actually be entering a new golden age, built on instantaneous engagement with social networks around the global, supported by data-driven capabilities. Most importantly, information needs to be built on a foundation of trust and engagement with the audience, which points to a new emerging role for news organizations.

First, let's take a brief look at what is happening with the old model. The news publishing business itself suffered substantial losses over the past decade, though these losses appear to have stabilized in recent years. Circulation revenue for U.S. newspapers recorded a second consecutive year of growth, rising 3.7% to $10.87 billion in 2013, according to preliminary data compiled by the Newspaper Association of America (NAA, 2014). Overall, total revenue for the multiplatform U.S. newspaper media business amounted to $37.59 billion in 2013, a slight decline from $38.60 billion in 2012.

Proceeds grew in several other categories — digital advertising, direct marketing, and other, newly-developing sources — while income from traditional print advertising channels declined. This trend reflects an industry evolving its business model in a significant way, taking advantage of developments in technology, consumer behavior, and advertiser interest, to grow audience and diversify its revenue stream. (Newspaper Association of America, 2014, para. 3)

The industry's numbers appear to reflect a precipitous collapse over the long term. Alan Mutter, a highly regarded industry consultant, points out that "combined print and digital advertising revenues at the 1,300-plus newspapers in the nation tumbled 55% from $46.2 billion in 2003 to $20.7 billion in 2013, according to the NAA (Mutter, 2014). Classified print advertising was hit the worst in the 10-year period, plunging by 74% to $4.1 billion in 2013. National print advertising dropped 61% in the decade to not quite $3.1 billion in 2013 and retail print advertising fell 53% to $10.1 billion in 2013."

There is also a dismemberment taking place of news content. The challenge was explored by Bill Grueskin, Ava Seave and Lucas Graves in a report out of Columbia Journalism School. (Grueskin, Seave, & Graves, 2011, p. 13). They note:

In the online world, content has become atomized, with each article existing independently of the next. It is as seamless for a reader to go from a tallahasseedemocrat.com story to a video on msnbc.com as it is to read back-to-back stories in Esquire magazine. The economic consequences of this fickle information-gathering are devastating for legacy news organizations, especially because they have ceded many of the benefits of aggregation to sources like Drudge Report, Huffington Post and Google News.

The challenge is to better connect with audiences, which have been leaving in droves for online sources, and this forms the basis of the new industry model that is now emerging. Entrepreneurs and venture capitalists have taken an interest in the news business in its evolving form, embracing digital media startups and outlets as the next paradigm of information delivery. In the process, there is a conversion taking place between the vestiges of the "old" media – print outlets – and the emerging digital class.

Justin Fox, a former editorial director of the Harvard Business Review and columnist for Bloomberg View, for one, says the venture capitalist community – which fuels the technology industry – is seeing potential in the emerging digital media model (Fox, 2014). Writing in *The Atlantic,* he points to some examples of new media organizations that have been surfacing in recent years: Amazon founder Jeff Bezos' purchase of *The Washington Post* for $250 million; eBay founder Pierre Omidyar's similar investment in First Look Media; and investments by Silicon Valley venture capitalists in news platforms such as Medium. Marc Andreessen, a storied high-tech investor who was the founder of Netscape Communications Corporation, which opened up the World Wide Web in the early 1990s, has been an avid proponent of digital news media.

The result is an emerging new paradigm for news delivery, undistinguishable on one level because it is simply delivery of information from newsgatherers and reporters over digital channels, versus being disseminated on paper through physical distribution channels. David Plotz, editor of *Slate* magazine, wholeheartedly agrees that this is actually a "golden age" for the editorial profession – to the point the world is now being overwhelmed by it. In a recent speech, he observed how "digital journalism has, for all intents and purposes, become journalism." (Plotz, 2014)

The move to digital is not drying up the pool of opportunities and innovation in journalism and content creation – if anything, Plotz continues, "There's way too much of it." *The New York Times* – the stalwart pillar of the old journalism world – now publishes 250 items per day online, he illustrates. This may sound like a lot, he adds, "until you realize *Huffington Post* publishes 500 per day. Fox News publishes 1,500 per day. Yahoo publishes 3,000 per day. That's just stories." As he notes, news reporting has not gone away, but is even more pervasive:

Digital journalism has metastasized, so that most journalists don't even spend their time reporting and writing stories, what with the tweets, Facebook and LinkedIn posts, vines, videos, podcasts and email blasts. Increasingly, it feels like everyone is publishing everything all the time, and no one actually has time to read any of it.

In addition to a plethora of news sources, there's an accessibility and permanence to it as well. That is, a news item no longer vanishes as yesterday's newspapers are put in the trash, or at the conclusion of a 60-minute television clip. All news content now remains accessible to anyone who wants to view it, at any time, for as long as it remains part of a website – which potentially could be decades, if not centuries. "Digital platforms extend the lifespan of journalism," write Grueskin, Seave and Graves. They note:

In the analog era, news stories were as ephemeral as fruit flies. An article was prominent for a day, then available only on a library's microfiche; a video would be broadcast to millions on the nightly news, then it would be sent to a network's vault. Journalism now can be freely accessible for as long as a publisher wills it to be. In the words of one programmer, there is no such thing as 'yesterday's news.' News organizations can make money from their archives as part of a subscription or pay-per-view service, or as part of a scheme to provide more content and build traffic and ad revenue. But as increasing amounts of content stream into archives, consumers may have greater difficulty finding what they want. (p.13)

Readership studies reaffirm that news consumption has been taking a dramatic upturn, due in large part to the proliferation of new, easily accessible digital channels. While there has been a well-documented demise in the circulation of many print newspapers and journals, online news consumption has been going in the other direction. Research by The Pew Research Center's Project for Excellence in Journalism tracks the trends shaping the way news is presented and consumed. "Online news consumption has risen sharply in recent years, following the rapid spread of digital platforms," write Jane Sasseen, Kenny Olmstead and Amy Mitchell in an analysis of the findings of the Pew Research Center's 2012 News Media Consumption survey. (Sasseen, Olmstead, & Mitchell, 2012).

The rise in news consumption is attributable in no small part to its immediate availability to audiences that are now comfortable with a range of intelligent devices, from PCs to smartphones to tablets. "News is becoming more mobile, more social, and more real-time," writes Nic Newman, a digital strategist, in the latest report from the Reuters Institute and the University of Oxford. The latest survey "reveals continuing shifts in how, when, and where people access the news, with digital patterns becoming more entrenched – particularly amongst the younger half of the population. Audiences increasingly want news on any device, in any format, and at any time of day" (Levy & Newman, 2013).

The rise of technology on the consumer side is also driving the increased choices audiences now have. This has shifted the balance of power to the news consumer, who may pick and choose news content from a variety of content, representing a variety of approaches and viewpoints. "Content is content, long form or short form (our reporters have succeeded with both strategies)," according to Lewis DVorkin, chief product officer of Forbes Media (DVorkin, 2012, para. 11). As he describes it:

Content is not really print or digital. Media organizations — both new and traditional — place it where they do solely for business reasons. A new breed of voracious news consumer will simply discover it, consume it, talk about it, share it — and even create new content around it — whenever they want on the platform and device of their choice.

SOCIAL AND MOBILE

While news organizations have been scrambling to deliver more immediate, customizable and sharable content to audiences, social media channels have also evolved to become news providers in their own right. Social media has become an important piece of online news consumption – either as an alternative to dedicated news sources, or as an adjunct to existing media organizations. A June 2012 Pew Research Center study found that 19% of Americans saw news or news headlines on a social network "yesterday," more than double the nine percent who had done so in 2010. The acceleration is not just among the young, the research adds. "Roughly 34% of those aged 18 to 24 said they saw news on a social networking site yesterday, up from 12% in 2010, and so did 30% of 30-to-39-year olds, up from 19% in 2010. Social networking is now a part of this process as well: 15% of U.S. adults get most of their news from friends and family this way, and the vast majority of them (77%) follow links to full news stories" (Sasseen, Olmstead, & Mitchell, 2012).

"In 2012, social media continued to expand its role in the news ecosystem, establishing itself as an indispensable tool for distributing content and attracting new readers, as well as for building deeper engagement with current ones," according to The Pew Center. The 2012 Pew study also observes how Sree Sreenivasan, the chief digital officer for Columbia University and a professor of digital media at its Graduate School of Journalism, "counted 100 news organizations around the country that had designated social media editors. That number now stands at 184" (Sasseen, Olmstead, & Mitchell, 2012).

The availability of news content through a variety of digital channels may ultimately be boosting audiences as well, research also finds. The widespread availability of relatively inexpensive devices, such as smartphones and tablet computers, means audiences are capable of accessing the latest news information at any time or any place. "Most mobile news users are not replacing one platform with another; they are consuming more news than they had in the past," write Sasseen, Olmstead and Mitchell. A 2012 study by Pew Research Center and the Economist Group for example, found that 31% of tablet users actually spend more time reading the news, and at least 43% say using a tablet computer actually has increased their news consumption. In addition, digital news consumers aren't wedded to a single device or channel. The Pew survey also found that 77% of tablet news users indicate they also get news on a desktop or laptop computer; 54% also get news from a smartphone, and 50% get news in print. About 25% of tablet news readers report they get news through all four channels.

Mobile devices are also transforming the news environment through the rise of what is called the "second screen" phenomenon, in which users log onto the internet while also watching television. Although the practice goes well beyond news, it has become popular around live news events such as the U.S. presidential debates, election night or the State of the Union address.

The Pew Research Center asked whether people used two screens simultaneously to follow some election-rated events (rather than using a second device to do unrelated activities like e-mail or shopping). Of the 56% of the public who watched the second 2012 general election presidential debate between Mitt Romney and Barack Obama, 11% "dual-screened," reporting that they followed the debate on both a computer or mobile device and television at the same time, according to Pew Research survey data.

Dual-screening during live news events "has the most potential for news organizations, offering an opportunity to leverage viewers' desires to communicate online and to engage more actively with the content they are seeing on the screen, especially if the event is occurring live," according to Pew.

While the computer "remains the primary device for accessing digital news, the key underlying trend is about growth in access from multiple devices," says Newman. "One-third of our entire global sample now gets news on at least two devices and 9% use more than three. This is important because, along with other researchers, we find that as people acquire more devices they consume more news in aggregate (time spent) – but also access news more often throughout the day."

Some devices "are used more heavily for news than others," Newman adds. For example, "85% of computer users say they access news on that device each week, compared with 63% of smartphone users, 60% of tablet users, 54% of smart TV users, and only 17% for the e-reader."

But multi-platform is not just about digital news, Newman points out. "Across all of our countries, an average of 49% of those who access news on a tablet say they also read a printed newspaper at least once each week; 81% also watch TV news and we see similar patterns with smartphone users."

THE TRUST FACTOR

Behind all this ubiquitous access, however, audiences still seek to validate the information they are gathering. Historically, the reporter, followed by the editor, served as a filter between incoming information and the reader, serving to validate and authenticate information, and eliminate or put away for further investigation any information of questionable merit. With the directness of digital media and social media, that filter is either substantially weakened or eliminated altogether. The Reuters Institute survey also cast further light "on the importance of trusted news brands," Newman adds. "In all countries we asked if people agreed that they preferred to get news from sites they know and trust." (Levy & Newman, 2013, p.13) The figures were universally high, they add, with 82% supporting the proposition in the US, and 77% in the UK. The high levels of trust accorded to established news organizations also was boosted by the proliferation of devices used to access and view news stories, Newman observes:

Asking the question in a different way ('I don't notice which sites I'm looking at...') showed a slightly different picture. Trust in traditional brands was also high when compared with blogs or social media. Broadcaster websites in the UK were trusted by 79%, with newspapers showing over 60%. In comparison, Facebook (8%) and Twitter (9%) were widely mistrusted – although heavy social media users were significantly more likely to trust what they found. Trust in news brands increases significantly with the amount of usage, so it is not surprising that smartphone and tablet news users also show more trust in traditional brands. We also find, in terms of their behavior, that users of these devices are much more likely to go directly to a brand (50%) using a desktop icon, on a smartphone, compared to the overall sample (34%). The more devices – and the heavier the use – the better they tend to do.

CHANGING MEDIA MODELS

Behind the new sense of excitement for opportunities within the media business is the inherent ability to capture and leverage data – based on readership transactions and preferences – that is not only changing the media business model, but is also reshaping the way news and information is gathered, prioritized and presented to audiences. The data revolution, which is only getting started, is reshaping the media business, and is a vital part of the move away from print and to digital platforms. The digital platform – news delivered via social media, websites and apps – is a dominant force on the business side, and is shaping the news-gathering and selection process as well.

Only two decades ago, there were substantial barriers to entry in the news business. Establishing and managing a news outlet required substantial investments in infrastructure. Newspapers required printing presses, paper, and extensive distribution channels throughout their communities. Television and radio stations required production facilities and studios, as well as broadcast capabilities. Both print and broadcast media needed talented people to identify, pursue and present news stories. Now, thanks to the internet, these barriers are gone, unleashing a plethora of news sources, from "citizen journalists" to the traditional outlets. To survive and stand out from this unlimited competition, news organizations need to be able distinguish themselves and their content from the rest. Ken Doctor, a former executive with the Knight Ridder newspaper chain and editor of the Newsonomics blog, estimates that it takes less than $25 million – dirt cheap by business standards -- to a launch a significant digital news operation (Doctor, 2014, para. 15):

The price of entry is what's key in this new business. No printing presses or broadcast pipes. At this moment, the world has conspired to make relatively cheap entry — at $25 million or less — quite possible. It's also possible to project a new credibility for such new products: Digital audiences have become accustomed to taking new brands seriously, seemingly overnight.

The impact of these changes – and a more profound abundance of choices – is dramatically transforming the media industry, which in turn is reshaping the way content is identified, developed and presented to audiences. Fox observes that "on the national level, at least, there are all manner of experiments and signs of success. *The New York Times* has, thanks partly to the success of its metered paywall, returned to a 19th-century model whereby circulation brings in more money than advertising. Buzzfeed has, by astutely catering to the massive new distribution network that is Facebook, built a huge audience at relatively low cost, while bringing in revenue with clever (and clearly labeled) modern equivalents of the 'reading notice'" (Fox, 2014).

Fox also points to the burgeoning role of social media sites such as Facebook and Google in news delivery. Which openly compete "with media companies in that, like them, it makes money by delivering audiences to advertisers. These two are also possibly the most successful such enterprises ever."

This rise in online news consumption is creating increased competition and disruption to the publishing business model, says Newman. Nevertheless, he added, new readership data "offers some signs of hope for those investing in original news content. More people say they've paid for digital news in the past 10 months and we have data for the first time about the types and frequency of digital payment. Traditional brands continue to attract the largest online audiences and we find that trust in news brands remains uniquely valued by young and old."

In this brave new world, literally thousands of online news providers are competing for readers' attention. At the same time, it's likely the disruption of the news content delivery model will continue for some time to come. As Newman observes:

Most news organizations are reconfiguring their workflows for the multi-platform age – trying to drive more output to more platforms with the same number (or fewer) journalists Finding new audiences and revenues is proving more challenging. Some news organizations are looking to exploit niches, others are pushing for scale and paywalls are going up around the world. As ever, success will depend on a combination of clear strategies and a strong understanding of changing audience behaviors. (Levy & Newman, 2013, p.16)

DATA RULES

The rise of digital platforms is creating new models of journalism and content creation. One approach is to use digital tools to create new types of journalistic and editorial engagements.

For example, Enda and Mitchell point to an online forum, Contently, which provides an outlet for journalists. The site "connects thousands of journalists, many of them ex-print reporters, with commercial brands to help them produce their own content, including brand-oriented magazines." *Fortune* also has a similar forum, called *Fortune* TOC—Trusted Original Content, which is targeted at marketers for distribution on their own platforms.

At the same time, new, online-only publications have come to the fore. One prime example is the *Huffington Post,* an online-online news and opinion journal that became a dominant force in new media within a very short time since its founding by Arianna Huffington in 2005. In 2011, the Huffington Post property was purchased by AOL for $315 million. "In just six years, Huffington has built her site from an idea into a real competitor— at least in the size of its audience—with *The New York Times*," The Columbia Journalism School report observes. During this time, *The Huffington Post* "has mastered and fine-tuned not just aggregation, but also social media, comments from readers, and most of all, a sense of what its public wants." (Grueskin, Seave & Graves, 2011)

Aggregation is a particularly notable hallmark of the site, they add, helping "media companies, new and old, understand the appeal of aggregation: its ability to give prominence to otherwise unheard voices and to bring together and serve intensely engaged audiences, as well its minimal costs compared to what's incurred in the traditionally laborious task of gathering original content."

At the core of this formula for success has been *Huffington Post's* ability to leverage data analytics to reach and engage with audiences. "Huffington Post also developed an ability to respond quickly to the data that it was getting on traffic and usage—something that is a crucial component of success in digital journalism," Grueskin, Seave, and Graves state. "Indeed, data analysis has moved from being a required skill in media companies' finance departments to being an essential part of the résumé for editors, writers and designers."

This form of analytics is applied to build traffic to attract online readership, which can be readily measured, they add. "One method of building traffic is to hop onto hot topics," they relate, noting that internal guidance from AOL's editorial directors suggest that as an example that if 'Macaulay Culkin and Mila Kunis are trending because they broke up,' someone should 'write a story about Macaulay Culkin and Mila Kunis.' And editors are told to always keep expenses in mind. The cost of content can run from $25 for a freelance article that needs 7,000 page views to break even, to a $5,000 video that will require a half-million streams to recover its costs. Catchy headlines, such as 'Lady Gaga Goes Pantless in Paris' (from AOL site StyleList.com) are important to entice readers from search." Neel Chopdekar, vice president at AOL Media, called this "bionic journalism—the best of man and machine." (Grueskin, Seave & Graves, 2011)

Is bionic journalism – this mode of content selection – what's best for new media journalism and its audiences? Adherence to generating page views based on search engine optimization and resulting soft news – such as celebrity coverage – may be an ugly byproduct of this process. At the same time, the variety and scope of various online digital media provides greater choices for consumers who wish to seek out more personalized experiences, filtered to the types of information they seek.

There is risk in going too far with audience data collection. A reader may follow a link from a news aggregation site, for example, to a news organization's page, but may only spend a few minutes reading an article before moving on to another provider's site. Typically, the bounce rate – the percentage of readers who only read one article and leave the site entirely – may range around 50%, according to web experts (Hartwig, 2013). "Most readers spend far less time on digital sites than they did on legacy platforms," The Columbia report finds (Grueskin, Seave & Graves, 2011).

One hallmark of the digital new era, then, may be the phenomena of consumers "voting with their feet" – simply turning to alternative information sources. With the ease of simply clicking from one site to another – and with so many different news providers to choose from – news consumers are far more fickle with their choices of content, and are not likely to exhibit the loyalty that was seen for hometown newspapers or TV/radio outlets. For example, in a survey of 2,000 U.S. adults in 2013, the Pew Center found that "nearly one-third—31%—of people say they have deserted a particular news outlet because it no longer provides the news and information they had grown accustomed to. And those most likely to have walked away are better educated, wealthier and older than those who did not—in other words, they are people who tend to be most prone to consume and pay for news," according to research from The Pew Center (Enda & Mitchell, 2013).

The rise of choices in the digital media world may also ultimately promote more comprehensive coverage – there has been a movement seen across some digital properties to offer more in-depth, greater coverage and analysis of topics, including embedded graphical and visual elements, also referred to as "long-form" content. To gauge the public's view of how the industry's financial travails have affected news coverage, the Pew survey asked people whether they thought news stories were less complete than they used to be or whether there simply were fewer of them. About half—48%—of respondents said stories are not as thorough as they were before, while slightly less than a third—31%—said stories are fewer.

In the process, new modes of content presentation are evolving to meet these demands. "There is a shifting trend toward consuming long form content on mobile and tablet devices, whether it be articles, videos, TV series or movies - people are opting for the long story," according to a report from Coulls, a digital media advisory service (Coull, 2014). "It's all about giving the viewers what they want, something publishers are now able to do because the technology is available to provide it" (Coull, 2014, para. 39). "Within long form content we have videos that play while you're in amongst the content - galleries, advertising, music - it's all contextual. The experience for the user is multi-faceted and the potential for engagement is greater than ever." (Coull, 2014, para. 30)

Today's news sites generate a plethora of information that may or may not be captured. Not only which stories are being viewed, but also how they're being viewed, how much is being read, and what other types of content are being read along with it. That doesn't necessarily diminish the role of journalists and editorial professionals, but actually may enhance their ability to deliver timely articles of great quality and significance to audiences. Forbes' DVorkin describes how he is seeing this shift play out (DVorkin, 2012, para. 3):

The availability of statistics puts the journalist's tried-but-far-from-true gut feeling to the test in real time. Reliable user data just didn't exist in the medium's early days. Now, the numbers illuminate everything all the time for journalists-turned-product-people like myself. You can track the digital news consumer's first click, second and each one after that. You know how far down the screen they scroll. And most important, you learn what they think as the social conversation evolves. When we look at what's produced, commented on and shared on Forbes.com and digest all the data, what lies behind news usage today becomes clear. Speed, perspective and analysis are certainly important — but in-depth reporting that often starts its life in longer Forbes magazine stories is fast becoming one of the news enthusiast's most rewarding clicks.

DATA IMPACTS ON NEWS ORANIZATIONS

Disruption is the key word about what is happening in the news industry these days, and this disruption is taking many different forms. It is also having a significant impact on the many areas of the organizations and people gathering and synthesizing news content for audiences. At the corc of this disruptive process is data – the industry has evolved from a static state to one that is moved and shaped by the data it is generating and acting upon. The important thing to remember is disruption is not a bad word – it simply means new ways of doing business and new players have emerged that are challenging the status quo, while making news information more accessible to wider audiences.

There are a number of disruptions that result from digital media adoption – much of which is challenging, but much of which can have also a positive impact on the delivery of news and information.

For example, while technology has wiped away barriers to entry in the news business, it is also creating opportunities to develop stronger, more responsive news channels. "Digital platforms provide ways for audiences to build quickly with lower marketing costs than in traditional media," Grueskin, Seave and Graves point out. They also observe that "digital provides a means to innovate rapidly, determine audience size quickly and wind down unsuccessful businesses with minimal expense." No longer do substantial capital expenditures have to be made:

A video service need not build tall antennae atop the highest hills in town, and print publishers can avoid capital-intensive investments in printing presses. The large staffs associated with getting information to readers—whether they're camera crews or printing staffs—aren't as necessary. The development time from idea to market is shortened, greatly increasing efficient use of a firm's resources. But because competitors can imitate or adapt more quickly, it is difficult to cash in on innovations. The shorter cycles can lessen the length of time that innovations remain unique, relevant and valuable (Grueskin, Seave & Graves, 2011, p.12).

Additional benefits mentioned by Grueskin, Seave and Graves include the availability of real-time audience information, enabling editorial managers and journalists to not only see content that is popular with audiences, but also quickly get a sense of the profile of the audience, and how they are engaging with the content. In the process, publishing organizations have the opportunity to deliver highly targeted content to those audiences as well. However, they also caution, too much diversification may result in too many choices that news consumers may not have the time or attention span for too wide of a range of choices.

SOLUTIONS AND RECOMMENDATIONS

Collecting and monitoring audience data opens up new avenues for news organizations. There are a number of ways editorial organizations and journalists can participate in the revolutionary new model that is reshaping the industry. The following are recommendations for moving to a data-driven new operation:

- *Understand that news is now a two-way delivery channel.* Until recently, publishers and broadcasters took in information, and selected and packaged it up for consumption. Now, understanding and engaging with audiences is now an essential part of the news presentation process. News organizations need to be open to ideas and input from their audiences.
- *Employ the right tools.* News organizations need the right tools to capture the audience numbers. There is a need for standards in the types of data being gathered on audience types. Many of the data analysis tools developed in the business world for analyzing market trend data will be just as useful for opening up and advancing the news process. Just as importantly, many of today's data analysis solutions don't necessarily require statistician skills to mine and interpret results. Today's data analytics packages are available via Software as a Service (the cloud), or can be set up and installed relatively quickly onsite. Such tools offer highly graphical front-end dashboards that enable users to quickly spot trends see who the outliers may be. In addition, as Ken Doctor observes, "digital-only content management systems get the content out on all platforms with far fewer people and keystrokes. Ad automation and optimization maximizes revenue with fewer staff. Social sharing tools magnify voice for virtual pennies. NBC Universal, ESPN, and Vox can all extend their content and sales systems to serve their new properties, leveraging the digital technology investments they've already made" (Doctor, 2014).
- *Always question the data and the assumptions behind it.* Data may be delivering more a more accurate picture of audiences that anecdotal evidence or simple gut feel. But digital publishing managers and journalists should never take the data at face value. Data may always be flawed, as well as the sources behind it. Managers and journalists should apply the same level of critical thinking to the data they are working with as they apply to actual news content. Is the data clean? Is it verified? Why is a particular set of data being sourced?
- *Enlighten and educate management.* New organization executives and managers need to recognize the opportunity that data analytics provides to better serve audiences. News organizations may now rely on social media and website data for leads, as well as to determine trending topics. The author spoke with the director of a local television newsroom, which examines the trending topics at its website every morning to determine the priority of its news presentations.
- *Form partnerships.* With the rise of data-driven news and content consumption, digital media organizations will be providing many services that align with the types of services produced and generated by tech and social media providers. In many cases, this means competition for advertising dollars, as social media platforms replicate many of the same services formerly provided through print newspapers – such as classified advertising, help-wanted advertising, and even legal notices. While competing on one level, publishers will often find themselves in partnerships with the social media platforms as well. By marrying the journalistic competencies of news organizations with the platform development skills of tech vendors, digital media providers may be able to host more powerful and far-reaching properties than if they tried to go it alone.

- *Acquire or grow new skills.* Editorial and journalistic skills – which include the ability to dig into stories, get all sides, and ask the right questions – will increasingly be in demand, especially as digital media providers seek to gain a competitive edge against the many players in this space, as well as social media-based reporting. At the same time, news organization managers and journalists will need to have the flexibility and adaptability to learn from the data and analytics tools they employ. This includes critical thinking skills, and the capability to look at information in new ways.

FUTURE RESEARCH DIRECTIONS

Digital news organizations will increasingly arise from a fusion with the technology sector. For example, social media platforms have evolved into aggregators or supporters of community-based news, and thus, there is a convergence taking place. The relationship between the high-tech industry and the digital news industry needs to be examined. Issues that may be prominent include the ability to cover events in tech in an unbiased way, and retaining independence from deep-pocketed owners.

In addition, the types of data collected needs to be reviewed in greater detail, and there may be a need to standardize some of this across the channels.

The role of new digital media in meeting editorial and journalistic standards needs to be discussed – that is, citing multiple sources within articles, striving for impartiality, and presenting news that's relevant and pressing, even though it may run contrary to analytics. For example, celebrity gossip may drive traffic, but it's not always in the best interest of a news organization or its readers to stream large amounts of inconsequential news.

CONCLUSION

Welcome to what is clearly becoming an emerging golden era of journalism and content creation. The news media isn't on the wane, as many pundits are stating. Instead, the business model for media organizations is shifting, away from print, and away from the "gateway" approach to journalism and content creation, in which a few select articles are presented to audience. Instead, the new digital media model is creating a plethora of content, which may be overwhelming audiences. At the same time, the rise of digital media is providing consumers a far wider range of choices that is pushing media organizations to provide content more tailored to their audiences.

The bottom line is that journalism and editorial skills still matters – a great deal. "Our data show that there still is a yearning – in an ocean of content – for trusted news across a range of subject areas," says Newman. This is a role that established news organizations with journalistic traditions – as well as relative newcomers who understand the importance of journalistic and editorial integrity – can fulfill.

REFERENCES

Coull Newsletter. (n.d). *Long form -- The story audiences want.* Retrieved October 04, 2014, from http://coull.com/resources/long-form-story-audiences-want

Doctor, K. (2014, January 29). The newsonomics of why everyone seems to be starting a news site, *Nieman Lab.* Retrieved October 10, 2014, from http://www.niemanlab.org/2014/01/the-newsonomics-of-why-everyone-seems-to-be-starting-a-news-site/

DVorkin. L. (2012, February 23). Inside Forbes: How long-form journalism is finding its digital audience. *Forbes.* Retrieved November 14, 2014, from http://www.forbes.com/sites/lewisdvorkin/2012/02/23/inside-forbes-how-long-form-journalism-is-finding-its-digital-audience/

Enda, J., & Mitchell, A. (2013). *Americans show signs of leaving a news outlet, citing less information.* The State of the News Media 2013, Pew Research Foundation. Retrieved September 18, 2014, from http://stateofthemedia.org/2013/special-reports-landing-page/citing-reduced-quality-many-americans-abandon-news-outlets/

Fox, J. (2014, April 16). A New Golden Age for Media? *The Atlantic.* Retrieved October 22, 2014, from http://www.theatlantic.com/magazine/archive/2014/05/start-the-presses/359810/

Grueskin, B., Seave, A., & Graves, L. (2011). *The Story So Far: What We Know About the Business of Digital Journalism.* Columbia Journalism School, Tow Center for Digital Journalism. Retrieved October 10, 2014, from http://www.journalism.columbia.edu/news/448

Hartwig, E. (2013, November 22). How to lower your site's bounce rate. *Mashable.* Retrieved October 28, 2014, from http://mashable.com/2013/11/22/bounce-rate-metrics/

Levy, D., & Newman, N. (2013). *Reuters Institute Digital News Report: 2013.* Reuters Institute for the Study of Journalism at the University of Oxford. Retrieved November 15, 2014, from https://reutersinstitute.politics.ox.ac.uk/publications/risj-digital-report/2013.html

Luckerson, V. (2014, October 8). Fear, misinformation, and social media complicate ebola fight. *Time.* Retrieved October 17, 2014, from https://time.com/3479254/ebola-social-media/

Mutter, A. (2014, July 16). The newspaper crisis, by the numbers. *Reflections of a Newsosaur.* Retrieved October 22, 2014, from http://newsosaur.blogspot.com/2014/07/the-newspaper-crisis-by-numbers.html

Newspaper Association of America. (2014, April 18). Business model evolving, circulation revenue rising. Retrieved October 24, 2014, from http://www.naa.org/Trends-and-Numbers/Newspaper-Revenue/Newspaper-Media-Industry-Revenue-Profile-2013.aspx

Plotz, D. (2014, May 29). We are in a golden age for journalism. National Post. Retrieved [originally] October 23, 2014, from https://groups.yahoo.com/neo/groups/TYR/conversations/messages/61109 Retrieved January 30, 2015, from https://groups.yahoo.com/neo/groups/TYR/conversations/messages/61109

Sasseen, J., Olmstead, K., & Mitchell, A. (2013). Digital: As mobile grows rapidly, the pressures on news intensify. The State of the News Media 2013, Pew Research Foundation. Retrieved October 21, 2014, from http://stateofthemedia.org/2013/digital-as-mobile-grows-rapidly-the-pressures-on-news-intensify/#the-second-screen-phenomenon

KEY TERMS AND DEFINITIONS

Big Data: Datasets that are either relatively large in size (generally more than 100 terabytes); occur in unstructured formats, such as video, documents, or log files; and is being delivered real-time or close to real-time.

Bionic Journalism: The combination of human prepared headlines and storylines, with selections driven by metrics based on number of visits to articles.

Digital Advertising: Advertisements or announcements that are featured within Internet channels, such as on web pages or through mobile interfaces.

Digital Journalism: The practice of developing and delivering news and commentary over online channels.

Digital Media: The delivery of information in the form of news, feature articles, videos or audio formats through Internet channels.

Direct Marketing: Individualized communication about products, services, companies or other organizations that is delivered directly to consumers, by mail, telephone, email, web channel, or social media.

Print Advertising: Advertisements or announcements that appear on the pages of newspapers or periodicals.

Social Media: Online channels or platforms that enable end-users to communicate and exchange information, photos, videos and audio files within virtual communities.

Section 2
Harnessing the Power of Data

Chapter 6
Web 2.0 and News 2.0:
Utilizing Real-Time Analytics for Modern News Organizations

Kyle Gibson
BostInno, USA

Greg Gomer
BostInno, USA

ABSTRACT

This chapter examines the effects that Web 2.0 technologies have had on traditional news organizations and how those organizations have been forced to adapt their content style, speed of production, and distribution models. It specifically focuses on real-time analytics and how news organizations can utilize new opportunities presented by social media platforms and web usage mining to analyze their audience, the competition, and popular opinions. The chapter will explain in detail how a news organization can compile data from social media and web usage, gain insights from that data, and act upon those insights. To further examine real-time analytics, the chapter presents real examples from BostInno, an online news source, where real-time analytics affected content and distribution. To conclude, the authors will reflect on the impact real-time analytics has on the news industry and how it might affect it in the near future.

INTRODUCTION

News organizations have historically been the gatekeepers of news content. Up until recently, they were the agencies best equipped to mass produce media and distribute it to a large audience. News organizations operated the majority of industrial presses, radio towers, and television satellites, so they decided what newspapers, radio broadcasts, and television broadcasts went out to their audience. They also got to decide how fast their news media was produced and distributed. Hence, they were the "Gatekeepers of Content."

DOI: 10.4018/978-1-4666-8580-2.ch006

Advancements in communication technologies have repeatedly disrupted traditional news organizations' positions as "gatekeepers." Either a current form of media will be improved upon or a completely new form of media will be invented, and it will draw consumers away from older media technologies and brands. According to Robles (2015), a disruptive innovation is one "that transforms the complicated, expensive services and products into things that are so simple and affordable that you and I can use them." (p.123) An example of such an innovation in the news industry is radio news broadcasts. They disrupted newspapers' business by relaying information quicker and having a one-time cost of buying a household radio.

When these innovations inevitably arise, news organizations have to choose between competing with the new technology or adopting it. The first choice is most likely a losing battle, as Robles (2015) explains:

Disruptive innovations appeal to customers who are unattractive to the incumbents. Although they typically involve simple adaptations of known technologies, entrants almost always beat incumbents at this game because established companies lack the motivation to win. (p. 123)

In other words, consumers will typically adopt the newer technology instead of sticking with the old technology and its established brands, since the newer technology is typically more convenient and consumer-focused.

Recently, traditional news organizations have been struggling to adapt to Web 2.0 and its several disruptive technologies. The term "Web 2.0" is used to describe the transformation of the Internet from a static, read-only medium to a dynamic, open and user-based experience. The Internet became a full platform for business, social connections, collaboration, and more. Tim O'Reilly, who coined the term "Web 2.0" in 2003, described the movement as "the business revolution in the computer industry caused by the move to the Internet as platform, and an attempt to understand the rules for success on that new platform." Notable examples of innovative technologies that came with Web 2.0 are social networking sites, wikis, forums, and blogs. Facebook, Twitter, and Wikipedia are three success stories from the Web 2.0 movement, each of them being a massive social network with a meaningful international presence.

The new Web 2.0 gives everyone with an Internet connection great potential for communication, collaboration, and education. These technologies were designed with individual consumers in mind, aiming to personalize the Web and empower its users. Mark Zuckerberg (2010), creator and CEO of the social network Facebook, said of social networking: "This flow of social information has profound benefits—from driving better decisions to keeping in touch more easily—and we're really proud that Facebook is part of the shift toward more social and personalized experiences everywhere online." At the same time as empowering Internet users, these Web 2.0 advancements take away prior advantages that traditional news organizations used to have.

Consider this: a multi-national, muti-billion dollar news company has just as much ability with social media technology to produce and distribute content as every individual person with a simple Internet connection. Just as *The New York Times* can "tweet" a photo, a person's grandmother can as well. The grandmother and *The New York Times* have the same potential to "go viral" and reach a worldwide audience. Social media networks, along with other Web 2.0

technologies, are designed to be completely level playing fields. This makes it impossible for news organizations to be gatekeepers of any content online.

Beyond equalizing content creation and distribution power, Web 2.0 has also greatly improved the number of consumer choices there are for retrieving news. Now, more than ever, individuals can gain worldly or local information through no news organization's help at all. Instead, they can get their information straight from social media platforms like blogs, Twitter, or Facebook.

Consumers can also get their information straight from the source, since most popular figures and notable entities maintain public social media profiles. This "choice of no choice" has never before been something that could substantially affect news organizations.

Ofcom, the "communications regulator for the UK," conducted a large study in 2013 of consumers' consumption of news media. They focused on four types of news sources: newspaper, radio, television, and online. Almost one third of the respondents said that they use online news sources, and of the respondents that mainly use one source for news, a fifth of those mainly use online sources. Predictably, young adults were most drawn to online news, with three in ten respondents aged 16-24 listing websites or mobile apps as their most important sources of news.

Also in 2013, the Reuters Institute for the Study of Journalism conducted an international study on news consumption. Fifty percent of respondents aged 18-44 listed online sources as their main source of news. In the United States, 21% of news readers are likely to comment on news events through social networks, and 47% of respondents under the age of 45 said that they use social media to find most of their news. The overall data on the journalism industry shows a growing number of consumers going online for their news exclusively, as well as a growing trust in those digital sources.

Web 2.0 technologies have severely weakened the role of traditional news organizations in distributing information. This leaves news organizations with less control over their own content's relevance and usefulness, since consumers can see the original source of information and choose to get their information from free sources, such as blogs and other social media platforms. For example, according to a study done by Verizon during the debates of the 2012 presidential election in the United States, 39% of adults watching the debate were at least somewhat likely to follow live reactions from political reporters and other figures on social media. That is an example of Web 2.0 technologies completely circumventing the role of traditional news organizations, since a political reporter would traditionally write an article for a newspaper or give a television interview.

As disruptive as these advancements are, they also present positive opportunities to traditional news organizations. On social networks, for instance, users share content they find on the Web with their network of friends or community members. This can be an avenue for news organizations to gain large viewership on their websites, since their content can get shared across large networks of users. Another opportunity is for instant feedback. News organizations can set up proper channels for their readers to respond to their content, fix errors, voice different opinions, and generate user-created content that lives on the news organization's site. These two opportunities add value and relevance to a news organization that were never possible before.

The most powerful tool for news organizations presented by Web 2.0 technologies is real-time analytics. Every action a user makes online, from visiting a page to commenting on a video, is recorded as it occurs and immediately ready to be analyzed. There are full suites of analytical tools available to users, web-masters, or organizations that allow them to analyze large sets of data as they are being collected and extract meaningful insights. News organizations stand to gain a great advantage from real-time analytics, if they learn to use them effectively and appropriately. It can turn Web 2.0 from being traditional news' enemy into its savior.

BACKGROUND

To fully understand how traditional news organizations can utilize real-time analytics, it is necessary to understand basic web analytics first. "Analytics" refers to the search for meaningful patterns in data that can lead to insights or help make predictions. Data that are retrieved online are typically "Big Data," or, data that are too large to manipulate with conventional methods. As market researcher Hali et al. (2013) said, "The volume of information in digital format has increased to such an extent, that there is a growing need for sophisticated tools that help people locate, filter and manage this information in an efficient and optimal way." (p. 1)

Web analytics, also referred to as "Web Mining," is "an activity that focuses to discover new, relevant and reliable information and knowledge by examining the structure, content and usage of the web. The main focus is on learning about web users and their interaction with websites." (Mehak et al., 2013, p.1) There are three types of web mining: content mining, structure mining, and usage mining.

With content mining, automated scripts scan text, pictures, and videos hosted on web pages in order to determine their relevance to one another. Structure mining identifies the relationships between web pages through the links found on each page. There are "inlinks," which lead to another page on that website, and "outlinks," which lead to another website entirely. When usage mining, scripts keep a log of user actions, such as how long a user remains on a certain page. These three types of web mining can be used in conjunction to extract valuable insights from user activity and web structure.

With the advent of Web 2.0, many new types of web actions have emerged. Commenting, blogging, vlogging, "Tweeting," and "Liking" are all new actions that can now be logged and analyzed. "Webmasters," or, the developers who maintain websites, have many different tools they can use to log user actions made on their site. They typically log everything they possibly can, as to not lose any possibly insight-worthy data.

The most widely used analytical suite among webmasters is Google Analytics, which was so popular when it was first released that Google had to temporarily stop sign-ups (AdAge, 2005). It is a full suite of data tracking and visualization tools that allow a webmaster to personally or automatically analyze large sets of data mined from their own website. They can visualize these data on a "dashboard," a personalizable screen with several panels showing analyzed web data, such as the most popular pages for the last month, the five most popular keywords on search engines that have led users to their website, and the average load time users have experienced when browsing. These are all examples of real-time analytics.

"Real-time analytics" specifically means analyzing events as they are currently happening. With a Google Analytics dashboard, for example, a webmaster can monitor how many users are currently accessing his website from France. He can also check where each of those French visitors was "referred" from, which is how they got to the website. They could have come from a link on a social network like Facebook, a Google search, or clicked on one of the site's online ads.

Depending on the website and what a company does, webmasters and analysts can gain insights from analyzing these data in real-time. Maybe a flight booking company wants to capitalize on its website's newfound popularity in France, so the company might start offering discounted flights departing from French airports. It is extremely difficult to predict online trends, but with analytical tools like Google Analytics, it is easy to react quickly to trends as they coalesce.

Real-time analytics are already being used heavily in advertising and public relations. For instance, there are online advertising platforms that allow for "real-time bidding" on advertisements. Put simply, real-time bidding allows someone to bid on the chance to advertise to users with specified characteristics, such as the region in which they are located. When a user accesses a website with real-time bidding, the highest bidder for that user gets their ad served. This enables the most efficient spending on advertising possible, since the company only pays to advertise to people it specifically wants to reach. Real-time bidding also allows for extremely personalized advertising, which is beneficial for both consumers and advertisers.

There have also been advances in using real-time analytics in disaster response plans. Japan's government and international volunteers made use of social media networks' speed and identification qualities to "perform vital relief functions such as safety identification, displaced-persons locating, damage information provision, support for disabled individuals, volunteer organization, fund-raising, and moral support systems." (Peary et al., 2012, p. 1) Using the same web analytics tools as marketers, relief workers are now able to save lives and reconnect families quickly and reliably.

Using these web technologies and methods for disaster relief is obviously a well-intentioned form of use, but real-time analytics have come under scrutiny when used for marketing. Some feel that tracking users' activity is an invasion of their privacy. Schulz (2007), a digital culture scholar, said of tracking social media activity: "All these activities create monetary value, which is sometimes based on involuntary participation. Interfaces put only few hindrances in the way of contribution. However, it's a breach of the social contract if users don't know that they are used." He went on to suggest that "Typologies of participation on the Social web would need to start with a separation of voluntary and involuntary participation (e.g., data mining)."

Whether using data collected on users without their permission is exploitation or not, there is no disputing how secretive marketers are about their data-collecting activities online. Users will never see "Your activity on this site is being logged" on any websites, for instance. Having a message like that would certainly make users act differently when browsing a site, just as participants act differently in a focus group than in a field study. The phenomenon of subjects modifying their behavior because they know they are being observed is known as the Hawthorne Effect.

Marketers need consumers to act normally on their websites, or else the data they collect will not be representative of how consumers really feel and act. In a small sense, consumers are working for marketers when they are browsing websites and participating in social media. "From this perspective, customers are configured as uniquely skilled workers who, for the production of value-in-use to occur, must be given full rein to articulate their inimitable requirements and share their knowledge." (Zwick et al., 2010, p. 166)

Even though it's made so many technological advances, Web 2.0 is still in its infancy. There are no established social expectations yet for marketers or webmasters in regards to tracking user activity and analyzing that data. Still, those data are already highly valued by investors and company management, with social networking companies Twitter and Facebook both being worth billions of dollars.

There are marketing professionals who see fundamental problems in real-time web analytics, beyond the ethical issues. Les Binet and Sarah Carter (2014) of advertising agency adam&eveDDB published a paper criticizing real-time evaluation for campaigns, stating that,

... short term metrics are not a reliable guide to long-term growth. In fact, focusing on short-term goals can actually reduce clients' long-term profits(...)With no longer-term perspective, it becomes hard to monitor and build the long-term, consistent memory structures that are brands." (p.1)

Real-time analytics are better suited for short-term goals, and those are much easier to monitor and act upon. It can be easy for real-time evaluations to overshadow long-term goals.

Other critics point out shortcomings in the data used for web analytics. For example, the data being extracted by web mining are only data that users have chosen to make publicly available. Therefore, analysts cannot know what user actions web analytics is missing. Furthermore, historical data for web analytics are mostly unavailable, since the World Wide Web is still young. In terms of web analytics, an analyst has no substantial record of studies or results to reference. There are also issues with demographics. Most of the time, webmasters or analysts have an IP address with which to identify the user. Gender, age, and other demographic variables are only minimally available, in the cases where the user elects to provide that information. And even then, there is no way of verifying that information. These holes in the data lead some market researchers to mistrust web analytics. However, those holes are slowly being patched and the historical data are building up to support the web analytics' validity.

Along with these criticisms of real-time analytics, there is heavy support as well. Researchers point to the speed and scope of big data, saying "Big Data allows analysts to spot trends, provide niche insights that help create value and innovation much faster than conventional methods." (Hali et al., 2013, p. 1) To put it simply: bigger data gives you a bigger picture. And, quicker data makes for a better understanding of what's happening right now.

In "Putting Consumers to Work," researchers from the *Journal of Consumer Culture* propose that web analytics will lead to companies better serving their consumers. They say, "We consider these latest management and marketing schemes as part of a larger, ongoing exercise by producers to reduce the distance between production and consumption." (Zwick et al., 2010, p. 168) With a better understanding of the consumer's interests, news organizations will be able to deliver a better product quicker than they could have without the data allowed by Web 2.0.

Taking the consumer-oriented positives even further, the authors of "The Like Economy," a study into Facebook's impact on the Web, see users as having all of the power on the Web. When discussing Facebook and the impact of the "Like" button, they say: "While Facebook, webmasters, developers and Instant Personalization partners are co-producers of the data-intensive infrastructure or web content as frame for user engagement, it is the user who produces the actual data flows of the Like Economy." (Gerlitz & Helmond, 2011, p. 12) In those researchers' eyes, the users are in complete control over the Web, and they profit much more than webmasters or marketers can.

News organizations have to weigh the opinions of these critics and supporters when considering real-time analytics. If they take a well-researched approach at the practice, they can incorporate real-time analytics in many positive ways into their business strategy, allowing them to reach more people with better content, advertise more effectively for less money, and negate all of the ill-effects that Web 2.0 has had on the news industry.

GETTING STARTED WITH REAL-TIME ANALYTICS

When news organizations decide to start utilizing real-time analytics, they need to have an established online business model first. There are many different online business models that news organizations have adopted with the coming of Web 2.0, and there are surely ones that have not been invented yet. A popular model is similar to the subscription service of traditional newspapers, where users pay a certain fee for access to the content. It is important to have an established business model because real-time analytics work best when you have set long-term goals. Like Binet and Carter (2014) point out, "With no longer-term perspective, it becomes hard to monitor and build the long-term, consistent memory structures that are brands." (p. 1) For instance, if you're using a subscription model, you can use sign-ups as a key metric when evaluating campaigns and the overall performance of the website.

Once news organizations have set their long-term business goals, they can start adding analytical tools to their websites and monitoring web activity outside of their sites. Full suites such as Google Analytics are generally easy to implement on a website, since the bulk of the data manipulation is done by the service provider. For instance, Google stores and analyzes all of the data collected through Google Analytics' tools on their own machines. This makes web analytics tools affordable and maintainable for small news organizations. Google Analytics is even offered for free to websites with relatively small traffic.

There are three areas of the Web that news organizations should focus on with real-time analytics: the website, search engines, and social media. Monitoring the website will tell an organization about regular readers and it can help in improving website design and functionality. Regularly auditing search engine results can tell a news organization how it ranks among its competitors, and reviewing the current most popular search terms can tell the organization what news events it should focus. And finally, evaluating social media activity can lead to valuable insights into consumer attitude, as well as indicate what type of content is the most "share-worthy."

Within these three areas of the Web are several key metrics that, when analyzed, can give a news organization powerful knowledge about their consumers that they would have never had access to before the coming of Web 2.0.

MONITORING YOUR WEBSITE WITH REAL-TIME ANALYTICS

The first and foremost area that news organizations should focus on with real-time analytics is their own websites. Their websites are where their products live, such as original articles, interviews, videos, and images. It is also their brands' "face," or, what consumers' first impressions will be based upon. If their content does not work well online or their website has technical issues, it will cause a poor first impression with many consumers. Real-time analytics allow for news organizations to see their website in action and know about issues as they occur. It is the equivalent of a newspaper editor being able to watch over thousands of readers' shoulders while they read their morning paper.

There are hundreds of actions that can be made on any particular website, so it is important to know which actions are most meaningful. Trying to gain insights from data that are not very meaningful is a waste of resources, and worse, it can lead to false insights. The most important kinds of data to track while monitoring a news organization's website are:

- **Number of Users:** A "user" is counted whenever any individual on the Internet has a page from your website open on any device. Knowing the current number of users accessing the site is most useful in measuring short-term campaigns, such as an advertisement or social media event. If there is a significant upward spike in active users, it might mean that content on the site has gone "viral," meaning it is currently popular online. If the number of users stays at the normal range during an advertising campaign, it indicates that the campaign is not being effective. And finally, seeing a large drop in users' signals that the site has crashed.
- **Number of Pageviews:** A pageview is counted when a user has viewed an entire page on the website. This metric is often confused with "hits," which only count a specific piece of content being loaded, such as an image or a video. Pageviews are important for news organizations because, like a traditional newspaper, their content is often divided into single pages. Monitoring pageviews for all of pieces of content indicates what specific pieces of content are the most popular, what types of articles are the most popular, how large the audience is, and much more. Pageviews are useful for tracking the success of a specific piece of content, while the number of users is more useful for measuring the success of the whole website.
- **Referrals:** A "referral" occurs when a user is either brought to an organization's website through a link on another website, or they are sent to another website through a link on the organization's website. For example, referrals occur when a blogger links to a news organization's articles, and a user is sent to the organization's website through those links. Monitoring referrals is very important for marketers, as they can provide information about other websites that link to the organization's website often, what websites the organization's website links to often, and how much web traffic - is obtained from online advertisements. When a user clicks a paid advertisement and is brought to the organization's website, it is counted as an "acquisition referral," and demonstrates the value retrieved from that paid advertisement.
- **Duration:** Recording how long users spend on each page of a website can lead to valuable insights about content. For instance, if there is a long-form article on the website that should take 15-20 minutes to digest, and 30% of the users that view the page only stay for five minutes, it indicates that many users are skimming the article or abandoning the page. It is important to be aware of users' viewing habits. The majority of content should not be long-form articles if users don't prefer long-form articles. There are other applications of duration data as well, such as load times. If a website loads slowly, that is a poor experience for the user that in turn causes them to dislike using the website.
- **Path Analysis:** Analyzing the path that users take through the website is known as "path analysis." Users navigate a website through links found on that particular website which lead to other pages on the website, and all of those navigations can be logged. Knowing which paths users take

through the website indicates what areas they tend to skip, what areas they tend to go back to, and what areas they never go to. In conjunction with duration data, path analysis is the most useful tool in improving a website's convenience. For instance, if most users check the weather page before reading articles, an analyst or website designer can justly assume that putting the weather information on the homepage of the site would be a convenient feature.

- **Visitor Demographics:** Most of the time, the only information that can be learned about a specific user is his IP address, from which one can discern the user's geographic location. Through surveys and user sign-ups, users can be asked to give more information about themselves. All of this demographic information can be used to personalize the user's experience on the website. For example, if it is known that a user is accessing the site from Boston, local Boston news can be displayed on the homepage.
- **Browser Type/Platform:** A "browser" such as Firefox is an application used for accessing multimedia content on the Internet, while a "platform" is an entire device, such as an iPhone and system software. Knowing what browsers and platforms users have is very important for web development teams, as it lets them know where their testing should focus the most. Testing a website can be a long process, so knowing the most popular platform used by target users lets the team know which platform to prioritize. This information can also assure news organizations if it would be worth the time and resources to develop a native application for specific platforms. For instance, if user research indicates that 75% of mobile users are using android devices, then it would be worthwhile to develop a native Android application.

Greg Gomer, Senior Vice President from BostInno, an online news source, explains how important it is to monitor your own website with real-time analytics:

Understanding real-time data about our website and the content that we produce has been crucial to our success. The data has allowed us to stay ahead of our competitors and drive change instead of reacting to it. Through tools like Chartbeat and Google Analytics we can accurately monitor the success of each piece of content and ensure that we are delivering the best product to the user. For publishers it is very important to capture the data in real-time, but it is also very important to act on that data in real time. For example, if a piece of content is performing well on Chartbeat at any specific moment, it is very important to that a distribution strategy is acted upon immediately and that other writers begin crafting a follow-up story to continue feeding the users' desire.

MONITORING SEARCH ENGINES WITH REAL-TIME ANALYTICS

According to a recent study, 33% of consumers who get their news online primarily use search engines to do so (Digital News Report, 2013). Making an online search has become a more-than-daily routine for many consumers, making search a large avenue for news organizations to gain audience members. It is also where competition matters the most for news organizations, as rankings play a large role in consumer choice during an online search. There is now an entire career path based on improving organizations' rankings on search engine listings, which is called Search Engine Optimization or "SEO". SEO is becoming a more and more important among corporations.

SEO is a very complicated field of work, since there is no straightforward way to improve rank on a search engine. A search engine is described as follows:

A software program that searches the Internet (bunch of websites) based on the words that you designate as search terms (query words). Search engines look through their own databases of information in order to find what it is that you are looking for. (Seymour et al., 2011, p. 47)

It is a fully automated process, so besides the paid advertisements that search engines offer, there is no way of manually altering a search engine ranking. But, there are dozens of ways for SEO consultants to improve an organization's chances for high rankings.

It is important for a news organization to know how easily their website can be found by search engines, what their general ranking is, and what search terms are currently popular. These all tell the news organization where they stand with their competition in online search, and what topics they should focus on. The most valuable action on search engines for news organizations are "organic referrals," which is when a user comes to a website from a search engine and didn't come through a paid advertisement. Some call it "Free Advertising."

Using real-time analytics tools, a news organization can enhance their organic search numbers and keep track of their competition. The important aspects of search engines to monitor are:

- **Organic Referral Sources:** Using tools like Google analytics, news organizations can see what search engines are driving the most users to their content. It is important to know the most popular search engine among website users because many news organizations pay for advertisements on search engines. If, for example, an organization knows that the majority of organic referrals come from Yahoo! search, it should prioritize that search engine over others.
- **Keyword Referrals:** Knowing what search keywords have brought users to a website suggests what information consumers want most, what kind of content should produce more often, and what general topic the website is ranked well for in search engines. For instance, if Google Analytics shows a large number of referrals coming from the search term "stock tips," it indicates that the website has relevant content to stock tips that rank well in search listings. It is advantageous to build upon that popularity by producing more content related to stock tips.
- **Trending Search Terms:** Many search engines provide the day's most popular search terms. Google has a product called "Google Trends," which provides historical data for search terms. Monitoring these popular terms in real-time allows news organizations to know what consumers are interested in, and this in turn tells them what news events they should focus on with their content.
- **Search Rankings:** A website's search ranking depends heavily on the content that the website has on it. If news organizations regularly audit search rankings, they can see what topics that their competitors are excelling in, what topics they themselves are excelling in, and what topics have little news coverage. These can all lead to large opportunities for attracting an audience. For example, if an organization notices that there aren't many news sources that come up in a search for "Fitness startups," it can start producing content based on that topic and be ranked highly in future searches with those terms.

Monitoring search engines is a crucial component of real-time analytics. As Greg Gomer of BostInno indicates,

.. we are constantly monitoring what search engine terms have brought users to our website, as well as what search engine terms are currently popular. These let us know what content our consumers want the most, and we often prioritize our reporting based on those terms. For instance, during the World Cup of 2014, we were producing summaries of important matches. To determine which matches would be important, we looked at past search traffic from the last World Cup in 2010 as well as real-time search traffic concerning the 2014 World Cup. It would have been much more difficult to react to unexpectedly important matches without being able to see search traffic in real-time. Using all of this data, BostInno was able to prioritize the content that consumers wanted the most.

MONITORING SOCIAL MEDIA WITH REAL-TIME ANALYTICS

Social media networks are becoming increasingly interconnected with real life. More and more people every year are using social media to find friends, romance, employment, and news. The technology is also beginning to play a large role in politics. Hubert Kiss and Alfonso Rosa-Garcia (2013) propose that "Social media affect the evolution of protests in various ways. Social media help to inform audiences around the world about the unfolding of events, attracting international attention and provoking diplomatic pressure." (p. 1) Across the globe, social media is being used by individuals to express their personal opinions and discuss those opinions with others.

News organizations stand to gain tremendous value out of social media. Not only can they have their pieces of content "go viral" and be seen by millions of users, they can extract valuable insights through the monitoring of social media with real-time analytics. Unlike the numbers-only data they get on Google Analytics' dashboards, there are large amounts of sentimental data in social networks that can inform news organizations about popular opinions, under-reported news topics, how their content is being received, and how their competitors' content is being received as well.

There are many free or subscription-based tools for analyzing Big Data on social media networks. One free tool for analyzing Twitter is called "Twitonomy," which allows analysts to view such data as an account's average tweets per day, how many of those tweets are retweeted, and how many of them are favorited. It also allows for topic-based data, such as how popular a certain keyword is. A free tool for analyzing Facebook data is called "LikeAlyzer," which allows analysts to view such data as a Facebook page's average posts per day, and how many likes those posts receive on average.

Using these tools, a news organization can monitor their official social media profiles' activity. An important metric to monitor is how many impressions accounts receive per day, or, how many times users like a piece of content or retweet one of the tweets. These instances build upon brand awareness, reputation, and credibility. The more a user sees news organization operating beneficially in social networks, the more likely they are to become a regular reader.

It is important for news organizations to not only monitor their own social media activity, but also the activity of their competitors and the activity of their audience. There are valuable insights to be made from analyzing these data, insights that can propel a small news organization to being popular on a global scale. The essential methods that news organizations should make use of real-time analytics in social media are:

- **Feedback on Content:** Using the many free social media networks available on the Web, news organizations can maintain channels for their readers to provide instant feedback on their content. This can be helpful for catching errors in their content. More importantly, it can also lead to valuable insights into consumer preferences. The content that gets the most positive feedback will show a news organization what they are excelling at, and the content that gets the most negative feedback will show a news organization what they need to work on.
- **Opinions on Recent Events:** Many social networks have a "what's trending" feature that shows the current most popular keywords or content on that platform. There are also community-oriented aggregator sites like Reddit that allow users to determine what topics or content are most relevant or "share-worthy." Monitoring these real-time resources allows news organizations to gauge the popular opinion and interests of their audience. With this information, they can determine what topics they should focus on with their content.
- **Popularity across Platforms:** By tracking referral traffic data with tools like Google Analytics, news organizations can see what social networking platforms are driving the most users to their website. Using this information, they can choose where to utilize paid advertising, design their site to work better with those platforms, and run promotions specifically for those communities.
- **Under-Reported Events:** On social media networks, it is common for an individual to break a large news item before any news organizations are aware of the event. If news organizations utilize real-time analytics, they can become aware of these under-reported events before other news organizations, giving them a substantial competitive advantage.

Greg Gomer of BostInno explains how beneficial monitoring social media can be:

Monitoring social media in real time is crucial for a news organization. Historically, news was broken over the networks because they were the only ones with a megaphone. Today, everyone has a megaphone thanks to Twitter and Facebook. News can be broken and widely distributed just by a simple tweet from a witness. One major example from that is when a bystander accidently live-Tweeted the raid on Osama Bin Laden, because he heard the Blackhawk helicopters coming.

Another example is the Boston Marathon Bombings. News of the tragedy was discovered on Twitter before any media publication could craft a story on it. Twitter was crucial in this case to both distribute facts of what happened but also to consume and report on what was happening. The best reporters on the street that day were the innocent bystanders on Boylston Street tweeting out photos and first hand reports on what happened. At BostInno, we successfully curated the news of the day through Twitter. News organizations from all over the world, were citing and reporting on the Twitter profiles of regular citizens that day.

THE FUTURE OF REAL-TIME ANALYTICS

As with all technology, it is impossible to know for certain what real-time analytics tools will look like in the future. It is especially hard to postulate for real-time analytics because of how rapidly the Web is changing. In "What is social media?" author Anton Mayfield (2008) imagines that "There will no doubt be exciting new variants on current formats, and perhaps innovations that come to be thought of as new forms of social media. They will develop in response to our appetite for new ways to communicate and to the increasingly flexible ways that we can go online." (p. 31) In only a few years' time, there will be countless new web actions and analytics tools for news organizations to utilize.

One recent trend in online news reporting that is likely to become commonplace is user collaboration. User comments, pictures, and videos are being included in professional journalists' articles, helping to speed up the news cycle and distribute the workload of reporting. This might become commonplace among all online news sources in the near future. News organizations might also implement social media network technology into their own websites, such as the voting system used on the community aggregator platform Reddit. In that scenario, it would be the readers who determine what content makes the "front page" of a corporate news organization. It is this consumer-oriented collaboration that has driven all Web 2.0 advances, and those advances are coming to news organizations quickly.

One worry over this collaboration is the potential for amplified media bias. David Siegel (2013) of Duke University outlined this phenomenon in his paper on social media:

A biased media outlet that systematically under- or over-reports a poll of the population by only a few percentage points can in some cases swing aggregate behavior (e.g., turnout or vote share) by over 20% in either direction due to positive feedback within the network. (p. 786)

With a stronger connection between social media and mainstream media, this effect might be worsened. One thing is certain about the future of the Web: there will be more consumer choices. More search engines will be developed, more social networks will be populated, and more traditional news organizations will make the move to an online business model. This means there will be more avenues for real-time analytics to collect data from, which means more avenues for valuable insights. If they actively incorporate these new technologies, news organizations stand to improve upon their reporting and serve consumers with better content in more personalized ways.

CONCLUSION

Web 2.0 has opened up a treasure trove of real-time analytics tools, and news organizations stand to gain valuable insights from these advancements. While Web 2.0 has been a disruptive force in the traditional news industry, it has also opened up opportunities for consumer insights that were never before possible.

There are ethical dilemmas surrounding real-time analytics. Some call it an exploitation of consumers when they do not know their actions are being recorded. Society will eventually decide what is right and what is wrong about real-time analytics. In the meantime, news organizations have three areas of the Web on which they should be focusing: their own website, search engines, and social media.

Utilizing these technologies will allow news organizations to understand their readers' wants and opinions better than ever before, which enables them to produce the exact content that their readers want and deliver that content in a more personal manner. In the future, user-collaboration with news organizations could be more prominent; meaning news content is produced quicker and with less influence from mainstream media. In all, real-time analytics is the most beneficial aspect of Web 2.0 for traditional news, and it could propel the industry instead of disrupting it.

REFERENCES

Binet, S., & Carter, S. (2014, June). Mythbuster: The vogue for real-time evaluation. Admap, pp. 2-3.

Gerlitz, C., & Helmond, A. (2011, May). *The like economy: The social web in transition.* Conference Paper MiT7 Unstable Platforms - The promise and peril of transition. Paper presented at the MIT7 Unstable Platforms conference, Cambridge, MA (May 13–15).

Hali, V. M., Wagh-Koppar, A., & Arora, S. (2013, November). *Humanising big data: Applying a qualitative analysis lens to big data.* Paper presented at ESOMAR. Qualitative, Valencia: Spain, pp. 2-3. Retrieved June 20, 2014, from http://www.warc.com

Kiss, H. J., & Rosa-Garcia, A. (2013, July). On the mobilizing role of social media in revolutions: A game-theoretic approach. Discussion Papers; 2013/43. Institute of Economics, Centre for Economic and Regional Studies, Hungarian Academy of Sciences, Budapest. Available at SSRN: http://ssrn.com/abstract=2298662 or10.2139/ssrn.2298662

Mayfield, A. (2008). *What is social media?* Retrieved June 18, 2014, from http://www.icrossing.com/sites/default/files/what-is-social-media-uk.pdf

Mehak, K. M., & Aggarwal, N. (2013). Web usage mining: An analysis. *Journal of Emerging Technologies in Web Intelligence, 5*(3), 240+. Retrieved June 20, 2014, from http://go.galegroup.com/ps/i.do?id=GALE%7CA350977892&v=2.1&u=ecl_main&it=r&p=AONE&sw=w&asid=36dcec8a9d7b5866c79a6f4f3bc6ede2

Peary, B. D. M., Shaw, R., & Takeuchi, Y. (2012). Utilization of social media in the East Japan Earthquake and Tsunami and its effectiveness. *Journal of Natural Disaster Science*, *34*(1), 3–18http://www.jsnds.org/contents/jnds/34_1_1.pdf. RetrievedJune192014. doi:10.2328/jnds.34.3

Reuters Institute for the Study of Journalism. (2013). Digital news report 2013 (Research Report). Retrieved June 21, 2014, from http://www.digitalnewsreport.org/

Robles, E. (2015). How to identify disruptive new businesses. *Review of Business & Finance Studies*, *6*(1), 121–130. http://www.theibfr.com/ARCHIVE/RBFS-V6N1-2015.pdf Retrieved June 20, 2015

Schulz, T., & Hartzog, P. (2011). Towards a critique of the social web. Retrieved June 18, 2014, from http://osdir.com/ml/culture.media.idc/2007-11/msg00003.html

Seymour, T., Frantsvog, D., & Kumar, S. (2011). History of search engines. *International Journal of Management and Information Systems*, *15*(4), 47–58. http://www.cluteinstitute.com/ojs/index.php/IJMIS/issue/view/662 Retrieved June 18, 2014

Siegel, D. A. (2013). Social networks and the mass media. *The American Political Science Review*, *107*(4), 786–805. doi:10.1017/S0003055413000452

Zuckerberg, M. (2010). Building the social web together (blog post). Retrieved June 19, 2014, from https://www.facebook.com/notes/facebook/building-the-social-web-together/383404517130

Zwick, D., Bonsu, S. K., & Darmody, A. (2008). Putting consumers to work: `Co-creation` and new marketing govern-mentality. *Journal of Consumer Culture, 8*(2), 163–196. doi:10.1177/1469540508090089

ADDITIONAL READING

Al-Htaybat, K. A., Abdulrahman, N. I. Y., & Awad, A. M. M. (2013). Model for the adoption of smart mobile devices in corporate financial reporting. *International Journal of Business and Management, 8*(24), 1–16. http://www.ccsenet.org/journal/index.php/ijbm/issue/view/964 doi:10.5539/ijbm.v8n24p1

Apostolopoulos, E. (2012) A new framework for quantifying social media investments. *BostInno.* Retrieved June 18, 2014, from http://bostinno.streetwise.co/channels/a-new-framework-for-quantifying-social-media-investments-infographic/ or http://www.socialmediatoday.com/content/new-framework-quantifying-social-media-investments-infographic

Arvidsson, A. (2008). The ethical economy of customer coproduction. *Journal of Macromarketing, 28*(4), 326–338. doi:10.1177/0276146708326077

boyd, d. (2010). Social network sites as networked publics: affordances, dynamics, and implications. *Papacharissi, Zizi, ed.* In Z. Papacharissi *(Ed.), Networked Self: Identity, Community, and Culture on Social Network Sites* (pp. 39-58). New York: Routledge.

Breese, E. (2014). *Instagram analysis and the success of visual brands* (article). *BostInno.* Retrieved June 20, 2014, from http://bostinno.streetwise.co/channels/instagram-analysis-and-the-success-of-visual-brands/

Dataminr (2014). Mining for tweets of gold. *The Economist, 411*(8890), 71. Retrieved June 19, 2014, from http://go.galegroup.com/ps/i.do?id=GALE%7CA370316448&v=2.1&u=ecl_main&it=r&p=GPS&sw=w&asid=6aafcdbde3432c0e9c29d3509d77a65d

Davis, C. E., Keuer, W. P., & Clements, C. (2002). Web-based reporting. *The CPA Journal, 72*(11), 28–34. http://www.nysscpa.org/cpajournal/2002/1102/soon.htm Retrieved June 18, 2014

Ellis, B. (2014). *Real-time analytics: Techniques to analyze and visualize streaming data.* Indianapolis, IN: John Wiley & Sons, Inc.

Fishkin, R. (2014). Barnacle SEO: Leveraging other sites' rankings. *The Moz Blog.* Retrieved June 18, 2014, from http://moz.com/blog/barnacle-seo-whiteboard-friday

Foreman, J. W. (2014). *Data smart: Using data science to transform information into insight.* Indianapolis, IN: John Wiley & Sons, Inc.

Google. (2013). Getting started with analytics measurement for marketing campaigns: A brief guide. *Google Analytics Blog*. Retrieved June 20, 2014, from http://analytics.blogspot.com/2013/05/getting-started-with-analytics.html

Google. (2014). Improving your data quality: Google analytics diagnostics. *Google Analytics Blog*. Retrieved June 20, 2014, from http://analytics.blogspot.com/2014/04/improving-your-data-quality-google.html

Himel, A. (2011). Real-time analytics for social plugins. *Facebook Developers Blog*. Retrieved June 18, 2014, from https://developers.facebook.com/blog/post/476

Kinsey, M. (2009). Keeping count of sharing across the web. *The Facebook Blog*. Retrieved June 18, 2014, from http://blog.facebook.com/blog.php?post=165161437130

Levy, D. (2014). What content marketers and journalists need to learn from each other. *The Moz Blog*. Retrieved June 20, 2014, from http://moz.com/blog/content-marketers-and-journalists

Lyle, C. (2013) BostInno's guide to content marketing lino. *BostInno*. Retrieved from June 20, 2014, http://bostinno.streetwise.co/channels/bostinnos-guide-to-content-marketing-lingo/

Mayer-Schonberger, V., & Cukier, K. (2014). *Big data: A revolution that will transform how we live, work, and think*. Boston, Massachusetts: Houghton Mifflin Harcourt.

Meyers, P. J. (2012). An open letter to new SEOs. *The Moz Blog*. Retrieved June 20, 2014, from http://moz.com/blog/an-open-letter-to-new-seos

Moz (2014). The 2014 industry survey (research report). *The Moz Blog*. Retrieved June 20, 2014, from http://moz.com/industry-survey

Ofcom (2013). *News consumption in the UK* (research report). Retrieved June 19, 2014, from http://stakeholders.ofcom.org.uk/binaries/research/tv-research/news/News_Report_2013.pdf

Provost, F. (2013). *Data science for business: What you need to know about data mining and data-analytic thinking*. Sebastopol, CA: O'Reilly Media, Inc.

Qualman, E. (2012). *Socialnomics: How social media transforms the way we live and do business*. Hoboken, NJ: John Wiley & Sons, Inc.

Sasseen, J., Olmstead, K., & Mitchell, A. (2013). Digital: By the numbers. The *Pew Research Center's Project for Excellence in Journalism*. Retrieved June 18, 2014, from http://stateofthemedia.org/2013/digital-as-mobile-grows-rapidly-the-pressures-on-news-intensify/digital-by-the-numbers/

Siegel, D. A. (2013). Social networks and the mass media. *The American Political Science Review*, *107*(4), 786–805. RetrievedJune202014. doi:10.1017/S0003055413000452

Siegel, E. (2013). *Predictive analytics: The power to predict who will click, buy, lie, or die*. Hoboken, NJ: John Wiley & Sons, Inc.

Tenge, M. (2014). Leveraging public social software platforms for relationship marketing in the airport industry. *Journal of American Academy of Business, Cambridge*, *20*(1), 149–156.

Williams, A. (2014). *SEO 2014 & beyond: Search engine optimization will never be the same again!* CreateSpace Independent Publishing Platform.

KEY TERMS AND DEFINITIONS

Big Data: Data sets that are too large to be manipulated by conventional methods. They are usually retrieved online or in digital formats.

Browser: An application used to access and visualize the World Wide Web (i.e., Google chrome).

Dashboard: A personalizable web page showing several panels of visualized real-time data.

Platform: A standard for the hardware of a digital device which determines what software it can run (i.e., an iPhone or Windows PC).

Real-Time Analytics: Analyzing data as it has been recorded, while the event is occurring.

Referral: When a user is brought to a website after clicking on a link.

Search Engine: An online software application that searches the World Wide Web based on keywords you set as search terms and returns relevant content from its database of information.

Search Engine Optimization (SEO): A field of work that focuses on making an organization's content on the Web easy for search engines to find and catalog with the goal of earning more organic referrals.

Social Media Network: An Internet based application in which users can create public profiles, link their profile with peers, broadcast content, collaborate with other users, and create content of their own.

Web 2.0: The second stage of the World Wide Web, characterized by the change from static web pages to dynamic and user-generated content, as well as the growth of social media.

Web Analytics/Web Mining: The recording and analyzing of data retrieved from the World Wide Web in an attempt to uncover insights and key information.

Chapter 7
Shaping Content Strategies with User Analytics and Identities:
How User Analytics is Shaping Editorial Strategy, Driving Marketing, and Generating New Revenue

Tricia Syed
Penton, USA

ABSTRACT

User data has become the foundation of many businesses. The ability to increase the breadth and depth of user data to analyze trends is now the roadmap for information companies – providing direction for new business, content strategy, print to digital shifts and overall retention and engagement. In this chapter, the author will explore user identity and the three key core data buckets – Profile, Activity, and Behavioral – that define how to decipher audience members and their 'user records.' The chapter will specifically showcase how user identity shapes editorial strategy, marketing messaging and drives revenue. It will look at the impact specific technologies are having on what data can be captured as well as the complexities around data capture in general – standardization, preservation, storage, relational data opportunities and data optimization.

INTRODUCTION

Recently, the author was shopping online for family in preparation for summer. She needed children's bathing suits, new beach towels and some rack equipment for an automobile. She went to at least ten consumer sites, including Lands End, L.L. Bean, Amazon, Thule.com, REI.com and Zappos, comparing styles, prices and item availability. While shopping, she added items to her online cart, either purchasing them or abandoning them, and in some cases abandoning

DOI: 10.4018/978-1-4666-8580-2.ch007

the site entirely. Customer service as well as exit intent automation interrupted the shopping process to ask if any help was needed or to attempt to stop her from exiting the site(s). She did not interact with any online support and in the end did purchase merchandise from three sites.

As an expert in user marketing, the author is intrigued by the approaches companies use to process customer activity for upsell or follow up engagement opportunities. It is impressive when the process is well executed and, more specifically, when there is contextual relevancy and strong timing with the follow up. In this recent shopping expedition, Zappos was the clear winner of the day on both fronts. When checking Facebook while shopping, the author noticed almost within seconds that items left in the Zappos shopping cart or items viewed, or items like them were suddenly appearing in the margins and body of the Facebook feed. The same dynamics are shaping content delivery as well.

STRATEGIES WITH USER ANALYTICS AND IDENTITIES

Contextual Targeting and Retargeting

There will be those who are "spooked" by the Big Brother aspect of contextual marketing and retargeting, viewing these practices as creepy, disruptive or as an invasion of privacy. Yet for digital media and marketing professionals, it is interesting to observe the tactics and how well or poorly methods and technology are executed. Companies as well as news and media companies are in need to continually drive for increased sophistication in editorial and marketing practices to increase readership, user engagement and revenue.

In the contextual marketing space, contextually targeting shoppers based on online behavior makes a connection and/or a presumption about what the shopper is thinking. As one shops, companies that leverage contextual targeting are anonymously cookie-ing visitors so that they can follow their actions. By tracking what links are clicked, what pages are perused, and what items are searched, the business is investing in re-marketing to place their products in front of shoppers again and again as they surf the web. This level of data capture, or what is also referred to as activity data, has a short shelf life. The re-marketed ads are relevant for a limited period of time before the shopper makes a purchase and for a short period of time afterward. The companies that have built and sell this technology and level of targeting are attempting to create an experience that is tied to anecdotal or potentially statistically proven 'human nature.' They are trying to re-engage, remind or re-attract buyers to what they were initially considering for purchase.

Retargeting has become a big business. Companies such as Bizo, ReTargeter and Adroll specialize in retargeting. Adroll, for example, has been around since 2007 and today it partners with some of the largest online social companies such as Facebook, Google, Yahoo and Microsoft. Retargeting enables their clients to reach 98 percent of sites on the Internet. Adroll claims extremely high return on investment (ROI) values for clients and cites advanced targeted techniques as one of their main differentiators. Like Adroll, Bizo is a multi-channel business-to-business (B2B) marketing solutions company. They also partner with major companies allowing them to reach more than 90 percent of the business population in the United States. ReTargeter is a display advertising solutions company that specializes in audience targeting and retargeting, claiming to reach 98 percent sites on the Internet.

There are some lessons digital media companies can learn from early experiences in this space. Despite the improvements in contextual targeting, issues such as discrepancies, irrelevancy and intrusion still permeate the user experience. Intelligently targeting ads or content and making sure they are relevant still present challenges for businesses. Repeatedly displaying an ad for something the buyer has already purchased is not effective. As an example, the author recently registered to attend what looked to be an informative and interesting marketing conference, yet after the registration was confirmed, she continued to receive emails asking her to register for the conference. Now, instead of focusing on looking forward to the event, she is thinking, *get your act together*! Most consumer companies and B2B companies relying on retargeted ads or even their own marketing automation platforms do not go beyond 'recent activity' data and geo-targeting. If they collect deeper demographic and/or firmographic data (*organizational data or features tied to the company's industry*), as well as historical activity and behavioral data, they would be able to provide a more holistic view of users and their needs, interests and experiences. Imagine how this might impact predictability and higher conversion rates. Perhaps the problem lies with not enough data sets linking or not enough human influence attempting to better discern the patterns within big data.

The Impact of Big Data and Little Data

Big data has become a term that is influencing businesses, data analysts, technologists and journalists alike. Understanding consumers' viewing and purchasing behavior must extend beyond cookies, it requires careful management of the volume, multiplicities and speed in which the data are being cogenerated and stored. Thomas (2014) defines the types of data you can trust as companies maneuver through and attempt to cull out what is usable and valuable, versus the "noise" so much data can create. The data types range from experimental data to marketing-mix modeling data, which is the creation of an analytical database. Then there is the cleansing and normalizing of those data and the use of multivariate statistics and modeling to isolate and neutralize some of that noise. Sales data and social media data are also important, but Thomas finds the most value in the "little data," which are statistically significant subsets of the data.

"Corporate decision-makers often would be better served if they rely on tried-and-true tools and systems from the world of little data, rather than illusions from big data," Thomas says. Specifically, he talks to the validity of marketing research based on data derived from random sampling of target audiences. "Marketing research can be designed to be forward-looking and predictive, rather than backward-looking," he claims. "Experienced researchers can create alternative futures and measure the relative appeal of the differing visions of the future." Such "little data often provides a more accurate basis for sound corporate decision-making." With the ability to capture enormous amounts of data sets and fields, it's interesting to consider what might be categorized as the little data within the bigger data movement.

Shaw (2014, para. 1) references Professor Gary King of Weatherhead University who makes the case for quality over quantity in big data gathering:

There is a big data revolution. But it is not the quantity of data that is revolutionary. The big data revolution is that now we can do something with the data. The revolution lies in improved statistical and computational methods, not in the exponential growth of storage or even computational capacity.

"Doing something" with the data means accurate interpretation and appropriate actions to build new layers of the business and generate new revenue based on the user data.

Capitalizing on Big Data

Capitalizing on big data includes: a) defining the audience, b) defining the valued trends of the audience, and c) ensuring one has the tools and capabilities to conduct analysis and act on opportunities within those trends. User data has become the foundation for many businesses' marketing strategy. The ability to identify user segments and trends within key segments enables one to:

- Understand a company's product roadmap
- Predict interests and behaviors
- Pre-qualify an audience in advance of an offer or program
- Help direct content strategy
- Enable customer or user lifecycle transparency
- Apply value to users and their activities or behaviors

In a time when so many B2B media companies are making a shift from print ad dollars to digital offers, the ability to parse user data, predict behaviors and engage users is mandatory. With a combined methodology, alongside platforms that support data capture and data access, marketers, editors, publishers and sales representatives have an opportunity to make smarter choices for the business.

Developing the "Who" of User Personas

Whether it's big data or little data, content creation teams within successful media and information service companies need to be dedicated to truly understanding the *day in the life of the customer*. This entails the creation of user personas to better understand users and customers. The user persona identity that represents the ideal segment or class within the target audience includes demographics, firmographics, subscriptions, mediums of interest, job function and requirements, daily pain points, challenges within their lines of work, what technologies they rely on to access solutions, and the concerns of their like-minded peers. Persona data provides for improved user experiences and deep segmentation. They enable content creators, community managers and marketers to execute a sophisticated targeting and engagement by providing relevant content, solutions and connections.

The concept of developing user personas to identify like communities within a broader audience has been a common practice within the marketing field, as developed by Jenkinson (1994) in his paper, "Beyond Segmentation". He created a tool called *CustomerPrints* to better categorize customer segments beyond the traditional segmentation based on demographic and behavioral similarities. The purpose was to achieve a higher level of knowledge about a customer's daily life, needs and desires based on distinct groups of customers. Today, the challenge is choosing the platforms and technologies to support this user persona work and how to parse through at times, inordinate amounts of data – in essence, capitalizing on big data.

Developing user personas is an important technique in meeting the challenge of deep relevancy by contextual targeting and user transparency (see Figure 1). User personas enable media and information services companies to dissect and analyze user data to better understand their business roadmaps.

Capturing Audience Profile Data

The key to user access and interpretation is in understanding how to employ database methodologies, platforms and cloud technologies to generate user-centric analytics. Decision-makers must determine how to parse data, generate user health checks and extrapolate data to discover or uncover significant trends about content, topics, and industry impact so that they can better project and predict the needs and interests of content consumers. For news and information organizations, the first step in building a foundation to analyze user data is acquiring the ability to capture a person's complete, and ideally most up-to-date, demographic and firmographic information. The second step is to ensure there is a platform in place that allows for data analysis and marketing automation in order to segment users based on demographic differentiators. Before a media organization begins to evaluate service options, it must answer the question: who

Figure 1. Capture a person's complete profile data including and ideally most up-to-date, demographic, and firmographic information

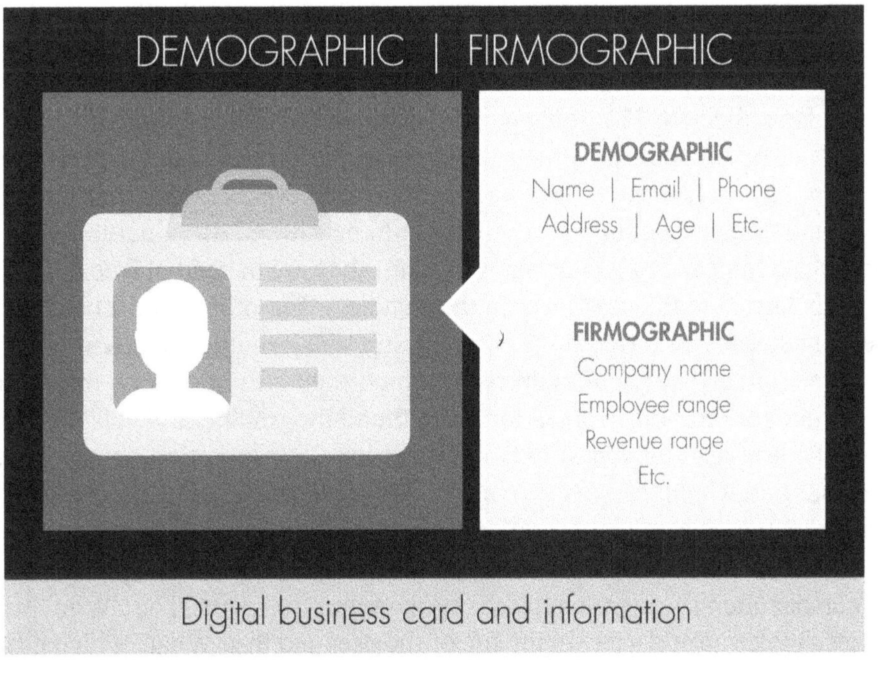

is the user? This is the starting point. Once established, the business can expand the definition with niche user segments that align with their content and product offerings.

When capturing demographic data, it's important to decide in advance what demographic fields or questions are important and impactful. Time invested in this sometimes-tedious process will be rewarded. Next, it is important to standardize how questions are asked – specifically, how registration forms collect the data as well as how the data are stored and accessed. Open fields in registration forms can create multiple variations of the same data point, unless a sophisticated system or dedicated data manager oversees normalization of the data. It's better to carefully define fields to prevent variations in user input.

Penton's Experience

There are web analytics platforms that can aid in data normalization. Web analytics platforms such as Omniture offer an option to upload backend user database fields and identifiers by email so that businesses can then track within Omniture what those records (or users) are reading and map it back to their unique record data. The process is called *Sainting.* At Penton, a professional information services company (the author's company), record data has been merged with Omniture to enable editors and marketers to see what topics people and companies are reading, downloading and revisiting. Here, the demographic data are imperative as they become the identifier of the activity and provide trends at both the individual and account level.

The user persona represents the reader, website visitor, or user who needs or willingly consumes content. At Penton, marketers and editors were recently tasked with implementing a phased approach to developing user personas. Penton is focused on five core industry segments, including agriculture, transportation, infrastructure, design & manufacturing, and natural products & food, and each also includes niche segments. As a result, the persona exercise is not one size fits all. Rather, each marketer was tasked to work closely with their editor, publisher and sales teams to define their key audience members. Fields being selected include target group, job title/function, geography, employee size, and company revenue.

Data on user daily influences, which include motivations, job pressure and industry pressures or needs, were also collected. The goal again is to ensure that the user universe and segments or user niches within the broader universe are understood. Once user definitions, user needs and clarity on their roles and challenges specific to those roles were collected, it was time to look at the topic level and content medium level that would be viewed as valuable. What content will resonate with the audience? For some user segments, they are in need of free or fee-based education to help propel them to the next level in their careers. For others, it's a better understanding of the scope of technologies based on their company size. Another segment is concerned with more information about the manufacturers on which they currently rely, or how new government laws will impact their business. Alongside the demographic and activity make-up of the user audience, Penton also looked at user habits around consumption based on the *day in the life of a consumer* and what it reveals. *Dayparting*, the process of dividing the day into different time segments, enables the adjustment of offers accordingly, which is critical to editorial and marketing efforts and the impact this has on response rates and user engagement.

The user persona identification exercise is broken into two parts. The "Who" which captures the demographic make-up and a day in the life of the user and the "What" which provides a list or roadmap of the content and assets for the user to engage. Because technology is influencing how and when users consume data, this exercise should occur at least annually, if not more frequently, to take into account new niche topics, changes in the industry and changes in content delivery and consumption. For example, with mobile content consumption, the recent focus is on responsive design to optimize the user experience, but this will also result in new data sets about how and when the users access that content on their mobile device.

In Penton's exercise with editors and marketers, it was emphasized to the team that analysis of user trends *within defined user personas* will become the roadmap for publishers. Before questions on the registration page can be finalized, the question of who is the audience must be answered. Are they small to mid-sized businesses, global enterprises or somewhere in between? Are the visitors c-level executives, directors and managers or developers? Once the segments – or buckets on where the user best fits – have been defined, one can begin to build on their identifiable record data by adding more complex data points that describe job expertise and areas of interest and more importantly, what are the specific concerns of the audience or audience segment.

The Role of Marketing Automation

Standardization, agreed-upon user data fields, consistent firmographic data particularly with enterprise companies with defined company naming conventions, company location and company size ranges, data optimization, data preservation, and relational data opportunities are critical steps to building a concise and minable user database. Companies today can find a faster path to get to quality data by investing in marketing automation software platforms designed primarily for marketing departments, but increasingly used by other divisions such as editorial to more effectively communicate across online channels. Marketing automation capabilities provide transparency on what resources users are consuming in terms of content (what newsletters they are opening, click through rates), where users are consuming content (social media sites) and when. These activities are track-able and users can be identified by the content-type, topics and social channels they access.

Garrison (2013, para. 2) explains the marketing automation approach as a means to quickly analyze key customer segments:

...most businesses have a broad customer base. And within that broad base are niche groups with distinct wants and needs, and unique motivations. A powerful tool to expand your understanding of those specific needs and motivations is to create a persona; this is an archetypal character that represents different user types within a targeted demographic that might use your product or service in a similar way.

There are over 200 marketing automation solutions from which companies can choose. Three of the more well-known include Eloqua, Marketo and Pardot. Many organizations have only begun to tap the power of these solutions. Of the B2B marketers using an automation platform in 2014, 85 percent of them feel that they are not using them to their full potential (Senatore, 2014).

When leveraged correctly, marketing automation provides companies with an opportunity to capture, store and define data segments that result in deeper data capture and new trends.

For a media or information services company relying on behavioral-based trigger marketing campaigns (*messaging the audience at preplanned points in time based on their behavior, for example, if they click on a certain link in a newsletter, they receive a contextually relevant follow up email associated to what they first clicked*), custom data cards that enable deep user segmentation and relevancy are less about driving leads, scoring leads or uncovering prospects, but more about engagement and understanding the user lifecycle based on topics of interest, mediums of interest and synergizing website traffic trends with the user base. Businesses rely on the marketing automation tool to enhance targeting and personalization. Trigger campaigns can be parsed according to user reaction. Marketers can subsequently create a series of unique messages based on the direction or lack of direction the user takes.

How Marketing Automation Platforms Work

Most marketing automation platforms provide insight and guidance on user persona or buyer persona best practices. These platforms foster deep segmentation, tight targeting, and the ability to retarget, nurture, and upsell. Companies including Marketo, Eloqua and Pardot offer marketing automation platforms that store, collect, optimize, normalize, and target data for email marketing efforts. Eloqua and Marketo have developed strong marketing communities. Pardot, part of Salesforce.com, also works with preferred partners, namely cloud applications such as SnapApps. They offer pre-configured interactive content, including interactive infographics, with the ability to capture user data and provide analytics. More specifically, Eloqua has created something it labels as Custom Data Objects (CDO), which enables companies to store additional information for user contacts, such as product purchase history or event attendance data, without cluttering up contact records. Marketers and editors can use these tools to maintain clean and organized databases, but more importantly, store data that can then be segmented at the contact level – to build out more sophisticated messaging based on the "Who" and the "What" of the audience.

Another provider in this space, Televerde, goes a step further by appending and enriching data at the program level based on a campaign to a specific audience. They provide data quality analysis to ensure data is current and accessible across multiple platforms. Another company and preferred partner of Eloqua, Sureshot Media, provides a variety of creative services for demand generation or targeted marketing programs driving visibility for a company's products, services, or brand awareness and one in particular is a set of apps called SparkPlugs. Sparkplugs help businesses extend the capabilities of their marketing automation application by addressing a variety of areas, including data quality and marketing channels. Specifically, these data quality apps integrate with third-party data providers to validate data, such as email and postal addresses and enhance data, such as appending company or contact information to records.

Data Optimization and Normalization

Once key demographics have been defined and a platform is in place to capture and communicate user records, the next critical step is data optimization and normalization. Despite the inconsistent data capture that might occur on a registration form or missing data as a result of a tiered registration approach, there are many service companies that can append demo and firmographic data based on unique identifiers such as email or company domain. Often these companies require access to a house file to do a match. They charge based on the data field or overall volume of appends. Such companies provide more complete and updated data to develop accurate segmentation and trend analysis. Typically, the cost of services is worth the investment. Traditional list services companies as well as cloud data companies can assist in this process.

Most of these service providers have proprietary databases and technologies. The costs of their services vary. It is important, as a company decides on which one to work with to consider data status, data health and business need. For example, the company Fresh Address focuses on email appending (adding email addresses to audience records by extrapolating or paying for the email through a list broker) and optimization. As an email database service provider around since 1999, Fresh Address services range from building, updating, segmenting and cleaning email lists from a customer's database. Televerde also provides appends like emails or address information, and data optimization, promoting data that are globally and socially sourced with several layers of validation to ensure job titles and job functions are up to date. Most likely they rely on companies such as LinkedIn and telemarketing outreach to ensure accurate data capture.

Some service companies are more niche focused. For example, iProfile is a sales and marketing intelligence provider that provides access to a database of company profiles and contact information for information technology decision makers. One of their unique offerings is a service of real-time deal alerts that notifies customers when IT purchasing decisions are about to be made. They also update clients when IT decision makers change jobs within their organization or move to a new company.

When enhancing or optimizing user data (updating demographic data or company data to ensure accuracy), a simple best practice is to test a small segment with one or more potential data vendors to ensure quality and engagement. As a rule, it is best to test small amounts of data with missing elements and conduct a permission pass campaign through email to trigger a response or conversion. This helps to ensure they are accurate and active before making a larger investment or commitment to enhance the user database.

Developing the "What" of User Personas

The next step in creating value and opportunity from the user persona is the "What." From the "What" of user activity data (see Figure 2), companies can begin to identify user interests based on content consumption including both content topics and content types. These content and product lifecycle patterns provide more sophisticated opportunities for user segmentation resulting in the three R's – relevancy, response and retention.

What are activity data? What can or should be captured? Most importantly how is this information used to direct content strategy, product strategy, and marketing to drive engagement? Simply put, activity data are defined as the record of any user's action.

Defining user activities is a key part of the user persona exercise and should be revisited often as industries and their audiences as well as the content channels and social platforms continually evolve. Activity data, as defined by Franklin et al. (2011), can fall into three key categories:

- ***Access:*** *Logs of user access to systems indicating where users have travelled (e.g., log in/log out, passing through routers and other network devices, premises access turnstiles).*

Figure 2. Activity, an individual's actions including the content and resources they access online

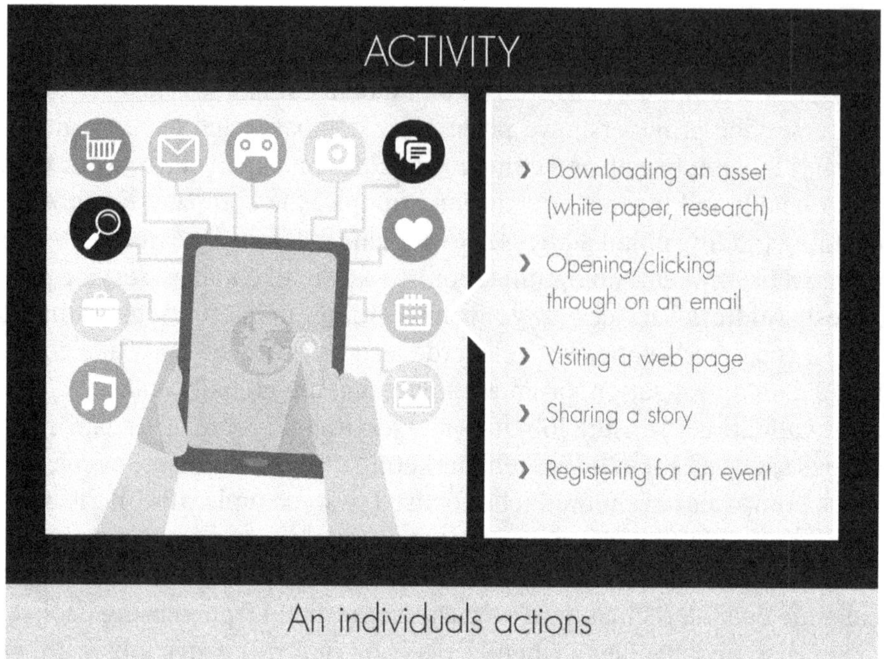

- ***Attention:*** *Navigation of applications indicating where users have been are paying attention (e.g., page impressions, menu choices, searches).*
- ***Activity:*** *'Real activity', records of transactions which indicate strong interest and intent (e.g., purchases, event bookings, lecture attendance, book loans, downloads, ratings).*

Once engaged in this process, there are important questions to ask, such as: Are all actions critical to track? Once tracked, how well can the trends within those activities be analyzed? If users are logged in to the system web analytics can be merged with user records. Even if users are not logged in and are not easily identified, web traffic can be tracked by IP addresses and geo-targeted to identify companies.

Some companies attempt to track traffic and identify users based on IP and geographic data in order to identify account-level data or the companies from which the traffic is coming. Sites can then take that information and map it against their internal databases to potentially locate look-a-like data or users from the same or similar companies, to better understand what topics are resonating across these organizations.

LSC Digital is one of those service companies focused on data processing that uses website tracking mechanisms employing profiling and mobility to build new segmentation plans. The end goal is to improve response rates and decrease promotion costs. This is the ability to locate profitable customers that companies can identify in their existing databases to support ongoing promotions and direct acquisition. This is an interesting approach because the desired outcome is a combination of the web traffic on sites alongside existing user base trends. If users are not logged in, it is typically not possible to track their activity back to their record data. With services such as that offered by LSC, one can at least see traffic trends and apply them to the internal audience.

Other service companies, such as Chartbeat, provide real-time analytics to editorial and marketing teams to help direct content- based on web traffic. With Chartbeat, one can see visitors, load times, and referring sites in real-time. The difference, unlike the *retargeters* of ads, is differentiating what people have clicked versus what they have read. Many think that the value lies not in what a user clicks, but what happens between the clicks. The goal for editors then becomes less about the click-through data and more about the attention of users, how long they stayed on a page or article, and their repeat-visit data.

Web traffic and website topics are one level of activity data. Companies such as LSC that track the type of traffic, or Chartbeat, which uncovers content value based on user consumption and attention rather than clicks, have the ability to better capture relevant organic traffic. Oncc these data sources are combined or the findings leveraged within the "member" database, one can begin to decipher deeper patterns and create a much richer, more relevant story for the target audience.

Haile (2014) of Chartbeat makes interesting and critical points on how best to maneuver through data and identify which actions are meaningful. For example, he writes, "As pageviews have begun to fall, brands and publishers have embraced social shares such as Facebook likes or Twitter retweets as a new currency" (para.14). He goes on to point out that data from these engagements tends to be misinterpreted:

...the people who share content are a small fraction of the people who visit that content. Among articles we tracked with social activity, there were only eight Facebook likes and one tweet for every 100 visitors. The temptation to infer behavior from those few people sharing can often lead media sites to jump to conclusions that the data does not support. (para.2)

Instead of an over-reliance on clicks or social sharing activities, Chartbeat contends that a more accurate relationship between content and engagement can be determined by the actual attention a reader gives to an article or what Haile refers to as "largest volume of total engaged time – or the Attention Web. (para.16)

Having access to topics of engagement from a media company's web traffic with tools like Google Analytics or Adobe, or more specifically enable editors to see what stories are being read; what topics are resonating with the audience and how long the audience spends with a particular article or story. Reader engagement data can help direct editorial strategy. Taxonomies, sub-topics, new content strategies can all be generated as a result of traffic patterns. Similarly, the same level of "attention" to the user base, whether it is data cards within an automation platform or some other form of data storage, should be given before emailing and marketing to audiences. What are the users reading, downloading, and signing up for? Are they logged in, are they repeatedly visiting the site, when do they access content (dayparting, or the practice of dividing a day into several parts and directing different forms of advertising to each part), and how long are their visits? These activities become the beginning of the process of applying value to users, as well as engaging them in a meaningful way.

How to Leverage Activity Data

At Penton, such activity data became the "What" of understanding users, customers, readers and members. "What" actions result in learning more about needs, pain points and interests as well as actions resulting in revenue for the business divisions. Each media company will create its own exercise, but in the case of Penton, the definition included a combination of website content access and consumption, including white papers, e-newsletters, webinars, virtual events, in-person events, fee-based habits and print subscriptions. Because Penton is an information services company that covers so many varied industries, there are multiple segments of user lifecycles or lists of activities. The values placed on those activities are also highly industry-specific.

How is activity data collected, and how is it best used? This may depend on the type of media used to access the information. In some cases, opening and clicking on an e-newsletter article results in the basis for critical activity data. Capitalizing on hot topics and an engaged subscriber base helps to drive needed traffic. It's important to look closely at the articles that do drive messaging for new subscriptions. Higher subscription counts lead to more internal traffic, as well as additional opportunity to capture more activity data per each user when they react, click and read. Activity data aligned with what articles users like to read (topics of interest) and the time of day they read (dayparting analysis) can then be used for other efforts.

The same exercise works with other media that require registration or user log in. By noting the actions taken on sites around media consumption, users become identifiable by the media to which they gravitate. In some industries, such as technology for example, where IT professionals have access to educational webcasts, white papers, learning guides, eBooks, interactive infographics, virtual trade shows, research and surveys, one can uncover interesting trends by record or record type. A researcher or analyst can begin to establish affinity lists based on the media users seem to repeatedly access.

In addition, it is possible to align the activity with a topic and create a segment within the medium to further target the audience. For example, some users rely on webcasts to keep up on the latest information or solutions around their roles. Others might gravitate toward white papers and others might register for a webcast with good intentions, but never attend. In all cases, user behaviors emerge and marketing or content outreach should be adjusted accordingly. An effective tactic for webcast attendees is to regularly send updates, rewards and or sneak peeks to maintain engagement. Those who register and never attend (have the intention but not the time for follow through) might benefit from a documented, high-level overview. Here they can still access the content, but in a different medium, such as an executive summary. If the goal is lead generation for the media organization, this is a win. If the objective is user paid activity, one may still win the conversion. If the goal is education and deepening thought leadership, the goal is accomplished with a condensed version of the presentation in a shorter format.

User Segmentation and User Lifecycles

Another best practice that results from capturing activity or content-type consumption data is dividing users up based on their preferences. Some users tend to read lengthier documents, some prefer brief summaries or roll ups, some gravitate to slide shows, and others participate regularly in virtual events, such as webinars and virtual trade shows. Understanding each user's content consumption preferences leads to better engagement and more upsell opportunities.

At Penton, users have also been identified as community participants by providing valuable user-generated content within niche communities. The user data compiled based on these activities provides email segmentation opportunities and trend analysis to better understand the personas – but most importantly, it provides the opportunity to glean user value or customer lifetime value. To determine this value, a weighted value is assigned to each activity. The more users engage, the more their value increases. Analyzing user patterns provides insight into user behavior around content consumption that leads to new ways to segment and ultimately reach the audience. There is no limit to these variables, as explained in Urbanski (2014, para.3):

Segments are everyone's business—increasingly, even B2B marketers. They recently asked a number of data suppliers to cite which common customer segmentation variables, such as size and industry type, they provide to clients. What Stevens and Grossman found surprised them: Some suppliers provide as many as 100 variables, including details on companies' installed technology and spending on items like insurance and legal services." Stevens goes on to make the point that "B2B data is richer in segmentation variables than most of us had thought.

Segmentation and the ability to act on activity data is not only about relevancy but agility. Much of the data collected has a shelf life or it evolves as the user takes more actions. Understanding user activities and building a data dictionary or encyclopedia to ensure that the entire team from marketing, to editorial, to sales understands how the audience is defined is important.

Defining, identifying and capturing activity data also leads to a clearer understanding of the user lifecycle. Companies can employ these techniques to understand user flow across content, content products, topics and frequency. User activity data, coupled with user demographics, becomes the foundation toward building user value and developing user lifetime value. Customer and user lifecycles are focused on reach, acquisition, conversion, retention, affinity, and brand loyalty. With so many options for content consumption as well as ways to measure activity, the "funnel" (the user's path from initial discovery to engagement or purchase) has become more complex. The question then becomes how to take advantage of user activity data to help define user or customer lifecycles. As editorial departments are more focused on content creation, topic relevancy, and user-generated content to increase readership and deepen engagement, the user lifecycle or user value is tied more to the types of activities and topics and how they impact the business.

Activity intelligence dashboards are just as relevant for the users as the buying customers. With data-capture tools and a platform that provides transparency beyond static data points, editors and marketers have the ability, with customization and user knowledge, to motivate behaviors based on what the user lifecycle data reveal.

Developing the "Why" of User Personas: Behavioral and Attitudinal User Data

The final and most complex aspect of analytics and big data with regard to readership or user persona is behavioral data – the "Why." Before delving into tools and methodologies on how to capture and assign behaviors, the author will first define behavioral data and differentiate it from attitudinal data (see Figure 3). Dupre (2013) interviewed Eric Tobias, VP of Web products at Exact Target, who observed there are significant differences between attitudinal and behavioral data:

Attitudinal data is explicit—asking customer questions such as through a survey and evaluating their direct feedback. Behavioral data is implicit— observing and inferring customer motivations based on actions such as online clicks. Independently, both types of data have virtues, but relying exclusively on one can leave gaps in understanding the customer's overall journey. For instance, neglecting attitudinal data can lead to a lack of understanding as to why a customer converted.(para. 2)

How do media companies today capture behavior (see Figure 4) and/or attitudinal data and more importantly, how can they use these data to guide editorial initiatives and business initiatives?

To gather these insights, implicit data can be collected via web analytics, opens, and clicks. Service companies such as Chartbeat are providing editors and community developers the ability to see in real time what their audience is accessing, reading, and where the hot spots are throughout the day. The goal is to provide quality data – not volume data – and to provide key metrics around user behavior that editors can use to make smart decisions. The differentiator with this platform from other web analytics platforms is that the focus is on readers' experiences – namely how much time they spent on an article, what they read next, and which articles resulted in valued actions or return visits. The ability to measure audience attention by article

Figure 3. Attitudinal, insights gathered from research, website click data

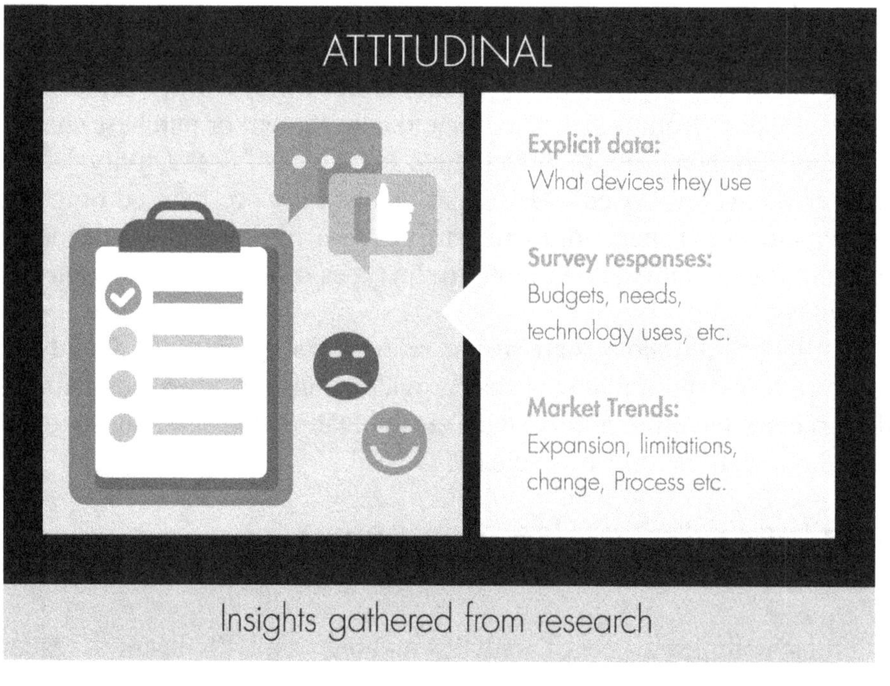

Figure 4. Behavioral, insights gained from a collection of activities

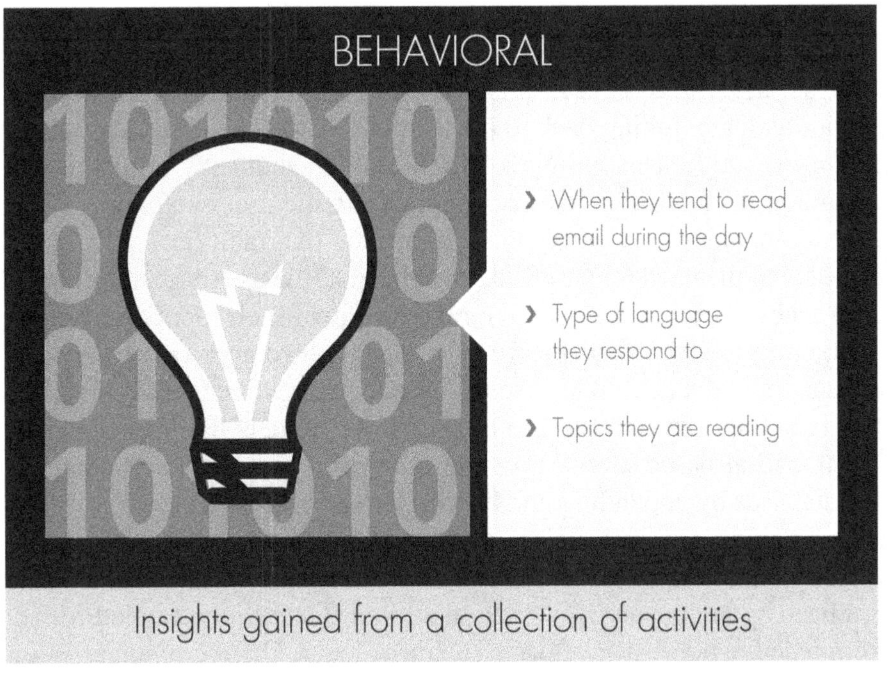

in real time is referred to by Chartbeat as "engaged time." This level of analytics, along with geographic data and platform usage data, begins to tell a story or stories about readership and what articles, pathways, and external sites are triggering the most valuable responses.

Similar to Chartbeat, Evergage is software aimed at helping sites create a highly personalized user experience in real-time to enhance customer engagement. In terms of attitudinal or explicit data, the best path is typically customer insight surveys, polls, field sales, and marketing outreach to obtain accurate and customized answers, which then become the measure for user satisfaction or consumption patterns. Then, the ideal is to combine these disparate data sources to enable a complete or holistic view of your audience (Dupre, 2013).

There are advantages to combining attitudinal survey data and behavioral data captured on the web, including content access as well as content premium access such as white paper downloads and webcast participation. Attitudinal surveys, much like registration forms, only measure what the audience self-reports, which is subject to inaccuracy, dishonesty, and bias. *Dayparting* and the level of engagement play an important part as well. Learning when to deliver surveys to audience types is critical in the success of and completion of lengthy surveys.

Self-reported data, coupled with behavioral data, provide a more transparent view into user interest as well as a comprehensive view of the segment to which each user belongs. Understanding behavior first can ultimately impact survey engagement, again knowing topics of interest, content medium of interest as well as time of day when users are more engaged. All of these behavioral data can help assist in positioning and deploying insight surveys with greater success.

The Role of Web Analytics

Web analytics plays a key role in understanding users. It's important to employ web analytics data that captures traffic trends to accurately reflect the motivations of the user base. Ensuring that web behavior data are linking back to the user base and enhancing user records provides a more comprehensive and transparent view into the audience than by simply profiling them. To reach this capability, it's important to attach behavior to the user database.

More service companies have emerged to go beyond the traditional services once provided by list brokers. Seeing the need for enhanced insights into the user base, they provide the ability to capture, gain access to, and act on behavioral data with a shelf life. For example, I-Behavior, a database marketing and behavior profiling company, leverages cooperative members who contribute transactional data to a database. In exchange, they receive higher-quality prospects for their own marketing, through the use of predictive models based on data about previous transactions. Behavioral-based service providers also offer capabilities that help enrich customers' in-house databases by appending and overlaying data elements such as interests, lifestyle, and behavior, to help increase the relevance of marketing messages to each customer.

Beyond these tools, another layer of capturing and interpreting behavioral data harkens back to the concept outlined by Jenkinson (1994) that like-minded behaviors coupled with demographics results in like-minded actions. In platforms such as Eloqua, these communities of like-minded behaviors are referred to as List Groups or Custom Data Objects. They enable personalization as a starting point. With a significant and increased uptake in digital content consumption, communities or user buckets are becoming more and more niche and more splintered. Users are falling into multiple sub-cultures of existing communities and the potential for over-messaging due to too much data which threatens relevancy, affinity, and a positive user experience. With personalized content being the key driver to user experience success, investing more time in defining the broader segments or buckets of the audience may pay off. For example, some broader segments and steps along the user lifecycle could be defined as *seeds*, *influencers*, *advocates*, and *influenced.* Conyard (2014, p. 9) explains one way to interpret the aforementioned buckets:

The idea is initially seeded through both idea creation and advertising (paid and unpaid). It is likely the idea will be picked up initially (but not exclusively) by existing advocates. Through them, the message will spread to those that will be influenced by the idea, namely further advocates and influencers within the market space. When conducted correctly, this can result in a snowball effect – an influencer aligns with an idea in a strategy and in turn encourages support from their own advocates, who go on to become ambassadors for the idea themselves." Similarly he points out that the counter here is one can also create extremely negative reactions that are subsequently "broadcast to a wider sphere.

Behavioral Data

Behavioral data help to more robustly uncover and define the user lifecycle. It is not just about implicit trends, interests, topics, and pain points. Lifecycle or implicit actions of the user are also contingent on the campaigns, content, and topical asset-types being consumed. Areas of interest, sub-categories, hot buttons, and community threads have a known shelf life. Campaign interest such as registering and attending a webcast on a particular topic provides insight into a user's medium of interest.

How long will the "topic" of interest be relevant? This harkens back to examining layers of the user persona and the, at times, unsophisticated delivery of retargeted ads to browsers. Is the product in the shopping cart still relevant? Is that behavioral data worth capturing? How long do editors and marketers developing persona-based databases in marketing automation platforms, hold onto these kinds of data? The answer lies in the ability to access audience segments by profile and activity along with behavioral data in real-time. Colwell, B. and Taylor, M. (2014) refer to the ability to target in real-time based on user behavior as "Always-On Marketing (AOM) or data-driven and content-led experiences that are delivered across channels and devices in real-time." Thcy surveyed 685 c-level marketing, technology, and business executives and found that fewer than "20 percent have the technology, creative execution, and integrated data to deliver a targeted experience to a recognized customer across channels."

Ultimately, the information collected needs to be actionable by the editor or marketer with the media organization. The success lies in companies that are able to generate unified views of their users or what might include the complete user persona (profile, activity, and behavior) with defined groupings or communities, "develop actionable rules for experiences in each moment across channels, with the creative assets pulling dynamically in each millisecond" (Colwell & Taylor, 2014). The Razorfish-Adobe study revealed that more than 75 percent of these companies, covering six vertical industries at company sizes with revenues exceeding $500 million annually, were unable to convert behavioral data into usable directives for targeted messaging. To address needs such as this, Razorfish and Adobe work in concert to bring together the ability to rapidly identify the roadmap needed to extract the most value from the client. The result is actionable plans to fill the gaps between marketing goals and identified roadblocks. This is just one example of how creative agencies and web and data analytics platforms are coming together to offer solutions, dashboards, formulas and speed to real-time data usage.

CONCLUSION

Now that components of user personas, analytical tools, access to big data capture, and methods for defining the audience have been addressed, how does all this shape the user experience and impact decision making on user and content strategies?

Although this chapter included many companies that support the ability to utilize data and better understand user persona, there is no perfect combination of tools, applications, platforms, and data structure. The answer will be unique based on a media company's needs, budget, and internal skill set. The trend is that all companies should consider the need for logic around user identities and broader segmentation. As Colwell (2014) points out, "It's just not good enough to invest in only the technology or data analytics skills. You need your digital marketing eco-system working together."

The following questions must be asked and answered in order to define each organization's ecosystem (see Figure 5): What should the ecosystem look like based on the direction of the industry? What are the customer insight surveys revealing coupled with implicit data capture? What are the user '*aha*' moments that define the user, content, and product roadmap?

Figure 5. Market segmentation defined by profile, activity, behavioral and attitudinal data

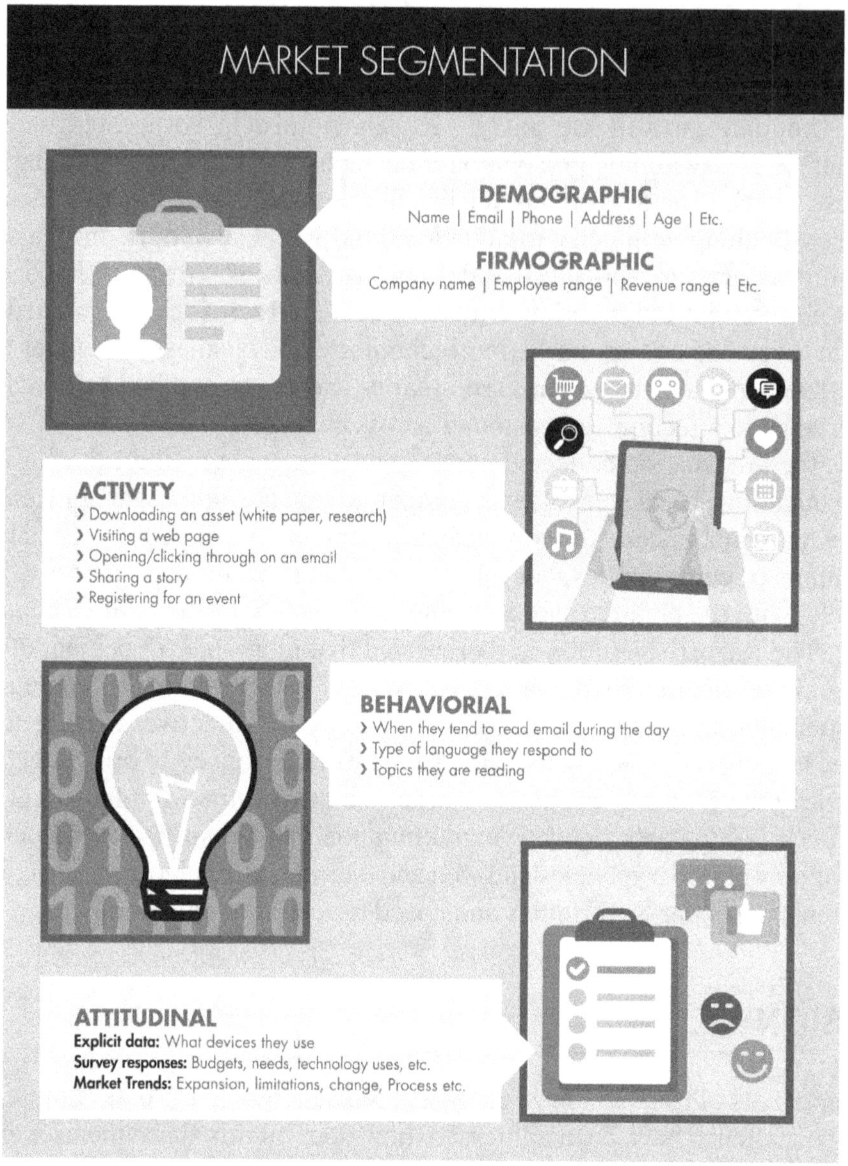

At the beginning of the chapter, the author described an online shopping experience. Her expectations for seeing relevant ads based on her user behavior and web perusing were not high. In contrast, the author has high expectations from this type of activity from media and information services companies, with which she has subscribed, become a member, or accessed premium, and gated content. Those activity-based and implicitly-based trends or choices should be capitalized upon. For these companies, there is an expectation that they are storing user's activities and will use these data to create more relevancies when messaging the user. Mining and intepretting user or audience data is a critical component of success in today's media and information services companies. Employing some of the strategies outlined here would be beneficial to align with this metrics-driven culture:

- Define personas and subcultures within each community
- Leverage the right tools to capture and append accurate demographic and firmographic data quickly
- Locate the right marketing automation platform and take advantage of segmentation, trigger programs and the ability to nurture and warm audiences intelligently
- Ensure data sets are linking – explore if and how the content contributors and the marketers and analysts unify
- Visualize the user path, make it a recurring exercise to recognize associations around activity and behavior to build out algorithms
- Set benchmarks to monitor increased affinity, loyalty and ROI – define what the user lifecycle looks like and what the trends are within the communities

Other questions to keep in mind include how the user personas evolve and represent the industry. Understanding users and defining personas is just a part of the user experience roadmap. What is the user's journey now and in the future? Do the content assets, products and channels align with the user-centric direction?

Data sources are increasing every year, from Google Analytics, Chartbeat, marketing automation data platforms, B2B contact lists, data appends, lifecycle processes, behavior profiling, consumer transaction databases, database service providers, and more. They all play a critical role. The job of editors and marketers is to determine which data are important and how to leverage them effectively.

Understanding the logical flow of data requires clarity with regard to the day in the life of the customer, reader, consumer or subscriber. Their logical interests and needs will vary based on profile data such as who they are, how senior their role, their concerns and areas of interest, company size or geography, and other firmographic information. Shaw (2014, para. 38) points out how important it is to turn data into visualizations. He states

To make sure that what we will be presenting to the user is understandable, which means we cannot show it all. Aggregation, filtering, and clustering are hugely important for us to reduce the data so that it makes sense for a person to look at

With regard to leveraging big data in terms of the relationship between data analytics and user experience, Shaw (2014, para. 38) indicates that

this is a different method of scientific inquiry that ultimately aims to create systems that let humans combine what they are good at—asking the right questions and interpreting the results—with what machines are good at: computation, analysis, and statistics using large datasets.

Relying on the little data within the larger data sets to impact user experience, editors, and marketers must form a collaborative team to clarify user personas in order to delve into the combination of technical solutions and platforms to support analytics directives.

REFERENCES

Colwell, B., & Taylor, M. A., & Razorfish. (2014). *The state of always-on marketing study*. Retrieved 2014, from http://www.alwayson.razorfish.com/#intro

Conyard, R. (2014). *Planning and creating a digital strategy*. Retrieved from https://www.red-ant.com/digital-strategy-whitepaper/

Dupre, E. (2013, November 1). Attitudinal and behavioral data: better together - Direct marketing news. *Dmnews.com*. Retrieved June 26, 2014, from http://www.dmnews.com/attitudinal-and-behavioral-data-better-together/article/317695/

Franklin, T., Harrop, H., Kay, D., & van Harmlen, M. (2011). *Exploiting activity data in the academic environment.* http://www.activitydata.org/

Garrison, K. (2014, June 18). 5 key questions to ask before developing customer personas. *It's All About Revenue: The Marketing Blog*. Retrieved June 26, 2014, from http://blog.eloqua.com/5-key-questions-to-ask-before-developing-customer-personas/

Haile, T. (2014, March 9). What you think you know about the web is wrong. *TIME.com*. Retrieved June 26 2014, from http://time.com/12933/what-you-think-you-know-about-the-web-is-wrong/

Jenkinson, A. (1994). Beyond segmentation, Journal of Targeting, Measurement and Analysis for Marketing, 3(1) 60-72. Henry Stewart Publications, London

Senatore, M. (2014, February, 20). *Eight is not enough: increasing adoption of marketing automation platforms | sirius decisions*. Retrieved February 20, 2014, from https://www.siriusdecisions.com/Blog/2014/Feb/Eight-is-NOT-Enough-Increasing-Adoption-of-Marketing-Automation-Platforms.aspx

Shaw, J. (2014, March-April). Why big data is a big deal. *Harvard Magazine*. Retrieved from http://harvardmagazine.com/2014/03/why-big-data-is-a-big-deal

Thomas, J. (2014, March 17). Little data vs. big data: nine types of data and how they should be used. *MarketingProfs*. Retrieved 26 June 2014, from http://www.marketingprofs.com/articles/2014/24670/little-data-vs-big-data-nine-types-of-data-and-how-they-should-be-used

Urbanski, A. (2014, January 1). 4 Modern Themes in Segmentation - Direct Marketing News. *Dmnews.com*. Retrieved 26 June 2014, from http://www.dmnews.com/4-modern-themes-in-segmentation/article/326267/

KEY TERMS AND DEFINITIONS

Activity Intelligence Dashboard: Activity intelligence dashboard provides a comprehensive view of a sales lead as well as the account associated with that lead.

Attitudinal Data: Attitudinal data attempts to determine how someone "feels" about a product or service by measuring the importance someone places on attributes of a product or service.

B2B: Business-to-business describes commerce transactions between businesses usually in the context of marketing and sales.

B2C: Business-to-consumer describes commerce transactions between businesses and consumers usually in the context of marketing and sales.

Behavioral Data: Behavioral data is a collection of all data on an individual's behavior. Behavioral data are typically collected online, but can also be derived from offline sources.

Big Data: Big data is a blanket term for any collection of data sets so large and complex that it becomes difficult to process using traditional database management tools.

Contextual Targeting: Contextual advertising is a form of targeted advertising on websites or content displayed in mobile browsers. The advertisements are selected and served by automated systems based on the content that is relevant to the user.

Data Normalization: Database normalization is the process of organizing the fields and tables of a relational database to minimize redundancy.

Dayparting: Dayparting is the practice of dividing a day into several segments and directing different forms of advertising to each segment.

Firmographics: Firmographics define the characteristics of organizations that are most likely to spend money on your product or service. What demographics are to people, firmographics are to organizations.

Infographic: Infographics or information graphics are visual representations of data presented in a form that is quick and easy for readers to visually interpret.

Little Data: The measurement, tracking, and analysis of the minutiae of everyday lives. Little Data is the small, unique preferences of users.

Marketing Automation: Marketing automation allows companies to streamline, automate, and measure marketing tasks and workflows, so they can increase efficiency and grow revenue.

Marketing Mix Modeling: Marketing mix modeling is a term for the use of statistical analysis such as multivariate regressions on sales and marketing data to estimate the impact of various marketing tactics on sales.

Organic Traffic: Organic traffic is traffic that comes to a website via unpaid links from other sites such as search engines, directories, and other websites.

Permission Pass Email: A permission pass involves sending out a new bulk email to your list asking the recipients to confirm that they want to continue to be subscribers.

Push Traffic: Push traffic refers to marketing promotions presented to large groups of people through channels such email campaigns and banner ads.

Retargeting: Retargeting is a cookie-based technology that uses a JavaScript code to anonymously ‘follow’ your audience all over the Web.

Retweet: A Retweet is a re-posting of someone else’s Tweet on the Twitter social media site.

Sainting: Sainting is a process where back-end user database fields are uploaded and merged with identifiers by email to track what users are reading and then map that data back to the user’s record data.

SMB: Small to mid-size business.

SME: Small to mid-size enterprise.

User Persona: A user persona is a representation of the goals and behavior of a hypothesized group of users. Personas are fictional characters created to represent the different user types that might use a site, brand, or product in a similar way.

Web Analytics Platform: A Web analytics platform is a tool that measures web traffic and enables businesses to measure, analyze and improve the effectiveness of a web site.

Chapter 8
Big Data, Text Mining, and News Content: Where is the Big Data?

Debora Cheney
University at Albany, USA

ABSTRACT

Mining the natural language text of news content has great potential for academic researchers seeking to understand and visualize patterns and relationships buried within everyday news coverage and content. Mining news can help researchers across many disciplines understand the impact of news, biases in news coverage, and language usage. It can also help them detect unknown patterns in news coverage. However, researchers must understand the challenges of using news text for text-mining-based research. Many challenges are inherent in the news form, including the complexity of the news environment; changing patterns of news consumption and distribution; growing use of social media; and the use of visual and audio information. Additional challenges relate to determining if the news content is available in a digital format, access and license restriction on use of the news text, and how complete and completely searchable the news text really is. This chapter explores these challenges and the impact they may have on how researchers gain access to news text, and methodologies used.

INTRODUCTION

Text mining can be broadly defined as a knowledge-intensive process in which a user interacts with a document collection over time by using a suite of analysis tools. In a manner analogous to data mining, text mining seeks to extract useful information from data sources through the identification and exploration of interesting patterns. In the case of text mining, however, the data sources are documents collections, and interesting patterns are found not among formalized database records but in the unstructured textual data in the documents in these collections. (Feldman & Sanger, 2007, p. 1)

DOI: 10.4018/978-1-4666-8580-2.ch008

Because of its daily, and, now minute-by-minute record of events, news text is an excellent reflection of news readers and where their interests lie—culturally, socially, and politically. Mining news text has become an important methodology and focus of contemporary research methods and data analytics in academic research (Housewright, Schonfeld, & Wulfson, 2013, p. 42). It is being used for a wide range of research, including an analysis of the impact Hong Kong finance news wire stories have on stock prices (Li et al., 2014); analysis of slave advertisements in the Richmond *Dispatch* from 1860-1865 (Nelson, n.d.); country comparisons of historical events referred to in news coverage from 1990-2010 (Au Yeung & Jatowt, 2011); analysis of hate blogs following the Obama presidential election (Sela, Kuflik, & Mesch, 2012); and ideological differences between local and international press coverage of Kenyan elections and post-election crises (Pollak, Coesemans, Daelemans, & Lavrac, 2011).

These examples illustrate the potential variety of news sources that may be used for news text mining, the potential for analysis across many decades, the possibility of international scope, and the wide variety of potential research questions. News text is used by academic researchers in many disciplines--history, political science, journalism, linguistics, rhetoric and communications studies, the humanities, business, marketing and advertising--to extract and visualize patterns and relationships within news text.

Because of the sheer scope of big data and text mining, it is possible to lose sight of the underlying characteristics of the news text data itself and the challenges they present, yet they are important. Some text mining projects may be more viable than others because of the nature and structure of the news corpus. Text mining social media, for example, may be appropriate for understanding how groups of individuals responded to an election, candidate or issue (Mohammad, Zhu, Kiritchenko, & Martin, 2015). Other research, for example, related to Civil War newspaper content, will be affected by how and whether the appropriate news text data and the necessary years are available in a digital form for text mining. It is important for researchers to understand that many challenges exist and to decide how they will be resolved in order to ensure that the research question and outcomes are articulated appropriately within the framework and to the extent allowed by the news text data.

Researchers engaged in news text mining research will experience significant challenges in two broad areas. One, challenges related to the form and function of the news, which pertain to the different types of news reporting and intended news readership, the changing patterns of news consumption and distribution, the growing use of social media, and the use of visual and audio news forms. Second, challenges related to accessing and identifying appropriate news sources for text mining research, which pertains to gaining access to the news text data in compliance with copyright and licensing law, and ensuring the needed news text data is complete, fully searchable, and available for the years or decades required of the research question.

THE FORM AND FUNCTION OF THE NEWS: CHALLENGES

In reality, there is no such thing as "the news." Today's news consists of many different types of news reporting with different purposes and intended readership, and an increasing array of methods used to attract readers. Although traditionally delivered on newsprint, today's news can be accessed and read on a smartphone app or on a website. It may be free or by subscription only, and, yet, it still can be delivered to a doorstep. All of these factors and many more will affect whether news text can be used for research.

The news media are a highly complex disaggregated network of for-profit news corporations (e.g., *The New York Times* and many others); non-profit organizations (e.g., *Poynter.org*); subject-focused news services (e.g., *Dow Jones Newswire*); and hyper-local and international news sources. Journalists work as professionals for a specific news organization. They may be citizen-journalists, or work free-lance. News organizations and journalists use social media in both formal and informal ways to distribute and deliver the news with the hope of gaining more (and different) readers. Thus, social media in some contexts represent a "free" expression of events, in other cases they are being used for purely commercial purposes.

Researchers who are mining news text data must be knowledgeable about how journalists practice their craft; how the news was distributed or delivered (e.g., via newspaper, wire service, website, blog, picture, or tweet); who and why it was read (by subscribers, followers or friends); and, even how it is aggregated, re-distributed, and re-packaged for different readers and purposes (wire services are a classic example, while re-tweeting is a more current example). Search engines are increasingly able to detect a reader's location and searching patterns and deliver information, including news, to the reader's desktop based on those patterns. Thus, whether the reader chooses the news or the news chooses the reader may impact readership and ultimately the way a research question can be framed.

Because news text data is complex in its content, organization, and how it can be found and read, researchers must select, analyze, and process the appropriate news sources using appropriate methodologies and technologies. The scope and nature of the research question will need to be framed within the context of the news source and its expected and real readers or followers. Just as researchers cannot argue that patterns within social media "made an event occur" they can argue the patterns of tweets constitute a "leading indicator of events unfolding" (Miner et al., 2012, p. 129). Or, a researcher text-mining scholarly research journals might omit the author, added keywords, and title because they might result in potential bias, when the abstract of a scholarly article is sufficient for analysis (Miner et al., 2012, p. 129). Similarly, the appropriate news corpus must be selected, analyzed, and processed with the appropriate methodology and technologies in order to "extract meaningful and useful information" from the text itself (Miner et al., 2012, p. 54).

There are many factors which challenge researchers and which will impact the research question, methodologies and news sources that will be used. The following sections explore challenges related to the form and function of the news itself that may impact the viability of a research project or the exact news sources which will be selected for text mining. These challenges include understanding that not all stories, blogs, or newspapers receive the same number of readers; news appears in many forms of media; and the news form may impact how readers perceive the news.

Not All Stories Receive the Same Number of Readers

All news media organizations have developed strategies that promote news readership and help readers sift through and find news most interesting to them. Sections of the newspaper (for example, the sports section) or the hashtag for tweets allow readers to pick those specific news stories they find most compelling and interesting.

Headlines, website design, tweets and news feeds to Facebook are all developed to attract readers. Stories which appear on the newspaper's front page, a newspaper section's front page, above the scroll on a website, at the top of an individual's Facebook news feed are all, theoretically, more likely to attract readers than those that appear below the fold or scroll, let alone later in the newspaper or further into a website.

Some of the most obvious elements of newspapers: a fixed page size and amount of space for "the news," the placement of a news story in an appropriate "news hole" depending on the importance of the story, the journalist, and other factors—influence readership and impact of a news story. In digital news forms editors are still aware of the length of a story (measured in number of words or column inches). More lengthy stories indicate that the news items are perceived as being important and will attract readership. Thus, the length of a story, placement of the story in the newspaper (e.g., front page, above the fold or the home page above the scroll) and whether it was featured as a social media posting, or re-posted or linked to on another news aggregator's website (e.g., *Huffington Post*), can, when taken together, mean some news has a greater impact on readership, behavior, and sentiment than other news.

Online stories can now contain links within the body of the story to related or earlier stories and create an experience designed to keep readers reading. A story that is linked-to from one related story to another, may have many more readers after it is "old" (yesterday's) news than it did on the day it first appeared in the news. All these ongoing relationships between news sources, readership, and impact are increasingly complex and may not be entirely accounted for within blunt-force text mining extraction and downloading methodologies. Thus, researchers must understand the news corpus they elect to use and apply appropriate and effective methods and tools for extracting, searching, or limiting research to specific types of text or stories to extract meaningful news text data from these big messy, data (Schöch, 2013). For example, it may require limiting the text mined to specific Twitter hashtags, including common metadata tags in the terms searched or mining text from carefully selected newspapers or wire services because of their intended audience or customer base.

The Same News Appears in Many News Media

News sources have a great deal of repetitive content when evaluated from one source to another. Just how much original reporting is taking place and which news organizations or journalists are providing that original reporting varies from source to source. Studies show the nature of the original reporting also varies depending on the country or news organization (Stray, 2010). In addition, the amount of original new news reporting has significantly declined over the years (Pew Research Center's Journalism Project Staff, 2010).

The news has always had repetitive content. In the 19th century large amounts of each newspaper were comprised of speeches, news stories, text-advertisements printed verbatim from other newspapers. Today the repetitive nature of the news includes a tweet or *YouTube* video that has been re-tweeted or linked to millions of times because it has "gone viral." Major newspapers and newswires generate the most original reporting which is purchased for reprinting or may simply be linked to by other news media or by a news aggregator (such as *Google News*,

Yahoo News, *Huffington Post* or many others). Due to methods for search engine optimization, the reader clicking through the news may be entirely unaware this is the same news story they read previously or which news organization originally reported the news. Researchers need to be aware that access to original or repetitive stories is impacted by:

- Ranking, clustering algorithms, and paywalls that influence what stories are more (or less) visible and likely to receive more (or fewer) readers, even when the same story is made visible (or less accessible) in many ways to a variety of readers (Sullivan, 2009);
- Newspapers that reprint stories within their corporate families (e.g., the Tribune or McClatchy newspapers) rather than from another newspaper outside the corporation, even when the reporting might be superior or more broadly read or viewed from another source;
- Many different newspapers reprint thousands of stories from newswires (e.g., *The Dow Jones Newswire; The Associated Press*, *Reuters*, etc.), thus these stories may be amongst the most widely accessible, although to the untrained eye, they may appear as original news reporting.

Aside from major newspapers and the wire services, a researcher seeking original reporting may look to local news sources, such as a hyper-local news site or a local newspaper, where the news reported may not appear anywhere else (e.g., marriages, real estate transactions, local news events, or, even, hymns) (Woodard, 2008) or may have a different ideological focus (Pollak, Coesemans, Daelemans, & Lavrac, 2011). However, the researcher should also be aware this local news (whether from a U.S. or from another country) might be quite different in word content, length of story, and in the placement and distribution of the story (Schmidt, Ivanova, & Schäfer, 2013; Jinzhi, 2010).

For many reasons it is difficult to determine the full extent of the readership of an online news story or how many newspapers reprinted a newswire story. However, the practice of reprinting and linking to news stories means that word frequencies will be skewed toward the words in the same story reprinted or linked to repeatedly. Readers may not see original stories about a news event, but rather the same news story delivered to them through multiple avenues. Or, stories of major events may not be widely reprinted or linked to because of the subject or reliability of the story's source. For example, a researcher counting word frequencies might conclude that some topics, subjects, or words appear more frequently than others by mining the stories in *Google News*. However, after removing the duplicate stories from the word results the researcher may discover there were far fewer unique stories, the words and subjects are not as prevalent as they may first seem. Researcher need to be aware of this impact and determine whether duplicate stories and words should be removed from the text data being analyzed because they will skew the results inappropriately. They might also examine whether this repetition of the same story received through various venues impacts in a positive or in a negative way reader behavior and sentiment, for example (Salzman, 2013; Ritter, 2008).

In content analysis research, there is recognition that the sample size and type of sample may need to vary depending on whether the news is an electronic sources or traditional news form (Connolly-Ahern, Ahern, & Bortree, 2009, p. 863). Similarly, researchers seeking to text mine news sources may need to modify their strategy to mine text or use appropriate statistical methodologies to ensure truly meaningful research outcomes. Researchers must understand how news content is different from text mined in scholarly research articles, literary forms (such as poetry or novels) or digitized books, all of which are structurally unique and whose distribution and readership are significantly different from news content.

Recognize the News Form

News stories, like scholarly research articles, have a basic structure—the headline, the lede paragraph, the byline (author) and a writing style. Beyond these basic structural elements, news stories have other very specific characteristics:

- Newspaper style can restrict what words are (and are not) used to describe events. A recent example is the discussion over the use of the words "illegal immigrants" which are no longer used by the *Associated Press* ("Words appearing in newspapers controversially," 2013), but many other examples occur and the ebb and flow of word frequencies can be influenced by these changes;
- Writing style includes many references to previous news events in order to place a current story in context. For example, a story about a school shooting today, will, most times include a reference to Columbine school shooting (Popescu & Strapparava, 2014);
- The lede paragraph is meant to grab the reader's attention, to pull them in—though not an abstract, the lede does attempt to capture the 5Ws (who, what, when, where, why) of the news story;
- Newspapers have many different types of content (aside from its advertising and visual elements): editorials, opinion, feature/human interest stories and short news announcements based on a press release. The language of the news media have become more informal, especially in social media and language can reflect the intended readership (e.g., a news source for business readers might include more specialized vocabulary), and narrative long form news stories are becoming more common in many newspapers;
- Local new sources have traditionally covered local crime, business, political, and social-economic news, which may reveal emerging patterns long before they appear in the national news or government statistics. News stories by local media result when community groups seek to raise awareness of a problem. For example, family homelessness on the rise in communities may indicate an economic downturn or changes in an industry or when reporters detect a pattern in the daily police crime report such as an increased number of rapes in a college town. Some features of newspapers, in particular, have begun to disappear—book, movie, restaurant reviews—except as information/blog postings by readers—but such text may still be mined from historical newspapers.

Generally, news organizations, and, increasingly, freelance and citizen journalists, are changing the once-predictable publication schedules, and, thus, the impact of the news (D'Angelo & Lombard, 2008). News outlets include a wide range of variant forms ranging from the *Huffington Post* (Silver, 2011) to *Buzzfeed.com* to *ProPublica*. Internet-based news aggregators who bring together stories based on a theme (e.g., *Yahoo Finance*) have exciting application for text-mining research. However, researchers need to be aware of who the readership is and source of the news story in order to ensure that the selection of words (whether mined or obtained through keyword searches) does not introduce additional terms or bias into the research.

For successful text mining-based research, the academic researcher should be aware that news text data reflects the context and purpose within which it is created. Because of these various forms, differences between intended and actual readership, and the scale of total expected (or hoped for) readers/subscribers/ friends/followers should be considered when determining which news source(s) will be most appropriate for the specific research question. Researchers should carefully select the methodology, and the software or tool that will produce results in keeping with the framework and context of the selected news text data. In addition, researchers will face challenges related to accessing and identifying appropriate news sources for text mining research, including gaining access to the news text data in compliance with copyright and licensing law, and ensuring the needed news text data is complete, fully searchable, and available for the years or decades required of the research question.

ACCESSING AND IDENTIFYING APPROPRIATE NEWS SOURCES: CHALLENGES

Data collection is often regarded as the easiest step of the entire analytical process, yet it is actually one of the most complex, with the quality of the collection and preparation processes impacting every other stage of the project. (Leetaru, 2011, p. 7)

Depending on the research question, interest, and context, the appropriate news text data may be stored in a variety of repositories and databases or it will need to be mined from Internet websites and social media. Because of the sheer visibility and perceived accessibility of today's news, researchers may not fully understand the complexity and challenges of identifying an appropriate news sources for a text mining research project. For many news readers, the news "appears" to be freely available and easily accessible for text mining. Certainly, researchers have a lot of news text data *potentially* available to them. In the last 20 (or so) years alone the form and function of news sources have undergone dramatic changes making today's news (or what passes as news) more visible and more accessible at the time it is read and distributed. Social media (e.g., *Facebook* and *Twitter*) are heavily used avenues for reading and distributing news (Matsa & Mitchell, 2014).

In addition, news also has deep historical and important international roots. The first American newspaper was published in 1690; there were 1,878 daily newspapers published in the United States in 1940; in 2005 there were 1,452 (Pew Research Journalism Project, 2007). There are thousands of newspapers published each day around the world ("The world's newspapers," 2011). Researchers should fully understand the role of the news source in a country. Some sources may be state or government owned; press laws can influence the freedom of the press within a country; some news sources have political party affiliations; and many other factors can influence what news is made available and in what forms within a country or media system.

When social media from another country is being used as the source of news text, researchers should consider how accessible the Internet is to the citizens of that country for reading, accessing, and for openly sharing or commenting on the news or country events ("Internet penetration," 2011). When comparative news coverage is being studied, language and other factors will also need to be considered (Schmidt, Ivanova, & Schäfer, 2013, p. 1239). Each of these factors can influence the news source that should be used for a research project. Researcher should carefully evaluate potential news sources while being thoughtful about their research question.

Once potential appropriate news sources are identified, researchers will then need to next determine how and whether they will be able to gain access to that news data text in order to search (or mine) it and further analysis. Many researchers will face issues related to a) whether the news content is available in digital format, b) access and license restrictions on use of the news text as data; and c) how to determine how complete and completely searchable the news text data really is.

Determine if the News Content Is Available in Digital Format

A review of text-mining research studies indicates the following trends: a) heavy use of social media, such as *Twitter* and *Facebook*; b) use of major newspapers with long publishing histories (e.g., *The New York Times*, *The Wall Street Journal*); c) use of Civil War or 19th century newspapers (Mussell, 2012); d) use of wire and news services (e.g., *Reuters)*; and e) use of specific country or subject-based news services (Li et al., 2014). Less frequently found are studies using local or regional news and studies conducted using newspapers published between 1924 and 1990.

There are reasons for these patterns. Text mining requires **access** to a large corpus of digital news content with relatively predictable form and complete content. The form and format of historical newspapers have many predictable elements and layout (Barnhurst & Nerone, 2001), which can make them ideal for text-mining. Once an appropriate newspaper or news source has been identified, researchers must do their due diligence to determine the exact nature/extent of the content and whether they will be able to access it in a digital form. They will encounter a very different situation for U.S. newspapers published before 1923 and news content (including newspapers) published after 1922. Copyright law related to news content and newspapers varies in every country and use of news content from other countries can present significant challenges for researchers seeking to use news sources for text and data mining (British Library, n.d.; European Commission. Directorate-General for Research and Development, 2014b).

Nineteenth and twentieth century newspapers present some of the oldest forms of U.S. news content. Newspapers published prior to 1923 are more likely to have been digitized. As U.S. Copyright Law (17 U.S.C. §§ 101 - 810) stipulates, they now reside in the public domain ("Copyright term and the public domain in the United States," 2014). After that date, availability of digitized newspapers varies greatly from title-to-title (Russell, 2012). Digitized newspapers can be found from many sources—some openly accessible and others available by subscription only on the Internet. The largest repository of openly accessibly U.S. pre-1923 digitized newspapers is the Library of Congress' *Chronicling America--Historical newspapers from 1836-1922* (see http://chroniclingamerica.loc.gov/). The researcher's library may provide access to sources that require a subscription or the researcher will learn where and how to most effectively access digitized newspapers by consulting a librarian. Libraries and historical societies are making great strides to digitize local newspapers as production costs decline and technology improves and much of this content can be found freely available on the Internet.

Copyright law would allow *some* newspapers published between 1923-1989 to be digitized under its "fair use" stipulations. In general, however, the availability of digitized newspaper content after 1922 changes significantly. Digitized newspapers for years after 1922 primarily occur when the newspaper itself, often in partnership with a library, an historical society, or a secondary publisher (e.g., Readex, ProQuest, or Gale) have undergone digitization projects for these years. Otherwise many newspapers may have only the years before 1923 digitized, if any years at all.

Another factor which impacts whether the newspaper is available in a digital format (thus the need for these digitization projects) is the change from analog to digital forms of newspaper production. Until the 1980's newspapers were largely produced through press production methods that did not produce a digital by-product. Once new production systems were adopted, the news text of the newspaper could be separated from the newsprint format, the images, and the advertising. By the early 1990s, major newspapers -- and to a large extent smaller newspapers -- had moved to digital production systems. Newspapers were then able to feed their news content to commercial database aggregators such as *LexisNexis*, *NewsBank*, and *Factiva,* which receive the text directly, in most cases, from the newspapers. They then provide aggregated news databases where many newspapers, wire services and other news sources can be searched or mined. Typically, access to these aggregator databases is provided to the researcher either through their library, by subscribing to the database as an individual, or by being granted limited access by the database vendor for research purposes. Researchers should consult with their librarian for recommendations and assistance.

The change in the delivery of the news to the Internet (rather than print-only products) and new social media forms, which have an important role in delivery of news content, has begun to change the strategies for mining news text data. News organizations may distribute the same news story through many different platforms, from newspapers, websites, *Facebook*, and *Twitter*. The growing impact of visual news elements and new forms of news that cannot be mined also present challenges to the researcher. News websites, for example, are very complex (Jeong, Oh, Kim, Lyu, & Kim, 2014). They include many different types of news stories, some original reporting and other content they may have linked to (e.g., breaking news from another news organization) or licensed (e.g., newswire stories). News websites provide a wide range of visual content such as advertising, video and photographs that cannot be searched (only the caption or close-captioning can be mined). Websites also provide comments related to a specific news stories that may reflect sentiment. However, this content can be difficult to mine and retaining the relationship between commentary and the news story can also be difficult. Some news websites will only allow subscriber access to their content.

All these factors impact, not only what can be mined directly from the website, but how it will be mined. For example, the *Internet Archive Wayback Machine (see* https://archive.org/web/web.php) may provide historical snapshots of websites, however, these snapshots are rarely complete in terms of the depth of website content. For example, the author took two snapshots of the *CNN.com* website from June 6, 2000, covering the Democratic National Convention. A quick check of many links shows that only a small fraction of the linking content is included with the snapshot. Whether that matters will depend on the research question. Research using website content is less frequent because the researcher must consider how they will extract content from websites and how much and which news text data they should extract.

For all these reasons, the availability of news text data varies with every newspaper. For example, *The New York Times* is highly accessible. Its entire print publication has been digitized (1851 to present) and continues to be digitized with only a three year delay by ProQuest. This digitized version is widely accessible through many libraries and to subscribers of *The New*

York Times website. In addition, the text-only content since 1985 is available in many different commercial database aggregators (although this content is less complete) and is also widely available in many libraries (Leetaru, 2011, p. 16). Finally, much of its content since the 1990's is also now available through its website, which is now largely restricted to subscribers. On the other hand, many other newspapers have no digitized content and may be accessible through a single commercial database aggregator. In addition, becoming a subscriber or having access through a library does not also automatically include the ability to mine large amounts of text. Additional caution should be exercised in terms of the full extent of the access provided by the license.

Determine Access and License Restrictions on Use

Generally, "many subscribe to the view that 'the right to read is the right to mine." Traditional publishers however distinguish between 'access' and 'mining', arguing that they are two different activities that require their own license and may bring with them different terms and conditions. (European Commission. Directorate-General for Research and Development, 2014a, p. 16)

An additional factor influencing the availability of news text data for mining is whether the researcher is prohibited by the terms of use license from downloading or mining large amounts of news text data. All aggregator databases will be alarmed and discontinue database access for the library (and thus the university or college) and academic researcher if they detect a researcher has begun to systematically download large amounts of text data from their databases. Researchers seeking to access data through a commercial database vendor should consult their libraries for license restrictions related to downloading or mining news content before they begin such work. Some publishers will grant use of news text data for limited purposes and time periods, particularly if the news text data is transformative or is disambiguated from the original news form (Smit & van der Graaf, 2011).

The willingness of *Twitter*, *Facebook* and other social media platforms and increasingly some repositories of digital news content to allow open-API access to their content has resulted in a wide range of studies using these sources. Because social media have an immediacy related to the news, and, because of their growing use, particularly by some demographic age groups, they are attractive for text mining projects. In all cases, the researcher's library, the publishers or the database vendor should be consulted when strategies other than open-API approaches are being used to download or mine news text data. This will help determine if the news corpus is complete and completely searchable.

Determine How Complete and Completely Searchable

Once a researcher has identified an appropriate news text source for searching or mining and confirmed content can be downloaded within copyright and license restrictions, he or she should take time to determine how complete and completely searchable or accessible the corpus is to text mining tools. Even when a newspaper has been digitized or the newswire feed is directed to a newspaper database aggregator, the content is never complete. Understanding what text, stories, images, or other content cannot be searched or mined is important for understanding the scope of the research question.

Newspapers that feed their content to aggregator databases also strip certain content such as newswire stories that were included in the newspaper or website. Local newspapers may omit from the feed some types of local content. What is removed can vary from newspaper to newspaper. In some cases, only a handful of the total news contained in a newspaper or website is included in the aggregator's databases (Leetaru, 2011, p. 14). Although the content in aggregator databases is more stable, newspaper content can be removed from an aggregator database, updated, and edited without notice (Leetaru, 2011, p. 8). Stories that may be identified as fabricated or plagiarized may (or may not) be identified only in the notes to the story, *if* this information is provided by the newspaper and practices vary widely.

Because access to news text data is so complex and involves many opportunities for the data and content to be changed, edited, or removed from aggregator and Internet sources, researchers should carefully document the source of the news text data, the specific search or mining strategy, and even those dates when the searches were conducted as part of the methodology of their research study. This will ensure future researchers can fully duplicate or understand the research framework. In addition, researchers should investigate whether their university library's institutional repository can be used to store the large amounts of data and working files that are created with the text mining process. Institutional repositories are designed to hold large data files and to allow access (public or private) to specific individuals and researchers.

In addition, some newspapers may be available in multiple aggregator databases, but the content can vary. With each database aggregator content can vary in a number of ways including abstracts only, different years included, different stories (business vs. news stories) due to their different clientele (Connolly-Ahern, Ahern, & Bortree, 2009, p. 865), or the selected content supplied through a news organization's newswire rather than directly from the newspaper itself. Database aggregators provide information about what content they provide for each news source that researchers should review carefully and compare with alternative sources for the same news content.

Various types of news blackouts (Leetaru, 2011, p. 16) are increasingly common and may be government mandated (Lefevre, 2014) or self-imposed by the families of victims (McBride, 2013). Historically, newspapers have chosen or been asked not to report on wartime events, presidential travel and journalists have been threatened and killed while reporting in some countries ("Journalists killed in 2013," n.d.). Press laws and what is allowed to be reported vary from country-to-country and can impact what is reported in traditional news media (Reporters without Borders, n.d.). Researchers have used social media to measure sentiment. However, researchers must understand that Internet access and literacy, for example, can impact how accessible these media are to the public and those seeking to read the news within a country (Emerson, Ghosh, & Smith, 2012).

Researchers should also be aware that even when a newspaper is digitized, it typically, but not always, includes the process of converting the text, via optical character recognition (OCR) to a digital form which can be searched or mined. However, the quality of the underlying OCR text, for even high quality digitization projects, can vary widely as much OCR software "reads" the image text from a newsprint page or microfilm and converts it to digital format (Brake, 2012). While newspaper content and print was largely predictable, the quality of the newspaper page, typeface, and many other factors can interfere with the quality of the OCR text, resulting in missing or garbled words which cannot be searched or mined.

Sources such as the *BBC Monitoring Library* or the *Foreign Broadcast Information Service* (FBIS) (compiled by the Central Intelligence Agency (CIA)) and similar sources must be evaluated based on the original purpose of the source and how the news text data were collected originally by the CIA. These sources represent a selection of news stories gathered for very different purposes and do not reflect a complete corpus of international news stories ("Foreign Broadcast Information Service (FBIS)," n.d.).

Finally, the researcher who is using aggregator databases to identify, search, and download text data will need to develop a thorough understanding of Boolean logic and other searching options (e.g., searching for word relationships within paragraph or sentence) offered by the database vendor (they differ with each database vendor). Searching news aggregator databases, rather than mining or scraping Internet and social media content, can provide the researcher with more control over what is actually searched within each story. Aggregator databases typically have their news text data in a more structured format that can allow the researcher to use Boolean search logic to limit the search to specific fields (e.g., the title and lede), by length or number of words, page or section, and some database aggregators also enhance the stories with additional keyword metadata and information about related photographs or illustrations and similar content. Whether this information is useful to limiting or focusing the search and resulting news text data that will be analyzed should be determined by the nature of the research question. However, judicious and careful use of these Boolean and field searching capabilities in news aggregator databases may result in less need to massage or analyze the text further once it has been downloaded (Leetaru, 2011, p. 25).

In summary, researchers in many disciplines will be able to use news text data from a wide variety of sources. They must understand, however, they will need to be prepared to work with large databases and repositories of news text data. Whether the researcher accesses the news text data through open-API scripts or through a database they should be prepared to work directly with news organizations; secondary publishers; news distributors; or their library and librarian to obtain access to news content for searching/mining and subsequent downloading. In addition, researchers may also use their university library's institutional repository to store and save their news text data for future use and to make the data available to other researchers.

CONCLUSION

Much news text mining research can be combined with geospatial and other visualization software, new statistical and mining methodologies, and a wide variety of traditional and new news forms. However, researchers will need to determine what source they want to use (social media, database or website content) and whether they can, either through their library or through an API script or crawler, be able to access and then search or mine the needed news text data.

To date, the news text data mining literature has largely focused on how increasingly sophisticated tools applied to very large amounts of text data mined or downloaded from large repositories. These methods can be used to reveal and understand underlying relationships and patterns between readers and the news. Another group of literature uses content analysis methodologies based on carefully selected articles or news text that has been searched (or mined) and subsequently downloaded for analysis. These methods present many opportunities for text mining research, but they should not ignore the challenges in using news content, which is inherently different from scholarly research articles, literary forms (such as poetry or novels) or digitized books. More research is needed to better understand how large-scale news text data repositories reflect the underlying patterns in how news content is delivered, consumed, and accessed. News text data repositories or social media alone do not fully represent how and where people receive, read, and interact with the news. The complexity of the news environment, changing patterns of news consumption, growing use of new forms of social media, and use of visual and audio news forms, which cannot be fully mined or searched for their inherent content, represent challenges for news text-based data mining research.

REFERENCES

Au Yeung, C., & Jatowt, A. (2011). Studying how the past is remembered: Towards computational history through large scale text mining. In *Proceedings of the 20th ACM international conference on Information and knowledge management* (pp. 1231–1240). Glasgow: ACM. doi:10.1145/2063576.2063755

Barnhurst, K. G., & Nerone, J. (2001). *The form of news*. New York: Guilford Press.

Brake, L. (2012). Half full and half empty. *Journal of Victorian Culture*, *17*(2), 222–229. doi: 10.1080/13555502.2012.683149

British Library. (n.d.). *Copyright at British library newspapers* [Text]. Retrieved June 16, 2014, from http://www.british-library.uk/reshelp/findhelprestype/news/copynews/index.html

Connolly-Ahern, C., Ahern, L. A., & Bortree, D. S. (2009). The Effectiveness of stratified constructed week sampling for content analysis of electronic news source archives: AP Newswire, Business Wire, and PR Newswire. *Journalism & Mass Communication Quarterly*, *86*(4), 802–883. doi:10.1177/107769900908600409

Copyright term and the public domain in the United States. (2014, January). Retrieved June 16, 2014, from http://copyright.cornell.edu/resources/publicdomain.cfm

D'Angelo, P., & Lombard, M. (2008). The power of the press: The effects of press frames in political campaign news on media perceptions. *Atlantic Journal of Communication*, *16*(1), 1–32. doi:10.1080/15456870701647391

Emerson, T., Ghosh, R., & Smith, E. (2012). Case study: Using the social share of voice to predict events that are about to happen. In *Practical text mining and statistical analysis for non-structured text data applications* (pp. 127–132). Waltham, MA: Academic Press. doi:10.1016/B978-0-12-386979-1.00007-4

European Commission. Directorate-General for Research and Development. (2014a). Standardization in the area of innovation and technological development, notably in the field of text and data mining: Report from the Expert Group. Luxembourg: European Union.

European Commission. Directorate-General for Research and Development. (2014b). The scope for special copyright arrangements for TDM (Section 3.5). In Standardization in the area of innovation and technological development, notably in the field of text and data mining: Report from the Expert Group (pp. 39–41). Luxembourg: European Union.

Feldman, R., & Sanger, J. (2007). The text mining handbook. Cambridge University Press; Retrieved from http://www.roelsbeestenboel.nl/text.pdf

Foreign Broadcast Information Service (FBIS). (n.d.). [Text]. Retrieved June 17, 2014, from http://library.uoregon.edu/govdocs/fbis.html

Housewright, R., Schonfeld, R. C., & Wulfson, K. (2013). *Ithaka S+R U.S. faculty survey 2012*. Ithaka S+R.

Internet penetration. (2011, June). Retrieved June 17, 2014, from http://www.oii.ox.ac.uk/vis/?id=4e3c0200

Jeong, O.-R., Oh, J., Kim, D.-J., Lyu, H., & Kim, W. (2014). Determining the titles of web pages using anchor text and link analysis. *Expert Systems with Applications*, *41*(9), 4322–4329. doi:10.1016/j.eswa.2013.12.033

Jinzhi, D. (2010, March 15). *The Google/China hacking case: How did the story flow through Chinese-language media*? Retrieved June 16, 2014, from http://www.niemanlab.org/2010/03/the-googlechina-hacking-case-how-did-the-story-flow-through-chinese-language-media/

Journalists killed in 2013. (n.d.). Retrieved June 24, 2014, from http://cpj.org/killed/2013/#

Leetaru, K. (2011). *Data mining methods for the content analyst: An introduction to the computational analysis of content*. New York: Routledge.

Leetaru, K. (2011). *Data mining methods for the content analyst: An introduction to the computational analysis of content*. New York: Routledge.

Lefevre, A. S. (2014, May 23). *Thai media chafe under post-coup blackout.* Retrieved June 17, 2014, from http://www.reuters.com/article/2014/05/23/thailand-protest-media-idUSL-3N0O80TZ20140523

Li, Q., Wang, T., Li, P., Liu, L., Gong, Q., & Chen, Y. (2014). The effect of news and public mood on stock movements. *Information Sciences*, *278*, 826–840. doi:10.1016/j.ins.2014.03.096

Matsa, K. E., & Mitchell, A. (2014, March 26). *8 Key takeaways about social media and news.* Retrieved from http://www.journalism.org/2014/03/26/8-key-takeaways-about-social-media-and-news/

McBride, K. (2013, December 13). *Newtown's media blackout forces journalists to do their jobs*. Retrieved June 17, 2014, from http://www.poynter.org/latest-news/creating-a-framework-for-ethical-decision-making-among-journalists-and-those-who-care-about-democracy/233342/newtowns-media-blackout-forces-journalists-to-do-their-jobs/

Miner, G., Elder, J. E., Hill, T., Nisbet, R., Delen, D., & Fast, A. (2012). *Practical text mining and statistical analysis for non-structured text data applications (1 edition.).* Waltham, MA: Academic Press.

Mohammad, S. M., Zhu, X., Kiritchenko, S., & Martin, J. (2015). Sentiment, emotion, purpose, and style in electoral tweets. *Information Processing & Management,* 51(4), 480-499. doi:10.1016/j.ipm.2014.09.003

Mussell, J. (2012). Nineteenth-century newspapers in the digital age. *Journal of Victorian Culture*, *17*(2), 221–221. doi:10.1080/13555502.2012.683147

Nelson, R. K. (n.d.). *Mining The Dispatch. Digital Scholarship Lab, University of Richmond.* Retrieved June 17, 2014, from http://dsl.richmond.edu/dispatch/pages/intro

Pew Research Center's Journalism Project Staff. (2010). *How news happens: A study of the news ecosystem of one American city*. Washington, D.C.: Pew Research Journalism Project. Retrieved from http://www.journalism.org/2010/01/11/how-news-happens/

Pew Research Journalism Project. (2007, March 12). *Number of U.S. daily newspapers, 5-year increments*. Retrieved June 17, 2014, from http://www.journalism.org/numbers/number-of-u-s-daily-newspapers-5-year-increments/

Pollak, S., Coesemans, R., Daelemans, W., & Lavrac, N. (2011). Detecting contrast patterns in newspaper articles by combining discourse analysis and text mining. *Pragmatics*, *21*(4), 647–683. http://elanguage.net/journals/pragmatics/article/view/3660 doi:10.1075/prag.21.4.07pol

Popescu, O., & Strapparava, C. (2014). Time corpora: Epochs, opinions and changes. *Knowledge-Based Systems*. 69, 3-13. doi:10.1016/j.knosys.2014.04.029

Reporters without Borders. (n.d.). *World press freedom index*, 2014. Retrieved October 26, 2014, from http://en.rsf.org/

Ritter, K. (2008). Study tracks news "fatigue" among younger readers. *Editor & Publisher*, (June 2).

Russell, J. G. (2012, March 19). *Copyright & the newspaper article*. Retrieved from http://www.legalgenealogist.com/blog/2012/03/19/copyright-the-newspaper-article/

Salzman, M. (2013, January 18). *2013: The Year fatigue set in*. Retrieved from http://www.huffingtonpost.com/marian-salzman/fatigue_b_2471860.html

Schmidt, A., Ivanova, A., & Schäfer, M. S. (2013). Media attention for climate change around the world: A comparative analysis of newspaper coverage in 27 countries. *Global Environmental Change*, *23*(5), 1233–1248. doi:10.1016/j.gloenvcha.2013.07.020

Schöch, C. (2013). Big? Smart? Clean? Messy? Data in the humanities. *Journal of Digital Humanities*, *2*(3). Retrieved from http://journalofdigitalhumanities.org/2-3/big-smart-clean-messy-data-in-the-humanities/

Sela, S., Kuflik, T., & Mesch, G. S. (2012). Changes in the discourse of online hate blogs: The effect of Barack Obama's election in 2008. *First Monday, 17*(11). doi:http://dl.acm.org/citation.cfm?doid=2063576.2063755

Silver, N. (2011, February 12). *The economics of blogging and The Huffington Post*. Retrieved from http://fivethirtyeight.blogs.nytimes.com/2011/02/12/the-economics-of-blogging-and-the-huffington-post/

Smit, E., & van der Graaf, M. (2011). *Journal article mining: A research study into practices, policies, plans....and promises*. Amsterdam: BF Bronfonteyn.

Stray, J. (2010, February 24). The Google/China hacking case: How many news outlets do the original reporting on a big story? Retrieved June 16, 2014, from http://www.niemanlab.org/2010/02/the-googlechina-hacking-case-how-many-news-outlets-do-the-original-reporting-on-a-big-story/

Sullivan, D. (2009, November 24). Under the hood: Google news & ranking stories. Retrieved June 16, 2014, from http://searchengineland.com/google-news-ranking-stories-30424

The world's newspapers. (2011, June). Retrieved June 16, 2014, from http://www.oii.ox.ac.uk/vis/?id=4e3c0222

Woodard, P. (2008). Hymns in North American newspapers 2000-2007. *Hymn: A Journal of Congregational Song, 59*(3), 26–38.

Words appearing in newspapers controversially. (2013, April 4). Retrieved from http://www.economist.com/blogs/johnson/2013/04/illegal-immigrants

ADDITIONAL READING

Barranco, J., & Wisler, D. (1999). Validity and Systematicity of Newspaper Data in Event Analysis. *European Sociological Review, 15*(3), 301–322. doi:10.1093/oxfordjournals.esr.a018265

Chronicling America (Library of Congress): About the site and API. (n.d.). Retrieved June 16, 2014, from http://chroniclingamerica.loc.gov/about/api/

Deacon, D. (2007). Yesterday's Papers and Today's Technology Digital Newspaper Archives and "Push Button" Content Analysis. *European Journal of Communication, 22*(1), 5–25. doi:10.1177/0267323107073743

Earl, J., Martin, A., McCarthy, J. D., & Soule, S. A. (2004). The Use of Newspaper Data in the Study of Collective Action. *Annual Review of Sociology, 30*(1), 65–80. doi:10.1146/annurev.soc.30.012703.110603

Fan, W., Wallace, L., Rich, S., & Zhang, Z. (2006). Tapping the power of text mining. *Communications of the ACM, 49*(9), 76–82. doi:10.1145/1151030.1151032

Internet Archive: Digital library of free books, movies, music & Wayback Machine. (n.d.). Retrieved June 16, 2014, from https://archive.org/

Li, X., Xie, H., Chen, L., Wang, J., & Deng, X. (n.d.). News impact on stock price return via sentiment analysis. *Knowledge-Based Systems.* doi:10.1016/j.knosys.2014.04.022

Liddle, D. (2012). Reflections on 20,000 Victorian newspapers: "Distant reading" The Times using the times digital archive. *Journal of Victorian Culture (Routledge), 17*(2), 230–237. doi:10.1080/13555502.2012.683151

Masawi, B., Bhattacharya, S., & Boulter, T. (2014). The power of words: A content analytical approach examining whether central bank speeches become financial news. *Journal of Information Science, 40*(2), 198–210. doi:10.1177/0165551513514928

Pew Research Journalism Project. (2014). *State of the news media 2014: Key indicators in media and news*. Washington, D.C.: Pew Research Center. Retrieved from http://www.journalism.org/2014/03/26/state-of-the-news-media-2014-key-indicators-in-media-and-news/

Piwowar, H., Dunham, J., & Lee, T. (2012). Text mining rights from three perspectives. In *32nd Annual Charleston Conference Issues in Book and Serial Acquisition*. Charleston, SC. Retrieved from http://2012charlestonconference.sched.org/event/fefb0c29aa6bbf91521e35efc2dd151c#.U6CJ7yjgeSo

Scott, S. (2013). The researcher of the future...makes the most of social media. *Lancet*, *381*, S5–S6. doi:10.1016/S0140-6736(13)60447-X PMID:23452936

Sirmakessis, S. (Ed.). (2004). Text Mining and its applications: Results of the NEMIS launch conference (Vol. 138). New York: Springer; Retrieved from http://www.springer.com/engineering/computational+intelligence+and+complexity/book/978-3-540-20238-7 doi:10.1007/978-3-540-45219-5_1

Smailović, J., Grčar, M., Lavrač, N., & Žnidaršič, M. (n.d.). Stream-based active learning for sentiment analysis in the financial domain. *Information Sciences*. doi:10.1016/j.ins.2014.04.034Thursda

Spinakis, A., & Paraskevi, P. (2004). Text mining tools: evaluation methods and criteria. In *Text mining and its applications: Results of the NEMIS launch conference* (Vol. 138, pp. 131–149). New York: Springer. doi:10.1007/978-3-540-45219-5_10

Truyens, M., & Van Eecke, P. (2014). Legal aspects of text mining. *Computer Law & Security Report*, *30*(2), 153–170. doi:10.1016/j.clsr.2014.01.009

Wei, W., Cao, N., Gulla, J. A., & Qu, H. (2011). ImpactWheel: visual analysis of the impact of online news. In *2011 IEEE/WIC/ACM International Conference on Web Intelligence and Intelligent Agent Technology (WI-IAT)* (Vol. 1, pp. 465–474). doi:10.1109/WI-IAT.2011.108

Yang, M.-C., & Rim, H.-C. (2014). Identifying interesting Twitter contents using topical analysis. *Expert Systems with Applications*, *41*(9), 4330–4336. doi:10.1016/j.eswa.2013.12.051

Youngblood, N. E., Bishop, B. A., & Worthington, D. L. (2013). Database Search Results Can Differ From Newspaper Microfilm. *Newspaper Research Journal*, *34*(1), 36–49. Retrieved from http://libproxy.albany.edu/login?url=http://search.ebscohost.com/login.aspx?direct=true&db=eft&AN=87083891&site=eds-live&scope=site

KEY TERMS AND DEFINITIONS

Copyright: Law protecting the use of an author's original creation by others; the specifics of the law vary from country-to-country and also for different forms (e.g., newspapers vs. photographs).

Database Aggregators: Third party companies who provide the storage and access to newspaper content and allow search and retrieval functions, many libraries subscribe to these database aggregators to provide news content to researchers.

Journalism: The profession of reporting news and events and the content journalists create in reporting the news.

Licenses: Allow or prohibit specific use of news content and may amend or further restrict copyright law.

Newspapers: The traditional physical format of news, however, the term is now increasingly used to refer to the online versions of newspapers.

Newswires: Companies (e.g., The Associated Press) who sell content to many newspapers and news outlets, use of this content is generally governed by license.

Social Media: A growing and changing variety of Internet sites and applications used by individuals to interact and share news and observations about their lives; the news media also use social media to distribute and share their news content more quickly.

Text Mining: Using a variety of computerized tools and software to search, retrieve, and analyze news content to determine patterns and relationships within the text.

Chapter 9 Using Market Research as the Basis for Successful Content Product Decisions

Judith Durgin Pilla
Independent Research Analyst, USA

Louis Pilla
Publishing Executive, USA

ABSTRACT

For publishers and content providers, basing content decisions on one's own perception of what users need can be fraught with peril. Adopting an "outside-in" approach to product development – in which customer needs, not internal desires of the organization, drive product development – leads to the greatest chances for success. When it comes to understanding the audience, content providers and product teams have a variety of methodological approaches from which they can choose. These methods fall into two overarching approaches: qualitative and quantitative research. This chapter provides descriptions of several qualitative and quantitative research approaches that are frequently used to inform publishing business decisions. The authors discuss the importance of researching a target audience and present methods to discover their needs. Through two case studies, they provide an example of how research methods are employed in real-world situations.

INTRODUCTION

All I know about getting out a magazine is to print what you think is good (or as near to your standard as you can get) and let nature take its course: if enough readers think as you do, you're a success, if not you're a failure. (Kunkel, 2001, p. 216)

DOI: 10.4018/978-1-4666-8580-2.ch009

So said Harold Ross, the esteemed founding editor of *The New Yorker* magazine, in a letter to the editor of the publication *Current Biography* dated June 23, 1943.

Closer to the present day, when asked what market research Apple did for the introduction of the first Macintosh computer, Apple founder Steve Jobs replied, "Did Alexander Graham Bell do any market research before he invented the telephone?"(Isaacson, 2011, p. 170). In these cases, the insights and intuition of these leaders resulted in enormous success. With Mr. Ross, his taste led to a publication that has survived for almost 90 years – *The New Yorker,* launched in February 1925. Apple's Macintosh, launched in 1984, continues to be successful some 30 years on.

While such genius can occur in any age, few content providers or product leaders can rely on their internal guidance mechanisms to provide such success. Even if an editor or product leader has toiled in an industry for decades, counting on one's own sense of what will delight an audience is a risky proposition. That is because the creator of the content is typically not an expert in the domain being covered, which is why qualitative and quantitative research needs to play such critical roles in content product design and development.

In this chapter, the authors discuss the importance of researching a target audience to inform publishing business decisions. They present specific research methods, as applied in a business setting, to discover audience needs. Through two case studies, they provide an example of how research methods are employed in real-world situations.

BACKGROUND

Those who would build new products face challenging odds. According to one eye-opening study, out of seven new product ideas, only one succeeds (Cooper, 2001, pp. 10-11). Among the reasons for product failure, poor market research sits at the top of the list. A study from The Conference Board finds that inadequate research is the number-one cause of failure. Other reasons included technical problems, insufficient marketing effort, and poor timing.

The concept of the "market-driven firm" sets out to prevent such problems. In a "market-driven" organization, "all decisions start with the customer and the anticipated opportunities for advantage. The entire organization then follows through to insist on providing superior quality and service on the customer's own terms" (Day, 1999, p. 359).

A structured framework for developing products based on understanding the needs of audiences and customers is required to succeed in delivering well-targeted content. Adopting an "outside-in" approach to content product development, where customer needs, not the internal desires of the organization, drive product development, leads to the greatest chances for success. This framework offers product managers, marketers, and others specific techniques to discover market problems and to craft products to meet those needs. There are highly regarded industry methodologies such as Pragmatic Marketing (see www.pragmaticmarketing.com) that provide guidance in establishing such a framework. If research is key to success, a content provider needs to understand the kinds of research available and the core value those techniques provide.

RESEARCH APPROACHES

When it comes to understanding the audience, content providers today have a variety of methodological approaches to choose from. Market research and product usability research provide a rich collection of these approaches. Methods fall into two overarching approaches: qualitative and quantitative research. The phrase *qualitative methodology* refers in the broadest sense to "*research that produces descriptive data: people's own written or spoken words and observable behavior*" (Taylor & Bogdan, 1984, p. 5). Exploratory in nature, qualitative research promotes discovery of a subject area. The techniques "emphasize depth of understanding, attempt to subjectively tap the deeper meanings of human experience, and intend to generate theoretically rich observations" (Rubin & Babbie, 1993, p. 33). The appropriate philosophical stance of the qualitative researcher is to enter into a project with an attitude of openness. Regarding oneself as knowing little, waiting to hear the knowledge of the customer, is the proper stance to take when using qualitative methodologies.

While the purpose of a qualitative research study is to explore and understand a subject area which was, before the study, completely or partially unknown, quantitative research allows the researcher to further probe the subject area in new ways. Once the overarching subject area is understood from a qualitative research perspective, the researcher can apply quantitative research methods to the findings to then ask specific questions about the data. Among other things, quantitative studies amass numerical data and use statistical analyses to provide evidence to affirm or refute a particular research question or to explain some phenomenon.

The following sections provide a brief summary of business-related concerns for both qualitative and quantitative research approaches. Four examples of research methodologies that are frequently used in business decision-making are discussed. While the chapter outlines qualitative and quantitative research adapted to business settings, it is not meant to be a comprehensive review of all possible methodologies.

Qualitative Research

Qualitative research studies have one goal: to provide a foundational grounding about a subject that is relatively unknown or unexplored. Qualitative research seeks a comprehensive, deep look at a subject to uncover all major topics about that subject that could influence the product's development or appeal. It is research that examines respondents' lived experiences of the subject being studied and depends on abundant information obtained from careful, comprehensive interviews (Mishler, 1986). For example, if a company wants to launch a specific online content product for the nursing profession, and does not have an in-depth understanding of the nuances of the profession, qualitative research will uncover the many different specialty roles in nursing, each with highly individualized needs. Qualitative research will provide a rich understanding of these specific needs to enable the content provider to design a desirable, useful product that is based on actual requirements of individual nurses.

Qualitative research focuses on a subject with great depth and breadth. Often the researcher conducts lengthy interviews using semi-structured interview guides. Relatively small sample sizes are used for qualitative studies, usually between 20 to 40 participants. The interviews will generate huge amounts of data. It is not unusual to have hundreds of pages of data produced by 20 interviews, which then must be analyzed to uncover common themes.

Qualitative research is considered "back-loaded" research, versus "front-loaded." Required at the "front," or beginning, of a qualitative study are open-mindedness; general, fundamental knowledge of the subject; a well-designed interview guide careful choice of participants; a highly skilled qualitative interviewer or facilitator; and abundant time for interviewing.

A long, strong effort must be put in at the "back" of a qualitative study once the data have been collected. At the back of a qualitative study, the analyst/interviewer spends days or weeks, depending on the sample size, combing through the data gathered from participants. This data search will reveal patterns of information that are then developed into themes by the analyst. These themes, and the research information that supports them, become the analytical findings of a qualitative research study.

Using the example of the online nursing publication again, a qualitative study could discover that there are many nursing specialties, each with particular characteristics. For instance, suppose it is discovered that emergency/trauma nursing is distinct from other nursing specialties in specific ways. One salient distinction is the finding that emergency/trauma nurses usually care for their patients only once, for a limited number of hours, as opposed to other nursing specialists who are responsible for patients' care over days, weeks, or months, such as visiting nurses who treat patients with chronic illnesses. It may prove vital for the publisher to design a content product that takes this difference into account. Content for emergency/trauma nurses is distinct from content for other nursing units.

Qualitative research methods could help the researcher uncover this distinctly important theme, which could be named "length of patient care experience." Once the importance of this theme is realized, the company may decide to expand this understanding to discover fully the impact that "length of patient care experience" has for every nursing specialty that is to use their product.

Products become highly appealing and desirable to audiences because they are responsive to users' needs or their real-world situations. Qualitative research can help to inform product design. Without it, a publisher could easily fail to develop content that audience members need in their everyday work or lives.

Qualitative Research Techniques

A qualitative study uncovers in-depth data by employing one or more research techniques. Each technique is designed with a particular objective in mind. The following are the most frequently used qualitative techniques for business research.

Individual, In-Depth Interviews

- **Purpose:** To generate a rich, substantive knowledge of a subject. Individual interviews produce a broad scope of information at a deep level. The knowledge gleaned will provide enough understanding to develop multiple themes relevant to a whole population as well as to subsets of the population, plus nuanced information necessary for complete understanding.
- **Structure:** Uses a semi-structured interview guide designed and administered by a professional qualitative interviewer. A huge array of interviewing exercises can be designed to achieve exactly

the information needed in an individual interview. The duration of an individual interview is 30 to 90 minutes, averaging 50 minutes for business-related research. High-quality interviews can be obtained either in-person or by telephone. Online individual interviews can be more expedient to conduct but will compromise the quality of information obtained, because vital interactions between interviewer and respondent are absent.

- **Sampling Information:** Typically 20 to 40 participants are needed, depending on the scope of the subject and other criteria specific to the study's requirements. A professional qualitative research designer will be able to specify relevant criteria to accurately determine the necessary sample size for any given study. The range of difference (heterogeneity) versus similarity (homogeneity) in respondent characteristics is one criterion that is important to understand and specify before choosing respondents.

Focus Groups

- **Purpose:** To generate novel, creative ideas for product development or to enhance an existing product by uncovering new, relevant ways that increase appeal and use. Focus groups also are useful for understanding the characteristics that define or describe a homogeneous sample of a population. However, focus groups are *not* the qualitative technique of choice for evaluating a product or discovering how customers use it. Any group of respondents will develop "group bias," based on the tendency for groups to align with a perceived leader or to resist a member who is negatively dominating or controversial. This human tendency results in "group think," which is counter-productive to the goals of evaluative research. In evaluating any concept or product, in-depth individual responses generally are more accurate and reliable.
- **Structure:** Uses a semi-structured interview guide designed and administered by a professional qualitative interviewer who is familiar with facilitating groups. As is true for individual interviews, a large array of focus group exercises is available. The duration of a focus a group is from 90 to 120 minutes, depending on the size of the group. Focus group exercises can emphasize group response or consensus, or they can focus on individual responses by individuating the response format. In many groups, both types of exercise are used.
- **Sampling Information:** Focus groups can range from mini-groups (triads or quads) to full-size groups of eight or nine participants. A group size larger than nine, however, dilutes the impact of individual responses and is difficult to facilitate effectively. A large group also demands a long duration to effectively obtain full responses from each member, and such a long duration will produce compromised data due to respondent fatigue.

One important question is whether to use a homogeneous versus heterogeneous group. Homogeneous groups have members who have in common certain personal traits, knowledge of the subject or levels of experience that could impact research findings. These groups are generally preferable. Homogeneous groups will produce less group bias, and group members will interact more easily with each other during research, producing more accurate results. Heterogeneous groups have highly disparate levels of knowledge, experience, or personal traits. They can be useful when it is desirous to spark differences or conflicting opinions for the purpose of eliciting novel or esoteric information.

Shadowing

- **Purpose:** To obtain a rich, nuanced body of information about a population that includes the environmental context of that population, because such contextual understanding is necessary to satisfy the research problem. Shadowing takes place in a specific environment because features of the environment are essential for understanding respondents and their roles.

Shadowing helps overcome two problems. The first is that customers don't always know what they want; the second is that customers don't know products as well as the product team. "You must do more than just asking them what they want in a new product or service. The simplest and most efficient method is to simply watch them as they do their day-to-day tasks" (Haselmaier, 2014, para. 11).

Business uses of shadowing research are sometimes mistakenly referred to as ethnography. Ethnography is a highly rigorous, often academically based research method that requires an enormous amount of skill, commitment and time to conduct (Denzin & Lincoln, 1994). It is not appropriate for business needs. Probably the most familiar example of ethnographic research is the work of the noted anthropologist Margaret Mead in the 1930s to 1950s, in which she lived with Pacific and Asian Islanders to research their culture.

- **Structure:** Shadowing is conducted by highly experienced qualitative researchers who embed themselves in the environment of research subjects. It is important to have a substantial understanding of this approach by consulting with an expert researcher before deciding to use it, as it is involved, quite detailed, and usually expensive.

As an example of shadowing, a researcher, to understand the day-to-day experiences and roles of an emergency/trauma nurse, would contract with a trauma facility to "live" in that environment for hours a day, for days at a time, to observe nurses as they do their work. Observation at a distance is the hallmark of shadowing research. However, individual interviews also can be conducted during shadowing.

Shadowing requires highly skilled researchers because it is easy for an untrained observer to make biased observations and unintended interference. For instance, the simple presence of an observer in a work setting can induce a subject to do things differently from normal, to try and perform better, or "look the part." Such different behavior will bias the findings and must be avoided by using experienced researchers who know how to minimize disruption in the setting.

- **Sampling Information:** Shadowing often takes place in work settings where several research participants can be observed and interviewed. Several settings with multiple participants may suffice to obtain the necessary data. However, each setting will exhibit its own culture and behaviors. Thus, it is important to understand that multiple settings, in different geographies and with different cultures, may be needed to provide a complete research picture. Typically, shadowing is elaborate and expensive research, due to the many hours required and the complex requirements of placing researchers in specific settings. These considerations also may tend to limit the size of the study.

Advisory Boards

- **Purpose:** To obtain the insights of thought leaders in the audience being researched to help content providers and publishers understand important industry themes. Thought leaders who make up expert panels serve as valuable repositories of insight into major dynamics and trends in the industry. Advisory boards can help a content product team understand where a profession is headed, major trends to which they should pay attention, and new opportunities to serve the audience.
- **Structure:** Advisory boards that are useful in understanding qualitative research subjects are *working* boards, experts whom product directors can rely upon to help understand the audience. The importance of advisory boards, or other types of expert panels, in a research effort is their ability to contribute actively, lending their insight, knowledge, and experience to add, enhance, or shape the direction that a content research project can take.

Advisory board assistance can be used in multiple ways to influence research efforts. Members can be asked to respond to questions about the direction a product might take, such as the content that might be most critical for the audience, which can then be researched further. Or they can be asked to make a presentation to the product team about a major theme affecting the audience, which might lead to additional analysis.

- **Sampling Information:** Because these are working groups, relatively small sizes work most effectively. Boards with more than 10 to 12 individuals may start to get unwieldy. Among the ways to utilize their expertise are web and in-person meetings, emails, and online surveys. As for frequency of contact, and given the usually busy schedules of the individuals involved, teleconference or web meetings held every six to eight weeks or so can work well, providing enough continuity and connection without overwhelming board members. Board members can be tenured for a certain time, say one year, and their terms renewed as needed.

Quantitative Research

The ultimate goal of quantitative research is to establish, through a series of specific questions, the extent to which a research problem is true or not true for the sample population being studied. Statistical analyses are used to determine if the observed differences between groups under study are statistically significant (i.e., did or did not occur by random chance). Quantitative research begins with a clear research problem, or overarching question, a hypothesis. The object of a quantitative study is to learn whether research findings prove or disprove the hypothesis. Whether the hypothesis is proved or disproved, a product team learns about the importance of the research problem for a representative proportion of the population being studied.

In the online nursing publication example presented earlier, during the qualitative study, nurses were asked about their practice, and different nursing specialties were uncovered, with an interesting theme developed about "length of patient care experience." Now, the content publisher wants to know more about the specifics of that theme, and whether, and how much, nurses' "length of patient care experience" will impact their use of a new online content product. In a quantitative study, a researcher might ask 3,000 nurses across the country, "To what extent will the length of your patient care time with an individual patient impact the level of interest you have in our product?" To determine length of care, the researcher may identify three different types of nursing units, each known to vary in the amount of time nurses spend caring for a patient. For instance, length of care in emergency units is short, length of care in pediatric units is medium, and length of care in geriatrics is long, and so on. The researcher could ask equal numbers of nurses in each of these units to rate the aforementioned question (e.g., 1 to 10 scale). The researcher could then compare if interest ratings differ by unit type or length of care. This is an example of a hypothesis: that length of patient care time will impact level of product interest. Obtaining responses from 3,000 nurses likely will provide a high level of confidence in the answer to this specific question. If nurses' responses are statistically significant in showing that patient care time *will* impact level of interest in the product, then content product developers know to make accommodations in their online publication concerning the length of patient care time readers experience in their work.

Quantitative research focuses on many, detailed questions with much less depth and breadth than qualitative research, because the purposes of the research are much different. By the time a quantitative study is designed, the deep, broad issues are understood. What is lacking is knowledge about *how important* all the specifics of these deep, broad issues are for the population as a whole.

Quantitative research is always "front-loaded," unlike qualitative research. "Front-loaded" means that much deliberation, design strategy, and intellectual effort go into developing the hypotheses, specific quantitative techniques, and wording of questions that make up a quantitative research tool. Only when the research tool, such as a survey instrument, is judged to be completely *accurate* and *reliable*, is it ready for use in a study.

All quantitative methods depend on statistical analysis, the particular methods of which will vary depending on the complexity of the research questions and the population's characteristics. This analysis is applied at the "back-end" of the research, once the complete data set is in hand. The reason quantitative research is considered "front-loaded" is that much effort, consideration, and time has to be put into designing each question to be asked at the "front" of the study. It is then relatively straightforward for a statistical expert to "crunch the numbers" at the "back-end" using all the data obtained. This is not to underestimate what is involved in "number crunching." Quantitative data analysis is highly complex and must be conducted by an expert statistician. However, the analysis at the "back-end" of a quantitative study depends on highly regimented analytical processes that do not have to be redesigned for each study. In the hands of an expert, they can be applied straightforwardly in all similar studies without the high degree of examination and effort that take place at the "back-end" of a qualitative study.

Referring to the online nursing publication example again, if a quantitative researcher administers a survey instrument to 3,000 nurses across the country, the instrument likely will contain dozens of questions that each nurse must answer about her or his practice. The questions are designed to cover all aspects of the themes developed in previous qualitative research that are deemed relevant to the product being developed. Perhaps the nurses are asked 75 questions about many aspects of their day-to-day practice. The statistical analysis done on the 225,000 questions (3,000 nurses X 75 questions each) will rely on mathematical procedures that have been specifically chosen at the front end of the study to address the type of problem being researched. Once these procedures have been chosen and put into place at the start of the study, analysis at the back end of the research is often less time-consuming.

Quantitative Research Techniques

There are many different quantitative research methods used in business settings that can examine a myriad of questions. Several specific methods will be discussed below.

Survey

- **Purpose:** Surveys, a frequently used instrument for quantitative research, generate data from a large number of respondents about a particular set of questions that have a unified theme or topic. Surveys can be used for descriptive, as well as explanatory or investigative purposes. They are excellent for measuring the attitudes and orientations of a large population (Rubin & Babbie, 1993).
- **Structure:** Surveys can be designed to be conducted in-person, by telephone, by mail, or online. They can be highly structured questionnaires that pose multiple questions in a single interview. More typically, survey instruments are composed of closed-ended questions with discrete, limited options for answers, usually based on a five-point scale.

Five- or seven-point scales are recommended over six-point or even-numbered scales, because an odd number of options forces respondents to choose an answer that is equidistant from a neutral midpoint. It also does not force a truly "neutral" person to select an option that is non-neutral. Even-numbered scales allow for a higher degree of unfocused vacillation on the respondent's part. They also force respondents to select options that are either at the high or low ends of the scale. Some open-ended questions, in which respondents compose their own, unstructured comments, may also be included in surveys.

Referring back to the online nursing example, the researcher could design a survey of 35 closed-ended questions concerning many aspects of a nurse's day-to-day practice. They may include non-scaled questions such as, "How many years of experience do you have as a nurse in your chosen specialty?" The survey likely will include scaled questions such as, "How important is the use of patient education materials on your nursing unit?" based on a five-point scale: 1) not at all important, 2) usually not important 3) somewhat important, 4) frequently important, 5) almost always important. An example of an open-ended question would be: "*Please describe in a few sentences the most important need you have in your nursing unit today that keeps you from doing your job at a higher level than you are able to now.*"

- **Sampling Information:** One of the most important reasons to use a survey is its capacity to understand the views of a large population when it would be impossible to interview the whole population directly. A well-designed survey uses *probability sampling* to collect original data from a *representative* subset (or sample) of a population. Once survey data are analyzed, results from this much smaller subset can be understood to apply to the whole population, within a reasonable margin of error. In other words, in a well-designed survey, a company can conclude from the responses of 3,000 nurses that the vast majority of the 2.7 million registered nurses in the U.S. today would have responses similar to those in the subset. The capacity to make a statistical inference from a *representative* sample to an entire population is called *generalizability* and is the crowning benefit of quantitative research.

Sample sizes for surveys usually are large but depend very much on the characteristics of the population being studied. An expert quantitative research designer will be able to provide precise estimates of the sample size required, based on the size and characteristics of the population being studied.

Attitude, Awareness and Usage Studies

- **Purpose:** Attitude, awareness and usage (AAU) research is frequently employed by those responsible for developing, selling, or licensing a product. It is considered fundamental research to understand the relationship between a product or a class of products and its customers. An AAU study examines customers' opinions as well as their behaviors. It thoroughly explores actual or potential customers' attitudes and opinions about a product brand, the level of their awareness of the product, its availability, its attributes, and the degree to which customers have used the product or function in the actual environment.
- **Structure:** AAU studies compare customers' perceptions of a branded product against perceptions of various other brands/products in the same or related categories. Specific questions elicit a detailed appreciation of how customers regard their own product in the context of a market containing similar products. Typically, qualitative research is done preliminarily to discover which attributes are most aligned in the customers' minds about the branded product and competitors. Once this attribute list is generated, a quantitative AAU study compares 1) how well the brand delivers this set of attributes, 2) how well other related products in the same market deliver the same set of attributes, and 3) how customers behave (purchase) products as a result of these perceptions. The result of an AAU study is a thorough understanding about the degree of "gap" that exists between the branded product, its competitors, and customers' perceptions of an ideal version of the product. Companies can use such gap analysis to develop or reshape products to fill these gaps and thus enhance their market share in the product category.
- **Sampling Information:** Larger sample sizes are required for accurate, reliable AAU studies. The specific sample size for an AAU study will be directly related to the market size of the product and its competitors. To reliably calculate the sample size required for an AAU study demands consultation with an expert quantitative researcher who is highly experienced in designing and conducting these studies.

Many companies make the mistake of insisting that they hire a researcher who is thoroughly familiar with the brand or category of product being tested. This is not a requirement. An expert researcher can translate expertise reliably from one brand/category to another. While basic knowledge about the industry is important, the more important criterion is the researcher's degree of experience with AAU studies, including sample size determination.

Market Segmentation Studies

- **Purpose:** A market segmentation study provides a detailed understanding of the entire market for a product by dividing that market into sections, or segments, according to characteristics that define each segment as distinct from another. All segments together constitute the product's entire market. Segmentation offers superior understanding of a product's likely audiences by identifying groups of individuals whose wants/needs and basis of purchasing decisions are related to each other, but different from those of other individuals. By dividing a market into segments defining unique wants/needs and bases of purchasing decisions, companies can better target a product by developing and marketing it according to the unique characteristics of each segment. This can be instrumental in growing market share.

- **Structure:** Quantitative segmentation studies are detailed and complex because there are many factors to consider when deciding how to determine market segments. Ideally, a company wants to know the economic value and potential for each segment, as well as having some idea about whether the value and potential of each segment is increasing or decreasing.

Given this overarching requirement, there are different methods to achieve market segmentation. A *needs-based segmentation* approach explores key drivers that stimulate individuals to use a product, resulting in identification of their needs based on trade-offs each person makes during the research testing. This needs-based segmentation uses a statistical method called conjoint analysis to split a category into different levels of functional performance.

A *usage segmentation* can be conducted by means of a Decile analysis or Pareto analysis, each of which split users into groups depending on their weight of use, from light users to heavy users. Decile analysis splits product users evenly into 10 groups. Pareto analysis splits users into the top 20% of high use from the bottom 80% of lower use.

Cluster analysis can be used as a statistical technique that groups together people with similar consumption attitudes. For instance, nurses who believe that "loyalty" to an online brand is more important than "new features" may occupy different segmentation clusters. The most basic way to obtain user segmentation is through *a priori segmentation*, where existing, established segments are used to target product development and marketing. For instance, nurses' ages, socioeconomic status, or other demographics can be used to define audience segments.

Returning to the online nursing publication example, on the face of it, it makes sense to think that emergency/trauma nurses are a distinct segment from other nursing specialties. However, perhaps it's not the category "emergency/trauma" that is most important to distinguish these nurses from others in terms of their likelihood to engage with an online venue. Emergency/trauma nurses may actually make content viewing choices that are the same as intensive care unit nurses. A well-planned and implemented segmentation study may show that a more useful segment for defining a product area for nurses may be the "length of patient care experience" defined earlier. In that case, all nurses who have short length of patient care experiences (perhaps school nurses as well as emergency/trauma nurses) will be more likely to purchase the product. If the company had mistakenly assumed that "emergency/trauma" nurses are a distinct segment, it would miss out on the revenues obtainable from school nurses.

- **Sampling Information:** Sampling for market segmentation studies uses criteria similar to those mentioned above for other types of quantitative research. A sufficient sample size for a segmentation study will be based on the size of the market to be studied and needs to be determined by an expert quantitative researcher.

Probability sampling is a requirement for all accurate and reliable quantitative studies. Probability sampling aims to identify a *representative* sample for the study – a sample that resembles the population from which it is drawn in ways that are important to the research problem. For instance, a sample of nurses used for a quantitative study must contain the same distribution of characteristics as the population of nurses as a whole, which is the population from which the sample was selected. Only by utilizing a representative sample can a company confidently generalize results from any study, including a segmentation study, to the whole population that is being targeted to use the product.

Pricing Study

- **Purpose:** Pricing a product is a critical decision for a company, and one of the most difficult to make. For publishers, it relates to the establishment of paywalls, subscription rates, and one-time purchases. A content product must be priced accurately to sell well. If a product is priced too low, the company may not be able to fund development costs or generate profit. If the product is priced too high, audiences will not purchase the product and revenues will be minimal, flatten, or decline. As a consequence, pricing research methods are an important contribution to quantitative marketing research. Since pricing research methods are widely used in a variety of industries, multiple approaches have been developed for understanding pricing. It is important for a company to determine which research approach best suits its product's needs.
- **Structure:** A research process called pricing optimization can help determine optimal pricing for a product. These processes range from faster and easier to complex and more accurate. A direct approach to pricing optimization is willingness to pay (WTP), which estimates an optimal price by asking consumers, once a full description of the product and its attributes have been provided, to provide a direct statement about what they are willing to pay for the product. Potential customers are asked, "What is the highest price you are willing to pay for this product?" There are several variations of this direct method.

Indirect pricing optimization methods, which are statistically more complex and provide more accurate results, include the Gabor-Granger model and the van Westendorp price sensitivity model (Lipovetsky, Magnan, & Polzi, 2011). Gabor-Granger relies on the use of a pre-determined set of prices that are randomly varied and presented to the research participant repeatedly in a specific pattern of higher/lower options. Ultimately, the highest price a consumer is willing to pay is determined.

Van Westendorp is a psychological price modeling method that correlates a customer's acceptable price with his perception of product quality. The pricing decision is determined by balancing price against perceived value, assuming there is a lower and upper limit to the price a consumer is willing to pay. The van Westendorp method is based on the assumption that an acceptable price exists for each segment of consumers and for each level of perceived value of the product.

Discrete choice methods offer a next, higher level of pricing optimization approaches. They are highly flexible and accurate because they attempt to replicate real-world market conditions. However, they are more complex and demanding than the Gabor-Granger or van Westendorp models, which are widely preferred for their usability and practicality (Lipovetsky, Magnan, & Polzi, 2011).

- **Sampling Information:** Sampling for pricing optimization studies uses criteria similar to those mentioned above for other types of quantitative research. A sufficient sample size for a pricing study will be based on the size of the market to be studied and needs to be determined by an expert quantitative researcher.

Throughout this discussion of quantitative methods, information about sampling has been an important topic. This is as true for pricing optimization studies as for other types of quantitative research. Quantitative research studies depend on wisely chosen, professionally recommended sampling techniques that are customized to meet the parameters of any given research study. A crucial understanding about the quality of quantitative studies, and their nature as "front-loaded" research, is the pithy saying, "garbage in, garbage out." If the sample employed in the study is not accurately defined and precisely obtained, all results of the research will be seriously compromised. Findings will be unreliable. They will not be generalizable to the population they are meant to describe.

Mathematical accuracy and reliability in quantitative research depends on random sampling. A random sample is one in which a portion (or sample) of a population is drawn so that each member of the population has an equal chance of being selected into the sample (Kerlinger, 1986). Any sample that provides accurate, reliable results needs to be highly descriptive and true of the actual population being studied. Without this precise replication of characteristics between the population as a whole and the sample chosen to represent that population, no research findings can be validly applied to the overall population.

All of this research can result in a large amount of data in various formats. Quantitative data often are stored in spreadsheets and survey tabulations; qualitative data in Word documents or PowerPoint presentations, as well as recordings of meetings and focus groups. To help promote sharing these data, teams can use such online tools as Microsoft SharePoint, especially if team members are not all located in the same office.

REAL-WORLD APPLICATIONS OF RESEARCH METHODS

The research methods described above can be used to address a multitude of important business decisions. Some content providers will utilize most or all of these approaches, plus others not discussed here. Most modify a "full-battery" approach to market research by tailoring research efforts to meet their own needs. Two frequent reasons to modify research efforts are company research budgets and time constraints. Two real-world examples are presented below as examples of what can be accomplished using variations of some of the research methodologies discussed above.

Example 1: Entering a New Market for an Information Product

Recently, an information company was considering whether to build a content website to serve an audience of clinicians in a new healthcare market with which the company was unfamiliar. The purpose of the website was to provide clinicians with reference information and electronic instruction. Historically, the firm's information products provided these tools to clinicians who required information related to acute-care patient needs only.

An important challenge for the company was to understand, through market research methods, the need for reference information and electronic instruction in non-acute-care settings. For instance, clinicians who care for patients in their homes do not have access to the same amount and type of medical equipment as their hospital-based colleagues. They also work in less-controlled environments and do not have immediate access to consultation with professional colleagues. The product team was aware of these general differences but needed a much deeper understanding of clinicians' specific requirements for reference information and electronic instruction in the non-acute-care setting as well as validation of the accuracy of such differences. The goal was to discover what content (such as skills information) and features (such as the ability to print more than one patient education handout at a time) were needed by clinicians in this new market. Ultimately, the company had to decide whether its research supported a substantial investment of effort, money, and talent to build this website and launch it into an exciting but unfamiliar market.

To understand the clinicians' needs, the firm used various marketing research approaches, including the following:

- **Initial Data Research:** The product team first decided to learn as much as possible about the non-acute-care setting by researching existing reports and general information about this market. They needed to understand such aspects as the size of the market, the general trends affecting it, companies serving the market, forecasts of growth, and other data. They consulted workforce data from the Bureau of Labor Statistics and market drivers from industry reports. They also studied demographic information and market size data by researching information from professional associations.
- **Initial Customer Research:** Besides the product team's efforts at conducting research, the company engaged an internal usability team to more fully understand day-to-day needs and workflows of these clinicians. This team specializes in researching customer needs and workflows and in designing a website's user interface and navigation. They accompanied the clinicians and watched them perform their daily work and noted the kinds of information required through their workday (*shadowing*). This team also conducted qualitative one-on-one in-person and telephone interviews to continue to build a detailed understanding of clinician needs. Based on the results of this research, the team obtained additional funding to build mockups and conduct a second round of this type of research.
- **Creation of Mockups:** In this second round of research, the usability team created product mockups, showed them to clinicians, analyzed the clinicians' reactions, and then modified the product design based on what the usability team learned. This helped ensure that the needs of the users informed the design process.
- **Deeper Data Analysis:** The product team commissioned an internal research department to unearth more information about the market. Using access to various healthcare databases, the research department discovered such information as revenues of the top healthcare organizations in this setting, cost per patient case segmented by geographic location (such as urban or rural), hourly mean wages, and more.
- **Advisory Board:** The product team created an advisory board of major thought leaders in the field, assembling a panel of six individuals who agreed to a one-year term as board members.

(One individual terminated her relationship before the one-year term expired.) Members agreed to participate in regular one-hour web meetings, advise on product strategy and provide insights into the profession. This feedback provided enormous help to further understand the overall direction of the market and how the proposed product would serve clinicians' needs.

- **Pricing Study:** An external consulting firm was engaged to conduct pricing research. As a result of using various approaches, including the van Westendorp methodology, the firm recommended a tiered pricing model for the product. After consulting with various internal stakeholders, the model was slightly modified to best fit the desired revenue goals and market segments of interest.

The online product was built in phases, with content and features added as development progressed. As each phase of the website product was completed, external users were asked to test various aspects of it for usability. For instance, users were challenged to find a specific piece of content and to report on this experience, indicating if they were successful or not. This "beta program" validated the results of market research and allowed the team to further refine the product design. Through user feedback, the beta program also uncovered ideas for enhancements that can be built in the future. The product was commercially launched into the market in October 2014.

Example 2: Determining the Appropriate Method for Providing a Mobile Version of the Product

In designing the above-mentioned product, the product, usability and programming teams had to decide on the approach for building a mobile version of the product, which would be crucial for success, as the users are an extremely mobile workforce. The approaches available included a downloadable app or a mobile website. An important difference between the two approaches was that a downloadable app would not require an Internet connection for users to obtain their information while a mobile website would.

From marketing research learnings, the product team had discovered that this audience would not have a reliable Internet connection at all times, for instance, when a user was serving a patient in a remote rural area. Thus, it was determined that a downloadable app would best meet the needs of potential users.

However, other real-world factors came into play. First, a downloadable app would be significantly more expensive to develop and this would put a strain on the product budget. Second, the app would take longer to build than a mobile website, and the product team needed to launch this product as quickly as possible. Third, far less maintenance would be required to maintain a single mobile website than apps built for multiple mobile operating systems, reducing ongoing maintenance and support costs.

Real-world constraints won out for the company's initial development decision. The product, usability and technical teams decided to develop a mobile website, which would meet the needs of a large percentage of the new market. Even though the company did not immediately invest in the downloadable app, which market research had determined would be the best option, their investment in research paid off. The technical team kept the market research results in mind, and they ultimately developed the mobile website in a way that could provide a basis for a future downloadable app. Because of the market research that was conducted, the company had increased confidence in the usefulness of their product for a large percentage of new customers, plus guidance for future product development.

CONCLUSION

Understanding and investing in a variety of appropriate research approaches helps to ensure that a content product team is basing decisions on sound information and analysis rather than instinct or "gut feel." The team has the assurance of knowing it has taken the necessary steps to understand audience needs as well as the best ways to meet those needs.

Also, well-conducted, appropriate market research can smooth the way for product funding. With fistfuls of market research findings in their hands, product team members can be much more confident of getting a resounding "yes" from management when they ask for financial investment in a new content product. The strong voice of research evidence speaks loudly to company decision-makers.

Groundbreaking product ideas are the "eureka" moments for which every publishing and digital media company searches. Market research can provide a critical foundation to ensure that an innovative product is as useful and profitable as it is original.

REFERENCES

Cooper, R. G. (2001). *Winning at new products: Accelerating the process from idea to launch* (3rd ed.). New York, NY: Basic Books.

Day, G. S. (1999). *Market driven strategy: processes for creating value*. New York, NY: The Free Press.

Denzin, N. K., & Lincoln, Y. S. (1994). *Handbook of qualitative research*. Thousand Oaks, CA: SAGE Publications, Inc.

Haselmaier, J. (n.d.).*Think you know how to meet customer needs?* Retrieved October 25, 2014, from http://www.pragmaticmarketing.com//resources/think-you-know-how-to-meet-customer-needs?p=0

Isaacson, W. (2011). *Steve Jobs*. New York, NY: Simon & Schuster.

Kerlinger, F. N. (1986). *Foundations of behavioral research* (3rd ed.). Orlando, FL: Holt, Rinehart and Winston, Inc.

Kunkel, T. (2001). Letters from the editor: The New Yorker's Harold Ross. New York: Modern Library.

Lipovetsky, S., Magnan, S., & Zanetti-Polzi, A. (2011). Pricing models in marketing research. *Intelligent Information Management*, *3*(5), 167–174. doi:10.4236/iim.2011.35020

Mishler, E. G. (1986). *Research interviewing: context and narrative*. Cambridge, MA: Harvard University Press.

Rubin, A., & Babbie, E. (1993). *Research methods for social work* (2nd ed.). Pacific Grove, CA: Brooks/Cole Publishing Company.

Taylor, S. J., & Bogdan, R. (1984). *Introduction to qualitative research methods: The search for meanings*. New York: John Wiley & Sons.

ADDITIONAL READING

Allred, K. (2010). How many data points do you really need? *The Pragmatic Marketer*, *8*(3), 20–22.

Cooper, R. G. (2001). *Winning at new products: Accelerating the process from idea to launch* (3rd ed.). New York, NY: Basic Books.

Day, G. S. (1990). *Market driven strategy: Processes for creating value*. New York, NY: The Free Press.

Isaacson, W. (2011). *Steve Jobs*. New York, NY: Simon & Schuster.

Krug, S. (2000). *Don't make me think*. Indianapolis, IN: New Riders Publishing.

Lashinsky, A. (2012). *Inside Apple: How America's most admired—and secretive—company really works*. New York, NY: Business Plus.

Nielsen, J. (2012). *Usability 101: Introduction to Usability*. Retrieved October 25, 2014, from http://www.nngroup.com/articles/usability-101-introduction-to-usability/

KEY TERMS AND DEFINITIONS

Back-Loaded: Back-loaded means that effort must be put in at the back of a study. For instance, at the back of a qualitative study, the analyst/interviewer spends days or weeks, depending on the sample size, combing through thc data gathered from participants.

Front-Loaded: Front-loaded denotes that much deliberation, design strategy, and intellectual effort go into developing the hypotheses, specific quantitative techniques, and wording of questions that make up a quantitative research tool.

Market Segmentation: Dividing a market into sections, or segments, according to characteristics that define each segment as distinct from another. All segments together constitute the product's entire market.

Qualitative Research: Qualitative research provides a foundational grounding about a subject that is relatively unknown or unexplored. It seeks a comprehensive, deep look at a subject to uncover all major topics about that subject that could influence the product's development or appeal. Qualitative research focuses on a subject with great depth and breadth.

Quantitative Research: Quantitative research establishes the extent to which a research problem is true or not true for the sample population being studied. Statistical analyses are used to determine if the observed differences between groups under study are statistically significant.

Shadowing: Researchers embed themselves in the environment of research subjects. Shadowing is sometimes mistakenly referred to as ethnography.

Usability: The art and science of understanding how people interact with machines. Usability techniques ensure that users can easily navigate websites to find the information they need or accomplish the tasks required.

Chapter 10
Research Methodologies, Data Collection, and Analysis at MailChimp:
A Case Study

Gregg Bernstein
MailChimp, USA

Laurissa Wolfram-Hvass
MailChimp, USA

ABSTRACT

Research plays a crucial role in understanding and improving the user experience. In this case study, members of software company MailChimp's Research team explain the company's data collection, analysis, and communication methodologies. Using methods that include customer interviews, big data, reports, and short films, the team moves through the research process, beginning with research questions and concluding with actionable insights.

INTRODUCTION

MailChimp develops a web application that allows users to create, send, and track email newsletters (see Figure 1). Many different industries use MailChimp's email platform to communicate to their particular audiences in a variety of ways: e-commerce and retail stores send messages promoting products or sales; non-profit organizations spread awareness of their causes; artists showcase their work; authors share their words; and entertainers promote their events. Though most often thought of as a marketing tool, MailChimp—at its most basic description—is a publishing platform from which its users can write and distribute information online.

DOI: 10.4018/978-1-4666-8580-2.ch010

Figure 1. MailChimp is an online service that allows customers to design, send, and track emails (©2013, MailChimp. Used with permission).

With millions of customers using MailChimp to share information, sell products, promote events, and more, knowing who these users are—and why and how they use MailChimp—is paramount. The MailChimp Research team plays a crucial role in gathering and sharing information that will help the company understand and improve the MailChimp user experience. Though this chapter focuses on software in general and MailChimp in detail, the methodologies and practices described herein apply to other industries and information services.

THE MAILCHIMP RESEARCH TEAM

The Research team at MailChimp is tasked with both synthesizing customer needs with the overarching goals of the company and then sharing those research findings among the company's various teams. The work of the Research team informs product design, feature development, support offerings, marketing materials, and more. Though each project the Research team undertakes is unique—varying in focus, scope, and duration—the team has whittled their toolbox of research methodologies down to a workable few, which the authors describe in this case study.

The MailChimp Research team consists of five generalists, with backgrounds in design, computer science, rhetoric, neuroscience, and account management. Due to their diverse backgrounds, each researcher has a unique set of skills they can apply to any research project, such as interviewing

MailChimp customers, conducting usability tests of new MailChimp features, or analyzing data from research surveys or site analytics.

The Research team works closely with the MailChimp designers and developers, who, in turn, work directly with engineers and quality assurance (QA) testers to create and maintain the MailChimp app. For each product update, these groups work together to plan, design, code, test, and release software. While some of the items in a release are iterations on previous features, others are new or wholly revised parts of the app that stem from a combination of company goals and customer needs.

RESEARCH METHODS

Each year, MailChimp's directors announce several broad themes for the company to focus its energies on—such as "Mobile," "Automation," or "International." These themes are kept intentionally broad, so that each team within the organization can interpret and tackle them as they see fit. Designers and developers, for example might build new tools or features that address those themes; the Knowledge Base team might expand their support documents to include more information on those tools; the marketing team might focus on how to talk about the year's themes with current and prospective customers. Much of the work conducted throughout the year can be directly tied to one of the year's themes.

The MailChimp Research team relies on these themes to guide research projects and maintain focus throughout the year. For instance, when Mobile was one of the company's annual themes, the Research team made mobile usage and behavior a focus or underlying topic in their research projects. They surveyed customers who use the MailChimp mobile apps, included mobile-related questions in customer interviews, and gathered information on the different apps customers rely on to conduct business throughout their day.

This chapter uses case study examples from MailChimp's research workflow to explain and describe research methods for collecting, analyzing, and reporting on results.

Stakeholder Discussions

At the beginning of each new project, it is crucial for researchers to align their goals with the objectives and expectations of stakeholders—the people who influence the company's direction. Therefore, the first step in the MailChimp research process is a stakeholder interview. The Research team meets regularly with the company's CEO and directors, forgoing a formal stakeholder interview in favor of a more relaxed, yet in-depth, conversation. Since most projects span multiple teams and departments, the Research team often meets next with other stakeholders, like the head of Engineering, manager of Client Relations or director of Marketing.

No matter the format of the stakeholder interview—a formal meeting, a hallway conversation, a quick email—this exchange provides the Research team with two bits of important information: context and exigency. Context helps create a proper background for a research project and makes sure everyone understands the objectives and expectations. Questions, such as these, can help researchers clearly define the kind of work they need to accomplish:

- Why are we studying mobile usage (or international customers or list management)?
- What does 'mobile' (or 'international' or 'list management') mean to you?
- What decisions are you hoping to make, based on this research?

Exigency, on the other hand, is the urgency or demand for something, which a researcher needs to know when prioritizing projects and setting schedules. This can be uncovered through asking questions, such as:

- Why now?
- What inspired this goal?
- What is the deadline for this project?
- Who is waiting on this information to make a decision?

The answers to this line of questioning influence not only the goals the Researchers set for themselves, but the research methods they use and the pace of their work.

As discussed by Sharon (2012) and Hall (2013), stakeholder interviews—and the discussions that follow—can expose preconceived ideas or assumptions, placing everyone involved in the research and design on common ground with shared expectations. For instance, the MailChimp CEO might ask the company to build more tools for "international customers" and enlist the Research team to help explore what international customers might need and what those tools should look like. However, what if the CEO thinks of "international" as "customers living and conducting business *outside* of the United States," while the researchers interpret "international" to mean "customers—both inside *and* outside the United States—who do business with people all over the world?" These are two very different groups of people—with different business models, different goals, and different needs. By discussing what "international" means to the CEO and the researchers, all parties are able to align their goals and streamline their efforts.

This initial conversation also creates an open line of communication between the researchers and company stakeholders throughout a project's life cycle. As MailChimp moves forward with projects, researchers meet regularly with stakeholders, designers, and developers to discuss progress and share preliminary results. Similar to the first stakeholder meetings, these periodic check-ins give everyone a chance to ask questions and share ideas or to adjust priorities and refocus efforts, if necessary.

Secondary Research Sources

Research sources fit into two broad categories: primary and secondary. Primary sources (which are discussed later in the chapter) are made up of any original research, first-hand research, or raw data. A secondary source is usually a document or some other published material that analyzes, interprets, or makes meaning of primary sources (see Table 1 for examples of each source type).

Researchers at MailChimp often start with secondary research, using what is already available to quickly gather information about a broad topic. They search through any available, relevant materials—from reports previously written at MailChimp or in academic journals to census data, news reports, and even blog posts—to uncover answers. Generally, drawing from secondary research is less labor intensive and more cost effective than conducting primary research.

Table 1. Examples of primary and secondary research materials

Primary Research	Secondary Research
Surveys	Census Data
Interviews	Published Papers
Case Studies	News Reports
Usability Tests	Competitor Websites and Documentation
Analytics	Past MailChimp Reports

By beginning with secondary sources, MailChimp researchers ensure they do not waste time repeating work and searching for answers that are already available.

Filtering through existing research can often narrow the scope of research projects. For example, with a new Mobile-focused initiative, the MailChimp team might filter through existing industry research to broaden their understanding of the mobile landscape beyond those who use the MailChimp app. The Pew Research Center, for instance, provides data surrounding trending topics like mobile device usage among different demographics. The consulting firm Nielsen Norman Group also conducts and publishes expansive research in the field of User Experience.

MailChimp researchers also closely watch the competitive landscape of email service providers to learn about product offerings. As noted by Hall (2013), "You need to know not only who your competitors are from the perspective of the business (that's generally obvious) but who competes for attention in the minds of your target users" (p. 95). In some cases, the Research team might methodically examine each feature a competitor offers compared to its MailChimp analog. This allows researchers an opportunity to spot opportunities for differentiation. They also track the nomenclature MailChimp competitors use to describe feature and actions, which helps the Research team ask questions and discuss ideas with the appropriate language as they engage in future research.

While secondary research can answer broad questions, like "What is currently the most widely used mobile device?" or "Who is more likely to use mobile devices—teenagers or business professionals?", it usually cannot answer more specific questions, such as "Why do customers visit MailChimp on a tablet?" or "Do MailChimp customers use a tablet or a laptop computer to accomplish different goals?" For questions such as these, existing research only serves as a starting point and provides the opportunity to identify gaps in the researchers' knowledge about the mobile landscape.

Primary Research Sources

Primary sources are products of original and self- (or organizationally-) generated research, such as surveys, customer support tickets, interviews, usability tests, and website analytics. Primary research is more time consuming than secondary, because the research is originally designed, collected, analyzed, and reported. The payoff, though, can be exponentially more valuable than secondary data, because it is specifically focused on MailChimp's goals and needs. The following sections describe the research methods MailChimp uses to collect primary data.

Web Analytics

A quick and easy way to answer basic questions, such as "How many people visit the MailChimp app?", "What time of day or day of the week receives the most traffic?", or "How many people use a specific MailChimp tool or feature?" is through web analytics. Services like Google Analytics and KissMetrics, among others, allow someone to not only count visits to their website, but also to discover information about who is visiting, how often, where they come from, and where their journey through the site took them. Depending on the particular analytics platform, the granularity of data ranges from identifying cohorts of users to specific individuals. By pairing web analytics with qualitative research tools (like usability tests or interviews), researchers can construct a more complete picture of their customers' interactions with their product (Kaushik, 2010, p. 170). MailChimp, for example, uses analytics to answer questions like "What are people doing?", while qualitative research answers questions like "Why are people doing those things?"

The MailChimp Research team leans on Google Analytics for this type of data (see Figure 2). It allows them to see the sequence of pages customers typically visit as they move from one part of the website to another, which buttons they click to get there, and what time of day all of this happens. Google Analytics does not inform researchers about who specifically does any of this, but it does help uncover patterns across a broad audience of users. For instance, a researcher might see that the iPad is the dominant tablet among mobile MailChimp users, and iPad use spikes in the morning and evening hours. Google Analytics also tracks the specific pathways the general iPad-using audience navigates through the MailChimp app.

Figure 2. Measuring pathways through MailChimp in Google Analytics

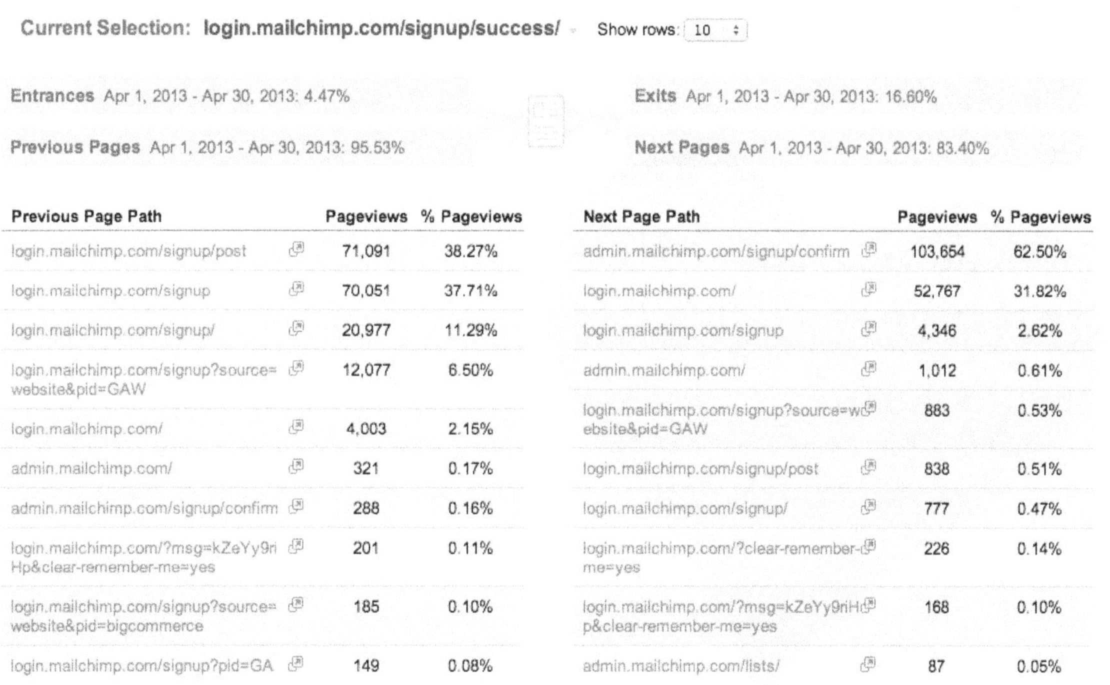
Current Selection: login.mailchimp.com/signup/success/ Show rows: 10

Entrances Apr 1, 2013 - Apr 30, 2013: 4.47%

Previous Pages Apr 1, 2013 - Apr 30, 2013: 95.53%

Exits Apr 1, 2013 - Apr 30, 2013: 16.60%

Next Pages Apr 1, 2013 - Apr 30, 2013: 83.40%

Previous Page Path	Pageviews	% Pageviews
login.mailchimp.com/signup/post	71,091	38.27%
login.mailchimp.com/signup	70,051	37.71%
login.mailchimp.com/signup/	20,977	11.29%
login.mailchimp.com/signup?source=website&pid=GAW	12,077	6.50%
login.mailchimp.com/	4,003	2.15%
admin.mailchimp.com/	321	0.17%
admin.mailchimp.com/signup/confirm	288	0.16%
login.mailchimp.com/?msg=kZeYy9riHp&clear-remember-me=yes	201	0.11%
login.mailchimp.com/signup?source=website&pid=bigcommerce	185	0.10%
login.mailchimp.com/signup?pid=GA	149	0.08%

Next Page Path	Pageviews	% Pageviews
admin.mailchimp.com/signup/confirm	103,654	62.50%
login.mailchimp.com/	52,767	31.82%
login.mailchimp.com/signup	4,346	2.62%
admin.mailchimp.com/	1,012	0.61%
login.mailchimp.com/signup?source=website&pid=GAW	883	0.53%
login.mailchimp.com/signup/post	838	0.51%
login.mailchimp.com/signup/	777	0.47%
login.mailchimp.com/?clear-remember-me=yes	226	0.14%
login.mailchimp.com/?msg=kZeYy9riHp&clear-remember-me=yes	168	0.10%
admin.mailchimp.com/lists/	87	0.05%

If the Research team wants to get data on an atomic, individual level, they could use a tool like MixPanel. This would allow them to see what a specific individual did on the MailChimp website, and—if that person is a customer—associate a name and email address with that person. This type of web analytics package is geared more toward customer acquisition and development. For the MailChimp Research team's purposes, the anonymous data of Google Analytics is sufficient.

Surveys

The easiest way to answer a question is to simply ask, and an easy way to ask is through an online survey (see Figure 3). According to Goodman, Kuniavsky, and Moed (2012),

Qualitative techniques such as interviews, think-aloud usability tests, and observational research give you insight into why people do the things they do when using your product and how some people use your product, but they can't accurately tell you the prevalence of characteristics and tendencies in user population. (p. 327)

Surveys, however, can, and MailChimp uses them extensively to target a specific audience (paid versus free customers, mobile users, people who use a particular MailChimp feature, people in Pittsburgh, etc.) and tailor questions that are relevant to them.

In order to learn more about the mobile landscape among MailChimp customers, for example, the Research team can isolate the customers they know use MailChimp mobile apps and send

Figure 3. MailChimp uses SurveyMonkey to send out surveys to specific groups of customers

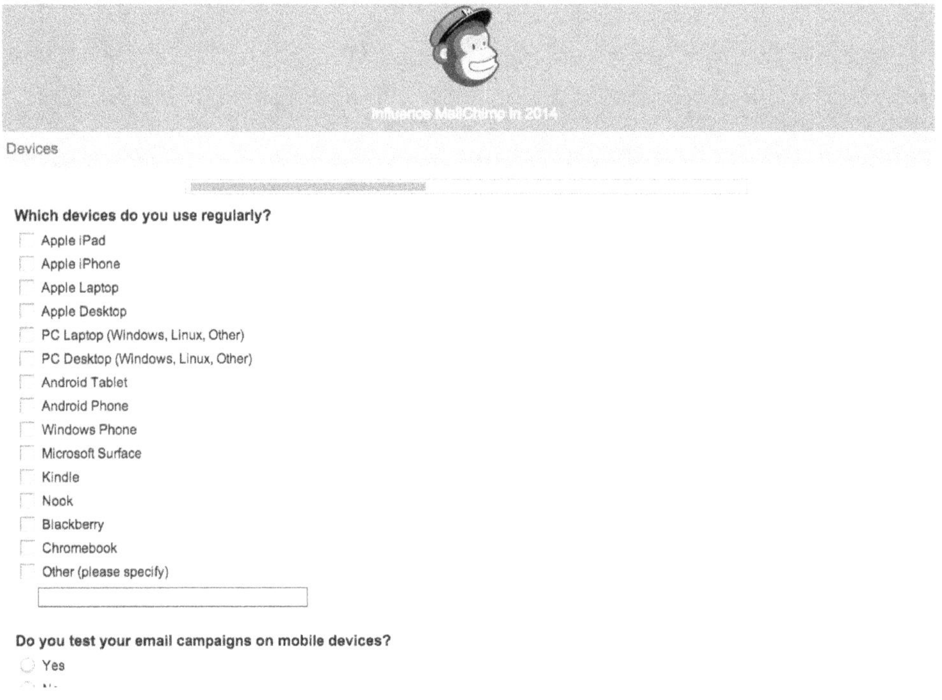

them an email requesting they take a survey. The survey might ask questions that provide context and depth—"Do you sell things online?" or "How old is your company?" It might also ask what email tools customers used before switching to MailChimp or what other apps they use in the course of a day. These questions lend clarity to the Research team's understanding of what MailChimp customers are doing.

Once the researchers receive enough answers to the survey, they match survey data to information in MailChimp's customer database, such as email list size, monthly payment amount, or industry. This provides additional dimensions to the survey data set. For instance, by combining customer information with survey responses, the Research team can specifically look at responses from paying customers who work in e-commerce. From there, they can mine the survey responses to see how that group of customers answered certain questions.

Customer Interviews

The MailChimp Research team uses survey responses to identify interview subjects. As they comb through survey data, they tag any interesting or puzzling answers as potential interview subjects. They then email these respondents to set up an interview over Skype or GoToMeeting.

According to Portigal (2013), customer interviews are essential to establishing the context in which customers work and live. By asking people, for example, about morning routines, commuting habits, and specific work-day scenarios, the MailChimp Research team enriches already-captured data from surveys or web analytics. Through the course of a conversation, a researcher may learn that many people use the train or bus commute home after the workday has ended to respond to emails on their mobile devices. This provides the opportunity for researchers to ask, "Why do you continue to work after you leave the office?" These conversations can uncover insight—mobile users are trying to recapture lost time—that would be impossible to identify from surveys responses or secondary data sources.

Repeating surveys and interviews over time allows for patterns to surface and theories to become fact. These patterns can then, in turn, be shared with designers and developers, who can use that information to inform and influence the tools or services they create for customers.

Contextual Interviews

Going further, MailChimp researchers use surveys to identify customers to visit. The Research team travels throughout the United States and abroad to visit customers and conduct in-person interviews. These are similar to the previously mentioned remote interviews, but being on-site provides contextual clues that, again, are impossible to glean otherwise.

Hall (2013) explains that spending a couple of hours with a customer provides the perfect opportunity to gather valuable clues and insights. On these visits, MailChimp researchers can gain a deeper understanding of the company culture, context, and environment in which users work. They get to see if someone works in a quiet office or at a front desk with constant interruptions. They observe if the computers in use are cutting edge or relics from another age. The décor of the cubicles, the volume of the office conversations, and the seating arrangements all provide rich data that fleshes out a researcher's view of the customers.

Usability Testing

As MailChimp designs, develops, and refines its software, it becomes necessary for them to work out unforeseen bugs and pain points through testing. This process can be as casual as asking a coworker to try things out or as formal as recruiting participants, scripting testing scenarios, observing as people move through the test, and timing and logging the results. No matter how spontaneous or formal, these tests can help pinpoint successes and failures of the software in a controlled environment.

Typically, the Research team at MailChimp relies on remote usability testing, rather than conducting tests in a formal lab or in the field. Bolt and Tulathimutte (2010) hold that remote testing is particularly useful for ensuring geographic diversity of participants. Because MailChimp customers are located across the world, remote testing allows the Research team to conduct tests from a pool of participants that most accurately represents their global customer base.

Remote testing can be done either unmoderated or moderated, and MailChimp finds both methods very valuable. With moderated testing, a researcher—or moderator—is present throughout the entire test—taking notes, prompting the testing participant, and perhaps asking questions at the conclusion of the session. For these types of tests, MailChimp typically uses services like Skype or GoToMeeting and records the users screen during the session. The moderator will send the participant a testing script, which will guide the participant through the session. These scripts might be very short and open-ended—with relatively little detail given—other than a simple objective, such as "Log into MailChimp, using the credentials we've given you, and send a test email" or "Add this list of subscriber names and emails to the MailChimp account we've given you." Or, the scripts might be longer, with specific scenarios (see Figure 4). Although the moderator's main objective is simply to observe and take notes during the test, he or she might occasionally prompt participants to share what is on their minds during the test through questions like, "What are you looking for right now?" or "Could you help me understand why you chose that particular option?"

For unmoderated tests, MailChimp uses a service called UserTesting.com that manages most of the testing process through its website. MailChimp is responsible for providing any materials needed for the test, like the testing script, account login details, and any other instructions, while UserTesting.com is responsible for everything else. UserTesting.com staff recruit testers from among their participant base and set up the test. Test participants complete the test using their own computers and allow UserTesting.com to record their screens and voices as they move through the test. Once the test is complete, UserTesting.com sends the recorded audio and video to MailChimp to analyze.

Both moderated and unmoderated tests allow researchers to observe first-hand how someone uses their product, step by step. They identify sections of the app that are confusing or misleading and, in the case of moderated tests, they delve into *why* certain sections might have been difficult. As researchers conduct more tests, they are able to spot common pain points or determine if a design appears to be successful.

Figure 4. Usability test scripts describe any scenarios the tester should place themselves in during the test, along with the objectives or goals they are to accomplish during the test.

Automation Usability Test Scenario 2

Scenario

You are the Marketing and Communications Manager for a clothing store that sells in their retail space and on their websites. You'd like to reward your mailing list subscribers with a 15% off coupon every year for their birthday.

You already have a mailing list set up with the following information:

- First name
- Last name
- Mailing address
- Customer ID
- Birthday
- Sign up date
- Clothing preference (Women, Men, Children)

Session Objective

Using MailChimp's Automation, set up an email that will go out to your subscribers 2 weeks before their birthday.

Please work through this task as you normally would at home or in your office, and use any resources you normally would (like Google or help articles) to help you along.

Also, please try to "think aloud" as you complete this task. Explain to me what's going on in your head as you work, explain the reasons behind your decisions, describe the problems you're running into, and voice any feedback or confusion you may have. I might prompt you occasionally and ask you to describe what you're thinking.

And remember: *You* are not the one being tested here; MailChimp is. You can't make any mistakes or do anything wrong.

Customer Feedback Loops

With surveys, interviews, case studies, and usability testing, the MailChimp Researchers seek customer feedback and data. They actively craft questions around particular goals and identify customer groups to contact. Conversely, data from customer support channels, social media, and email trickles in without prompting from the Research team. As customers work with the MailChimp app, they provide opinions, suggestions, and commentary through these different feedback loops, and their input shapes MailChimp's next steps. By paying attention to the voice of the customer, the Research team can quickly understand which particular customer groups face certain issues. This allows the company to rapidly iterate and refine the app for the user experience—or just note common complaints as something to keep an eye on for future exploration.

Big Data Analysis

The data that MailChimp researchers study is often limited to that which is captured via surveys, interviews, and other qualitative methodologies. To determine significance and to better understand the accuracy of this data, the Research team works closely with the company's Data Science team, who can parse larger data sets into actionable insights. According to Shron (2014), data can do things such as identify patterns, determine relationships, and gather support for decisions. By collaborating with data scientists, MailChimp researchers are able to join their qualitative findings with quantitative data—from web analytics or the MailChimp database—and create a more complete picture of a problem or scenario.

While the Research team focuses on small clusters of customers, the data scientists work at scale, measuring, and tracking statistics across millions of MailChimp customers. Their collection of data allows the researchers to compare observed behaviors to actions across the entire MailChimp app. The data scientists' quantitative analytical skills are particularly valuable when they are able to change customer demographics into projections ("At this rate, we'll have twice as many customers in Pittsburgh by 2004."), feature usage into forecasts ("Our iPad app is only going to become more popular."), and financial data into risk assessments ("Expanding our marketing to Antarctica isn't going to generate much revenue for us.").

Putting It All Together

MailChimp's Research team cycles through all of these research methods throughout the year. Much like how a carpenter selects a specific set of tools for every task, researchers carefully select the methods that are most useful for each individual project, based on project goals, currently available data, deadlines, resources, or other limitations.

Some projects, like sign-up form completion, might start with a study of Google Analytics data, which can tell researchers at what page or step in the signup process large numbers of people are abandoning the process. At that point, researchers might conduct a usability test of the signup process, paying careful attention to the page they identified as problematic through Google Analytics. The usability test and conversations with the test participants can uncover specific issues with the page—like confusing instructions or validation errors.

Other projects, like understanding new features the company should build for customers who sell products or services online, may follow a very different research process. The Research team might first start by reviewing feedback they have collected from past interviews, support tickets, or feedback forms. From there, they might design a survey, sent directly to the customers who use email to sell products online. Based on the survey responses, they might contact several of those customers for more in-depth interviews.

CONNECTEDNESS

All of the data collected by the Research team has potential to inform the work of other teams throughout the company. The Marketing team might consider how customers talk about their work and MailChimp and use that to communicate better with current and potential customers; the designers refine (or, in some cases, redesign) the app's appearance based on customer needs; developers and engineers use research to build new tools to help customers work more efficiently.

To facilitate this process, the Research team feeds all of their findings into a shared Evernote account that functions as a central research database. They use Evernote to store, add to, search for, and peruse company-wide data. Each week the Research team funnels MailChimp site analytics reports, app feature usage statistics, interview transcripts, development features, survey data, customer emails, social media responses, testing videos, and more into the account.

Although there are more sophisticated research storage systems available, a tool like Evernote makes it fairly simple for anyone in the company to access and contribute data.

Making the data accessible to all inspires a sense of autonomy and empowerment—anyone can research anything. Those initial questions at the start of a new project, like "What do we know about how customers use our segmentation feature?" or "What's happening with mobile?" might easily be answered by a quick search through the information researchers have already collected. As the Research team adds more information and data to Evernote, they increase the collective body of knowledge, which accelerates their own research process.

While the MailChimp Research team is dedicated to gathering, analyzing, and sharing user insights, many teams in the company contribute to these efforts. Successful customer research is the product of a company united in its efforts to learning about and designing for the user. So while research is the sole objective of the Research team, research is not limited to that one team. Many MailChimp teams possess valuable customer insight: the Support team analyzes customer tickets, engineers have access to information about feature use, Marketing brand managers talk frequently to customers within their business verticals, and data scientists make meaning out of big data from the app's database. In his article "Seeing the Elephant: Defragmenting User Research," Rosenfeld (2013) encourages companies to consolidate customer insights from all of their teams, in order to create a more accurate and complete picture of their customers' experiences with their products. Through collaborative tools like Evernote and maintaining open lines of communication between departments, MailChimp strives to keep customer research circulating and readily available throughout the company.

Sharing and Analysis

While understanding users is important, that is only one part of the research process. The job of the Research team does not end after the final survey response has been submitted, the audio recorder has been turned off, or the last usability test has ended. User research—no matter how methodologically sound, relevant, or interesting—is essentially worthless if it is not used to improve a company's products or services. One of the most important parts of a researcher's job is making sure their research findings reach the people who make decisions about products and services. This means translating findings into actionable insights and sharing them with executives, team leads, designers, developers, marketers, writers, and support staff—anyone involved in constructing and influencing users' experiences.

A research project might generate pages of notes, hours of audio or video, and massive spreadsheets filled with data. In those forms, all of that information is not particularly useful. A researcher *could* just consolidate all of her notes and spreadsheets, package up the audio or video files, and send them to designers, developers, and stakeholders—but there is a good chance that information would be overwhelming, and it would just sit there, untouched. Products would never improve. Instead, the goal of the researcher is to take all of that data, analyze it, generate meaning from it, and then communicate it with colleagues in a way that is meaningful to them.

Creating research deliverables without keeping colleagues specifically in mind is like trying to design for users without knowing anything about them. At MailChimp, the Research team spends a lot of time talking to and getting to know colleagues on other teams. This helps researchers discover several things:

- The projects different teams are working on (which could benefit from ongoing research).
- What information is most important to which team?
- What are the team's goals?
- What information do teams already have (and would therefore be redundant)?
- What communication styles appeal to them?
- What learning styles are most effective for them?

For the MailChimp researchers, one of their biggest challenges is finding the most effective way to share information among several hundred people and across several different teams. They experiment frequently with different formats for sharing research and pay close attention to how colleagues receive and respond to that information.

Reports

The traditional, printed research report is the most familiar method for sharing findings and insights, but it is often not very effective. Reports tend to be densely packed with potentially valuable information, but they usually require more time to read (and write) than most people are willing to spend. At MailChimp, reports are usually read by just a fraction of the company; they're first shared with leads, who then might pass them along to someone on their team if the research relates directly to a current project.

Reports are most effective when kept short (five to ten pages), which doesn't demand much from readers. For the sake of consistency and organization, MailChimp research reports take on a formal structure, with typical sections like Introduction, Executive Summary, Methods, Conclusions, etc., but researchers use clear, plain language (and, at times, even humor), which makes reports easier to read and digest. Researchers also include visuals in their reports as much as possible—charts and graphs can communicate numbers and comparisons more clearly and quickly than paragraphs of text and numbers. Rather than printing and passing around copies of reports, researchers write and share them in Google Drive, which allows researchers to draft and edit collaboratively. Google drive can also facilitate discussion among colleagues and teams after a report is shared, via its commenting features.

Posters

Reports do not appeal to everyone, though, so the Research team has experimented with communication forms that are more visually interesting to keep research engaging and accessible. Posters are a way to summarize and present high-level information that people can absorb and digest at a glance. In 2013, the MailChimp Research team conducted extensive research to develop five different personas that represent five of MailChimp's primary user groups (see Figure 5). They created a poster for each persona and hung them near the company espresso machine, where colleagues gather on a regular basis.

These posters only scratched the surface of the team's research, but the team's intentions for the posters were not to communicate *all* the research they had on personas. Instead, the goal was just to create something that would introduce the company to the personas, spark company-wide interest, and make them curious to learn more. This proved to be very effective; the posters

Figure 5. User personas rendered as printed posters that were displayed around the MailChimp office (©2013, MailChimp. Used with permission).

prompted conversations, questions, and ideas. The company began thinking of customers in new ways, and that changed the way they worked: the Marketing team brainstormed how they could reach out to different types of customers, the Quality Assurance team began structuring their testing differently, and the Support team began categorizing and talking about customer issues in new ways.

Coffee Hour Talks

On Friday mornings, MailChimp holds a company-wide Coffee Hour. These events might feature someone from the company or outside guests who come in and speak about everything from their personal creative process or charity work to information security, nutrition, or design. Several times a year, the MailChimp Research team takes the floor for an hour and presents a summary of research from the past few months (see Figure 6). These talks tend to focus on things that affect the entire company, such as broad customer trends and patterns.

During one Coffee Hour, for example, the Research team summarized research findings from an annual survey of over 18,000 users. Survey data focuses primarily on numbers and percentages, which can become tiring for an audience after a while. Rather than present slide after slide of statistics, the Research team contextualized survey results within specific use-cases from customers they had spoken with or visited in the past year.

Information from Coffee Hours is usually available to colleagues in other places, like in a Google Drive report or in MailChimp's Evernote research database. The in-person presentation, though, is often more dynamic and engaging than a report—and more likely to reach a wider audience of colleagues.

Figure 6. Presenting research at a Coffee Hour
(©2013, MailChimp. Used with permission).

Usability Lunches

MailChimp designers and developers are very user-conscious and open to the insights the Research team shares with them, but nothing fosters a deeper sense of empathy and motivates action more than watching someone struggle with the MailChimp app. As often as possible, the Research team hosts usability lunches and invites a small group of colleagues to join them. Everyone gathers in a large room and enjoys a catered lunch, while the researchers project the testing participant's computer screen onto the wall. A facilitator runs the test, while everyone else looks on, pausing periodically for questions.

Running a usability test in front of a live audience is not the typical way of doing things, and many people may not be comfortable participating in this type of setting. However, once potential participants realize it is the MailChimp app being tested, not them, recruiting becomes less difficult.

Everyone at MailChimp learns a great deal from these hour-long lunches, and at their conclusions the room is usually buzzing with conversations about the issues encountered and how various teams could quickly address them. The lunches have been so helpful that developers have asked if the Research team could conduct them more often.

Internal Research Newsletters

Every month or so, the Research team uses the MailChimp app to send out an internal newsletter to the company, summarizing some of their current research. These newsletters are very short (only about a page or two long) and are a collection of insightful stats on a very specific topic, such as international growth rates, integrations usage, or certain customer behaviors. Researchers pair the numbers with a brief explanation or analysis and often try to compare them to other research conducted previously. The researchers also encourage other departments to use this as a channel for research or insights they have gathered. The end of the newsletter usually features a link or directions to where readers can go if they would like to learn more.

Case Study Research Videos

The Research team learns so much from visiting customers, chatting with them, and observing as they conduct business. It is important that the rest of MailChimp is able to also catch a glimpse of its customers in this setting. With customers' permission, MailChimp researchers interview and film customers and their workspaces. They ask customers questions about how their businesses function, how they communicate to customers, and how MailChimp fits into their workflows. After returning home, the Research team filters through the recorded media for salient points, edits it down to the core story, and creates short documentaries that they can share with colleagues.

Videos capture people's attentions and communicate a message with greater impact than a written report. They introduce MailChimp employees to their customers and help develop a sense of empathy toward them. With videos, the idea of a customer shifts from descriptions on a page to living, breathing human beings with unique stories, business goals, and challenges.

Because each mini-documentary is focused on just one customer, these videos are effective supplements to other communication forms, like reports or presentations. Videos provide additional context to quantitative data by attaching faces or specific use cases to broad patterns and trends.

Internal Research Websites

The Research team has experimented with creating internal web-based reports for sharing and for making research more interactive. With the help of the MailChimp Design team, the Research team has the goal of creating digital reports with a narrative format that are information-rich, visually interesting, and engaging. Since these reports contain user information and internal company research, the team keeps the data secure by restricting IP access to only the MailChimp office.

While the standard printed report primarily communicates information in a static, linear format, online reports can take advantage of the affordances the digital medium has to offer. Digital formats allow researchers to easily use a mix of images, videos, and text. The researchers are free to use an abundance of images (without worry about page count or the expense of ink) or embed clips of customer interview videos. They can pair charts and graphics that visually display quantitative data with long-form written analyses. They might also play with text color, size, typeface, and arrangement to reinforce organization and hierarchy or to emphasize important information. The Research team's ultimate goal with these kinds of reports is to present research findings that are not only informative but also a pleasure to read.

Though the MailChimp research sites are not quite as detailed, the authors of this chapter list several sites that have served as inspirations for this project in the Research Websites section at the conclusion of the chapter.

Research Evangelists

An unspoken part of a researcher's job at MailChimp is just "being around" and promoting research whenever he or she can. The Research team is open to serendipitous moments around the office when they can contribute tidbits of research to a conversation they are a part of. This does not mean monopolizing conversations and droning on and on about a current study—it just means being aware of when research might inform the work of others.

MailChimp tries to keep the organizational walls between teams low, so ideas can move and flow freely throughout the company. Researchers play an important part in making that happen. By working across the many different groups at the company, researchers can see how the work of one team might impact another. When talking to colleagues, researchers are in a strategic position to serve as diplomats, bridging gaps and making connections among different teams.

Multi-Channel Communication

There is no perfect communication method. Each of the channels the MailChimp Research team uses serves a different purpose:

- Posters provide a snapshot—a small collection of information that can be understood and digested quickly—but by nature, posters cannot offer deep understanding.
- Mini-documentaries develop a stronger sense of empathy by giving the company a glimpse into customers' everyday lives, and they allow the company to hear customers describe their MailChimp experiences in their own words. Videos can be watched anytime, paused, and replayed.
- Coffee Hours and Usability Lunches are dynamic, interactive, and can provide a forum for answering questions and exchanging ideas.
- Reports are rich with detail, and they are read and digested slowly. However, many people do not want to take the time to read them.
- Internal newsletters provide a brief snapshot of a certain issue or area of research. They are not very in-depth, but they can be gleaned quickly for information.

All of these communication forms have their place, and the MailChimp Research team is learning that the best way to reach all of their colleagues is to repeat information in different ways through several of these different channels.

The Research team wants to spark conversation, get people interested, and inspire curiosity about the people who use their company's services and how they can create better products for them. Ultimately, the goal is to empower colleagues with information so they can make better decisions about their work.

CONCLUSION

The act of making better design and development decisions brings this chapter full circle—to the need for research in the first place. Simple questions beget further questions and complex answers that end up influencing the direction of a company. At first, the process of continuously questioning and seeking answers is exhaustive, as is the act of delivering findings.

A big part of researching the user and product experience is simply determining both what is valuable and what is effective in that organization—the lay of the land, so to speak. Researchers should be able to turn the mirror of analysis back on themselves and their companies to understand what their collective needs are, so they can tailor research accordingly. Until that time, everyone in the organization is flying blind.

The more the research process repeats, the more data and insight accumulate, and the more researchers can experiment with sharing findings. Over time, both process and patterns emerge, and it becomes easier to align a type of problem to the best possible research methodology and communication channel. The cycles required to answer research questions shorten because so much data has accumulated from previous projects.

REFERENCES

Bolt, N., & Tulathimutte, T. (2010). *Remote research*. Brooklyn, New York: Rosenfeld Media.

Goodman, I., Kuniavsky, M., & Moed, A. (2012). *Observing the user experience*. Burlington, Massachusetts: Morgan Kaufmann.

Hall, E. (2013). *Just enough research*. New York: A Book Apart.

Kaushik, A. (2010). *Web analytics 2.0*. Indianapolis, IN: Wiley Publishing.

Portigal, S. (2013). *Interviewing users*. Brooklyn, NY: Rosenfeld Media.

Rosenfeld, L. (2013). Seeing the elephant: Defragmenting user research. *A List Apart*. Retrieved July 24, 2014, from http://alistapart.com/article/seeing-the-elephant-defragmenting-user-research

Sharon, T. (2012). *It's our research*. Burlington, MA: Morgan Kaufmann.

Shron, M. (2014). *Thinking with data*. Sebastopol, CA: O'Reilly Media.

RESEARCH WEBSITES

Battan, C. (2013). Janelle Monae. *Pitchfork Magazine*. Retrieved July 17, 2014, from http://pitchfork.com/features/cover-story/reader/janelle-monae/

Himmelman, J. (2013). A game of shark and minnow. *The New York Times Magazine*. Retrieved July 17, 2014, from http://www.nytimes.com/newsgraphics/2013/10/27/south-china-sea/

Ikea. (2014). Life at home. *Ikea*. Retrieved July 17, 2014, from http://lifeathome.ikea.com/

Lax, J., & Teehan, G. (2013). A place for sharing ideas and stories. *Teehan+Lax*. Retrieved July 17, 2014, from http://www.teehanlax.com/story/medium/

Quartz Marketing Team. (2014). Global executive study. *Quartz Insights*. Retrieved July 17, 2014, from http://insights.qz.com/ges/

ADDITIONAL READING

Boslaugh, S., & Watters, P. A. (2008). *Statistics in a nutshell*. Sebastopol, California: O'Reilly Media, Inc.

Foreman, J. (2013). *Data smart: Using data science to transform information into insight*. Indianapolis, Indiana: John Wiley & Sons, Inc.

Krug, S. (2006). *Don't make me think*. Berkeley, California: New Riders. [GB4]

MailChimp. (n.d.). *The UX newsletter*. Retrieved December 18, 2014, from http://www.theuxnewsletter.com/

Norman, D. (2002). *The design of everyday things*. New York: Basic Books.

Walter, A. (2013). Connected UX. *A list apart*. Retrieved July 24, 2014, from http://alistapart.com/article/connected-ux

Wroblewski, L. (2008). *Web form design: Filling in the blanks*. Brooklyn, New York: Rosenfeld Media.

KEY TERMS AND DEFINITIONS

Big Data: Big data is the collection and analysis of large and multi-structured data sets.

Contextual Interview: A contextual interview is a research method that combines with observation of the participant working or conducting their everyday activities. It is sometimes referred to as a case study, mini-ethnography, deep hangout, or contextual inquiry.

Primary Research: Primary research uses original, self-generated data.

Qualitative Research: A method of research used to understand underlying human behaviors. It is often used to answer questions such as "Why?" and "How?" Typically, qualitative research involves exploring an issue more deeply with a smaller, specific samples of people.

Quantitative Research: A method of research that explores questions through numerical means. It is often used to answer questions like "What?" "How many?" or "How often?" Typically, quantitative research involves exploring a specific issue across a larger sample size.

Secondary Research: Secondary research relies on existing data and available materials.

Stakeholder: A stakeholder maintains interest and influence in the direction and decisions of a company or organization.

User Experience: User experience is the study and practice of how a user interacts with a product or service.

Web Analytics: Web analytics are the myriad data points surrounding website traffic and activity.

Section 3
Measuring the Future

Chapter 11
Spreading the News: Spreadable Media, Social Networking, and the Future of News Production

Robert J. Baron
Austin Peay State University, USA

ABSTRACT

This chapter is concerned with the process of "spreading the news" through social media. It suggests a method of rhetorical analysis that focuses less attention on the content of news productions and more attention on analyzing how audience members might make use of the news. This transition of focus from content to audience use should lead news producers to see the value of content that engages with audiences and enables audience members to engage in the sharing and spreading of news content. The purpose of this chapter is twofold: 1) to help journalists design content that engages their audiences in the process of spreading the news in ways that can go far beyond the reach of traditional news formats and 2) to provide journalism scholars with a means of understanding the ways in which audiences and the news media interact in social media-rich communication environments.

INTRODUCTION

More people are getting their news from social networking sites (SNSs) such as Twitter, Facebook, and Instagram, while more traditional news formats like newspapers and TV broadcasts decline. The Pew Center's 2012 study of trends in news consumption finds an overall decrease in the percentage of people getting their news from television (55%), radio (33%), and newspapers (29%). The same report noted that amid all of these decreases in traditional news formats, the number of people *regularly* getting news from social networks rose from 7% to 20% (Pew Research Center, 2012, September 27). The Pew Center's 2013 *Social Media Update* cites "73% of online adults now use a social networking site of some kind" (Duggan & Smith, 2013, p. 1). A

DOI: 10.4018/978-1-4666-8580-2.ch011

more recent report by the Pew Center highlights the role that news content plays in social media use and finds that 30% of adults use Facebook and 8% of adults use *Twitter* to get news (Matsa & Mitchell, 2014, March 26). Social media provides many opportunities for news producers to reach new audiences, but it also provides its own set of unique challenges. On social media platforms, photos from last night's party, status updates from far-flung family members, and "hard news" all wage battle for a user's attention. When journalism, as a discipline, discusses new and emerging trends in news production and news research, it must account for these new means of accessing "the news." At the same time it must also examine how these new ways of accessing news content affect news production, distribution, and analysis.

The modern social media user is not *only* a passive consumer of information. He or she is engaged in a constant blur of activity: creating, consuming, repurposing, and sharing content from a variety of sources to tell his or her own social media story within a community of other social media users. In light of this, it's important for journalists and journalism scholars to recognize that today's social media users can, and often do, play an active and important role in spreading media content among their social networked peers.

Journalists need to be cognizant of this new second-hand, socially-mediated flow of content and must actively engage with their audiences as a part of the digital media information economy. Journalism scholars must account for this new means of "spreading the news" when trying to understand the impact of a story, or trying to make sense of how news audiences encounter and work content into their social media interactions and daily lives. This shift, from a passively consuming audience to an actively sharing audience, requires journalism to place a greater emphasis on user experience and search for new analytics that can explain the role that sharing can play in spreading the news.

With all of this in mind, this chapter is concerned with the process of "spreading the news" through social media communities. It looks at the rhetorical dynamics of sharing and offers a way of analyzing the news that focuses less attention on the content of news productions and more attention on analyzing how audience members might make use of the news. This change of focus, from content to audience use, should help lead journalists and other news producers to see the value of content that both engages audiences and allows opportunities for audience members to assist in the process of sharing and spreading news content. The goal of this chapter is to help journalism scholars gain a deeper understanding of the ways in which the news media operate in a social media-rich communication environment. At the same time, journalists can use this information to design content that engages audiences in the process of "spreading the news" in ways that go far beyond the reach and scope of traditional news formats. In doing so, it provides a new analytic lens with which to view news content.

In order to understand the ways in which social media is changing journalism, and the powerful role that audiences can play in this larger process of "spreading the news" through social media platforms, this chapter proceeds in three sections. The first section examines the role of what Jenkins (2008) terms "convergence culture" in creating the current media landscape. It looks at how media convergence has shaped the modern media economy and the key role that social media plays in an increasingly converged media culture. The second section draws upon Kenneth Burke's rhetorical concept of "identification" as a means for understanding how social media communities function rhetorically, the rhetorical aspects of sharing, and the role that community plays in social media interactions. It also draws on the recent work of Jenkins, Ford, and

Green (2013) and examines their concept of "spreadable media" as a model for understanding the flow of media messages in converged, social media communities. It looks at the question of how one analyzes and understands media content (including news content) in this new spreadable, socially-mediated media environment. The third section asks the important question: how does one create content that will succeed in a spreadable social media environment? In doing so, this chapter seeks to equip future journalists with tools and concepts they can use to succeed in the current, social media moment.

BACKGROUND: CONVERGENCE CULTURE, COMPETITION, AND THE ROLE OF SOCIAL MEDIA

In order to understand the importance of "spreadability" for future news analysis and production, one must first understand the current media context. At the risk of stating the overly obvious, the rise of digital media technologies has drastically altered the global media landscape. Media industries, including journalism, have been changed at every level by the introduction of what is collectively referred to as "new media." News production, distribution, and consumption are all drastically different today than they were even ten years ago. One could easily fill several pages listing the myriad changes enabled by the increased distribution of digital technology. However, perhaps the most important change for this chapter's discussion of social media, community, and news media use is the rise of what media scholar Henry Jenkins labels as "convergence culture."

In describing convergence culture Jenkins (2008) notes that the rise of "new media technologies enabled the same content to flow through many different channels and assume many different forms at the point of reception" (p. 11). At the core of convergence culture is the breaking down of barriers between formerly divergent media formats. Today journalists live and work in a highly converged media environment. For younger media consumers, raised within this convergence culture, it is increasingly difficult to imagine a world where one would experience a "newspaper article" as only a page of newsprint, or experience a local newscast as only a discreet 30-minute television broadcast. Instead, modern media consumers expect to be able to access the content they want, when they want it, and in whatever format best suits their particular media needs. Convergence culture's emphasis on "different channels" and "different forms" has drastic consequences for media producers. The journalist that only works in a "single format" has already lost his or her audience.

The need for journalists, like all media producers, to embrace challenges of convergence is not a new concept. Students in the earliest stages of journalism training are being increasingly told to develop multimedia skills. For example, Roschke's (2009) survey of high school journalism educators finds a growing recognition of the importance of media convergence-related skills:

> *This research found that high school journalism educators are also creating convergence programs in an attempt to keep up with university programs and the professional media industry. Survey respondents recognize the importance of providing a curriculum that will adequately prepare students for a journalism-related job, which means teaching convergence topics alongside traditional reporting and writing skills. (p. 63)*

Quinn (2005) notes that both journalists and publishers "need to find a way to gather and fund news for different platforms without compromising the needs of their audiences, and while maintaining ethical business practices. In essence they need to find ways to blend the twin aims of telling the truth and making money" (p. 37). The need to create multimedia content that addresses a converged media market is clearly on the minds of news producers and journalism scholars at all levels.

This cultural shift makes it is easy to find value in offering multimedia content to an audience that craves it, but convergence culture also brings its own host of challenges. The shift to a convergence culture encourages producers to be flexible and cross traditional formatting boundaries. This means that in a converged media environment everyone is, practically, everyone else's competition. Long gone are the days when the *New York Times* and *The Washington Post* were one another's main rivals. News producers find themselves competing against an increasing number of media creators, all offering converged media content. The rise of media convergence and digital media technologies have drastically changed the ways in which journalists and journalism scholars need to think about several, formerly unrelated, media formats. Content creators across the full spectrum of media formats now find themselves in direct competition with one another. Today, a writer for *The New York Times* must be equally concerned with competition from national television news sources such as *CNN* or *Fox News* and vice versa. Additionally, these national news organizations must also consider competition from: local news sources, a multitude of international news sources, amateur citizen journalists, and the ever-present lure of non-news related content.

In addition to these new sources of inter-media competition, it's important to note the "disruptive" aspects of convergence culture that comes with audience empowerment. Jenkins notes "convergence doesn't just involve commercially produced materials and services traveling along well-regulated and predictable circuits… It also occurs when people take the media into their own hands" (Jenkins, 2008, p. 17). The shift to a convergence culture means that media consumers find themselves increasingly empowered by the media technologies they use and can, as a result, do more with the media they access. Jenkins further elaborates that, because of this empowerment, audiences find themselves in a more powerful position in relation to media producers than they do in a non-converged media culture:

The advent of new production tools and distribution channels has lowered barriers of entry into the marketplace of ideas. These shifts place resources for activism and social commentary into the hands of everyday citizens, resources which were once the exclusive domain of the candidates, the parties, and the mass media. (Jenkins, 2008, p. 293)

Thus far this chapter has discussed the increased competition and need for diverse multimedia skills among professional media producers that come with convergence culture, but journalists and journalism scholars must also consider the ways in which audiences themselves become a new source of "competition."

As an example of this, consider the rise of amateur journalism content provided by independent blogs and citizen journalists armed with social media. While these amateur news producers cannot compete logistically with larger, more established, national news producers, both amateur and professional news increasingly circulates in the same converged media channels like social media platforms. This new source of amateur competition is forcing media scholars to reconsider how they understand journalism. For example, Christian Fuchs (2014) discusses the changes brought about by the increase in competition and the fragmentation of news production in his review of citizen journalism on social media. Fuchs cites changes in McQuail's definition of journalism, which shifted from 2000's definition: "'paid writing (and the audiovisual equivalent) for public media with reference to actual and ongoing events of public relevance'" to 2010's definition: "a person who creates 'informational reports of recent or current event of interest to the public'" (Fuchs, 2014, p. 225). Such a transition in framing highlights the ways in which this new wave of empowered amateurism is forcing media scholars to reconsider some of the basic questions inherent to journalism as a profession.

Reactions to this new wave of digitally-enabled audience empowerment have been mixed. Back in the early stages of the rise of convergence culture, Tapscott and Williams (2006) celebrated audience empowerment and highlighted the important communal aspect at play in link-sharing news aggregator websites like *Slashdot* and *digg*. They suggest part of why digitally empowered "prosumers" flock to these social websites is because these websites' creators "have learned how to make news a social pastime. And, like all other facets of their lives, prosumers want in on the conversation" (Tapscott & Williams, 2006, p. 145). Conversely, Keen (2007) argued that the rise of sophisticated amateur media producers was leading to an increasingly crowded online media environment and, in turn, devaluing the work of media professionals in all fields. Keen argued, "Amateur journalism trivializes and corrupts serious debate. It is the greatest nightmare of political theorists through the ages, from Plato and Aristotle to Edmund Burke and Hannah Arendt—the degeneration of democracy into the rule of the mob and the rumor mill" (Keen, 2007, p. 54).

Setting aside the debate over how to value amateurism and increased audience engagement/empowerment, convergence culture has clearly changed the relationship between media producers and audiences. Rather than viewing audiences as competition, audiences should, instead, be viewed as a resource for gaining even broader audience access. Leading audience members to engage with their chosen media more deeply provides journalists and other media creators with an opportunity to enlist the audience in the process of content distribution. In this converged media reality, the most successful journalists will not necessarily be the ones that create the "best" content, but rather the ones that garner and mobilize the largest audience for their content.

While convergence culture creates a whole host of challenges for established, professional media creators, it also provides many answers to those challenges as well. In a world where all media have converged into a singular, digital marketplace of ideas, cultivating audience engagement and focusing on user experience become key skills that media producers need to develop. Media producers that want to stay current and tap into this marketing opportunity need to think about how they can engage audiences. News organizations that develop and foster these skills will find their engaged audiences to be powerful allies in the constant battle for greater attention.

Social media takes paramount importance in the process of spreading the news in a convergence-enabled media marketplace. Just as the development of digital technologies led to a convergence culture, the development of mainstream social media websites like Facebook and Twitter have created new ways for internet users to interact and have enabled new patterns of media communication. Social media codifies and reinforces social connections among individual users, and creates new media distribution channels that challenge old understandings of mainstream distribution. In doing so, social media platforms have created new opportunities for media content creators to interact with their audiences. When looking at the future of the news industry it is important to account for these new opportunities and the questions of how and why audiences choose to interact with news content.

Media convergence has created a new media reality. Convergence culture leads media creators to think about new ways of making their content accessible, and social media creates a new means of accessing an audience. These converged social media interactions put far greater emphasis on creating personal connections and "sharing" information as opposed to simply creating content. With this in mind journalists are left to consider: new ways of engaging and connecting with audience members through social media, new ways to build deeper connections between content creators and audiences, and new ways to leverage those connections to expand an audience. At the same time journalism scholars need to consider new theories and analytics methods that make sense of these new rules of engagement. At the core of this new media paradigm is the increased competition among media producers to provide audiences with content that best tells their own social media stories. The next section will look at how the concept of spreadable media offers a means of understanding this new media paradigm.

SPREADABLE NEWS: RHETORIC, COMMUNITY, IDENTIFICATION, AND "SPREADABLE MEDIA"

The study of rhetoric is, at its core, the study of communication, community, and interaction within a greater social context. Rhetorical actions are always situated within the greater social realities of those seeking to communicate. Even the earliest formulation of rhetorical theory focuses attention on the contextual nature of rhetoric. In Book 1, Chapter 2 of *on Rhetoric*, Aristotle clearly defines rhetoric as "an ability, in each case to see the available means of persuasion" (2007, p. 37). From this point of departure Aristotle goes on to lay out his techniques for achieving persuasion in various, particular, cases. However, at the core of Aristotle's concept of rhetoric remains this key observation of persuasion always occurring in a particular context or set of contexts. Rhetoric, then, takes on an even greater importance when looking at a community-driven communication environment such as social media.

As a way to understand how and why people appropriate, share, and spread news media messages as their own on social media, it may be helpful to consider Kenneth Burke's rhetorical concept of identification. In Burke's formulation of rhetoric, community is a powerful tool for message creators. Rather than *simply* existing, community is created, defined, and reinforced through rhetorical "identification." In *Rhetoric of Motives*, Burke explains the basis for his concept of identification:

A is not identical to his colleague, B. But insofar as their interests are joined, A is identified with B. Or he may identify himself with B even when their interests are not joined, if he assumes that they are, or is persuaded to believe so. Here are ambiguities of substance. In being identified with B, A is 'substantially one' with a person other than himself. Yet at the same time he remains unique, an individual locus of motives. Thus he is both joined and separate, at once a distinct substance and consubstantial with another. (1950, pp. 20-21)

At the core of this Burkean identification lies the concept of "consubstantiality" or the sharing of motivations and "substance": "To identify A with B is to make A 'consubstantial' with B" (1950, p. 21). Under such a theory of rhetoric, community becomes the most important consideration for understanding communication.

As for the relation between 'identification' and 'persuasion': we might well keep it in mind that a speaker persuades an audience by the use of stylistic identifications; his act of persuasion may be for the purpose of causing the audience to identify itself with the speaker's interests; and the speaker draws on identification of interests to establish rapport between himself and his audience. (Burke, 1950, p. 46)

Similar experiences provide the first step toward the creation of consubstantiality, but beyond these experiences, message creators must rely on the use of symbolic language and rhetoric to create identification and bridge the gap between message creator and audience.

Social media users share the unifying characteristic of their participation in a shared social media network. As such, a certain level of underlying "virtual consubstantiality" always exists among social media users. While the users of various social media platforms may have drastically different motives, they are all linked by the very act of being on the same social media platform. Put another way, people join social media networks because other people are already there. At the same time, while all social media users may share certain universal experiences, they are also separated from one another and subject to their own internal motivations. As Burke notes, while language enables communication and identification, it also creates division. While, "In pure identification there would be no strife. Likewise, there would be no strife in absolute separateness, since opponents can join battle only through a mediatory ground that makes the communication possible" (Burke, 1950, p. 25).

Communal action requires that individuals work together and so they must use symbolic language to overcome the inherent conflict created by differing motivations. This chapter argues that this concept of virtual consubstantiality is central to understanding how users interact within the mediated experience of social media platforms. By virtual consubstantiality, the author means the whole set of mediated experiences designed into any digital environment, from computer games to social media platforms, which all users share. These common experiences act as a kind of social glue that draws a potentially disparate group of users together and bonds them into a cohesive online virtual community. This focus on community and virtual consubstantiality drastically reframes the relationship between journalists and their audiences. Rather than consumers that simply receive content, audiences instead become collaborators that help journalists spread their story through social media sharing.

When viewed through this lens, sharing content on social media becomes a kind of rhetorical act. It creates a set of common symbols that are shared across a community of social media users. This ever growing body of symbols and social media practices lead users to see one another as virtually consubstantial. Consubstantiality and virtual consubstantiality provide a way to make sense of why people share what they share on social media. Media content is not just something to read, watch, or listen to; rather it is the material out of which users forge identification with one another.

As an example of this consider one of the author's Facebook friends, "Simon." Simon is both openly gay and very open about his political views. He frequently posts to Facebook (often several times a day) and his posts most frequently involve providing links to news stories. He pulls his shared news stories from several different news organizations, often seemingly based on what will help him articulate his views on a number of issues important to him (gay rights, American gun culture, the latest political misstep by a conservative politician, etc.). One way to look at his sharing could be a simple matter of convenience or quality of the content, but instead consider what Simon's sharing accomplishes as a part of his Facebook community of friends. Simon's posts are ideas and experiences that he and his like-minded friends can share. By sharing this content, Simon's group of friends is provided with a body of symbols that they can, in turn, share and comment on amongst themselves.

This growing collage of media content becomes the thing that makes this group of Facebook friends consubstantial with one another. For example, when Simon shares news of his state's legislature voting to legalize same sex marriage, or links to entertainment blog articles about the latest *Marvel* movie, or posts and comments on an article from an alternative weekly newspaper criticizing leading right-wing voices, he is creating identification with his friends and integrating this media content into that community identification. If this content were less accessible, for example if the only way to access a news story was in the actual weekly printed publication or access to their articles was locked away behind a paywall, then Simon would, obviously, be either less likely, or even unable, to share content. News producers need to be mindful of the rhetorical power of sharing content. When crafting news content journalists need to keep in mind the ways in which their words and stories will become the building blocks of their reader's online communities. News organizations need to make choices as to when, where, and how users can access and share content. By entering into community with their audiences journalists and other news producers not only enable their news to be a part of the process of online community creation, they also gain a powerful new means of distributing content.

As a follow up to Jenkins's work on convergence culture, Jenkins, Ford, and Green (2013) offer the idea of "spreadable media" as a way to understand these new distribution channels. The three authors define spreadable media as,

The technical recourses that make it easier to circulate some kinds of content than others, the economics structures that support or restrict circulation, the attributes of a media text that might appeal to a community's motivation for sharing material, and the social networks that link people through the exchanging of meaningful bytes. (Jenkins, Ford, & Green, 2013, p. 4)

They offer this concept as a corrective to the long-standing concept of "stickiness" in media production. As they define it, "sticky" media put a greater emphasis on demanding attention, focusing on visitor monitoring, and generating data on the visitors to specific sites on the internet (p. 5). To see examples of "sticky media," one need only look to any website that locks the majority of its content behind a paywall. Users must come to one location and access the locked-down content only in the ways in which the creators deem appropriate. This "locked-down" approach to content creation and distribution puts creators in control and limits the power of audiences.

Instead, Jenkins, Ford, and Green's spreadable media paradigm puts more emphasis on user empowerment and, in doing so,

Assumes a world where mass content is continually repositioned as it enters niche communities. When material is produced according to a one-size fits-all model, it imperfectly fits the needs of any given audience. Instead, audience members have to retrofit it to better serve their interests. As material spreads it gets remade: either literally, through various forms of sampling and remixing, or figuratively, via its insertion into ongoing conversations across various platforms. This continuous process of repurposing and recirculating is eroding the perceived divided between production and consumption. (Jenkins, Ford, and Green, 2013, p.27)

This more open approach to content creation and distribution puts greater agency in the hands of audience members. As such, the spreadable media paradigm pushes content creators to assume that empowered audience members will rework media content that doesn't fit their purposes to fit their purposes. For example, a consumer might add a comment to a story before sharing it on social media, or might extract a photo or screen-grab from a video to help give their own account of an event. By making it easier for media consumers to share, reshape, and reuse content, media producers can increase their content's spreadablity. In doing so consumers become partners in a longer chain of media distribution, carrying content to audiences that the original producer may not have ever considered and increasing the reach of the spreadable media message.

News production, as a media industry, is also highly affected by these shifts in convergence culture and empowerment of audiences. News producers find themselves struggling to capture their audience's attention when audience members are able to choose news content from a multitude of sources. As Jenkins, Ford, and Green note,

Newsrooms are still struggling to figure out what their roles may be in an environment where the demand for information can be driven by affect and shaped by what happens within online communities, where citizens may make demands on what journalists cover and may cobble together information from a range of resources if traditional news outlets fail to provide desired information. (Jenkins, Ford, and Green, 2013, p. 42)

In a situation of increased competition, understanding the rhetorical dynamics at play in how and why online communities share content amongst themselves is of the utmost importance. To navigate this complex web of communal action means learning the internal dynamics of social media communities and looking at what those communities do with the content they choose to access. News stories can no longer be considered in a vacuum, instead journalism scholars must look at the ways a news story tries to engage multiple audiences and the ways in which those audiences will ultimately use the provided content.

Analyzing news content through this larger rhetoric of identification, consubstantiality, and spreadablity involves asking questions that look at the user experience, media "use," and "communal value." Considering what an audience values and how they might use media content necessarily leads journalism scholars to think about a different set of analytical questions.

When journalism scholars analyze an article, photo, or video they still need to ask important age-old questions such as "how does this frame the story?" However, scholars now also need to consider the following new types of questions as well:

- Who is the audience for the story?
- How might that audience interpret the way in which the story is framed?
- What will the audience do with this story?
- Does each of the multi-media elements in a news story tell the same story?
- If not, what story does each element tell individually?

These are more difficult considerations as they ask journalists to take into account questions that journalists are not always well equipped to answer. This new emphasis on user experiences, audience engagement, and social-use analytics will require both journalists and journalism scholars to engage with and learn from their audiences.

By understanding what each audience on each social media platform is looking for, one can craft content that most engages the audience where they live and best develop content with which the audience will actively engage. Journalists need to ask new audience-based questions like: how is the story told? How can text, photos, audio, video, and other "new media" tell a compelling and easily reusable story? Most importantly, considering news content from the standpoint of identification and spreadability asks journalists to consider what "added value" a news production carries with it for its audience. Does a news story perfectly encapsulate a complex issue in a single media text? Does a news story take an event that seems large and difficult to understand and make it simpler to understand? Does that same story help audiences articulate their own opinions? Is there a particular "viralness" to the story that will make someone want to share it among their peers on a social media network? Is there a single, iconic image or passage that a social media user might use to tell his or her story? Does a news piece engage an audience so as to help them tell their story?

The effect of this focus on spreadable media is a drastic reframing of the relationship between media content creators and audiences. A focus on spreadable media transforms social media users from passive consumers of content into partners that can act as a resource for news organizations and other media producers. More open, spreadable, media content creation allows messages to flow across platform boundaries. By letting audience members actively engage with content in multiple ways and share the content they find useful across their own social networks, media content becomes more spreadable.

When analyzing media content for its spreadablity, journalism scholars need to focus on media "uses" as well as the content itself. The above questions address why SNS users might help to spread a story, but this list is far from exhaustive. It is ultimately up to each scholar and analyst to engage and understand his or her selected audience. To only treat audiences as passive consumers leaves them unempowered. As journalism as a discipline looks at new ways of analyzing news content in the 21st century, it must be mindful of the ways in which community has taken center stage in the larger discussion of media consumption. While journalism has always been concerned with covering events as they happen, now journalists should also consider who will be most interested in their coverage of the event and how they might best access the largest audience for their coverage. By engaging with social media communities and working to provide the means for a group of social media users to build their identification among themselves and become an active part of the community.

Telling a Spreadable News Story

The preceding section looked at the rhetorical dynamics of sharing among social media users. It also presented a set of analytic questions meant to help journalists and journalism scholars begin thinking about the rhetorical work that sharing news content provides for social media audiences. This section offers news producers ideas to consider as they go about trying to create spreadable media stories. Jenkins, Ford, and Green offer several considerations that can make media productions more spreadable:

- News content should be available when and where audiences want it.
- Content needs to be portable.
- Content needs to be easily reusable in a variety of way.
- Content needs to be relevant to multiple audiences.
- Content needs to be part of a steady stream of material (2013, pp. 197-198).

Rather than look at each of these specific considerations individually, it is, perhaps, more helpful to consider what they actually amount to for media producers. To that end, crafting spreadable news content involves doing two specific things: 1) making content easy for audiences to access and use, and 2) engaging with and participating in audience communities. Doing both of these things should, ultimately, enable news content to be more easily and readily shared and, thereby, become more likely to be worked into the virtual consubstantiality linking together various social media communities.

Ease of access and use: Making content available, accessible, and easily usable is perhaps the most important aspect of making content more spreadable. After all, people can't share what they can't access. News producers should always seek to maintain archives of their content in perpetuity. This not only allows for content to spread when it is first released, but also increases that story's longevity. After all, it's impossible to know when an old story will find new life. Allowing users to gain easy access to content and maintaining this easy access allows content to be more easily shared. By making sure that audiences can access the stories they want, in the formats they want, and when they want, journalists can ensure that audiences will be better able to share content.

Closely related to this idea of ease of access is the concept of media portability. Here, portability does not necessarily mean creating content that media sharers can easily and quickly access on mobile devices. Rather, it refers to creating content that is easily linked to and easily shared among social media users. Simply having content available digitally is an important first step, but journalists and news producers can also increase the portability of their content by preformatting it for specific social media. For example, a local broadcast station can maintain a Facebook public profile and share links to video clips and stories on its main website. Doing so enables Facebook users to easily share the posted content. A journalist can maintain a Twitter profile and tweet short 140 character story summaries and links to her stories that her followers can then easily retweet. Doing so creates an ongoing stream of content that audience members can share and puts the journalist "in community" with her audience.

Finally, news producers can make their content easily reusable by offering different kinds of content within a single story. For example, a traditional "internet news story" can easily be linked to text-based social media like Twitter or Facebook, but that can also be supplemented with photos that could be shared on more visual social media platforms such as Instagram and Pinterest or short video loops that could be posted on *Vine*. To do so will require journalists and news producers in every medium to embrace media convergence and cross traditional media boundaries (i.e., a news writer may need to shoot video). Each of these different media add a different potential way in which the story can be reused by an audience and create a richer user experience. Enabling reusability means embracing divergent uses for the content journalists create, no matter how strange, in the interest of getting the maximum amount of audience coverage.

These suggestions may seem like common sense to someone well versed in the power of digital technology and it's easy to say that someone should do all of these things. However, it's important to note that making all media more accessible and reusable requires an important change in journalists' mindsets. News producers need to become more comfortable with working in multiple formats and in multiple media. At the same time, and on a more fundamental level, this also may require news producers to loosen the reins over who can use their content and how they can use it. This change from a mindset where exclusivity and controlled access are the norm to a mindset that embraces audience participation, cooperation, and eventual co-ownership is not something that a single media producer can enact on her own. Rather, it will require journalism, as a larger discipline and profession, to accept and embrace new kinds of relationships between media producers and audiences and, moreover, to put consideration of these relationships at the forefront.

Engaging in community participation: As noted above, social media platforms capitalize on the communities created by their users. This means that in order for content to be shared it needs to be relevant to those communities. In part this means that journalists like all media producers, need to learn who their audiences are and work to engage those audiences. At the same time audience relevance also requires media producers to leave some room for the audience to be able to make their own use of news stories. Rather than focusing on being the singular and definitive voice for a news event, spreadability encourages news content to which others can and will add their own voices. This is perhaps the most drastic shift from more traditional conceptions of journalism.

The rapid pace of digital life also means that media producers need to get into the conversation early if they want their content to be spread. Rather than focusing on long-format journalism, spreadable journalism could take the form of several smaller "reports" checking in as news happens. Rather than one-and-done projects, spreadable journalism involves keeping audiences informed and engaged with a steady stream of updates punctuated by longer stories that offer deeper coverage. For example, a more spreadable type of campaign coverage would involve a reporter following his or her subject throughout the day. During the coverage the reporter might tweet what the candidate is doing, post photos of the candidate with brief quotes, and finally end the day with a longer narrative putting the preceding content into a larger context for the social media audience. Such an approach gives audiences several possible social media texts to share. They might retweet the reporter's updates, or they might like or share the photos and add their own comments or captions to help show their support, or criticism, of the candidate being followed, and they might ultimately share and comment on the story that the journalist posts at the end of the day. In any case, this style of coverage gives the audience options for what and how they might share. Any one of these digital "breadcrumbs" might potentially lead additional social media users back to the original content, and in the end, build out the audience for this new kind of journalism. Social media rewards community membership and participation. The journalist that can insert him or herself into the community of his or her audience will be well prepared to have his or her voice heard in the new social media marketplace of ideas.

Such an approach changes the nature of the newsroom and the relationship between journalists and their audiences. Rather than acting as lone authoritative voices, this new approach emphasizes the role that journalists play as members of greater online communities. Rather than writers that can, or should, labor to create the single definitive account of who, what, where, when, why, and how, this new approach leads journalists to engage in dialogue with their audiences and deliver the news as a part of the communities they serve. Rather than news producers, this new approach transforms journalists into storytellers that give their audiences the building blocks of community identity. By offering engaging, sharable, and, ultimately, spreadable content, journalists can become partners with their audiences and thrive in today's converged, and cluttered, media environment.

FUTURE RESEARCH DIRECTIONS

Focusing on news content's spreadability offers several new potential research directions for journalism scholars. First, one could empirically investigate the nature of news media spreadability across multiple social media platforms. One could examine which news stories spread more readily across social media platforms and survey social media users regarding specific questions of when, how, and why they share content. This chapter lays out some of the theoretical framework necessary for understanding and making more sharable and spreadable news content, but offers little in the way of examining specific user intentions. Research participants could be given a range of different content options and asked which one they would be most likely to share and how they might share them. Such a study would provide a powerful metric for *how* users integrate content into their social media engagement and give journalists clear indications of how best to encourage engagement among audience members.

One could examine spreadable media within the context of specific social media platforms. This chapter presented social media in the broadest terms possible so as to make allowances for changes in social media platforms. As such, it doesn't offer specific suggestions into exactly how news content operates on one social media platform compared to another. For example, news content designed to be spreadable on Twitter will be drastically different than news content designed to be spreadable on Instagram. By looking at examples of successfully spreadable content in each of these settings, one might be able to better define the exact nature of what spreadable media looks like on each social media platform. This would allow for deeper analysis and more targeted content.

Using the Burk's concepts of identification, consubstantiality, and rhetorical community pushes journalism scholars to look at the larger question of how news content gets woven into the fabric of various audience communities. Put another way, how do users actually make use of the news content they share? Looking at patterns in how users share content: if they pass it along as is, add their own comments, rework content into another form, etc... would provide insight into the key questions of how the news functions rhetorically. News scholars and journalists can gain new insight into the exact work that news content carries out and how users actually engage with one another through the content they link to and share. In what ways does the news become the symbolic text that makes audience members feel consubstantial with one another? Looking at exactly how communities of social media users utilize shared content, can offer insights into both social media communities and news content as a whole.

CONCLUSION

The goal of this chapter was to raise critical questions about the role that social media plays in the future of journalism. In doing so, it looks at social media as something more than a place where users post links to online content. Media convergence, convergence culture, and the rise of social media have brought about drastic changes in the relationship between audiences and media producers. Understanding these changes and the rhetorical dynamics of sharing social media content presents a way to conceptualize a larger role for the news on social media platforms. As journalists and journalism scholars consider the role that news content and news production play in a socially-mediated world it is important to keep these concepts of identification, consubstantiality, and spreadability in mind. Journalists and journalism scholars need to understand the increasingly important role that audiences play in the distribution of news content. Journalists need to look for new ways to engage audiences and empower them to help tell the stories that need to be told.

Gone are the days when a successful news story could only live in one location and only be accessed under a very particular set of circumstances. The news producer of the future needs to account for this new multitude of options and avenues for spreading news content. No longer should journalism consider the audience as the final destination. Rather, journalists and journalism scholars should consider the initial audience to be simply another step in the long process of spreading the news. To succeed in this new digitally mediated economy requires all media producers to re-evaluate their relationship with audiences. Journalists can either choose to maintain the *status quo*, not embrace audience empowerment, and watch their profession be subsumed in a sea of new media competition and lose their place, or they can embrace their role as the teller of people's stories, and use their work to help people tell their own stories. Social media makes every user an empowered media producer at some basic level. Journalism can either fight this change or embrace it. In embracing this change, journalism can gain a powerful new channel of content, and a powerful ally in social media audiences.

REFERENCES

Aristotle, . (2007). *On rhetoric: A theory of civic discourse* (2nd ed.). (G. A. Kennedy, Trans.). New York, NY: Oxford University Press.

Burke, K. (1950 [1962]). A rhetoric of motives. Berkley, CA: University of California Press.

Duggan, M., & Smith, A. (2013, December 31) *Social media update 2013*. Retrieved from: http://www.pewinternet.org/files/2013/12/PIP_Social-Networking-2013.pdf

Fuchs, C. (2014). *Social Media: A critical introduction*. Thousand Oaks, CA: Sage. doi:10.4135/9781446270066.n2

Jenkins, H. (2008). *Convergence culture: Where old and new media collide* (revised ed.). New York, NY: New York University Press.

Jenkins, H., Ford, S., & Green, J. (2013). *Spreadable media: Creating value and meaning in a networked culture*. New York, NY: New York University Press.

Keen, A. (2007). *The cult of the amateur: How blogs, MySpace, YouTube, and the rest of today's user-generated media are destroying our economy, our culture, and our values*. New York, NY: Doubleday.

Matsa, K. E., & Mitchell, A. (2014, March 26). 8 key takeaways about social media and news. *Pew Research Center's Journalism Project*. Retrieved from http://www.journalism.org/2014/03/26/8-key-takeaways-about-social-media-and-news/

Pew Research Center for People and Press. (2012, September 27). *In changing news landscape, even television is vulnerable*. Retrieved from http://www.people-press.org/files/legacy-pdf/2012%20News%20Consumption%20Report.pdf

Quinn, S. (2005). Convergence's fundamental question. *Journalism Studies*, *6*(1), 29–38. doi:10.1080/1461670052000328186

Tapscott, D., & Williams, A. D. (2006). *Wikinomics: How mass collaboration changes everything*. New York, NY: Portfolio.

ADDITIONAL READING

Baym, N. K. (2010). *Personal connections in the digital age*. Malden, MA: Polity Press.

Benkler, Y. (2006). *The Wealth of networks: How social production transforms markets and freedom*. New Haven, CT: Yale University Press.

Chandler, D. (1995). *Technological or media determinism*. Retrieved from: http://www.aber.ac.uk/media/Documents/tecdet/tecdet.html

Gurak, L. (1997). *Persuasion and privacy in cyberspace: The online protests over lotus marketplace and the clipper chip*. New Haven, CT: Yale University Press.

Gurak, L. (2001). *Cyberliteracy: Navigating the internet with awareness*. New Haven, CT: Yale University Press.

Hauben, M., & Hauben, R. (1997). *Netizens: On the history and impact of usenet and the internet*. Los Alamitos, CA: IEEE Computer Society Press.

Howard, P. N., & Jones, S. (2004). *Society online: The internet in context*. Thousand Oaks, CA: Sage.

Lessig, L. (1999). *Code and other laws of cyberspace*. New York, NY: Basic Books.

Lessig, L. (2004). *Free culture: The nature and future of creativity*. New York, NY: Penguin Books.

Lessig, L. (2008). *Remix: Making art and commerce thrive in the hybrid economy*. New York, NY: The Penguin Press. doi:10.5040/9781849662505

Levine, R., Locke, C., Searles, D., & Weinberger, D. (2009). *The cluetrain manifesto (10th Anniversary Edition)*. New York, NY: Basic Books.

Levinson, P. (1999). *Digital McLuhan: A guide to the Information Millennium*. New York, NY: Routledge.

Levy, P. (1997). *Collective intelligence: Mankind's emerging world in cyberspace* (R. Bononno, Trans.). New York, NY: Plenum Trade.

Levy, P. (2001). *Cyberculture* (R. Bononno, Trans.). Minneapolis, MN: University of Minnesota Press.

Li, C., & Bernoff, J. (2011). Groundswell, expanded and revised edition: Winning in a world transformed by social technologies. Boston, MA: Harvard Business School Press.

McLuhan, M. (1964 [1994]). Understanding media: The extensions of man. Cambridge, MA:MIT Press.

McLuhan, M., & Fiore, Q. (1967 [2001]). The medium is the massage: An inventory of effects. Corte Madera, CA: Ginko Press.

Pacey, A. (1983). *The culture of technology*. Cambridge, MA: MIT Press.

Solis, B. (2011). Engage! (Revised and Updated Ed.). Hoboken, NJ: Wiley and Sons.

Terranova, T. (2004). *Network Culture: Politics for the information age*. Ann Arbor, MI: Pluto Press.

Turkle, S. (1995). *Life on the Screen: Identity in the age of the internet*. New York, NY: Simon and Schuster.

Webster, J. G., & Lin, S.-F. (2002). The internet audience: Web use as mass behavior. *Journal of Broadcasting & Electronics*, *46*(1), 1–12. doi:10.1207/s15506878jobem4601_1

Weinbeger, D. (2007). *Everything is miscellaneous: The power of the new digital disorder.* New York, NY: Times Books.

Williams, R. (1974). *Television: Technology and cultural form. London.* Fontana: Collins. doi:10.4324/9780203426647

Winner, L. (1977). *Autonomous technology: technics-out-of-control as a theme in political thought.* Cambridge, MA: MIT Press.

KEY TERMS AND DEFINITIONS

Consubstantiality: The rhetorical concept of shared substance and identification that links the members of a community together; formed by the sharing of common symbols.

Convergence Culture: A media culture enabled by media convergence which features, among other things, increased audience participation and increased competition among media producers.

Identification: Seeing likeness or similarity in the motives and interests of another person.

Media Convergence: The breaking down of technological barriers between several, formerly separate, media technologies due to the rise of digital technology.

Prosumer: A portmanteau of "professional" and "consumer." Media consumers that have access to, and utilize, professional-grade media tools.

Social Media Platform: A specific social media service that may encompass several different means of accessing that service; for example, an app and a website that both access the same service.

Social Media: Websites, smartphone applications (apps), and other digital services that allow users to connect with other users and share content amongst themselves. For example, MySpace, Facebook, Twitter, Instagram, etc.

Spreadable Media: Media content that enables, and encourages, audiences to share, reuse, and reshape the media message in ways that best fit their needs.

Virtual Consubstantiality: Consubstantiality built specifically upon shared digital experiences.

Chapter 12
Visualizing Social Network Influence:
Measurement and Case Studies

Jeremy Harris Lipschultz
University of Nebraska at Omaha, USA

ABSTRACT

Billions of social media users communicate via Web and mobile platforms. A variety of measurement tools may be used to advance research methodologies in the study of computer-mediated communication (CMC). Social networking sites (SNS), such as Twitter, allow researchers to conduct exploratory data scraping and create visual mapping of possible relationships between social network accounts. The nature of the visualization depends upon the number of accounts within the social network, the amount of communication activity, the direction of specific communication, the amplification of messages across the network and other factors. A major challenge of this research method is disclosure and verification of individuals operating online identities. Additionally, most free research tools fail to disclose algorithms for generating scores and ranks. The purpose of this chapter is to explain how individual position, or centrality, is one reflection among many in the measurement of social network influence.

INTRODUCTION

The study of personal influence has played a central role in development of communication theory, methodology, and research. Katz (1971), for example, explored a two-step flow that tracked diffusion of messages across time, communication channels, and social structure. In a traditional agricultural community, for example, word-of-mouth (WOM) was more influential in learning about new ideas and practices than use of the mail or media, yet colleagues were "increasingly important as *later sources* which come to *add* information and to exert influence"

DOI: 10.4018/978-1-4666-8580-2.ch012

(p. 783). Proximity, therefore, may be an important communication variable then and now. In a social media context, this process may reveal important aspects about online influence.

Global SNS platforms are rapidly growing in terms of numbers of users and accounts, even though data suggest large numbers of accounts exist but are not used. Still, the billions of users imply importance of communication across these channels. From Facebook, Twitter, LinkedIn, and Pinterest to mobile apps, such as Instagram, Snapchat and Vine, these networks exist within the larger context of social media communication (Lipschultz, 2015). "Social media interfaces engage us through interactivity and the appearance of co-presence, community, and, in the end, the appearance of social connection" (Hunsinger & Senft, 2014, p. 9). Our online interactivity, then, involves hardware and software connections that may blur human cognition about reality.

Social Media in Business

Baer (2013) focuses on three facets of SNS use for social business: self-serve information, radical transparency, and real-time relevancy:

With marketing of this type, your success is scenario-specific, which is why it's so critical to be truly, inherently useful. If you are, your audience will keep your marketing close... You don't have to be "found" – at least not after initial discovery – because your customers and prospects already know where you are and what you offer. When they need you, they'll engage (pp. 92-93).

Vaynerchuk (2013) similarly emphasizes the need to be native to a particular social media platform:

Twitter speaks to an iconic, urban audience that loves hashtags. An earnest post like "We love our customers!" would probably be soundly ignored. It sounds funny here, and yet posts like these are everywhere, proving that most brands are ignorant about what is native to a platform (p. 17).

From a social marketing perspective, consumer data tracking may be incomplete, yet valuable in targeting consumer demand (Kaye, 2014)

Albarran (2013), addressing social media influence on business, admits there are many questions: "We have a far from complete understanding of the social media industries, no doubt due in part to the nascent stage of development" (p. 232). Given the rate of change, it should not be shocking to find social and legal conflict. Stewart (2013) identified social media cases covering free speech, defamation, privacy, intellectual property, commercial speech, information and leaks, student speech, obscenity, use in courtrooms, journalist policies, and advertising and public relations. Global social media may create legal risks, as well as the potential blurring of private and public life (Mcnamara, 2014).

For journalists, broadcasters, public relations practitioners, advertisers and marketers social networks offer new tools for reaching audience members. At the same time, social networks have activated some audience members to interact with each other, traditional media and organizational representatives. This chapter will explain the growing interest in social network visualization and the movement toward real-time data analysis to inform social media engagement, influence and trust.

General Issues of Social Media Measurement

Measurement of social media rests upon general principles of social research methodologies, search engine optimization (SEO), and new tools to explore user behavior within social networks. From the early years of the Internet, social researchers explored credibility of authorship, sponsorship, point of view, references, verifiability, and currency (McBurney, 2001, pp. 36-37). Fundamental research principles – variables, measurement, reliability and validity – must be considered when evaluating all research, including social media data. As websites developed, proliferated and commercialized, SEO became an important business principle (Fleischner, 2013). Crucial data can be found in the research of "meta tags" (p. 26), "keyword development and placement" (p. 44) and other on-page and off-page variables impacting results. Google, the leader in search, provides extensive free online SEO training and certification (Google, 2014). The Analytics Academy offers basic and advanced courses.

SEO offers a basis for understanding online traffic flow and destinations, including how users progress through clicks toward a variety of actions from gaining awareness by reading to donating, volunteering, and purchasing. Alexa.com, for example, offers global page rank, engagement (through page bounce rates, daily page views and time on site), demographics of users (gender, education, and browsing location), and "upstream" sites visited before going to a page. Although the data appear to answer important questions, Hohmann (2014) and others challenge a lack of transparency in algorithms. It is common to see users on Facebook, YouTube or Google leaving to go to a specific website. These ideas connect SEO to social media and have been extended into understanding user behavior within social networks.

Sterne (2010), a marketing expert, identified 100 social metrics – buzz, fans, followers, friends, likes, pageviews, links, influence, sentiment, customer satisfaction and others (pp. xx-xxv). From a business perspective, there is an interest in Key Performance Indicators (KPIs) and Return on Investment (ROI) based upon three typical goals: lowering costs, raising revenues, or increasing customer satisfaction (pp. 4-5). Marketers focus on goals and benchmark data with a common goal of conversion to sales (Marketo, 2011).

While marketers focus on business goals, academics seek to understand the basis for social network behavior. Johnston et al. (2013), for example, explored the connection between social capital and Facebook friends: "Results indicate that intensity of Facebook use plays a role in the creation of social capital, but is particularly significant regarding the maintenance of social capital in the South African context" (p. 35). Of course, exploratory research needs to be developed further, as social network platforms mature and expand global reach. Facebook offers page content managers insight data including:

- **Page likes**: increases and decreases linked to date of change
- **Post reach**: organic (free) and paid related to likes, comments and sharing of content
- **Visits**: from within Facebook's timeline and elsewhere, and external SEO related traffic from websites, Google and other sources
- **Individual post data**: reach and engagement
- **People**: demographic data

Similarly, Twitter offers page brand managers data about:

- **Impressions**: number of times users saw a tweet
- **Replies**: tweet reply action
- **Retweets**: distribution of content
- **Favorites**: identifying specific content as favored
- **Engagement rate**: responses divided by impressions

Beyond the page manager data, a variety of online sites offer some free data collected and analyzed from the relatively open Twitter social network site.

Twitter itself offers uses measurement of number of tweets, as well as number of user followings and followers. At any moment, Twitter tracks trending activity by location. Topsy.com tracks searched terms on Twitter. For example, on the afternoon of October 20, 2014 there were 36,186 tweets using "Ebola" worldwide in just one hour. Over a 30-day period, there were more than 25 million tweets using the word. Twitter trends may be tracked for the previous month. Topsy also measures sentiment (positive or negative), links, photos, videos and influencers. Similarly, SocialMention.com allows a researcher to use a term, such as Ebola, and measure reach, strength, passion and sentiment in real-time. The absence of human coders and reliance on machine coding, however, can be criticized because it may fail social science requirements of reliability and validity. Frequently, words are used in a variety of communication contexts. Thus, the machine coding may not capture references that should be filtered from the analysis. It is simpler for an online search engine to count top keywords, users, hashtags, and sources. So, sentiment ratios should be considered very exploratory findings. Some companies do engage in relatively expensive human coding and computer programming designed to improve reliability over time.

TweetReach.com allows analysts to import personal user data to measure reach, exposure (impressions), activity time, and key contributors to activity. HowSociable.com tracks a variety of social network sites and estimates an overall magnitude score based upon activity on YouTube, LinkedIn, Google+ and Foursquare. Likewise, Klout.com aggregates social data across specific accounts and compares users. While these snapshots of data may be useful, they fail to explain the nature of conversation within social networks.

Winchel (2014) offers five points in collecting and analyzing social media data:

1. *Let your audience guide you to new places.*
2. *Topic-specific interests trump demographics.*
3. *Vanity and engagement numbers should tie into ROI.*
4. *Numbers and sentiment outside branded profiles matter.*
5. *Context is everything (pp. 1-2).*

Real-time social analytics may help media professionals engaged, but only through targeting influence: "Social media is just highlighting the importance of finding those who care about your message" (p. 2). A contextually based analytics model should work outward from the center of influential social networks.

Social Network Analysis

Social network theory and methods may be applied to the visualization of influence within traditional media events. Case study data in this chapter explores amplification of social media messages during the 2013 and 2014 Berkshire Hathaway shareholders meetings in Omaha, Nebraska. CEO and celebrity billionaire Warren Buffett was a center of attention, along with his friend Bill Gates – often considered the wealthiest person on the planet. One of Buffett's Berkshire Hathaway company Twitter accounts, rather than his personal account, developed online content during both annual meetings. At the same time, his favorite business journalists' coverage of Buffett placed their Twitter accounts near the center of influence. Examining Buffett's wider social media footprint as seen through top free measurement platforms will contextualize these data.

The interest in systematic study of individual interaction within social settings has intrigued researchers for decades. Tubbs and Moss (1983), for example, traced the nature of "popular" or "overchosen" and "unpopular" or isolated people within social groups (pp. 108-109). Social interaction was visualized through the "sociogram," which showed positive traits, such as enthusiasm and maturity, may be related to judgments about "sincerity" (p. 110). It is easy to see how this theoretic base of popularity may be applied to current media interest in trust, credibility, authenticity, branding, message amplification and dispersion, and opinion leadership within social networks and media.

BACKGROUND

Traditional cognitive information processing theory and models recognized message flow through media channels, audience perception, situation and context (Severin & Tankard, 2001). From Heider's balance theory and Festinger's cognitive dissonance theory, researchers related these concepts to social judgment (Milburn, 1991). Evaluation is important, as individuals filter people and the information they share. Online behavior includes various aspects of social interaction. The development of the Internet and the World Wide Web in the 1990's drew scholarly attention to the blurring of media production and consumption across global "linkage and connections" that help define core meaning of the Web, communication "modes" and intersections: "…the Web is simultaneously a mass-mediated *and* one-to-one form of communication… incredible cultural consumption *and* cultural production and makes it harder to establish the boundary between these two activities (Burnett & Marshall, 2003, p. 59).

At one level, large social network platforms, such as Twitter and Facebook, were seen as new channels to push content to mass media audiences and drive traffic to websites by including content links. However, social networks also may be online spaces for engagement with other users. The decision to adopt a new tool, such as Twitter, is the first diffusion adoption decision among many. Once an account is created, a user must decide how to present a profile that reflects an identity, whether or not to regularly use the account, which accounts to follow, and how to respond to followers. Content creation and distribution decisions happen within this context. While a journalist may find Twitter value in researching story ideas, a company may see the same tool as a way to develop brand identity, engage with customers, and offer public relations, marketing and advertising. In this way, social networking has a basis within computer-mediated communication (CMC) and Human Computer Interaction (HCI).

SOCIAL NETWORK ANALYSIS

Issues, Controversies, Problems

CMC and social network analysis extend interpersonal communication theory and methods to the study of online identity and "shifting boundaries" – anonymity, language, narcissism, and gender (Burnett & Marshall, 2003, pp. 78-80). Some have argued that this online chatter does not constitute meaningful interpersonal communication, while others see it as an extension of traditional talk. SNS research (Boyd & Ellison, 2007) contends that higher educated users leverage social capital through number of acquaintances and bridging behaviors (Brandtzaeg, 2012).

The current chapter explores Twitter and a specific international media event, Warren Buffett's 2013 and 2014 Berkshire Hathaway annual meetings, for evidence of CMC interaction and media online community building. Examining visualization of relationships between accounts over time may enhance social network analysis. Such longitudinal research programs offer potential to study changes, as online relationships mature and shift.

Online Social Networks and Twitter

Twitter user analysis seeks to identify "visual patterns found within linked entities" (Hansen, Shneiderman & Smith, 2011, p. 32). A diagram in three-dimensional space can be seen as a heuristic device that offers insights to deeper questions raised by communication structure. Researchers have proposed and developed methods for analysis of structure and grouping of categories and clusters in a social network. One model is called Group-In-A-Box (GIB):

One particularly important aspect of social network analysis is the detection of communities, i.e., sub-groups of individuals or entities that exhibit tight interconnectivity among the other wider population. For example, Twitter users who regularly re-tweet each other's messages may form cohesive groups (emphasis added) within the Twitter social network. In a network visualization they would appear as clusters or sub-graphs, often colored distinctly or represented by a different vertex shape in order to convey their group identity. (Rodrigues, Milic-Frayling, Smith, Shneiderman, & Hansen, 2011, para. 2)

Some researchers call the network graph that is produced by analysis software a "sociogram," which has "vertices (also called nodes or agents) and edges (also called ties or connections)" (Hansen, Shneiderman & Smith, 2011, p. 33). In social network analyses, Twitter users are connected by a series of lines in social space. The maps represent a center of people at the core of a network, as well as isolated users at the periphery (Smith, 2014):

There are at least six distinctive structures of social media crowds, which form depending on the subject being discussed, the information sources being cited, the social networks of the people talking about the subject, and the leaders of the conversation. Each has a different social structure and shape: divided, unified, fragmented, clustered, and inward and outward hub and spokes. (p. 3)

Communication on Twitter may range from crowds that gather online within a tight social space, but they may also resemble a traditional media broadcast audience with mostly one-way communication and little feedback to senders. The mapping of Twitter data, though, may be considered controversial because of the nature of accounts. In brief, communication between accounts may or may not represent actual emotional or affective closeness, but the visualization method suggests temporary social distance that could be difficult to validate over the long-term. A passing exchange may be nothing more than briefly sharing an online space, or it might indicate existence of a meaningful social network.

Social Network Theory

The earliest graph theory can be found about three centuries ago, and when applied to social network analysis offers the opportunity to visually represent any set of connected relationships from the perspective of any individual within the grouping (Hansen, Shneiderman, & Smith, 2011). Thus, observer position is an important variable and context. In politics, for example, social network analysis may enhance understanding about information flow and collaboration (Heaney & McClurg, 2009), and information interpretation as a matter of ideology and political orientation. Garton, Haythornthwaite, and Wellman (1997) describe social network analysts as examining relational patterns, observing core and periphery actions, and they "examine how involvement in such *social networks* helps to explain the behavior and attitudes of *network members* ...They use a variety of techniques to discover a network's densely-knit clusters and to look for similar role relations" (para. 3).

Network clustering may represent clues to understanding personal influence. Cooley (1909, 1966) identified key communication factors: expressiveness, permanence, swiftness, and diffusion of communication and viewed the extension of messages as "enlargement" and "animation" (pp. 149-159):

Social contacts are extended in space and quickened in time, and in the same degree the mental unity they imply becomes wider and more alert. The individual is broadened by coming into relation with a larger and more various life, and he is kept stirred up, sometimes to express, by the multitude of changing suggestions which this life brings to him (p. 150).

Baran and Davis (2006) suggested that influence of opinion leaders may be understood through similar interests and social stratification of leaders and their followers. At one time, the shift from interpersonal to mediated communication reduced feedback (Westley & MacLean, 1957), but the lines between interpersonal and media communication have now blurred. Even so, Gumpert and Cathcart (1986) concluded that, "Every type of communication, from face-to-face to mass communication, is still basically an interpersonal communicative act" (p. 19).

Influence may disperse from the center of a social network. This influence often accelerates when a leader is "stimulating" what has been called "virtual communities" within two decades of CMC research (Koh, Kim, Butler, & Bock, 2007, p. 70). In order to be sustainable, though, the researchers contend that four principles must exist: clear purpose/vision, clear member role definition, moderator leadership, and *online/offline events* (emphasis added) (p. 70-71). Events and special interests, in fact, play a key role in strengthening member identification within a social network.

Social Network Analysis Methodology

Any event in which individual social network users communicate in real-time may be used to study patterns. From large media events to breaking news, social networking leaves a trail of past behavior. In some cases, the postings also have geo-tags that broadcast user location. The 2013 and 2014 Berkshire Hathaway annual meetings were rich social contexts to explore traditional and new media relationships, as they may be observed on Twitter.

The Berkshire Hathaway annual meeting is the largest U.S. gathering of stockholders for any corporation. Chief Executive Officer Warren Buffett, among the wealthiest people in the world, drives intentional media interest and coverage. Buffett and longtime partner Charlie Munger speak for hours each year to shareholders. Additionally, Microsoft founder and philanthropist Bill Gates, now a Berkshire board member, joins Buffett in presenting various photo opportunities for media and social network user cameras (Bloomberg, 2013).

Data analyses were performed using Twitter raw data and NodeXL software on the #BRK2013 and #BRK2014 hashtags during a one week period, May 4-10, 2013, and again from May 1-7, 2014. Twitter activity data were collected beginning with the Saturday morning official opening of the 2013 annual meeting. Based upon the results, Twitter activity before, during and after the 2014 annual meeting provided new insights for future research. The analyses sought to identify central positions within social networks, the nature of information flow and influence, and key content.

Researchers collaborated with a national media monitoring company that had white-listed access to Twitter data in 2013. A white-listed company can retrieve Twitter data at a far higher limit (18,000 to 20,000 queries per hour) than a common Twitter user, limited to 150 queries per hour. Researchers used NodeXL, which is a social network analysis template tool for Microsoft Excel and is specifically designed for non-programmers to collect, analyze and visualize network data from social media sites, such as Twitter and YouTube, as well as employer Outlook email. Additionally, researchers examined 2014 data from key Twitter accounts, as well as a visualization generated by The Social Media Research Foundation and presented in the NodeXL online gallery (Social Media Research Foundation, 2014).

The focus of this work was Twitter networks of people whose tweets contained specific hash tags and keywords. Once the 2013 data were imported, NodeXL's graph metrics feature was used to calculate the betweenness, eigenvector, and clusters. All of the graph metrics were calculated automatically and inserted into columns in the Excel worksheets. There are five worksheets and a simple graph built into the NodeXL workbook. A vertices worksheet was created to graph the network maps. NodeXL was used to filter the graph data based on numeric attribute values for betweenness and eigenvector centralities. Low values were "ignored by NodeXL" and removed from the graph. This allowed only Twitter users with the higher values (the top "tweeps") in the graph. The Fruchterman-Reingold layout algorithm was used in a force-directed algorithm that attempts to minimize edge crossings. This layout produces a clean output with minimal lines crossing over another – creating starburst looking maps. The Google PageRank algorithm for measuring the importance of web pages and the eigenvector centrality are key parts of this measurement. NodeXL uses this same eigenvector centrality metric for identifying important users in a Twitter network. To accomplish this, the NodeXL filter removed "tweeps" with a low eigenvector centrality. In a Twitter network, there are times when researchers are less concerned about a tweep's importance and more concerned about his or her position in the network. A tweep's position in the network may have something to do with having access to information, or the flow of information. For example, a PR practitioner may appear near the center, if she or he is disseminating new information to be used by electronic news media. Thus, it was important to examine the betweenness centrality measurement. Utilizing the NodeXL filter, tweeps with a low betweenness measurement were removed. This resulted in a focus on the Twitter users with the shortest connections between others in the network. The participants with short connections are important because their position in the network acts as a bridge between two or more relationships, connecting them to the network. NodeXL has the capability to identify clusters or cliques of tweeps based upon the network structure. The software uses an algorithm that looks for groups of densely clustered tweeps that are only loosely connected to other tweeps in another cluster.

The 2013 study focused on #BRK2013 and followed the social network analysis approach of Russo and Koesten (2005), which addresses the concepts of centrality and prestige. Within a network, an individual can be placed within a social space occupied by others:

An actor's centrality (out-degree) represents his or her ability to touch others in the network. In particular, centrality is a measure of potential influence and popularity based on who an actor seeks to interact with within the social network... An actor's prestige (in-degree) represents the degree to which others seek out a particular actor in a social network. (p. 256)

It is possible to examine centrality of network positioning, as contrasted with being on the periphery, to determine importance in the flow of information. A person at the center of a network has a lot of information flowing through them. Prestige is another way to say that influence happens when others seek out an individual in the network. For example, a financial journalist may be sought out by a PR person with a goal of gaining media attention for her or his event. Centrality and prestige may place an individual in the role of being "the object of communication," (p. 256) without necessarily being the original source.

The 2014 NodeXL graph filtered for #BRK2014 and represented 223 Twitter users "replied to or mentioned... from a data set limited to a maximum of 18,000 tweets" on May 5 and 6 (Smith, 2014). The method visualizes edges for mentions and replies within the network of hashtag users (see Figure 1). Smith's (2014) "graph's vertices were grouped by cluster using the Clauset-Newman-Moore cluster algorithm," and "laid out using the Harel-Koren Fast Multiscake layout algorithm." This visualization utilizes edge weight values and follower values. Additionally, #BRK2014 was examined through key accounts identified in the visualization by searching through all tweets before, during and after the meeting.

Figure 1. #BRK2014 Twitter Visualization. NodeXL Social Network Analysis #BRK2014 Visualization
Courtesy: The Social Media Research Foundation (May 2014). http://nodexlgraphgallery.org/Pages/Graph.aspx?graphID=19466

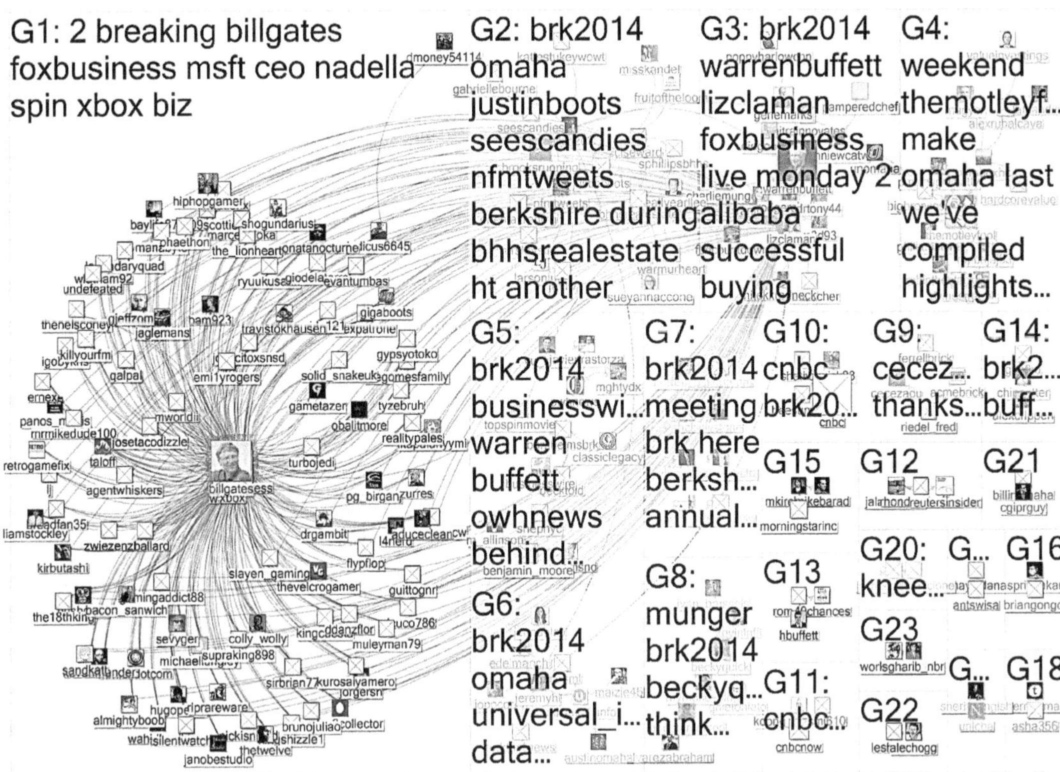

Created with NodeXL (http://nodexl.codeplex.com) from the Social Media Research Foundation (http://www.smrfoundation.org)

Exploratory Social Network Research Findings

More than 30,000 people attended the May 4, 2013 Berkshire Hathaway annual meeting. Of those, 665 users actively tweeted using #BRK2013, which was the official hashtag designated by the corporation. The #BRK2013 demonstrated a large amount of activity. There were a total of 1,517 mentions and re-tweets using the hashtag between May 4 and May 10. The top 10 influencers included key business websites and media. According to their Twitter bios (and June, 2013 N of followers), they were:

1. **Andrew Sorkin**: @andrewrsorkin – "New York Times Columnist & CNBC Squawk Box (@SquawkCNBC) Co-Anchor. Author Too Big To Fail. Founder, @DealBook." (442,413)
2. **The Motley Fool**: @themotleyfool – "Helping the world invest… Fool on! Alexandria, VA – fool.com." (423,175)
3. **Q Savage**: @QSAYTHAT – "Everyone follow me on #Instagram QSAVAGE & go like my page http://www.facebook.com/qsavagepromotions… Baton Rouge, La." (127,474)
4. **The New York Times**: @dealbook – "News from The New York Times about deals and those who make and break them. New York, NY – nytimes.com/dealbook." (66,377)

5. **The Street**: @TheStreet – "Stock market coverage with an edge. Valuable information. Unique insight. Strong opinions… From the Heart of Wall Street – thestreet.com." (64,045)
6. **Lixiaolai**: @xiaolai – Individual's site in "Beijing – lixiaolai.com." (56,004)
7. **Director's Talk**: @DirectorsTalk – "the most followed in the UK providing London Stock Exchange AIM news and interviews with Directors of leading PLC's. DirectorsTalk.com." (54,813)
8. **Trends Map**: @TrendsSthAfrica – "Real-time South Africa Twitter trends South Africa – trendsmap.com/south+Africa." (54,036)
9. **Becky Quick**: @beckyquickcnbc – "Co-host of CNBC's Squawk Box from 6-9 am Eastern with Joe Kernen and Andrew Ross Sorkin. Fortune Columnist. Former WSJ reporter. Rutgers grad."(52,919)
10. **Maria Latella**: @MariaLatella – SKY TG24 Italian television personality following "Wall Street - https://www.facebook.com/marialatellapaginaufficiale." (47,263)

Three of the top ten influences – Andrew Sorkin, DealBook and Becky Quick – *all* had direct connections to the CNBC business news channel. A fourth, The Motley Fool, is an influential business blog site. These were all found within the center of the complex social network, which did not feature any Berkshire companies. The remaining six top ten influencers were found along a well-defined edge of the social network within three distinct sub-areas. The Street, Trends Africa and Directors Talk were distanced from the top four influencers. QSAYTHAT and xiaolai were connected to Becky Quick. Maria Latella's main connection was with Andrew Sorkin.

The social network map showed six accounts that had fewer Twitter followers than the top ten, but generated significant re-tweets:

1. **Alex Crippen**: @alexcrippen – "Tracking all things Warren Buffett for http://CNBC.com's Warren Buffett Watch blog."
2. **Insider Monkey**: @insidermonkey – "Finance blog following insiders and hedge funds. Our small-cap hedge fund strategy beat the S&P 500 index by 18 percentage points per year."
3. **Alec Hogg**: @alechogg – "Writer, broadcaster, entrepreneur, thinker, striver for an open mind; founder Moneyweb…tweets breaking news and links to interesting info. Johannesburg, Gauteng – alechogg.com."
4. **Borsheims**: @borsheimsbrk – "The ultimate guide for updates about Warren Buffett's annual Berkshire Hathaway shareholder's meeting – brought to you by Borsheims Fine Jewelry & Gifts. Omaha, NE – borsheimbrk.com."
5. **Jenna Blan**: @jennablan – "Editor of US Investment Strategy at Reuters. Sharing my world in covering biggest, most influential US investors. Barron's alum (wrote Current Yield column)."
6. **Vitaliy N. Katsenelson**: @vitaliyk – "Investor - CIO at IMA, educator, writer - author of The Little Book of Sideways Markets and write monthly column for Institutional Investor Magazine. Denver, CO – activevalueinvesting.com."

Borsheims, an Omaha, Nebraska jewelry store, was the only Berkshire company to appear in the graph as an influencer. The Borsheims' Twitter account began using the #BRK2013 days before the annual meeting, and their placement among media as a main re-tweeter of content was important. The @borsheimsbrk account was the main official voice for Berkshire during the annual meeting in 2013 and 2014.

The 2014 visualization which was generated by The Social Media Research Foundation two days after the annual meeting on May 3, 2014, identified top influencers based upon verticies and betweeness centrality. According to their Twitter bios (and May, 2014 N of followers), they are led by Warren Buffett's account. He has tweeted only five times since joining in 2013 and had no tweets since February of 2014.

1. **Warren Buffett**: @WarrenBuffett – Chairman and CEO of Berkshire Hathaway, Omaha, NE – berkshirehathaway.com" (830,000).
2. **Liz Clayman**: @LizClaman – "Fox Business Anchor, New York" (31,100)
3. **Ralph Witkin**: @ralkin203 – "Ralph Witkin, Connecticut" (58)
4. **The Motley Fool**: @themotleyfool – "Helping the world invest… better. Have a question, comment or PR inquiry? Tweet @Matt_Trogdon. Fool on! Alexandcria, VA foolk.com (485,000).
5. **Bill Gates**: @billgates – "Sharing things. I'm learning through my foundation work and other interests. Seattle, WA thegatesnotes.com" (15,900,000)
6. **Jeremy H. Lipschultz**: @JeremyHL – "Isaacson #Professor, UNO School of #Communication – U of #Nebraska at #Omaha - #author #socialmedia #journalism #education" (2,940).
7. **Justin Boots**: @justinboots – "The Justin Boot Company Since 1879, Fort Worth, Texas – justinboots.com" (27,100).
8. **Top Spin**: @topspinmovie – "A documentary about teenage table tennis athletes – @ AriellHsing, @LilyAnnZheng & Michael Landers – Fighting for Olympic glory, 2014 release. Bay Area and New York – topspinmovie.com" (892).
9. **Fox Business**: @FoxBusiness – "The official twitter page of FOX Business Network: Capitalism lives here. Ask your cable provider for FOX Business in your neighborhood. New York, NY – foxbusiness.com" (201,000).
10. **Borsheims**: @Borsheimsbrk – "The ultimate guide for updates about Warren Buffett's annual Berkshire Hathaway shareholder's meeting – brought to you by Borsheims Fine Jewelry & Gifts" (1,227).

To see the #BRK2014 Twitter visualization, visit the NodeXL Graph Gallery and search for number 19466 in the public archive (NodeXL, 2014).

Qualitative Data

Analyses of the text of the tweets confirmed that Warren Buffett's words, as well as those of longtime business partner Charlie Munger, were the drivers for much of the social network activity. For example:

RT @beckyquickcnbc: .@WarrenBuffett at #BRK2013: When it comes to investing knowledge "it's all cumulative." That's how he can make snap decisions now.

RT @beckyquick: .@WarrenBuffett #BRK2013: Of our $49b, we haven't moved any of it to #BitCoin.

RT @andrewsorkin: Munger: "'New normal' is less than we've enjoyed in our lifetime. #brk2013

RT @dealbook: Dodd-Frank's Limited impact on Berkshire. http://t.co/zRFraGf3k7#brk2013

RT @andrewsorkin: Buffett: "I've got a lot of faith in Bernanke." #brk2013

Core Ben Graham belief RT @alechogg: #BRK2013 WB: "...People get fearful en masse. When we see falling prices we see opportunity." #Omaha

By analyzing the visual appearance of the network we can see that most of the users ringed an oval shaped social network dominated by CNBC affiliated and other business opinion leaders. Most of the audience for tweets was not tightly connected to the media sources. Users are paying attention to each other, and there is a symmetric exchange of attention and information in this social network (Hansen, Shneiderman, & Smith, 2011). The top-ten influences clustered around four major starbursts and triads between users with strong social ties (Hansen, et al., 2011). The users with the highest betweeness centrality revealed the bridging users. These users are vitally important to the structure of the network and are important for three reasons: 1) these users are in a better position than others in terms of having access to information; 2) these users are a bridge to *different people in other networks,* which have the potential to carry the message further and thus increase the reach; and 3) these users are connected to *different people*, and they have greater chances of having access to *different information.*

In the #BRK2014 data @BeckyQuick (75,900 followers) had faded by the end of the hashtag activity, but she remained central as one of the media questioners at the 2014 meeting. The account Buffett activity began April 23 with a re-tweet promoting her CNBC interview with Buffett that day following an annual lunch and auction. That same day, the account retweeted news from the interview:

RT @DonnaBurton – "Have not sold and have no intention to sell Coca-Cola shares" Warren Buffett tells @BeckyQuick #CNBC $KO

The story about a controversial Coca-Cola (Buffett controlled 9.1 percent of shares and son Howard is on the Board of Directors) would become a major media theme for the 2014 annual meeting. Three days later, Quick's Twitter account again retweeted about Buffett:

*RT @ezraklein – "Warren Buffett's web site is hilariously ugly:ttp://*bit.ly/1j0hk1P

The annual meeting tweets began May 2 with Quick promoting an upcoming interview with Bill Gates by retweeting an historical photo of Gates' 1977 mugshot.

@BeckyQuick: "Our guest Mon am on @SquawkCNBC ! @CNBC RT @HistoryInPics: Bill Gates, arrested in 1977 for speeding in his Porsche. pic.twitter.com/o2Ka1TPce7*"*

On the morning of the annual meeting, May 3, Quick tweeted one of the many popular photos of Gates and Buffett tossing newspapers in the convention hall before the question and answer session, but she failed to use the complete hashtag:

@BeckyQuick: "Warren Buffett & Bill Gates warming up at the BRK mtg. BRK2014 pic.twitter.com/LjMFjO4pJf

Quick, however, later used the full hashtag in a less popular photo:

@BeckyQuick: "… And Kathy Ireland w/Warren Buffett. #brk2014 pic.twitter.com/qguPBcpr9o

In Quick's final convention hall photo, she frames the image with the words "media scrum," and this image also has the full #brk2014 tag.

@BeckyQuick: "Media scrum following Warren Buffett at BRK meeting. #brk2014 pic.twitter.com/h6lN4SYSqm

During the questioning, Quick's account continues by live-tweeting Buffett quotes from inside the arena:

@BeckyQuick: "Buffett on Coke vote: 'I don't think going to war is a very good idea in most cases."

Twitter data showed 10 retweets and 11 favorites, which seems quite low given Quick's more than 75,000 followers and television audience. Media are not allowed to record or broadcast the questioning, and the Twitter stream has become a popular way to learn what Buffett and Munger are saying. Quick retweeted The Warren Buffett Watch in one exchange:

RT @alexcrippen: "Munger: 'I think you handled the whole situation very well.' Buffett: 'And Charlie remains vice-chairman!' #BRK2014"

This tweet also had little traction – six retweets and two favorites. One of the most popular Quick tweets, with 29 retweets and 22 favorites, quotes Munger:

@BeckyQuick: "'We're pretty good at ignorance removal. The nice thing on that is we have a lot of ignorance left to remove.' #BRK2014"

Quick also commented on and showed Gates' willingness to stand with fans for "selfie" photographs, and this modified retweet received 20 retweets and 15 favorites:

@BeckyQuick: "Watched about 100 people ask Bill gates for a selfie here @ #BRK2014 He agreed to all MT @siyuansun pic.twitter.com/JAFoD8GvL4

Perhaps because Twitter attracts those interested in technology, one of the most popular Quick tweets was on Buffett's thoughts about Google's self-driving cars and possible impact on his insurance businesses:

@BeckyQuick: "Buffett on self-driving cars: If it happens 'that is a real threat to auto insurance industry.' #BRK2014:

The tweet received 93 retweets and 28 favorites. This initial activity may be amplified by those retweeters with audiences of their own that may send the message along to other followers. Additional conversation also is generated by replies to the tweet:

1. @jonstank: BREAKING "@BeckyQuick: Buffett on self-driving cars: If it happens "that is a real threat to auto insurance industry." #BRK2014
2. @Nikki_Flash28: @BeckyQuick @CNBC Good. I'm sick of seeing @GEICO and @ Progressive commercials
3. @windycityamar: @BeckyQuick @CNBC I don't think it'd be a big threat. Accidents happen w/ self driving cars and gov will still require insurance.
4. @windycityamar: @BeckyQuick @CNBC Premiums will reduce significantly though.
5. @lamTay: Oh, I'd love to punch-in an address, let the car take me! Then I can text, read, talk on the phone-illegal while driving

These may be seen as attempts at engagement with the core of the social network, but these users were left hanging without any response from the accounts. In a Monday morning Omaha interview following the annual meeting, Quick seemed to capture the medium with a selfie of her, Gates, Munger and Buffett:

@BeckyQuick: Hey @joesquawk check out this selfie! @cnbc Buffett, Gates and Munger live n SquawkCNBC now pic.twitter.com/W5G4Po5oxr

The photo received 167 retweets and 170 favorites on Twitter. Clearly, popular photographs and witty quotation were the most engaging social media content that traveled out along the Quick's social network and beyond. In a moment typified by the social media #selfie photograph, Becky Quick's use of it resonated with the online crowd. Warren Buffett, though, with the much larger network, ignored the opportunity to amplify the content. Without a retweet, most of his large number of followers likely missed the photograph.

Other Analytics Data

The larger context of a social network analysis may be found within an analysis of other available data. Starting with the Berkshire Hathaway website in October of 2014 and accepting Alexa lack of data transparency for discussion here, Alexa.com suggested that the Berkshire global rank is 73,429, although Web traffic peaked during the annual meeting at the beginning of May (when annual meeting tickets are ordered here). The site had a bounce rate of 39.7%, an average of 2.11 daily page views per visitor, and an average daily time on site of 1:54. Its most likely viewer is a male with graduate school education visiting from work in the United States (44.8%), India (9.2%), Germany (3.8%), United Kingdom (3.6%) or Canada (3.5%). About 27.5% of visitors found the page by searching: "Berkshire Hathaway" (69.77%), "Warren Buffett" (8.69%), "Berkshire" (4.64%), "Buffet" (3.7%) or "Berkshire Hathaway Inc" (1.42%). The top sites visited before coming to the home page were: Google (29.8%) and Wikipedia (3.8%). It is important to note here that website owners have access to more reliable and accurate Google Analytics, but researchers must rely on secondary data.

On Twitter, @WarrenBuffett had only five tweets as of late 2014 since joining in May of 2013, yet more than 895,000 followers. A Topsy.com analysis, however revealed 2,824 tweets in 15 days (sentiment score = 72) and 10,766 tweets with "Warren Buffett" (sentiment score = 38) (Oct. 21, 2014). Sentiment is a controversial measure of positive and negative comments typically coded by a computer algorithm and inconsistent across various tools. There is movement toward using a combination of automatic and traditional human sentiment coding, which can be checked for reliability in a conventional content analysis. In this case, over 30 days, there were about 90,515 tweets (algorithm sentiment score = 56). There were five top influencers of @WarrenBuffett, including Becky Quick with three tweets tagging Buffett:

@beckyQuick: RT @OnTheMoney: "You will not make money trying to buy or sell stocks daily or weekly." @WarrenBuffett to@BeckyQuick pic.twitter.com/vtVxJpgKl6

@beckyQuick: RT @matthew_quayle: Get up early for a special hour with @WarrenBuffett starting at 8 a.m. ET on@SquawkCNBC @BeckyQuick http://t.co/cFhLai...

@beckyQuick: RT @OnTheMoney: See highlights of @BeckyQuick's conversation with @ WarrenBuffett ow.ly/Cg4cU *this Sunday@CNBC at 730pET. http:...*

For "Warren Buffett," the top influencers on Twitter during the period of analysis were: The Guardian, CNBC, Business Insider and Market Watch:

@TheGuardian: Warren Buffett sells more Tesco shares gu.com/p/42fhz/tw *via @guardian*

@CNBC: Warren Buffett says buying this stock was a "huge mistake": cnb.cx/11rU9Zw pic.twitter.com/yMgGO1EDMh

@BusinessInsider: Warren Buffett dumps Tesco after losing $700 million read.bi/11s5it5

@marshacollier: The 3 Most Important #Business Lessons @BillGates Learned From Warren Buffett read.bi/1sUKmFK

@marketwatch: Why Warren Buffett isn't worried about this market: on.mktw.net/1wN9xsJ Photo/Gettypic.twitter.com/NmVq6ev5Xc

Outside the Berkshire Hathaway annual meeting, and beyond the @WarrenBuffett tag, there was less message control. It resulted in what appeared to be less positive sentiment.

A TweetReach.com analysis suggested that messages about Warren Buffett travel far and wide. For a single day in late October of 2014, there were 365,499 impressions, and 323,526 accounts reached. In a 37 minute period alone, there were 50 tweets from 49 contributors. A single tweet by Canadian social entrepreneur Enzo Calamo (@EnzoCalamo) had more than 249,000 impressions:

@EnzoCalamo: Earnings season has not been good to Warren Buffett http://fb.me/3r8m7fiaE

The most retweeted influence came from two media organizations – Fortune (8 retweets) and Yahoo (2 retweets), such as:

@FortuneMagazine: IBM and Coca-Cola have cost Warren Buffett about $2 billion so far this week. Here's whyfor.tn/1tIPgYC

@Yahoo: Warren Buffett and Bill Gates are the richest people in their states; how about the other 48? yhoo.it/1DxksLxhttp://t.co/pE21dpeaM3

On SocialMention.com, Warren Buffett had mixed sentiment – 90 positive tweets, 145 neutral and 22 negative. These came from 152 unique authors and 44 retweets. Top keywords were Warren (304), Buffett (285) and link (74). The #Buffett hashtag was at the top with three uses on this particular day. The influence came from a range of platforms: Twitter (99), YouTube (50), Delicious (50), Reddit (24), Facebook (16), Ask (9), Topix (8) and Yahoo News (1).

HowSociable.com also measures brand influence across top sites. Warren Buffett had a one week brand magnitude score of 9.9 equally spread across Twitter, Facebook, and YouTube.

Finally, Klout.com compares social media influence among influencers. The @WarrenBuffett official account (score of 48) was presented as having less online influence than one called @ WarrenBuffettEffect (61). The unofficial account had more than 13,000 tweets and more than 25,000 followers. It appeared to promote a WarrenBuffettStrategies.com website. These contextual analyses could provide input into deeper social network analyses of various subgroups interested in Buffett topics and issues.

EVENT ENGAGEMENT RESEARCH

The social network studies discussed in this chapter focused on one annual international media event over two years, as well as follow-up analyses of branding and influence. In the annual meetings the level of sponsor engagement, the size of the event, the presence of news media, and the previous Twitter activity of participants all may have an effect on the visualization of the social network. The decision by key participants – especially those with large followings – to take on the role of opinion leader is important. The nature of the event did not produce significant social conflict among members, and this would be an important area for future study.

There were a series of limitations in this study: 1) The nature of the Berkshire Hathaway annual meeting and the type of people drawn to it and investing information: Future research should gather larger and random samples from a wide variety of events; 2) Social network theory is relatively new and not well understood within an interpersonal communication theory context; 3) This study examined only the #BRK2013 and #BRK2014 tags – not #Buffett or the @WarrenBuffett account; 4) The visualization maps take into account only those attendees participating by communicating through Twitter, we cannot see other social media conversation, people watching on Twitter but not tweeting, or all of the face-to-face communication happening at the annual meeting; 5) Although the follow-up analyses provided some context, they still constituted a snapshot of data rather than continuous and long-term observation of communication behavior; and 6) Theory and method need further development. We need to move beyond labeling of graph characteristics and begin to understand and predict fluid movements within each network over time.

Social network analyses continue to evolve as scholars refine methods (Butts, 2008). In particular, the methods used to define social network centrality and boundaries are open to discussion. As additional events are analyzed – from #Ebola to #Ferguson and beyond – it should be possible to begin to predict participation behavior (Howard, 2008; Wright, 2011). The inclusion of geo-location data from tweets offers future research possibilities for a multi-step, real-time analysis technique that might look like this:

1. Real-time social listening and monitoring on Twitter for *trending* conversations.
2. Use of geo-tag *mapping* applications to locate hubs of social media conversation in physical space.
3. Scraping of *rich media* data, such as photographs and videos.
4. Qualitative analyses of the nature of *interactions* between accounts.
5. Use of social network analysis visualization to *identify influence* and other communication patterns.
6. Multi-method approaches to connecting social network data to traditional *ethnographic observations*, interviews and other data collection methods.

Early communication studies demonstrated an understanding about group behavior, sharing, socialization, entertainment, and following (Schramm, 1972). Social networks have introduced new interpersonal communication questions about leadership, behavior, and online social influence (Huffaker, 2010; Greenhow & Robelia, 2009). Researchers need to extend existing communication theories to the social networking landscape. By performing future systematic content analyses of language used in online interaction, for example, it may be possible to discover emerging patterns of interaction and engagement. Facebook is changing journalism consumption (Somaiya, 2014), for example, and academics and professionals need data to develop social media best practices. Specifically, PR practitioners would want to know more about:

- Media brand loyalty among opinion leaders at the center of an event network
- Potential to grow through key network hubs and spokes brand loyalty among isolates
- Topic resonance within a social network forming around different event types
- Comparison of a news media channel's social network popularity with competitors

Greene (2014) suggested four tips for measuring a PR campaign: 1) identification and alignment of objectives and expectations; 2) demonstration of ROI through rapid results; 3) widely shared content; and 4) business impact results reporting (paras. 4-7). Changes in data collection and analysis should be expected to continue within a context of measuring "ideal" content characteristics (para. 1).

In other words, theory and practice of social network graphing has potential to be increasingly important for media and PR industries, along with academic researchers. Such research should strengthen understanding about the nature of popularity, social isolation, opinion diffusion and social network leadership.

SOLUTIONS AND RECOMMENDATIONS

Smith (2014), generalizing through the ongoing analyses of thousands of visualization maps, suggests that this inductive research method does not directly address issues of reliability, validity, and theory construction. A stronger future approach would be to ground analysis within established social theory of communication. A multi-method approach would also address other social media platforms and simultaneous face-to-face and mass media communication happening during the Twitter activity under study.

When a user says nothing about a specific tweet, but she or he clicks "favorite," there is subtle communication behavior worth studying. Yet, in traditional social network analysis, it is not clear what weight should be given to this compared to a reply or retweet in terms of defining a core or periphery. Likewise, a basic "RT" versus one with comment should suggest user level of involvement. Similarly, a tweet with a URL link to a website generates other communication activity, from reading to clicking and even buying products. It is not yet clear how to judge these related interactions, such as those measured with Google Analytics as Search Engine Optimization (SEO).

While Twitter offers a relatively open social network, Facebook is a walled or gated community. Page operators have insights data about likes, shares, and comments. These are indicators of engagement, but they do not directly reflect an online community and its social network.

FUTURE RESEARCH DIRECTIONS

Each social network account is full of important variables – number of followers, number following, number of updates, number of replies and so on (Lipschultz, 2015). While those in the social media industry have created algorithms to approximate influence, trust, popularity and engagement, these have not been connected in a systematic way with social network analysis. Relational patterns, while interesting, need to be connected to theory, method, and other useful and valuable data. These data return us to fundamental questions, such as Lasswell (1966) and his:

Who
Says What
In Which Channel
To Whom
With What Effect? (p. 117)

It is matter of structure *and* function: "(1) The Surveillance of the environment; (2) the correlation of the parts of society in responding to the environment; and (3) the transmission of social heritage from one generation to the next" (p. 118). Whether or not communication is one-way or two-way, we must ultimately be concerned with social values:

In every society the values are shaped and distributed according to more or less distinctive patters (institutions). The institutions include communications, which are invoked in support of the network as a whole. (p. 123)

This supports the idea that personal influence frequently is effective in the sharing of information, ideas and opinions (Katz, 1966):

While the opinion leader may be more interested in the particular sphere in which he is influential, it is highly unlikely that the persons influenced will be very far behind the leader in their level of interest. Influentials and influencees may exchange roles in different spheres of influence. Most spheres focus the group's attention on some related part of the world outside the group... In every case, influential have been found to be more exposed to these points of contact with the outside world. (p 364)

The vast amount of social networking content would suggest the need to reexamine how users filter it through indexing and interpretation (Tannenbaum, 1971). It is likely that such research would also account for "deep culture, which:

...refers to the unconscious meanings, values, norms and hidden assumptions that allow us to interpret our experiences as we interact with other people. These shared meanings form a framework which acts as a starting point for our sense of what it means to be human, what constitutes normal behavior, how to make moral or ethical choices and what we perceive as reasonable. (Shaules, 2007, pp. 11-12)

The visualization of social network structure, then, is an over-simplified indicator of deeper tendencies to interact in online social spaces.

CONCLUSION

Social network analysis has many theoretic and methodological limitations, yet the approach offers opportunity. For decades, communication researchers have wanted to be able to observe and track interpersonal communication influence as it travels through opinion leaders and those repeating messages. Smith, Ranie, Himelboim, and Shneiderman's (2014) interpretation is that map structure may be identified as "polarized" crowds, "tight" crowds, brand or community "clusters," and broadcast or "support networks" (p. 9). Group size, interconnection levels and behavior of isolated group members all may have something to do with actual group activity. Measurement of behavior on Twitter, however, remains an indirect assessment of involvement or other traditional group communication social measures. So-called "support networks on Twitter, for example, "are often dominated by one or two accounts interacting with many others" (p. 52). One empirical question is obvious: Does this behavior align with traditional group research findings about communication leadership and audiences? It is tempting to become enamored with the colorful Twitter visualization that depicts account activity, but, as social scientists, researchers must resist jumping to the conclusion that these data fully represent communication behavior. "Insights" into online communication (p. 54), though, may be valuable within their limited context.

Some may question the value of traditional communication theory in the study of social networks. Clearly, this chapter argues that word-of-mouth influence may be mediated, yet it is potentially similar to face-to-face conversation. A multi-method approach may come closer to capturing important data. In the case of the global Ebola conversation, for example, millions of social network messages would require a clear protocol to sort these over time, across nations and languages, and within subgroups of influencers. An initial review of these data suggest a rich a complex pool of data for researchers. It seems obvious that any interest in influence would require better understanding of centrality and network position. If personal influence flows from the center of a social network, the individuals or social network accounts at the center strike to heart of diffusion of new ideas.

For students, learning social research methods, search engine optimization techniques and social media measurement tools, the potential exists to not only find work in business, but also critically think about social media usage. Data visualization is in its infancy, but it offers potential to reach greater understanding about the nature and practice of personal influence.

REFERENCES

Albarran, A. B. (2013). *The social media industries*. New York, NY: Routledge.

Baer, J. (2013). *YOUTILITY, Why smart marketing is about help not hype*. New York, NY: Portfolio/Penguin.

Baran, S. J., & Davis, D. (2006). *Mass communication theory* (4th ed.). Belmont, CA: Thomson Wadsworth.

Bloomberg (2013, May 6). *The Berkshire Hathaway shareholders' meeting*. Retrieved May 8, 2013, from, http://www.bloomberg.com/slideshow/2013-05-06/the-berkshire-hathaway-shareholders-meeting.html#slide5

boyd, d. m., & Ellison, N. B. (2007). Social network sites: Definition, history, and scholarship. *Journal of Computer-Mediated Communication 13*(1), article 11. Retrieved June 30, 2013, from, http://jcmc.indiana.edu/vol13/issue1/boyd.elison.html

Brandtzaeg, P. B. (2012). Social networking sites: Their users and social implications – A longitudinal study. *Journal of Computer-Mediated Communication, 17*(4), 467–488. doi:10.1111/j.1083-6101.2012.01580.x

Burnett, R., & Marshall, P. D. (2003). *Web theory*. London, UK: Routledge.

Butts, C. T. (2008). Social network analysis: A methodological introduction. *Asian Journal of Social Psychology, 11*(1), 13–41. doi:10.1111/j.1467-839X.2007.00241.x

Cooley, C. H. (1909, 1966). The significance of communication. In B. Berelson & M. Janowitz (Eds.), Reader in public opinion and communication (2nd ed.; pp. 147-155). New York: The Free Press.

Fleischner, M. H. (2013). *SEO made simple, Strategies for dominating the world's largest search engine* (3rd ed.). Lexington, KY: Fleischner.

Garton, L., Haythornthwaite, C., & Wellman, B. (1997, June). Studying online social networks. *Journal of Computer-Mediated Communication, 3*(1). Retrieved from http://jcmc.indiana.edu/vol3/issue1/garton.html

Google. (2014). *Google analytics*. Retrieved from http://google.com/analytics/

Greene, B. (2014, October 22). 4 tips for successfully measuring your PR campaign. PR News Online. Retrieved October 22, 2014, from, http://www.prnewsonline.com/water-cooler/2014/10/22/4-tips-for-successfully-measuring-your-pr-campaign/

Greenhow, C., & Robelia, B. (2009, July). Old communication, new literacies: Social network sites as social learning resources. *Journal of Computer-Mediated Communication, 14*(4), 1130–1161. doi:10.1111/j.1083-6101.2009.01484.x

Gumpert, G., & Cathcart, R. (Eds.). (1985). *INTER/MEDIA, Interpersonal Communication in a Media World* (3rd ed.). New York: Oxford University Press.

Hansen, D. L., Shneiderman, B., & Smith, M. A. (2011). *Analyzing social media networks with NodeXL*. Burlington, MA: Elsevier.

Heaney, M. T., & McClurg, S. D. (2009, September). Social networks and American politics. *American Politics Research*, *37*(5), 727–741. doi:10.1177/1532673X09337771

Hohmann, L. (2014, October 13). Disturbing mystery affecting your favorite news sites. *WND*. Retrieved October 14, 2014, from, http://www.wnd.com/2014/10/your-favorite-news-sites-shafted-by-amazon/

Howard, B. (2008, November). Analyzing online social networks. *Communications of the ACM*, *51*(11), 14–16. doi:10.1145/1400214.1400220

Huffaker, D. (2010, October). Dimensions of leadership and social influence in online communities. *Human Communication Research*, *36*(4), 593–617. doi:10.1111/j.1468-2958.2010.01390.x

Hunsinger, J., & Senft, T. (Eds.). (2014). *The social media handbook*. New York, NY: Routledge.

Johnston, K., Tanner, N., Lalla, N., & Kawalski, D. (2013). Social capital: The benefit of Facebook 'friends.'. *Behaviour & Information Technology*, *32*(1), 24–36. doi:10.1080/0144929X.2010.550063

Katz, E. (1966). The two-step flow of communication. In W. Schramm (Ed.), *Mass communications* (pp. 346–370). Urbana, IL: University of Illinois Press.

Katz, E. (1971). Social interary of technical change. In W. Schramm & D. F. Roberts (Eds.), *The process and effects of mass communication* (revised edition, pp. 761–797). Urbana, IL: University of Illinois Press.

Kaye, K. (2014, October 27). A data lab rat in the city: Why trackers couldn't trap this city dweller. Retrieved October 27, 2014, from, http://adage.com/article/dataworks/data-trackers-trap-city-dweller/295562/

Koh, J., Kim, Y.-G., Butler, B., & Bock, G.-W. (2007, February). Encouraging participation in virtual communities. *Communications of the ACM*, *50*(2), 69–73. doi:10.1145/1216016.1216023

Lasswell, H. D. (1966). The structure and function of communication in society. In W. Schramm (Ed.), *Mass communications* (pp. 117–130). Urbana, IL: University of Illinois Press.

Lipschultz, J. H. (2015). *Social media communication: Concepts, practices, data, law and ethics*. London, UK: Routledge.

Macnamara, J. (2014). *The 21st century media (r)evolution, Emergent communication practices* (2nd ed.). New York, NY: Peter Lang.

Marketo. (2011). *Marketing metrics & analytics, The definitive guide*. San Mateo, CA: Marketo.

McBurney, D. H. (2001). *Research methods* (5th ed.). Belmont, CA: Wadsworth.

Milburn, M. A. (1991). *Persuasion and politics*. Belmont, CA: Wadsworth.

Node, X. L. (2014). *The Social Media Research Foundation Graph Gallery*. http://nodexlgraph-gallery.org/Pages/Graph.aspx?graphID=19466

Nudd, T. (2014, October 24). Infographic: The ideal length of everything online, from tweets to YouTube. *AdWeek*. Retrieved October 25, 2014, from, http://www.adweek.com/adfreak/infographic-ideal-length-everything-online-tweets-youtube-videos-160972

Rodrigues, E. M., Milic-Frayling, N., Smith, M., Shneiderman, B., & Hansen, D. (2011). *Group-In-A-Box layout for multi-faceted analysis of communities*. Retrieved June 7, 2013, from, http://hcil.cs.umd.edu/trs/2011-24/2011-24.pdf

Russo, T. C., & Koesten, J. (2005, July). Prestige, centrality, and learning: A social network analysis of an online class. *Communication Education*, *54*(3), 254–261. doi:10.1080/03634520500356394

Schramm, W. (1972). Nature of communication between humans. In W. Schramm & D. F. Roberts (Eds.), *The process and effects of mass communication* (Revised ed., pp. 8–32). Urbana, IL: University of Illinois Press.

Severin, W. J., & Tankard, J. W. Jr. (2001). *Communication theories* (5th ed.). New York, NY: Longman.

Shaules, J. (2007). *Deep culture: The hidden challenges of global living*. Buffalo, NY: Multilingual Matters LTD.

Smith, M. A., & Ranie, L. Himelboim, & Shneiderman (2014). Mapping Twitter topic networks: From polarized crowds to community clusters. Washington, D.C.: Pew Research Center, Feb. 20, 2014.

Sterne, J. (2010). *Social media metrics, How to measure and optimize your marketing investment*. Hoboken, NJ: John Wiley & Sons.

Stewart, D. R. (2013). *Social media and the law, A guidebook for communication students and professionals*. New York, NY: Routledge.

Tannenbaum, P. H. (1971). The indexing process of communication. In W. Schramm & D. F. Roberts (Eds.), *The process and effects of mass communication* (revised edition, pp. 313–325). Urbana, IL: University of Illinois Press.

Tubbs, S. T., & Moss, S. (1983). *Human Communication* (4th ed.). New York, NY: Random House.

Vaynerchuk, G. (2013). *Jab, jab, jab, right hook, How to tell your story in a noisy social world*. New York, NY: HarperCollins.

Westley, B. H., & MacLean, M. S. Jr. (1957). A conceptual model for communications research. *The Journalism Quarterly*, *34*(1), 31–28. doi:10.1177/107769905703400103

Winchel, B. (2014, October 20). 5 things to look for in social media analytics. *PR Daily*. Retrieved October 21, 2014, from, http://www.prdaily.com/Main/Articles/17473.aspx

Wright, A. (2011, May). Web science meets network science. *Communications of the ACM*, *54*(5), 23–23. doi:10.1145/1941487.1941497

ADDITIONAL READING

Hesmondhalgh, D., & Toynbee, J. (Eds.). (2008). *The Media and Social Theory*. London, UK: Routledge.

Lievrouw, L. A., & Livingstone, S. (Eds.). (2006). *Handbook of New Media (Updated Student Edition)*. London: Sage.

Welser, H. T., Gleave, E., Fisher, D., & Smith, M. (2007). Visualizing the signatures of social roles in online discussion groups. *The Journal of Social Structure*, *8*(2). Retrieved from http://www.cmu.edu/joss/content/articles/volume8/Welser/

KEY TERMS AND DEFINITIONS

Computer-Mediated Communication (CMC): Online, mediated communication that approximates at varying levels face-to-face (f2f) interaction.

Electronic Word of Mouth (eWOM): Use of CMC for online conversations via SNS, email, messaging or other means with the potential to spread personal influence.

Global Page Rank: A number reflecting website relative position among all others.

Search Engine Optimization (SEO): A variety of methods that improve Google Analytics and search engine results.

Social Media Metrics: A large number of measurable variables, such as reach, page visits, impressions, likes, re-tweets, favorites and shares.

Social Network Analysis: A framework for measuring relative position and distance between SNS users within an account or topical network.

Social Network Sites (SNS): Online computer platforms that make it possible for mediated interpersonal communication to flourish.

Chapter 13
The Disruptive Impact of Emerging Technology

Gordon J. Murray
Kent State University, USA

ABSTRACT

In this chapter, context for understanding the phenomenon of "big data" and disruptive innovation is introduced relative to current changes affecting the future of the journalism industry. Perspective is provided on market forces and emerging technologies that now shape the demand for data journalism. Current best practices and strategies to analyze, scrape, personalize, visualize and map data are presented. Trends and resources to access data and effectively analyze information are outlined for journalists to use when researching and reporting online. Three contemporary case studies explore the day-to-day operations and decision-making processes of media organizations struggling to remain profitable; adapt to changing consumer demands and try to serve a new demographic that is increasingly global, wireless, mobile and socially networked.

BIG DATA AND DIGITAL DISRUPTION

Data matures like wine, applications like fish. —James Governor, Principal Analyst and founder of RedMonk

Humans have been producing volumes of data—collecting, storing and aggregating them in one form or another for millennia. Researchers studying clay balls from Mesopotamia have discovered clues to a lost code used for record-keeping about 200 years before writing was invented. The clay balls may represent the world's "very first data storage system," said Christopher Woods, a professor at the University of Chicago's Oriental Institute (Jarus, 2013).

Data are plain facts and alone, are fairly useless. One of the clay balls found in Mesopotamia contained 49 pebbles and a cuneiform text. When data are processed, analyzed and interpreted to determine true meaning, they are transformed into information. The cuneiform text is now

DOI: 10.4018/978-1-4666-8580-2.ch013

thought to be a contract commanding a shepherd to care for 49 sheep and goats. Four thousand kilometers northwest of Mesopotamia in Wiltshire, England, there is an astronomical calculator that can calculate times in the solar year and the lunar month. We now know ancient worshippers may have used the calculator—Stonehenge, to collect the data required to predict eclipses on a 56-year cycle.

The capacity of our data storage devices has improved remarkably since the days of clay balls and stone monoliths. According to the *Oxford English Dictionary,* the first attempts to acknowledge the volume of data, or what has popularly been known as the "information explosion," is encountered in 1941, when the term first appeared in the common vernacular. In *A Very Short History Of Big Data,* author Gil Press (2013) marks many of the significant milestones on the continuum of how our digital data—now stored microscopically on silicon—became so big. Highlights from the timeline include:

1944: *The Scholar and the Future of the Research Library*, (Rider, 1944) estimates American university libraries were doubling in size every sixteen years and speculates the Yale Library in 2040 will have "approximately 200,000,000 volumes, which will occupy over 6,000 miles of shelves… [requiring] a cataloging staff of over six thousand persons.

1961: *Science Since Babylon*, (Price, 1961) charts the growth of scientific knowledge and concludes the number of scientific journals and papers has grown exponentially rather than linearly, doubling every fifteen years and increasing by a factor of ten during every half-century.

1971: In *The Assault on Privacy*, Miller (1971) writes, "Too many information handlers seem to measure a man by the number of bits of storage capacity his dossier will occupy."

1980: In *Where Do We Go From Here?* Tjomsland, (1980) says, "Those associated with storage devices long ago realized that Parkinson's First Law may be paraphrased to describe our industry—'Data expands to fill the space available'…. I believe that large amounts of data are being retained because users have no way of identifying obsolete data; the penalties for storing obsolete data are less apparent than are the penalties for discarding potentially useful data."

1996: Digital storage becomes more cost-effective for storing data than paper (Morris & Truskowski, 2003).

2000: Lyman & Varian (2000) published, *How Much Information?* the first comprehensive study to quantify, in computer storage terms, the total amount of new and original information created in the world annually. The study finds in 1999, the world produced about 1.5 exabytes of unique information, or about 250 megabytes for every man, woman, and child on earth. It also finds "a vast amount of unique information is created and stored by individuals" (what it calls the "democratization of data") and "not only is digital information production the largest in total, it is also the most rapidly growing." Calling this finding "dominance of digital," Lyman and Varian say that "even today, most textual information is 'born digital,' and within a few years this will be true for images as well."

WE ARE DATA STORAGE

Two men were examining the output of the new computer in their department. After an hour or so of analyzing the data, one of them remarked: Do you realize it would take 400 men at least 250 years to make a mistake this big? —Nicholas Negroponte Chairman Emeritus of Massachusetts Institute of Technology's Media Lab

Just as data have grown, technologies correspondingly have become more pervasive. Innovations are now so imbued with human development that Nobel Prize-winning economist, Robert W. Fogel, argues humans are experiencing a "technophysio evolution." Fogel discovered the size and shape of the human body has a lot to say about economic and social changes throughout history, and vice versa. An example: the average adult man in 1850 in America stood about 5 feet 7 inches and weighed 146 pounds; average life expectancy was 45 years. In the 1980s the typical man in his early 30s was around 5 feet 10 inches tall, weighed 174 pounds and was likely to pass his 75th birthday. This technophysio evolution, powered by remarkable advances in food production and public health, has so outpaced traditional evolution that 21st century humans stand apart—not just from every other species, but from all previous generations of Homo sapiens as well (Cohen, 2011).

Not coincidentally, sociologist Samuel H. Preston, one of the world's leading demographers interviewed by Cohen for the article in *The New York Times,* observed Fogel's greatest achievement was in figuring out a way to measure the changes in human height, weight, disability, and longevity. Fogel and a team of researchers spent three decades examining a "monumental" amount of raw data to piece together health records of thousands of people in different countries, and Cohen notes, "Much of the evidence—childhood growth, mortality, adult living standards, labor productivity, food and manufacturing output—was available, but no one had put it all together in this way before."

With history, technology and data so inexorably linked to human destiny, it begs the question, "What has happened recently to make our data so suddenly *big*—and our technology so *disruptive*?" Almost sixty years after the "information explosion" was observed, we can trace the first academic use of the term, "big data," to University of Pennsylvania economist, Francis X. Diebold, in his paper, "*Big Data" Dynamic Factor Models for Macroeconomic Measurement and Forecasting.* In it, Diebold (2000, p.115) says:

Recently much good science, whether physical, biological, or social, has been forced to confront–and has often benefitted from–the "Big Data" phenomenon. Big Data refers to the explosion in the quantity (and sometimes, quality) of available and potentially relevant data, largely the result of recent and unprecedented advancements in data recording and storage technology. In this new and exciting world, sample sizes are no longer fruitfully measured in "number of observations," but rather in, say, megabytes. Even data accruing at the rate of several gigabytes per day are not uncommon.

In hindsight, it is easy to see Diebold may have underestimated the volume of potential data accrual possible to be considered in a big data analysis. For example, as the Large Hadron Collider explores the secrets of the universe—the European Organization for Nuclear Research

(CERN) is reporting experiments generating one petabyte of data *every second* (Worth, 2011). Digital technology is changing how information and data are created and recorded—how words; ideas; images; actions and behaviors proliferate; and how all are studied and analyzed.

The *idea* of big data had a decade to foment and by 2012, the term and the phenomenon were experiencing a breakout year. Everyone from marketers to scientists, hackers, new startups, media outlets and IPOs wanted to hitch their analytical wagons to the big data train. By this time, even Francis Diebold was compelled to re-enter the discussion. He acknowledged his follow-up inquiries into the genesis of the term proved to be "a journey of increasing humility" (Lohr, 2013). Even though there is little challenge to his first introduction of the term to a scholarly audience, Diebold (2012, p.2) concluded: "The term Big Data, which spans computer science and statistics/econometrics, probably originated in the lunch-table conversations at Silicon Graphics in the mid-1990s, in which John Mashey figured prominently."

As public and private data stores continue to grow, and with so many organizations interested to engage in big data analysis for profit, a clear definition is needed. But the field is still maturing, and new terms and new ideas are affecting big data—not just in how one approaches the problems to which big data analysis is applied, but also in how he or she thinks about the people involved in the process. In defining big data, it is important to first understand that the comprehensive volume is comprised of unstructured and multi-structured data.

Unstructured data does not have a pre-defined data model. It is not organized or easily interpreted by traditional databases, and typically, it is text-heavy. Metadata, Twitter tweets, and other social media posts are examples of unstructured data.

Multi-structured data refers to a variety of data formats and types and can be derived from interactions between people and machines, such as web applications or social networks. An example is web log data, which includes a combination of text and visual images along with structured data like form or transactional information.

While many variants of working definitions for big data may be found, Gartner, a leading American information technology research and advisory firm, provided an early framework that has proven to be resilient for understanding big data in its many forms, and the framework has now become ubiquitous (Laney, 2012) (see Figure 1).

Big data is high volume, high velocity, and/or high variety information assets that require new forms of processing to enable enhanced decision making, insight discovery and process optimization.

Laney defined data growth challenges and opportunities as being three-dimensional: increasing volume (amount of data); velocity (speed of data in and out); and variety (range of data types and sources). Gartner, and now much of the industry, continue to use this "3Vs" model for describing big data (Gartner, 2011).

- **Volume:** The increase in data volumes within enterprise systems is caused by transaction volumes and other traditional data types, as well as by new types of data. Too much volume is a storage issue, but too much data are also a massive analysis issue.
- **Velocity:** This involves streams of data, structured record creation, and availability for access and delivery. Velocity means both how fast data are being produced and how fast the data must be processed to meet demand.

Figure 1. Big data: what is it, what kind of data and how much?
Courtesy: Martha L. Stone, CEO World Newsmedia Network (2013.) Sources: Mushroom Network, Deep Blue Analytics, MBAOnline, IBM, Gartner.

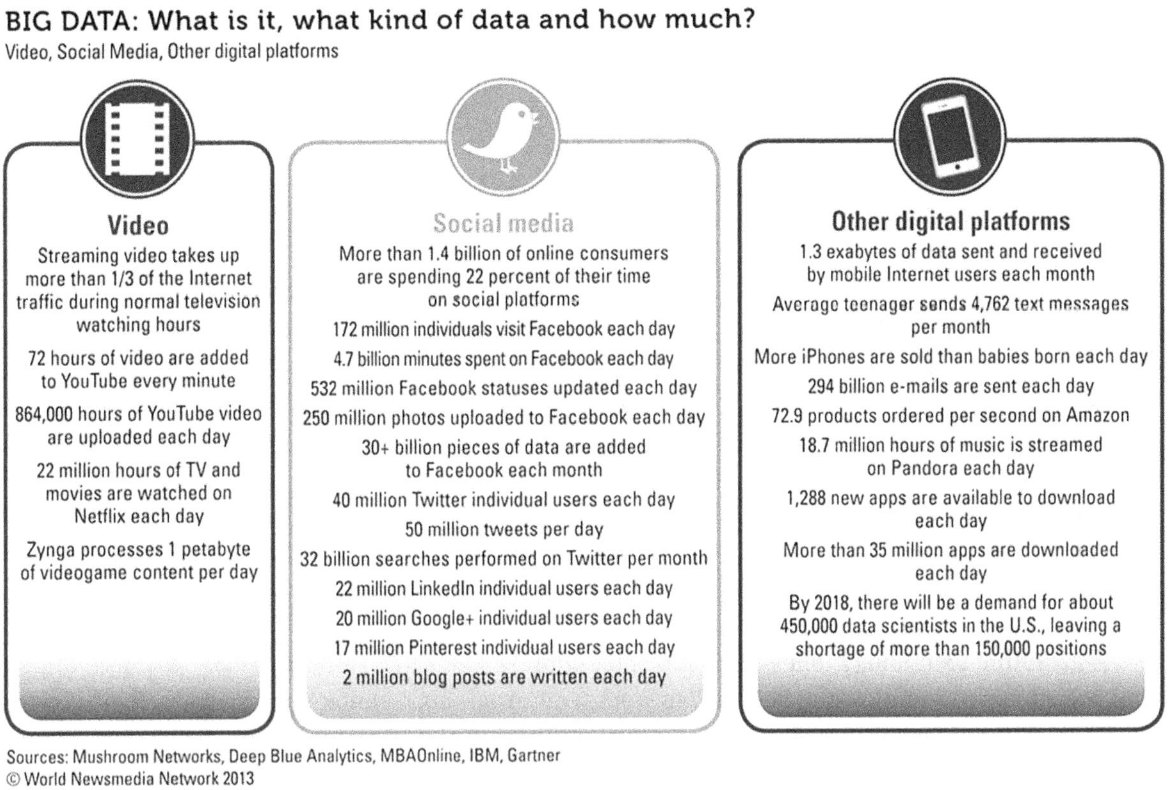

- **Variety:** Information technology leaders have always had an issue translating large volumes of transactional information into decisions—now there are more types of information to analyze—mainly coming from social media and mobile (context-aware). Variety includes tabular data (databases), hierarchical data, documents, e-mail, metering data, video, still images, audio, stock ticker data, financial transactions and more.

Gartner analyst Svetlana Sicular (2013) provides additional insight on Laney's original model and says the most interesting of the 3Vs is *variety.* She points out companies are "digging out amazing insights from text, locations or log files." Elevator logs, according to Sicular, have helped to predict vacated real estate; shoplifters have tweeted about stolen goods right next to the store; and emails have contained communication patterns of successful projects. She says, "Most of this data already belongs to organizations, but it is sitting there unused—that's why Gartner calls it dark data. Similar to dark matter in physics, dark data cannot be seen directly, yet it is the bulk of the organizational universe."

Sicular calls *velocity* the most misunderstood data characteristic, saying it is "frequently equated to real-time analytics." Yet, velocity, she says "is also about the rate of changes, about linking data sets that are coming with different speeds and about bursts of activities, rather than habitual steady tempo." She says, "It is important to realize that events in data arise out of the available data and that available data forms its own 'social network'. This means some data serve as a 'canary', other data influences, and yet more data results in decisions." And, while *volume* is commonly interpreted as the quantity of actual data analyzed, Sicular suggests it is also "about the number of big data mentions in the press and social media."

INNOVATION'S UNRULY SIDE

Never invest in any idea you can't illustrate without a crayon. —Peter Lynch, American businessman and stock investor.

For insight into the meaning of *disruptive technology* and a means to describe a new technology that unexpectedly displaces an established one, we turn to Harvard Business School professor, Clayton M. Christensen. Christenson actually coined the term, "*disruptive innovation*" in his best-selling book, *The Innovator's Dilemma* (1997). The term, "disruptive technology" has been widely considered a synonym of "disruptive innovation," but the latter is now preferred. Market disruption typically is less a function of technology itself, but rather, is attributed more to its changing application. Christensen separates new technology into two categories: sustaining and disruptive.

- **Sustaining technology** relies on incremental improvements to an already established technology. Most large corporations are designed to work with sustaining technologies. They excel at knowing their market, staying close to their customers, and having a mechanism in place to develop existing technology. Conversely, they have trouble capitalizing on the potential efficiencies, cost-savings, or new marketing opportunities created by low-margin disruptive technologies.
- **Disruptive technology** lacks refinement, often has performance problems because it is new, appeals to a limited audience, and may not yet have a proven practical application. (Such was the case with Alexander Graham Bell's "electrical speech machine," which we now call the telephone.)
- **Disruptive innovation**, describes a process by which a product or service takes root initially in simple applications at the bottom of a market and then relentlessly moves up market, eventually displacing established competitors.

When Christenson began his search for an answer to the puzzle of why the best firms can fail, a friend offered some sage advice. "Those who study genetics avoid studying humans," he noted. "Because new generations come along only every thirty years or so, it takes a long time to understand the cause and effect of any changes. Instead, they study fruit flies, because they are conceived, born, mature, and die all within a single day. If you want to understand why something happens in business, study the disk drive industry. Those companies are the closest things to fruit flies that the business world will ever see."

Christensen took the advice, investigated the evolution of the hard drive and extrapolated. His research demonstrates how it is not unusual for a big corporation to dismiss the value of a disruptive technology because it does not reinforce current company goals. Likewise, he illuminates how the corporation can be blindsided as the technology matures, gains a larger audience and market share and threatens the status quo. The vast majority of innovations are sustaining, according to Christensen—meaning companies tend to make existing products better for existing customers, which is usually to the advantage of successful incumbent companies. Disruptive innovation, on the other hand, is different. "I made a big mistake when I called it 'disruptive,' because it has so many different connotations," he said nearly 16 years later. "A lot of people think it's just new and different, or radical." Instead, disruptive innovation changes industries not because it is radical, but because it makes complicated and expensive processes simple and opens them up to a wider audience (Ellis & Donovan, 2013) (see Figure 2).

In October 2011, the professional networking site, Focus.com, teamed up with social media site Mashable to look at seven companies that rolled out new products, lowered prices, approached markets in unheard-of ways, even created new markets—and changed the world. Netflix was among the list including Apple, Skype, Google, Zynga and Tata Nano.

Nowhere are the effects of disruption from technological innovation more evident than in the journalism industry. Journalist Tyler Marshall and the Pew Research Center's Project for Excellence in Journalism (2008, para. 1) conducted interviews with senior newsroom executives at more than 250 newspapers across the country and offered this composite description of the contemporary American daily newspaper:

It has fewer pages than three years ago, the paper stock is thinner, and the stories are shorter. There is less foreign and national news, less space devoted to science, the arts, features and a range of specialized subjects. Business coverage is either packaged in an increasingly thin stand-alone section or collapsed into another part of the paper. The crossword puzzle has shrunk, the TV listings and stock tables may have disappeared, but coverage of some local issues has strengthened and investigative reporting remains highly valued. The newsroom staff producing the paper is also smaller, younger, more tech-savvy, and more oriented to serving the demands

Figure 2. Innovation abounds

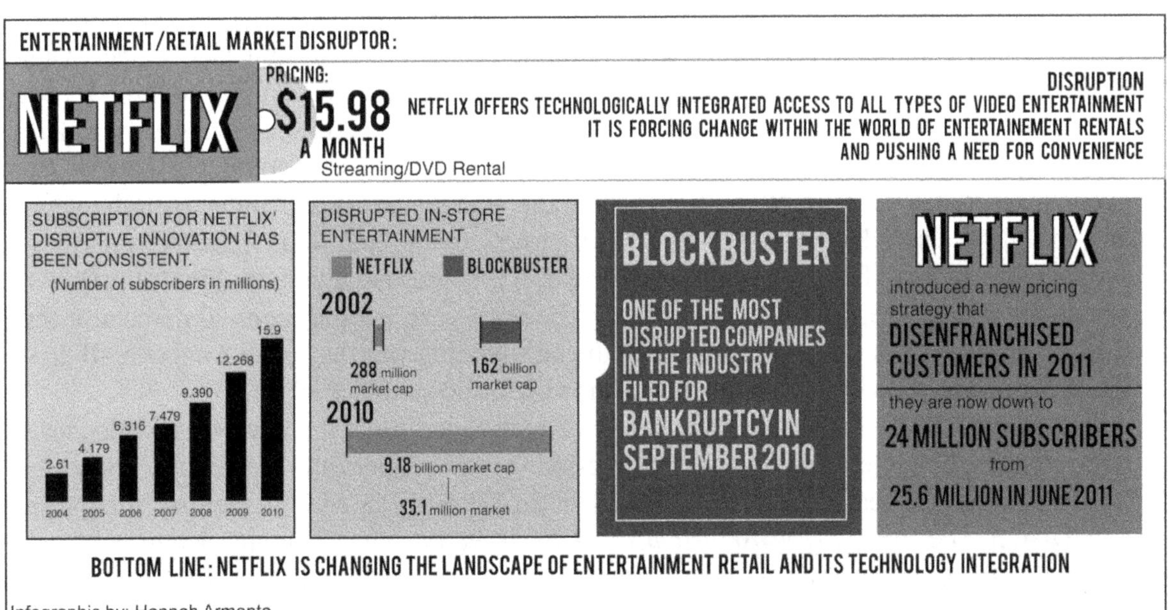

of both print and the web. The staff also is under greater pressure, has less institutional memory, less knowledge of the community, of how to gather news and the history of individual beats. There are fewer editors to catch mistakes.

The Pew study noted two powerful, but contradictory, forces are transforming the journalism industry. On one hand, the report says financial pressures sap journalism's strength and threaten its very survival. On the other, the rise of the web, the evolution of smartphones and the mobile Internet now boost competitiveness, open up innovative new forms of journalism, build new bridges to readers and offer enormous potential for the future. Despite the image of decline, more people today in more places read the content produced in the newsrooms of American daily newspapers than at any time in years.

An interesting example of disruption in the journalism industry is found in aggregation. Aggregating news stories has been a key part of journalism since Henry Luce first tried it out with *Time Magazine*—in 1923. Even though aggregation reappears in various forms since then, the concept and practice still seemed to surprise many in the Internet era. In journalism, the Internet, wireless and other technologies have broadened the market for information. News aggregators like *The Huffington Post* and *Buzzfeed* have emerged and are often lambasted for reusing content from other sources while producing little of their own. Yet as each organization matures, we see they are repositioning themselves with new strategies, with more room for distinctive, often original content (Skok, 2012). By 2014, nearly 43 million people were visiting the *Huffington Post* monthly. The same year, *Buzzfeed's* cocktail of humorous lists, celebrity gossip, picture stories and breaking news had captured a booming demand for material to share with friends. The six-year-old company was valued at about $200 million and recently announced plans for international expansion.

The Pew Research Center reports 91 percent of Americans now own a cell phone and almost two-thirds use their phones to access the Internet. The Pew survey (Duggan, 2014) found smartphones are replacing traditional computers as the go-to device many Americans choose to get online. The proportion of mobile Internet users in the U.S. doubled between 2009-2013. The trend appeared to be most common among people with lower incomes. The survey also found 34 percent of American mobile users choose their phones as their primary Internet device, instead of a desktop, laptop or tablet computer. By comparison, in China, the state-run China Internet Network Information Center (CNNIC) reports some 80 million mobile web users were added in 2013. The growing popularity of mobile devices in China increased the country's Internet users to over 618 million—80 percent of which access the web via their smartphones. In the United States, mobile is also taking a bigger share of Internet advertising. Mary Meeker, a partner at the venture capital firm Kleiner Perkins Caufield,& Byers sees great potential for future growth on the small screen. Meeker (2014) reported in the prior year, people spent 20 percent of their time on mobile devices, yet only 5 percent of the ad spending was there. A strong overall driver in the accelerating growth of mobile traffic was video, she said (see Figure 3).

The American Press Institute (2014) reports Americans follow the news on a wide variety of devices, including television, radio, print versions of newspapers and magazines, computers, cell phones, tablets, e-readers, and devices such as an Xbox or PlayStation that link the Internet to a television. The survey, *How Americans Get Their News*, suggests many Americans prefer to receive news across devices, using whatever device or technology is most convenient when they want to follow the news (see Figure 4).

Figure 3. Cell phone activities of Americans in 2013
Source: Pew Research Center Internet & American Life Project Spring Tracking Survey (2013.)

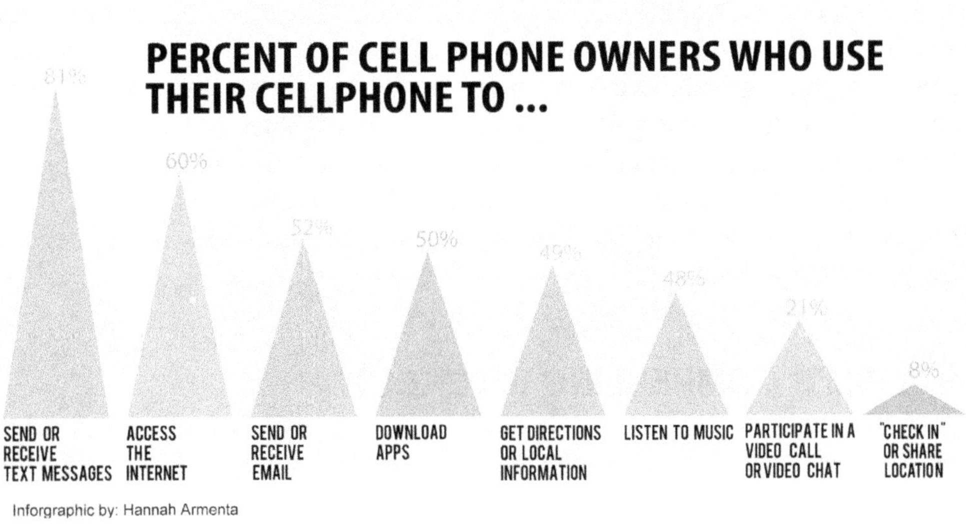

Figure 4. Question: please tell me if you used each device or technology to get news in the last week, or if you did not
Source: American Press Institute, (2014) How Americans Get Their News.

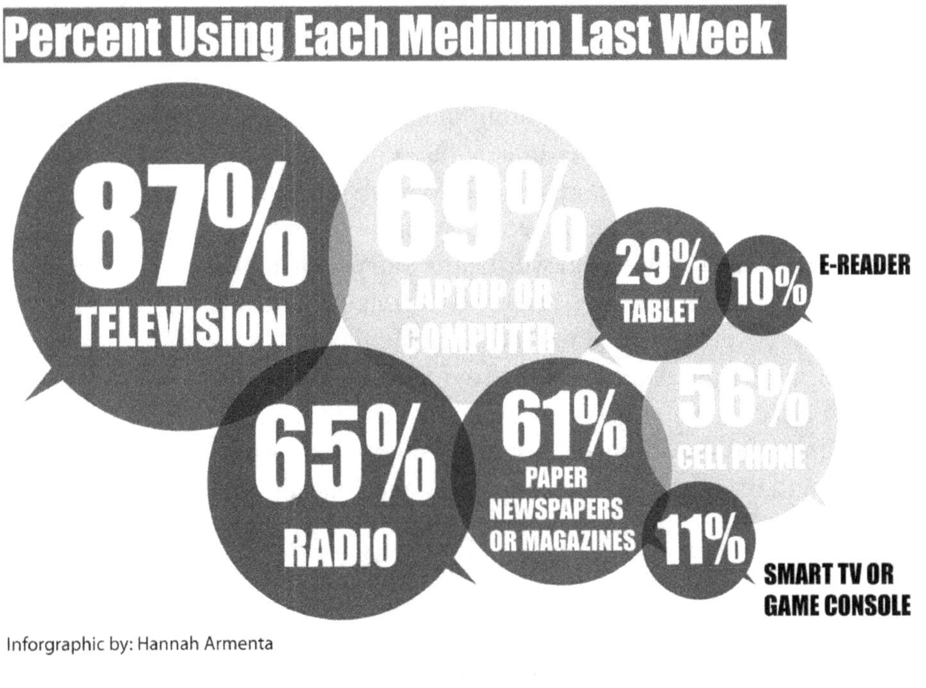

The survey data also show the powerful connection between the growth in mobile Internet technology and social media. Adults with an Internet connected cell phone are much more likely than those without one to find news through social media. Similarly, adults with smartphones are also much more likely than non-mobile users to get news through search engines; online news aggregators; sharing with friends via email, text, or other online methods; and electronic news alerts. Similar patterns emerged for owners or users of tablets.

While people use different media for news each week, and only half express a preference for a device, most Americans do care about the means of discovery, or where they first hear the news. More than 6 in 10 Americans say they prefer getting news directly from a news organization compared with any other way.

JOURNALISM'S COMPELLING INTEREST

Torture the data, and it will confess to anything."—Ronald Coase, British economist and author

One of the significant influences that brought *data journalism* into prominence was the way media organizations like *The Guardian* and *The New York Times* handled the large amounts of data released by *Wikileaks*. The term essentially describes how journalists are using data to improve coverage and augment in-depth investigations into particular newsworthy topics.

When journalism is great, it always is based on adding context, clarity and compelling storytelling to facts. Correspondent Alex Howard made this observation after a year of investigating data based journalism for *O'Reilly Media*—just as big data's disruptive presence was beginning its dramatic expansion into the global media landscape. Howard (2012) reports that while the tools for researching, covering, and packaging the news have improved; it is the "explosion of data, that provides new opportunities to think about reporting, analysis, and publishing stories."

Today, the aim of the journalistic enterprise remains the same as always: explain the *who, what, where, when* and *why* behind the story. What is different today is that where a single photograph once was worth a thousand words in a story, consumers now expect video and audio; multimedia; narrated photo essays; interactive infographics; animation and simulation to be part of the overall coverage and news package. Media outlets seeking to gain market share, relevance and profitability are stretching to provide this content. Data journalism is the newest means to help visualize the news and make the news, and the media organizations themselves, more relevant online. The art of journalism must adapt to incorporate new and emerging tools and also serve an audience that is more socially connected, mobile, and global.

This adaptation does not come easy for many traditional news organizations and media companies. *Buzzfeed* obtained a 96-page internal *New York Times* report that quoted a committee led by the publisher's son warning "Our journalism advantage is shrinking." The report largely ignores legacy competitors and focuses on the new wave of digital companies, including *First Look Media*, *Vox*, *Huffington Post*, *Business Insider*, and *BuzzFeed*. "They are ahead of us in building impressive support systems for digital journalists, and that gap will grow unless we quickly improve our capabilities," the report says (Tanzer, 2014).

Box 1. Case study on The Columbus Dispatch

The Columbus Dispatch

By Jan Leach, Kent State University

The *Columbus Dispatch* has a number of databases published on its website and also maintains a database of public information for its reporting staff to use. The paper is well known for computer-aided reporting and data-crunching journalism. Most newsroom employees are using *Twitter* and *Facebook* to connect with readers and sources. Some of their data-driven reporting involves surprising investigative work: A series on bad teachers resulted in changes to the law to protect school children from predators; ongoing coverage of data-scrubbing in Columbus schools prompted changes at the state and local levels.

Secrecy 101

In May 2009, The *Dispatch* published in print and online a two-part series titled *Secrecy 101*, in which two reporters detailed how college athletic departments keep NCAA violations big and small secret, citing federal FERPA laws, which are supposed to protect the privacy of students' education records. Within the series, reporters Jill Riepenhoff and Todd James conveyed, through statistical data and their own carefully constructed databases, that Ohio State University reported the highest number of NCAA violations of any bowl-division school.

That single reported nugget—Ohio State had more NCCA violations than any other school in the country (at the time)—has now been passed along and published so frequently that virtually no one knows or remembers where it originally came from. In fact, Riepenhoff, said people often ask her why the *Dispatch* doesn't report that detail about Ohio State, a question that still shocks her. "Take newspapers out of the mix and that statement is used so frequently now that people aren't even checking it and don't know who did the reporting of it," she said (Riepenhoff, 2014). But the reporting of that fact is significant, Riepenhoff and *Dispatch* Managing Editor-News Alan Miller said. It took the journalists six months to find and validate the material. People should know where the information comes from, that it's verified and that it's not speculation. That's why the *Dispatch* focuses heavily on data-based reporting and verification of facts (Miller, 2014).

A New Nose for News

Data journalism is reporting that combines "the traditional 'nose for news' and ability to tell a compelling story, with the sheer scale and range of digital information now available," according to Paul Bradshaw in *The Data Journalism Handbook* (Gray, Chambers & Bounegru, 2012.) It is arguably one of the disruptive innovations driving news organizations, separating conjecture from fact and bolstering (or diminishing) media credibility. Data analytics and data visualization have become both necessary and desired in newsrooms big and small. The *Dispatch* is one of those newsrooms.

With about 145,000 daily/265,000 Sunday circulation and 160-plus editorial (news) employees including those working on the newspaper's website, the *Dispatch* has carved a niche covering Columbus, Franklin County, the statehouse, Ohio State-OSU athletics, and central Ohio frequently using databases and data analytics and offering news and information in multiple, varied platforms. At the *Dispatch*, Editor Ben Marrison has been pushing data-based reporting for at least 20 years. According to Miller and Riepenhoff, Marrison believes in the concept of data reporting and fostering the skills to do it. "There really is recognition that that's (data) what sets us apart," Riepenhoff said.

From news to features to sports to business, the *Dispatch* is telling stories with data. There are quick daily pieces on things such as farmer's markets and pedestrian accidents and longer stories on topics such as home foreclosures or disciplined teachers. Most data-based stories also include web extras such as lists, charts, interactive graphics and tables. The payoff for the Dispatch's commitment to data reporting may be in credibility. Readers, web and mobile viewers might see a story that's interesting. If they also see data behind the details they're more likely to believe it, according to Riepenhoff and Miller. "It's not just big projects; it's across the board. Our stories have been elevated and have far more impact. People notice and really appreciate it," Miller said (2014).

The paper's website also conveniently includes a separate section/tab labeled "data" that various simple lists and charts on any number of topics such as census, schools, crime, sports and more (*Dispatch.com*, 2014). This compilation does not accompany any story, nor is a story necessary to understand the data; it's there for consumption and usefulness. Again, the idea is to convey news and information to consumers in any format they want it, Miller said.

continued on following page

Box 1. Continued

Demanding Consumers

The future success of media entities like the *Dispatch* may depend on the rich detail of data journalism and multi-platform availability of the journalistic work. Consumers of all ages are more demanding. Once news is consumed, it may be saved, shared via social media like *Facebook*, blogged and spread. Gary Kiefer, *Dispatch* managing editor-new media, said media organizations have to adapt their work to consumers' habits. He said there is wide and common adoption of technology by the potential audience, which makes it easier to reach more people but that more people demand more—a Catch 22 that may be key to survival of the news industry. "Trying to obtain information in a digital fashion is no longer foreign, including for older audiences," Kiefer said. *Facebook* sharing, for example, is a big way to reach an audience that's not only local. "We see our stuff spread far and wide," he added (Kiefer, 2014). Miller said some in the *Dispatch* audience still want print, others want digital and still others want news on their phones. "The bottom line is we are delivering all the news we put in print and more and delivering online and more and in any format you want it but we have not done enough to tell people we are your 24-hour news operation in any format you wish."

Data, disruption; multiple platforms—all will continue to contribute to journalism's success. Combined, these concepts and commitment to them will likely improve media literacy and credibility. The proof is apparent: After the *Secrecy 101* stories were published, legislators called for changes in FERPA use, colleges and the NCAA examined, and sometimes changed, their interpretation of FERPA. And one other thing. "That nugget about OSU leading the nation in NCAA violations literally cost the Dispatch thousands of dollars because *Secrecy 101* was a six-month investigation, yet people pass around that information (to this day) as if it were free," Riepenhoff said.

Source: Jan Leach, Kent State University

The *Poynter Institute* (http://www.poynter.org) and the *Global Investigative Journalism Network* (www.gijn.org) each maintain excellent lists of resources and tools to support data based journalism. The tools can be grouped into five broad categories each with specific tools and methods:

1. **Data analysis** is supported by a broad range of powerful tools that include: Microsoft Excel, IBM ManyEyes, Google spreadsheet, Qlikview, SQL, Python, Django, Ruby on Rails. All facilitate the process of inspecting, cleaning, transforming, and modeling data to discover useful information.
2. **Semantic analysis** often uses online tools like DocumentCloud, Semaphore, NOD3X that can import hundreds of documents and show who and what is being mentioned on particular dates making it possible to examine the most newsworthy facets.
3. **Scraping** is becoming an increasingly useful method to get the answers that a journalist needs—not just the story someone else wants to tell. It is a particularly powerful way to gain insight from public data on the web. Scraper, OutwitHub, Beautiful Soup, Scraperwiki are popular with journalists who consider scraping faster than a Freedom of Information Act (FOIA) request and frequently provides more detailed and structured results than a public records request. Scraping for Journalists (Bradshaw, 2013) is a popular guide to learning the techniques behind writing scripts to grab information from the web.
4. **Personalization** provided by Internet forums, weblogs, wikis, social networks, crowd-sources and content communities bring new meaning to the old saying that all news is local. Capabilities provided here connect people to stories—underscoring how it affects you, based on the details you may have provided relative to your education, age, marital status, employment, geography, affiliations and interests.

5. **Visualization and Mapping** applications incorporate the capability of real-time and stored GPS data to help journalists visualize multi-dimensional data sets using tools like Wolfram Alpha, Google Earth, Google Maps, PostGIS, SpatiaLite, Fusion, and Tableau.

Box 2. Case study on Digital First Media

Digital First Media

By Susan Zake

Digital First Media, Inc. is a newspaper management company known for its innovative business practices on multiple platforms. It manages the *MediaNews Group*, *Digital First Ventures*, and *21st Century Media* and is headquartered in New York City. As of 2012, the company's newspapers and online media outlets had 66.6 million readers. According to *its* CEO, *DFM* prioritizes delivery of news and information on the platform of the customer's choice—including web, mobile, SMS and social media.

Digital First, Print Last

When John Paton started a blog (Paton, 2010) to have a "dialogue with employees and the public on how newspaper companies can adapt and thrive," he called it "Digital First." Since then, the expression "digital first, print last" has become an industry catch phrase symbolizing the order in which readers want news. It also suggests the potential solution to replace print revenues that Paton believes will "inevitably disappear." (Kirchner, 2011).

As CEO of *DFM*, a management company first formed in September 2011 to manage the *Journal Register Company*, now *21st Century Media*, and *MediaNews Group* properties, Paton blogged at the time about the immediate changes he made to the *Journal Register's* structure and challenged its employees to "start thinking differently about how we conduct business." Paton's communications with his staff, along with continually emerging new initiatives, are aimed at overcoming the disruption in the newspaper industry caused by the implosion of and continuing drop in print advertising revenue.

In April 2010, Paton launched *The Ben Franklin Project*. On his blog, he said the project was intended to help employees learn how to work in "the new news ecology to see where we as professional journalists fit in this new system and how we best serve our communities." Employees from *The News Herald* in Lake County, Ohio and the weekly newspaper at *Montgomery Media's Perkasie News-Herald* had 30 days to reinvent themselves and, "from assigning to editing–create, publish and distribute news content on the web and print, using only free tools available on the Internet" (Cooper, 2010).

Effects of Participant Journalism

Continuing on a path of innovation, Paton launched *Project Thunderdome*, (2014) "designed to deliver high-quality, non-local content to all Digital First Media newsrooms and, in turn, free local journalists to focus on local content and audience engagement." The project created a central team of digital journalists led by Jim Brady, the editor in chief of *DFM*, and Robyn Tomlin, the editor for *Thunderdome*. Steve Buttry, the Digital Transformation Editor for *DFM*, said his job was "to help our newsroom move further, faster and smarter down the digital path," (Buttry, 2014).

Buttry sees the biggest disruption in the newspaper business model of the bundle, "Where in one package, we used to sell investigative reporting and sports coverage and features and recipes and horoscopes and advice and comics and crosswords." Buttry said, "Different people like different things in that bundle, so that lots of people bought it even if they were buying it for different reasons." Further, the "disrupting of the bundle—disrupting is almost too mild a word for what it did to the business model—the ability to sell that many ads, to charge that much for them is just gone."

Buttry is critical of the industry for not seeing the opportunities presented by technology and for not becoming the local marketplace that sells "stuff directly to people, like *Amazon* and *EBay* and airlines and hotels do. Rather than sell the businesses in our community eyeballs—we're selling them customers, we're making transactions, we're selling their shit." The newspapers' ability to capture market share was a missed opportunity. "Nobody can gather local audience the way we do. If we had thought of that …we'd have been much more successful," (Buttry, 2014.)

Brady said mobile phones are the newest disruption. Instead of having one platform on the Web, or one site for all browsers to use, the mobile phone changes everything all over again. But he also thinks "the mobile phone is the first really huge development that plays into the hands of local developers," because knowing your audience's location will be everything. Buttry characterized the important part of what *Thunderdome* accomplished as raising "the data skills around the company." The establishment of a discussion list, plus efforts company-wide, helped pull together a community of interested journalists with "up to 120 people who were learning and practicing some data skills with varying levels." Throughout the company, Buttry said, "our people were able to do more things to analyze the data and play that watchdog role with government."

continued on following page

Box 2. Continued

The Need for Expertise

Despite the gains made at *DFM* during his tenure, Buttry says there is still too little growth in data journalism and "most newsrooms don't have enough data journalism expertise." Buttry says, "I was subjected to the term, *computer assisted reporting*; I thought that was like saying telephone-assisted reporting or notebook-assisted reporting. It's just an essential tool a reporter has to know how to use—and most of us don't know how to use it—except for writing a story or surfing the web. I think it's still too much of a specialty, but it certainly has grown as a specialty."

Brady sees data as an opportunity to gain greater insight into readers and deliver information that is of interest to them, along with a custom experience based on what the data says about the reader. "Data is not letting anything hit the floor that we can use."

Another initiative, "Project Unbolt," (2014) which Buttry launched in January 2014, was an effort to take "a massive wrench to the culture and workflow of our newsrooms and unbolt them" so they are "Digital First in culture, processes and priorities." Paton's response to low digital ad prices, where revenue compared to print ads was like "trading dollars for dimes," was to "start stacking dimes" and stop whining (Kirchner, 2011). Columbia Journalism Review's Bill Grueskin (2011) said "the gamble is that the Journal-Register Co. will be able to cut costs and increase its online audience quickly enough to compensate for the lower revenue that online advertising brings."

Paton's (2013) efforts met with some success—he said digital revenue at *DFM* rose 89.2% from 2009 to 2012, although total revenues were down 11.5%. The company outperformed Lee Enterprises and the McClatchy Company in the same period.

Upwardly Mobile

Most *DFM* newsrooms have crossed the 50% threshold of having most of their Web traffic coming from mobile, Buttry said, although that number is not broken down between tablets and phones. The trend year to year is that mobile traffic is rising steadily within the company. News organizations do two things, Brady said. They still perform the "water cooler function", which is "to raise an issue that's important and get people talking about it." They also fulfill the "personalized ATM model," which delivers information that meets an individual's needs. He thinks media need to "become a real central part of peoples' lives."

Despite assertions that Thunderdome would be "central to Digital First Media's future and will fuel the company's growth, (2011)" Paton announced April 2, 2014 the centralized newsroom would be shut down. Media analyst Ken Doctor (2014) attributed the closing to ongoing budget cuts and the "impact of unending high-single-digit loss in print advertising. The ongoing devastation in print is overwhelming even *DFM*'s relatively faster pace of digital innovation."

A New Toolbelt for Journalists

But in his blog, Paton (2014) attributed the closing to less of a need to centralize skillsets, because "what once were fairly isolated skills located in one place are now skills shared by many in our Company … we now have divisions taking their own Digital First initiatives. That means it is time to change again." Brady said he sees the journalist most prepared for the future as one "who goes out everyday and has a carpenter mentality. They look in their tool belt and figure out the three or four best tools for the job."

He said journalists should be:

1. Great at one thing.
2. Competent at a few things.
3. Know something about everything else.

Buttry said most of the *DFM* newsrooms are still run "by traditional newspaper editors who have been learning lots and lots of digital" and that "digital chops are a big part as we fill newsroom leadership positions." Since the closing of Thunderdome, Brady and Buttry have left *DFM*—Buttry will become the Lamar Visiting Scholar at Louisiana State University's Manship School of Communication. Brady will head to Temple University, where he will teach while incubating a news venture called Brotherly.

Brady's successor at *DFM*, David Butler (2014), said in a press release that despite the changes the company is experiencing *DFM* is still committed to "aggressively pursuing a new and exciting digital future while continuing to produce superb, exclusive, local enterprise reporting that makes a difference in the lives of our readers, including those who cherish print."

It will continue the work of Buttry, who said of his *DFM* tenure: "we pushed digital transformation. Changing your workflow, engaging with the community using data, using social media, curating the community conversation, crowd sourcing, all of those techniques. Certainly as aggressively as anybody."

Source: Susan Zake

Integrating data, big and small, in journalism allows journalists to move beyond anecdotes, and base their stories on facts and evidence. Almost all subjects journalists typically cover including: sports, elections, disasters, crime investigations and money flows produce data which can be analyzed through the use of *computers and social science techniques*. Steve Doig, Knight Chair at the Cronkite School of Journalism provides guidance to develop ideas and incorporate data in journalistic storytelling (Doig, 2014):

1. *Consider the statements you want to make.* Start with a hypothesis such as "crime is getting worse in my area." For this hypothesis, you might want to make statements like: Crime has increased by x amount; The amount of crime per 1000 people is greatest in our area, etc.
2. *Think of the variables required to make the statements.* Visualize a table of information. Columns typically include variables, and rows are for the individual data points. There are two kinds of variables: categorical and numerical. Categorical variables might include gender, type of crime, or zip code. Numerical variables might include counts, number of crimes, number of accidents, or number of arrests. An example of these variables working together might make it possible to report: type of crime; population of the places where crime is happening; date of crime; time; location; number of victims; and whether or not an arrest was made.
3. *Search for the data you need.* Once the variables are identified, research who collects the data. Government agencies, organizations and corporations and websites all collect a lot of information that might be useful to your story.
4. *Obtain the data.* Most countries have Freedom of Information laws, or an official way to request data from public agencies. There are many data formats—know which is required by the tools you choose. When working with the data, seek assistance from places like the National Institute for Computer-Assisted Reporting and Investigative Reporters & Editors NICAR-L listserv; The School of Data Archives; and The Data Driven Journalism website.
5. *Clean the Data.* Raw data in general, is messy. A classic example is found in campaign finance records where volunteers often compile the data. Names of people and cities are frequently misspelled, causing problems in the analysis. Spreadsheets and text editors that provide search and replace features can help cure the problems. Google's OpenRefine.com also makes it possible to clean data and transform it between different formats.
6. *Look for patterns.* Examine the data to scan for highs, lows, maximums, minimums and averages. Assess the shape of the data, look for outliers and anything that seems unusual. Many stories have been discovered through the simple sorting of data.

The scale and scope of data journalism often benefits from working in teams. There are many roles to cover, including: reporters, editors, graphic artists, photographers, videographers, page designers, web designers, app developers and analysts.

Box 3. Case study on The Akron Beacon Journal.

AKRON BEACON JOURNAL
ohio.com *There's something in it for you.*

The Akron Beacon Journal
By Hanna Armenta

Though the Akron Beacon Journal was one of the first papers in Ohio to take advantage of the web in 1997 with a sports site dedicated to the then-hot Cleveland Indians baseball franchise, the newspaper has struggled to make online news a priority in the newsroom and with readers. Print circulation continues to decline. Web visitors are increasing but many in the newsroom are hesitant to think digital first. Some of this may have to do with union issues.

continued on following page

Box 3. Continued

Updating a Legacy Since its inception, the *Akron Beacon Journal* has always striven for high-quality, provocative journalism that could not be found anywhere else. The outstanding reporting at the *Beacon Journal* has won many awards and national recognition for the newspaper. However, with the rise of the Internet, shrinking circulation caused advertising to take a hard hit in a time when profit margins needed to be high. In 2011, the *Beacon Journal* was at the forefront of other headlines when *Knight Ridder*, the second-largest newspaper publisher in the United States, sold to *The McClatchy Company* for $4.5 billion in cash and stock. The sale shocked the industry, but *Knight Ridder* was ahead of the curve. "Within the next year everyone else was doing it, and they were doing it even more dramatically," said Doug Oplinger, *Beacon Journal* managing editor (Oplinger, 2014). After the sale to *McClatchy*, the *Beacon Journal* was then sold to David Black of the privately owned Canadian publisher *Black Press Group Ltd.*, a wholly-owned subsidiary of *Sound Publishing Holdings*. With the sale to *Black*, the operation of the *Beacon Journal* would change dramatically. The newsroom would shrink by 25 percent—including replacing then Editor Debra Adams Simmons. The newsroom continued to downsize until 2014 to 75 full and part-time employees, compared to 197 employees in 2001. With the rise of the Internet and downsizing of the staff, the problem then became how to stay innovative and keep up with a 24-hour news-hungry public and a community that was changing. "If we don't find a way to monetize what we're doing, we're going to die too. The disruption comes in the way information moves through our communities," Oplinger said.
Going Digital Like most newsrooms, the Internet caused a shift in how news is reported, and on how we receive our news. Having instant access to information creates a pull for 24-hour news coverage that some newsrooms can't keep up with. While some see the Internet as being a major disruption, Rich Desrosiers, metro editor for the *Beacon Journal,* sees it as more of a distraction. "Anybody can put any kind of comment on a story; anyone can have a blog; anyone can post something on their *Facebook* page—completely un-vetted—and there are lots of times when we are chasing false leads or rumors and speculations that become the truth on the Internet," (Desrosiers, 2014). "We find ourselves wasting a lot of time trying to authenticate something that we know in our heart isn't true, but we have to check it out," he said. *Ohio.com* was initially created as a way to report on the Cleveland Indians. Since then, the site has grown to become the online version of the *Beacon Journal*, with digital extras like daily blogs. However, the size of its dedicated staff has gone from roughly 20 full-time employees in 2000, to six people who run the site and manage the social media in 2014. The *Beacon Journal* is having trouble making its digital presence as strong as some of its competitors—largely due to the *Beacon Journal* being a "print-first" newsroom. "The newspaper is the cash cow. If circulation is declining then the ripple effect of that effects everything," Desrosiers said. The desire to have a stronger web presence is there, he says, but the question becomes how to make that shift to a "web-first" newsroom when the median age of the *Beacon Journal* newsroom is 55. Many career journalists at the *Beacon Journal* have excelled at doing the same thing the same way for 30 years, he said, and "it is a challenge for them to embrace change."
A Change in Community The Internet and *Ohio.com* have forced the *Beacon Journal* to look beyond the geographical dissemination of their newspaper, and focus on the communities they are reaching via the Internet. "The *Beacon Journal's* traditional readership numbers have declined every year for the past decade, but the number of people reading our stories online has increased every year because of our partnership with *Ohio.com* and some of our other newspaper partnerships sharing our stories," Desrosiers says. *Ohio.com*, the Internet and social media are making it easier for the *Beacon Journal* to reach new audiences and open them up to a whole new generation of readers.
Getting Smart Internet-enabled smartphones now make it possible for news to be at the tips of our fingers 24 hours a day, seven days a week. Where news comes from and how consumers choose their favorite sources creates fierce competition for news organizations to upgrade and stay relevant. Everywhere you go, people are looking at their cell phones. They are getting the latest news from their friends, from *Twitter*, and *Facebook*, Oplinger says. The mobile space "is the disruption that will kill us unless we figure out how to penetrate that," he said. Smartphones are not only changing the way people get news, but also are changing the way news can be reported, Desrosiers says, "I know I can send somebody to a flash flood with an iPhone and basically get anything I want; I can get pictures; I can get video, and they can type a story and email it to me without ever leaving the scene." The ease of both reporting and receiving news makes discussion of eliminating print editions a common debate in the journalism industry. But at the *Beacon Journal*, with 90 percent of the revenue coming from print, Oplinger says it is not easy to let it go. "One of the problems of online advertising is that the little square on the right side of the page is not generating more money, it's generating less," he says.

continued on following page

Box 3. Continued

Learning to "Like" and "Tweet" Like many newspapers struggling to keep their digital presence as current as possible, the *Beacon Journal* now encourages reporters to create an online presence and cultivate relationships with their readers and in essence build their own communities. "How do we get people to understand that [the circulation department] is no longer doing all the work? You need to figure out how to do it yourself," Oplinger says. In 2014, the *Beacon Journal* began requiring reporters to use some form of social media like *Facebook* or *Twitter* to promote their stories. The *Ohio.com* team is also working on new strategies to improve its online presence to encourage and increase reader engagement with all news content.
The Cost of Digital With an increased push for digital content, the *Beacon Journal* is going to establish a new charge for the *Ohio.com* service they hope will raise revenue in the print circulation. Readers will be charged a monthly fee if they read more than seven stories on *Ohio.com*. If they have a subscription to the print newspaper they will have access to *Ohio.com* and to the digital *Replica* edition that is available to consumers with iPads and e-readers. While the *Beacon Journal* recognizes shortfalls, its true commitment remains the same: save democracy, empower people and play a constructive role in their community.

Source: Hanna Armenta

A NOT-SO-FINAL-WORD

I still believe that if your aim is to change the world, journalism is a more immediate short-term weapon. —Tom Stoppard, British dramatist and screenwriter

It has been more than a generation since author John Naisbitt penned the famous quote, "We are drowning in information but starved for knowledge" in his 1982 book, *Megatrends*. This was a year before the *DynaTAC* mobile phone launched on Ameritech's first 1G network. The phone cost $100 million to develop, and took over a decade to reach the market. It sold for $3,995 and took ten hours to charge for a talk time of just 30 minutes. Looking back, there has never been a time in our history when we have produced more data, nor has the challenge to understand it been more acute. Today, there is a lot of data, but also many *types* of data, created, managed and accessed in new ways. Over 6 billion hours of video are watched each month on YouTube—almost an hour for every person on Earth and the service now reaches more U.S. adults ages 18-34 than any cable network (YouTube, 2014). A variety of web sources estimate there are almost 450 million English language blogs active in 2014 with a new blog created somewhere around the globe every half-second.

What's compelling about big data is journalists now have tools that let them see the data and actually use it. But while the tools are new, the interest in analyzing big data is hardly a new phenomenon. The financial industry is a prime example of data analytics in action, ranging from the processing of credit scores at the retail level to high frequency quantitative trading in the stock markets. The airlines have been crunching passenger data for years to optimize everything from ticket prices to flight schedules. The manufacturing and utility industries collect myriad data points, typically at intervals of a few minutes, from thousands of sensors located in plants and other facilities and use these data to optimize operations. Consumer packaged goods operations owe their entire success to analyzing vast amounts of sales and marketing data. Pharmaceutical companies collect and analyze data from the drug discovery stage to large post-approval population studies. The insurance industry has been analyzing actuarial data for generations.

More recently in this generation, at a monitoring center in Salt Lake City, technicians working for *SecureAlert* sit in front of computer screens filled with multicolored dots looking for patterns of suspicious behavior. Each dot represents someone on parole or probation wearing one of the company's location-reporting ankle cuffs. The company works with law enforcement agencies around the U.S. to keep track of about 15,000 ex-cons, meaning it must collect and analyze billions of GPS signals transmitted by the cuffs each day. The more traditional part of the work consists of making sure people under house arrest stay in their houses. But advances in the way information is collected and sorted means *SecureAlert* isn't just watching; the company says it can employ algorithms to look for patterns in the data to actually predict when a crime is about to occur (Vance, 2011).

Every time you go shopping in a store or online, you share intimate details about your consumption patterns with retailers. Many stores are able to capture demographic information like your age; whether you are married and have kids; where you live; how long it takes you to drive to the store; your estimated salary; whether you've moved recently; what credit cards you carry in your wallet and what web sites you visit. Retailers can buy data about your ethnicity; job history; the magazines you read; if you've ever declared bankruptcy or got divorced; the year you bought (or lost) your house; where you went to college; what kinds of topics you talk about online; whether you prefer certain brands of coffee; paper towels; cereal or applesauce; your political leanings; reading habits; charitable giving and the number of cars you own. All those data are meaningless, however, without someone to analyze and make sense of it.

Many retailers study these details to figure out what you like, what you need, and which coupons are most likely to make you happy. *Target*, for example, discovered they could examine 25 items purchased by shoppers in various sizes to assign a "pregnancy prediction" score. The giant retailer notes women in their first trimester tend to purchase calcium, magnesium or zinc supplements as well as unscented lotions. From that small piece of information, Target can then look at other purchases to make related predictions about a woman's pregnancy—like her current trimester and even her due date.

In a controversial news story from 2012, the *New York Times* (Duhigg, 2012) reported Target, after analyzing the purchasing habits of a high school girl in Minneapolis, predicted she was pregnant and subsequently began mailing coupons to her father's house for her to use. Her father was incensed at the store's attempts to "encourage" pregnancy in teens and complained to the management. A few days later, the Dad who was embarrassed called the manager to apologize; it appeared his daughter actually was pregnant. Since then, Target realized sending baby ads to expectant mothers who have not announced their pregnancies could be intrusive. So now, they often mix in random ads for other products to make the pregnancy ads less noticeable. This practice has helped Target earn over $67 billion in retail sales in 2010 at a time when many stores were going bankrupt, proving other businesses could benefit from this type of data collection.

Journalists are on the frontlines of finding stories in the data, and turning that data into knowledge. Interpreting the data can be burdensome; yet reporting them correctly is imperative. The journalism industry faces a number of challenges from emerging technology, but perhaps the greatest challenge is in embracing the resulting change it causes to current best practices and the world of work within a particular organization. In a conversation with David Skok for the *Nieman Journalism Lab*, Clayton Christensen says companies should resist seeing their customers through the lens of demographics and instead think about the jobs they would hire their products to do (Ellis & Donovan, 2013). The customer, Christensen says, is the wrong unit of analysis; "it's the job you need to understand if you want to survive disruption." An example: Think of the job of delivering messages across distances. Western Union did that well—but they framed their business through their technology, the telegraph. As technology advanced, Western Union was left behind—even though the job of delivering messages across distances remained. Skok, who was working in broadcast for Canada's *Global News* at the time, said his department was a standalone unit with its own budget, trying to be revenue neutral or better within the company; it is "patient for growth but impatient for profit," he said. Every decision, Skok advised, "is based on whether a new initiative will allow us to scale in a way that lets us grow but also maintain profitability."

New threats and opportunities for media industries will continue to develop as current innovations mature and new technologies appear on the horizon. The Organization for Economic Cooperation and Development (2010) and other sources from around the web have noted a number of trends:

- Online readership is more ad hoc, irregular and sporadic.
- Search is the new culture.
- Accuracy, quality and diversity of news are at risk.
- Relaying information of a third party is becoming commonplace.
- Responsibility, integrity and standards for news reporting are diminishing.
- Creation of news content is at risk of commoditization (robo-journalism).

So what should new journalists train for specifically with regard to data journalism? There are some generic base skills, such as the ability to use spreadsheets, but many think focusing on tools is the wrong approach. It's always best to be led by your editorial needs: if you are interested in a field that involves public institutions, then FOI is useful; if not, then scraping may yield results more efficiently. If you are dealing with science, financial or health stories, statistical literacy is more important—although some literacy is a good idea in any field. If you want to make useful tools, then learn programming. If your story is about striking facts and figures, then perhaps learn how to use visualization tools and languages to show the data in an easy to understand form.

Data journalism will always involve new challenges, new tools, and new opportunities. An important skill for a journalist to have is a willingness to learn new things—but not at the expense of skills like good writing, ethics, news judgment, and an ability to investigate thoroughly and verify facts. These fundamental skills will be more important than ever as audiences search for credible news on the web.

Recent changes in technology—in particular the widespread availability of big data infrastructure—have made big data accessible to a much larger group of companies, from the smallest startups to the biggest enterprises (Harford, 2014). That, in turn, is going to spawn a huge wave of big data apps, and ultimately, a new set of billion dollar tech companies. Tim Harford, writing for the *Financial Times,* points out "as our communication, leisure and commerce have moved to the Internet and the Internet has moved into our phones, our cars and even our glasses, life can be recorded and quantified in a way that would have been hard to imagine just a decade ago." As with so many buzzwords, Harford reminds us big data still is "a vague term, often thrown around by people with something to sell." Harford cautions when it comes to data, size isn't everything. In a messy pile of raw, found data there must always be a question about who and what is missing. Kaiser Fung, (2013) a data analyst and author of *Numbersense*, warns against simply assuming we have everything in the data that matters. "N=All is often an assumption rather than a fact about the data," he says. Indeed, looking back at the famous story of Target's statistical sorcery to determine the pregnancy scores of customers, Fung, who has spent years developing similar approaches for retailers and advertisers says, "There's a huge false positive issue." What this means is that in the shock and awe of discovering the depth of insight yielded in the correct analysis and unintended results, we didn't get to hear the countless stories about women who received coupons from Target for babywear—but in fact, were not pregnant.

According to David Spiegelhalter, Winton Professor of the Public Understanding of Risk at Cambridge University, "There are a lot of small data problems that occur in big data, they don't disappear because you've got lots of the stuff." Big data and disruptive innovation are an integral part of the media landscape and while big data promise much to scientists, entrepreneurs, governments and now, journalists—the results are doomed to disappoint us if we ignore some very familiar statistical lessons.

REFERENCES

Bradshaw, P. (2013, May 13). Ebook interactive: what do you think of it so far? *BBC News*. Retrieved June 19, 2014, from http://www.bbc.co.uk/blogs/collegeofjournalism/entries/e7addb23-3f6d-3cb7-9b5c-4cd8035d41cd

Christensen, C. M. (1997). *The innovator's dilemma: when new technologies cause great firms to fail*. Boston: Harvard Business School Press.

Cohen, P. (2011, April 26). Technology advances: Humans supersize. *The New York Times*.

Desrosiers, R. Interview by Gordon Murray. Phone interview. June 5, 2014.

Diebold, F. X. (2003). *Big data dynamic factor models for macroeconomic measurement and forecasting: a discussion of the papers by Lucrezia Reichlin and Mark W. Watson*. Cambridge, MA: Cambridge University Press.

Diebold, F. X. (2012). *A personal perspective on the origin(s) and development of 'big data': The phenomenon, the term, and the discipline*. Department of Economics, University of Pennsylvania.

Doig, S. (2014, May 13). Data driven journalism. *From Idea to Story: Planning the data journalism story*.

Duggan, M. (2013, September 19). *Cell phone activities 2013*. Pew Research Centers Internet American Life Project RSS.

Gartner. (2011, June 27). *Gartner Says Solving 'Big Data' Challenge Involves More Than Just Managing Volumes of Data*. Gartner.

How Americans get their news - American Press Institute. (2014, March 17). American Press Institute RSS. Retrieved June 18, 2014, from http://www.americanpressinstitute.org/publications/reports/survey-research/how-americans-get-news/

Howard, A. (2012, November 26). Investigating data journalism. *Radar*.

Jarus, O. (2013, October 10). Clues to Lost Prehistoric Code Discovered in Mesopotamia. *LiveScience*.

Kiefer, G. Interview by Jan Leach. Phone interview. June 18, 2014.

Laney, D. (2012, January 14). *Deja VVVu: Others Claiming Gartner's Construct for Big Data*. Gartner Blog Network.

Lohr, S. (2013, February 1). The origins of 'big data': An etymological detective story. *The New York Times*.

Lyman, P., & Varian, H. (2000, January 1). About the project. *How Much Information?*

Marshall, T. (2008, July 21). *The changing newsroom*. Pew Research Centers Journalism Project RSS.

Meeker, M. (2014, May 28). *Internet trends*. Internet Trends 2014 Code Conference. Kleiner Perkins Caufield Byers.

Miller, A. Interview by Jan Leach. Phone interview. June 19, 2014.

Miller, A. R. (1971). *The assault on privacy*. Ann Arbor, MI: University of Michigan Press.

Morris, R. J., & Truskowski, B. J. (2003). The evolution of storage systems. *IBM Systems Journal*, *42*(2), 205–217. doi:10.1147/sj.422.0205

National Institute for Computer-Assisted Reporting. (n.d.). Investigative reporters & editors. Retrieved June 19, 2014, from http://www.ire.org/nicar/

Oplinger, D. Interview by Gordon Murray. Phone interview. June 11, 2014.

Press, G. (2013, May 9). A very short history of big data. *Forbes*.

Price, D. J. (1961). *Science since Babylon*. New Haven, CT: Yale University Press.

Rider, A. F. (1944). *The scholar and the future of the research library. A problem and its solution* [Advocating the use of micro-cards.]. Middleton, CT: Hadham Press.

Riepenhoff, J. Interview by Jan Leach. Email interview. June 24, 2014.

Riepenhoff, J. Interview by Jan Leach. Phone interview. June 19, 2014.

Riepenhoff, J., & Jones, T. (2011, Sept. 15). Secrecy 101. *The Columbus Dispatch*.

Sicular, S. (2013, March 27). Gartner's big data definition consists of three parts, not to be confused with three "V"s. *Forbes*.

Skok, D. (2012, January 27). *Aggregation is deep in journalism's DNA*. Nieman Journalism Lab.

Statistics, O. Data & Demographics. (n.d.).The Columbus Dispatch. Retrieved June 25, 2014. http://www.dispatch.com/content/sections/news/databases.html?cmpid=tplnnv

Tanzer, M. (2014, May 15). Exclusive: New York Times internal report painted dire digital picture. BuzzFeed. Retrieved Nov. 1, 2014 from HYPERLINK "http://www.buzzfeed.com/mylestanzer/exclusive-times-internal-report-painted-dire-digital-picture" \l ".iiy184wX2" http://www.buzzfeed.com/mylestanzer/exclusive-times-internal-report-painted-dire-digital-picture#.iiy184wX2

Tjomsland, I. A. (1980). Where do we go from here? Digest of Papers: The Gap between MSS Products and User Requirements. In *Proceedings of Fourth IEEE Symposium on Mass Storage Systems*. IEEE.

Worth, D. (2011, June 23). CERN experiments generating one petabyte of data every second. V3.co.UK. Retrieved June 8, 2014, from http://www.v3.co.uk/v3-uk/news/2081263/cern-experiments-generating-petabyte

ADDITIONAL READING

Anderson, J., & Rainie, L. (2014, March 14). Internet of Things. Pew Research Centers Internet American Life Project RSS. Retrieved June 24, 2014, from http://www.pewinternet.org/2014/05/14/Internet-of-things/

Arthur, C. (2010, November 22). Analyzing data is the future for journalists, says Tim Berners-Lee. The Guardian. Retrieved June 24, 2014, from http://www.theguardian.com/media/2010/nov/22/data-analysis-tim-berners-lee

Big data now current perspectives from O'Reilly Media: 2012 edition. (Kindle ed.). (2012). Sebastopol, CA: O'Reilly Media.

Bradshaw, P., & Rohumaa, L. (2011). *The online journalism handbook: skills to survive and thrive in the digital age*. Harlow: Longman.

Brockmeier, J. (2011, August 11). Gartner adds big data, gamification, and internet of things to its hype cycle. ReadWrite. Retrieved June 24, 2014, from http://readwrite.com/2011/08/11/gartner-adds-big-data-gamifica

Feinleib, D. (2012, May 24). Tech's Next Billion Dollar IPOs. Forbes. Retrieved June 24, 2014, from http://www.forbes.com/sites/davefeinleib/2012/05/24/techs-next-billion-dollar-ipos-big-data-apps/

Grabowicz, P. (2014, June 1). The transition to digital journalism. Print Editions Decline. Retrieved June 24, 2014, from http://multimedia.journalism.berkeley.edu/tutorials/digital-transform/

Gray, J., Chambers, L., & Bounegru, L. (2012). The data journalism handbook. Sebastopol, CA: O'Reilly; http://www.datajournalismhandbook.org/1.0/en/index.html, Retrieved June 24, 2014.

Journal, I. R. E. (n.d.). IRE Journal. Retrieved June 24, 2014, from http://ire.org/publications/ire-journal/

Leonhardt, D. (2014, April 22). Navigate news with the upshot. The New York Times. Retrieved June 24, 2014, from http://www.nytimes.com/2014/04/23/upshot/navigate-news-with-the-upshot.html?rref=upshot&_r=2

Manishin, G. (2014, January 10). 5 industries facing disruption in 2014 - disruptive competition project. Disruptive Competition Project RSS. Retrieved June 24, 2014, from http://www.project-disco.org/competition/011014-5-industries-facing-disruption-in-2014/

Narisetti, R. (2014, April 7). We need to talk: 26 awkward questions to ask news organizations about the move to digital. Nieman Journalism Lab. Retrieved June 24, 2014, from http://www.niemanlab.org/2014/04/we-need-to-talk-26-awkward-questions-to-ask-news-organizations-about-the-move-to-digital/

Needham, J. (2013). *Disruptive possibilities how big data changes everything*. Sebastopol, CA: O'Reilly Media.

Origin and Growth of Big Data Buzz. (2012, May 31). The Origin and Growth of Big Data Buzz. Retrieved June 24, 2014, from http://it.toolbox.com/blogs/infosphere/the-origin-and-growth-of-big-data-buzz-51509

State of the News Media 2014 Key Indicators. (2014, March 26). Pew Research Centers Journalism Project RSS. Retrieved June 23, 2014, from http://www.journalism.org/2014/03/26/state-of-the-news-media-2014-key-indicators-in-media-and-news/The

Tynan, D. (2008, March 18). The 10 most disruptive technology combinations. PCWorld. Retrieved June 24, 2014, from http://www.pcworld.com/article/143474/the_10_most_disruptive_technology_combinations.html

Walters, A. (2012, March 3). Strata week: Google offers big data analytics. OReilly Radar. Retrieved June 24, 2014, from http://radar.oreilly.com/2012/05/google-bigquery-data-journalism-open-data.html

KEY TERMS AND DEFINITIONS

Big Data: Big data is high volume, high velocity, and/or high variety data assets and information that require new forms of processing to enable enhanced decision making, insight discovery and process optimization.

Data Analysis: Data analysis is the process of transforming raw data into usable information, often presented in the form of a published analytical article, in order to add value to the statistical output.

Data Journalism: Data journalism is a journalism specialty reflecting the increased role that numerical data is used in the production and distribution of information in the digital era. It reflects the increased interaction between content producers (journalist) and several other fields such as design, computer science and statistics.

Disruptive Innovation: Disruptive innovation describes a process by which a product or service takes root initially in simple applications at the bottom of a market and then relentlessly moves up market, eventually displacing established competitors.

Disruptive Technology: Disruptive technology does not have a pre-defined data model. It is not organized or easily interpreted by traditional databases, and typically, it is text-heavy. Metadata, Twitter tweets, and other social media posts are examples of unstructured data.

Multi-Structured Data: Multi-structured data refers to a variety of data formats and types and can be derived from interactions between people and machines, such as web applications or social networks.

Personalization: Personalization of news occurs when content is made for, or directed, or adjusted to a particular individual or group.

Scraping: Scraping is a technique in which a person or computer program extracts data and information from websites and other data sources for analysis and incorporation into news stories.

Semantic Analysis: Semantic analysis is the process of relating words, phrases, clauses, sentences and paragraphs to their language-independent meanings to look for patterns and examine the most newsworthy facets.

Sustaining Technology: Sustaining technology relies on incremental improvements to an already established technology.

Unstructured Data: Unstructured data does not have a pre-defined data model. It is not organized or easily interpreted by traditional databases, and typically, it is text-heavy.

Chapter 14
Transformational Content and Relationships:
Research, Analytical Tools, and Big Data in Shaping the News User Experience (UX)

Stuart Schwartz
Liberty University, USA

ABSTRACT

This chapter outlines the trend toward research within news organizations based upon big data and the increasing emphasis of growth-oriented companies on promoting a positive and passionate User Experience (UX). It discusses the implications of digital research techniques developed by successful technology and consumer merchandising organizations, and links the 24/7 nature of digital research methodologies to the development of more user-responsive and successful news organizations. A journalistic organization that wants to grow in the digital age must revamp its operations to take advantage of the continuous big data research cycle. This means creating a feedback loop from the organization to the information consumer and back, viewing journalism as content to be shaped to the UX through constant modification and change based on growing sets of user behavior and preference data.

INTRODUCTION

The evolution of new research in reaction to the explosive growth of big data has the potential to be every bit as intense and impactful as the changes and challenges of the digital era. This revolution is made possible by the increasingly sophisticated technology of consumer measurement, along with the ability of news producers to create, aggregate, and store an almost limitless amount of digital data on individual market behavior. This may assist news organizations in not only surviving, but thriving, in the digitally-driven 21st century. Ultimately, the winner in all of

DOI: 10.4018/978-1-4666-8580-2.ch014

this is the news and information consumer. Consumers may increasingly find that contact with news channels shaped by big data immeasurably increases their likelihood of a satisfying User Experience (UX), while increasing affinity between news organizations and their audiences.

There are three critical elements that will enable a news organization to employ big data to positively transform the UX. These same three elements are the natural result of a news organization adopting, as an integral part of operations, the research tools and analytics essential to big data and its corresponding methodologies. The three elements:

First, *the use of the big data research approach will promote a consumer-oriented worldview rather than the traditional journalistic view of the world.* This is largely due to a perceptual shift accompanying the use of digital research approaches. This shift may pull a news organization from its conventional journalistic view of the world, wherein the news product is traditional journalism and the news consumer needs to be informed by what the newsroom views as the necessary topics of the day, to an evolved view that sees the news product as content and the audience as users—rather than the objects of journalism—in need of a long-term relationship with the news organization.

Second, the UX can be dramatically transformed by the adoption and use of a new research and analytics paradigm, enabling an interactive approach over the one-way capabilities of older tools. This approach relies in large part on the constantly evolving digital analytics that are already part and parcel of successful digital-based information organizations, as pioneered in both the consumer merchandising and technology sectors.

And, third, effective use of big data research tools and analytics demand a commitment to a continuous research process, integrating user analysis into the everyday operations of news/content teams. This process empowers the audience, consumers of news and information products, and makes them part of a continuous product-improvement process. The focus of news organizations is shifting from "doing journalism" to producing an interactive connection between news providers and consumers through an intelligent UX.

BACKGROUND: TRANSFORMING TRENDS

Paired together, big data and UX have become—in the age of technology-powered data collection and analysis tools—drivers of insight and, consequently, market empowerment (Svilar & Chakraborty, 2013). This has happened to such an extent that 21st century organizations, and even slow-to-change news enterprises, cannot adequately market and operate without the use of these tools, which in turn have attracted an army of software suppliers (see, for example, Schiff, 2012). Along with this, research has been elevated to a central place within organizations' competitiveness. News organizations will increasingly rely on big data and its affiliated research tools to shape content, while research methodologies continually push them toward the use of metrics that assume a well-targeted UX as a primary goal.

It's trite but it's true – you are what you measure. The constantly expanding arsenal of digital research tools assumes an affecting and passionately positive UX as the pot of gold at the end of the rainbow for an organization. The tools were developed and continue to be developed with the single-minded notion that progress in a market demands positive users, and extraordinary progress demands extraordinarily positive users.

Some brief definitions important to understanding the research that will lead to a positive UX include the following:

- **Big Data:** Big data is the variety, volume and value of data that results from the combination of the tracking and storing of the digital footprints left by consumer behaviors and habits. The acquisition and employment of digital analytics that correspond to the product-related behaviors related to an organization's markets (Bertolucci, 2013), and the ability to join all of this with other relevant data collected as part of the marketing and operations of an organization (Tien, 2013), all combine to provide insight that increases the ability of an organization to create and enhance relationships with audiences, customers and affiliates.
- **User Experience (UX):** UX emphasizes users' experiences with digital products or services. This is an encapsulated reference to the need for an organization in the digital age to emphasize the experience with its products and/or services of the individuals who comprise the segments of its markets. As part of this definition, an organization concentrates on discerning and managing the experience of its products and/or services by the consumer. The UX was originally developed by software developers, hardware designers, and marketers as a way of getting minute-by-minute feedback on the use of their products or services and, consequently, using that to influence succeeding product and design improvements. In practice, this developed into an iterative process, whereby the UX became a key determinant of strategy at all levels and stages of the organization and its products. This, in turn, produces continuous innovation that, building off of previous steps, positively impacts users (Dadich, 2013). The UX, then, has become shorthand for continuous improvement to the experience that users have with an organization and its products, incorporating a continuous interactive feedback process between the organization and its affiliates that relies on the ongoing creation and analysis of big data.

It may appear that the UX approach is actually at odds with traditional journalistic approaches, both in practice and academia. Traditionally, news has been regarded as the product of designated journalists who take it upon themselves to decide the content and formats through which the audience will be informed. Often, this selectivity rests upon a philosophical and ethical belief system of social responsibility, as documented within the in the seminal work of Fred S. Siebert, titled *Four Theories of the Press: The Authoritarian, Libertarian, Social Responsibility, and Soviet Communist Concepts of What the Press Should Be and Do* (1956). Journalists in the United States have enthusiastically viewed the social responsibility theory as the raison d'être for an approach that values what journalists prefer over the preferences and opinions of average news consumers. The result is (1) the development of a moral framework for both professional practice and journalism education, and (2) the positioning of journalism and journalists as social advocates. This view is reinforced periodically by reports of self-censorship imposed by news organizations. Representative of this genre is, for example, Bernard Goldberg's *Bias: A CBS Insider Exposes How the Media Distorts the News* (2002) or the more recent *Stonewalled: My Fight for Truth Against the Forces of Obstruction, Intimidation, and Harassment in Obama's Washington* by Sharyl Attkisson (2014).

The result of this is the notion that journalism is not just creating content for consumption; using self-proclaimed expertise and understanding of societal needs, journalists are determining, what information is appropriate to filter through to audiences, with the understanding that that information will assist in the social engineering of American society. This social engineering is part of the considerable efforts of both journalism educators and practitioners to be regarded as knowledge elites (Donsbach, 2014).

On the other hand, the effective research use of big data and UX is based upon the market-oriented notion that individuals are in the best position to determine what is and what is not important to them, and big data research techniques are singularly useful in helping researchers understand the minds of consumers. Newsrooms will find themselves closer to a true understanding of and engagement with readers and viewers when these tools are worked into the news creation and dissemination process.

- **Snapshot Research:** Snapshot research comprises the existing methodologies traditionally used by news organizations to assess the status of its news product in the market. It includes survey and other types of research related to panels, questionnaire design, measurement, and sampling tools, and is episodic in nature. The major characteristic of this is periodic data-gathering and analysis deliveries, commonly done on a pre-arranged schedule by a news organization (depending largely on the size of the organization, it may be done monthly, quarterly, or annually), and trending data and analytics are more often than not offered in year-to-year comparisons.

There are a range of potential advantages to news organizations and their audiences in embracing this digital big data/UX research paradigm. This approach has been the foundation of advances in the technology and consumer merchandising market sectors, and involves the real-time and enhanced collection and storage of data, as well as continually tracking the behaviors and preferences of consumers.

Never before has research played a more central role in the operations of consumer-oriented industries (Svilar, Chakraborty & Kanioura, 2013). The need to collect, aggregate, and analyze an exponentially expanding collection of consumer behavior and preferences has become critical to the shaping of product. A similar effect is now being seen within the news industry. The insights yielded by data research processes have the capacity to transform the worldview and, consequently, the work products of those producing the nation's news. For the news industry, the adoption of the big data approach to research and its attendant advances in digital tools and analytics offer the possibility of providing the insight necessary to bring responsive news organizations closer to their audiences. This, in turn, puts the goal of a more positive UX at the center of the news gathering and creation process. This increases the potential for a digital future in which news organizations will not just survive, but thrive based on their relationships with users and correspondingly enhanced UX.

The worldview that incorporates strategic use of big data and the primary goal of a more positive news UX is all about relationships, particularly the relationship of an organization with its affiliates – readers, viewers, audiences. News organizations are fast acquiring the ability—through websites, social and interactive media devices—to know what individuals are viewing, doing, even thinking, through the ability, for example, of viewers to comment upon individual content items, express preferences, enter contests, or interact with news producers. Because of this, the news industry has the opportunity to move from a journalism model that has been resulting in record losses of audience in recent years, to a broader content creation worldview. The latter will create a bond between the audience and news organization that mirrors that of the most successful global consumer marketing organizations. A content creation worldview challenges the ability of a news organization to create and publish editorial product—content—that connects with the attitudes, values, and information needs of users. At the heart of content, rather than journalistic news strategy, is the impact that effectively used big data has on the ability of an organization to strengthen the relationship with its customers and dramatically improve the UX. The foundation is the integration of research into the content strategy operation. Unlike the business and social scientific research tools of the last half century that have largely been used to periodically inform news producers (what we are calling Snapshot Research), this new digital research era requires a vastly increased awareness of user behaviors, attitudes, and worldview, all of which are assumed in effective use of big data analysis tools. The result: the news business is being pushed to become closer to its customers.

The path to future growth for the news industry runs through the adoption of a more customer-friendly orientation. The successful news producer will join its counterparts in the consumer marketing industry, marshalling a variety of editorial tools and techniques, powered by the continuous research and analysis demanded by big data, and the needs of the passionately positive UX assumed as a goal in big data analysis and metrics. As news becomes consumer-oriented and the focus shifts from a journalistic product to the UX, the gap between the research methodologies and tools being used by consumer organizations will close. Savvy news production will come with a corresponding ability to more closely understand and positively impact the view of the news consumer for a journalistic product. The news industry will increasingly view affiliates as news "users," versus the more passive designations of "viewers" and "readers." Along with this has come a corresponding shift in the nature of research tools, from the occasional to the continuous use of research as, in and of itself, a major factor in shaping a more positive and passionate UX.

RESEARCH TAKES CENTER STAGE

Snapshot research classics that have been a staple of audience research for years, will continue to have an important part to play in the digital future of news operations. However, they will play an altered and supporting role, morphing from a periodic snapshot of consumers to a critical snapshot—providing additional information to be added to the individual records of segments of a population—to a continuing collection of data from specific individuals with whom the organization has developed a relationship. These data will be activity and interest-specific, rather than being used as a sample that represents a population.

The information that has been produced with these tools has offered valuable insights as to the nature of audiences and their preferences. Gains over the years in sampling theory and techniques, for example, have allowed news organizations to generate increasingly accurate portrayals of an organization's affiliated population of readers, or the news consumers. At the same time, technology-driven strides in statistical modeling and decision techniques have allowed both editorial and marketing portions of news organizations to provide more accurate direction for both the news and business sides of their organizations.

These same strengths apply to the periodic surveys offered by sales and marketing departments to gain an understanding of audience shopping and buying habits, invaluable for working with advertisers. But the tools that have been used in the past will still be used in the future, providing valuable information that, when combined with the avalanches of insight offered by big data in pursuit of a passionate UX, promises to dramatically improve the news creation and management capabilities of news organizations.

In terms of data collection, there is increasingly little difference between the news industry and other consumer product categories. Researchers in news organizations are joining their counterparts within the consumer sector in shifting from episodic surveys and market snapshots to the 24x7 collection and analysis of user behavior and characteristics. The ability to gather instantaneous information regarding the habits and behavior of users also enables the industry to continually shape the experience of its users through analysis, followed by reaction to continuing feedback. The result is a continuous loop of product offering-reaction-measurement-revised, offering-reaction-measurement.

Continuing assessment, done correctly, leads to continuing improvements in the UX. This is where the experiences of other industries can provide a glimpse of the future for the news business. It is rare to find a successful brand that does not gather information about the experience of users. From hard goods to soft goods, from tableware to software to the soft drink category, consumer marketers and merchandisers have evolved a continuing series of measurements and analytics that enable them, on the one hand, to intensify the bond between their brands, products, and services and consumers. This, in turn, has resulted in greater customer affinity and loyalty.

The successful news organizations of the future will look more like the successful consumer marketer of the present, as news producers emphasize and measure affinity and loyalty. Affinity and its measurement are critical goals for the news organization, as it emphasizes the importance of the underlying and positive strength of the bond between the news organization and its audience; at the same time, loyalty as both a goal and the object of a continuing series of operational research measurements is critical to understanding whether the affinity created between the organization and its audience is leading to more frequent and intense use of the news products.

THE UX OF THE NEWS FUTURE: ENGAGED, SATISFIED, AND POSITIVE

The successful news organization of the future will weave research into news and information operations. The digital era of content brings with it an almost limitless information marketplace, forcing information outlets to shape content (news) in such a way to provide a UX that leaves individuals feeling *engaged*, *satisfied*, and *positive*. Regardless of the monetization approach (advertiser supported, subscription, or other revenue paths that unfold along the way) that news organizations take as they increasingly become digital content organizations, their success depends upon engaged and frequent users, which in turn depends upon a positive and passionate UX.

In news, as in all life and consumption, the more positive and intense the UX, the greater the loyalty and affinity of the user, and the more value users attach to enterprises' products and services. In the digital age, driven by big data and metrics focused on the UX, research will play a critical role in helping an organization create content that provides a positive UX. User behaviors, attitudes, and values—as discerned through continuing user interaction with the organization—will inform story creation, development, and staging—just as it does in successful consumer product categories. The news producers who thrive in the big data age will continually test and react to understand the impact of various UX elements – such as color, theme, video/audio, slant, length, typography, and comment friendliness – that must be manipulated to produce news content. Each news organization must produce its own "look and feel" that both sets it apart from an Internet filled with competitors, and evokes a passionately positive UX. The more intense and positive the UX, the greater, longer, and more intensely engaged the viewing, reading, and buying of news and related products and services.

ALL YOU NEED IS LOVE

The tools used by effective consumer marketers have enabled them to intensify the UX, increasing the positive affect and creating relationships that grow in affinity and loyalty. This relationship cycle is something that the successful news organization, with the aid of research integrated into operations, will be able to emulate with the digital research and analysis tools associated with big data. These tools are integral to the digital research capabilities generated by online, social, and interactive delivery systems that are now standard fare for consumer marketing organizations, and are fast becoming available to the news business. The savvy and successful news organization will incorporate this continuing research to obtain feedback on the effect of the content products and service activities that will power growth for news organizations with an appropriately big data/user experience worldview. The relationship between the news organization and the user is analogous to human relationships, in which feedback is a natural part of daily communication and a key part of involved and attractive associations.

Although involving many moving parts and vast amounts of data, the underlying assumptions of the use of big data to improve the UX is simple. The more you love something—be it a person, product, or service—the more willing you are to spend time and money in service of that relationship. "All You Need is Love" is not just a song written by Beatles John Lennon and Paul McCartney during the golden days of British rock; it is also a handy way of achieving greater affinity, and thereby greater use, of the content that is the product of a news organization.

The following example illustrates the underlying big data, UX, and analytical assumptions:

Mother's Day is coming and Junior sends Mom flowers. Mom finds them at her front door, reads the card, and breaks into tears. "Oh, Junior," she exclaims, "Oh Junior, Junior, Junior—you remembered me after all!" And, caught in the emotion of the moment, Mom whips out a cell phone, calls her attorney, and puts Junior back in her will, ceding him a share of his sister's inheritance—she had previously been in line for all of Mom's wealth, as Junior had previously angered Mom by being the prototypical prodigal son. Junior, recognizing the worth of a good relationship with Mom, sends another batch of flowers as he manages the association in the hope of capturing an additional share of his sister's inheritance. Mom, as a participant in the parent/child relationship, has had a positive UX. Junior is managing the relationship, which is acquiring, analyzing, and acting upon a foundation of ever-increasing data. Data point: Mom called him within minutes of receiving the gift; previously, she only called him every other year (data point); she added him to her will (data point); with more flowers, a few calls, and the occasional box of chocolates, she gives him a larger share of her estate (more data points). As the data piles up, Junior has a better understanding of his mother, of how she reacts to gifts by type and occasion, her affinity for various types of flattering notes, and a gauge to growing her positive affinity and consequent loyalty. Mom may also have a better understanding of her son. Thanks to big data and a positive UX (by Mom), these two individuals have a positive, engaged relationship and Junior now has a path to a sizable chunk of inheritance, if not the whole estate.

Data provide insight. And big data—done right—provide increasingly actionable and effective insight of the kind that could facilitate more intense relationships of journalistic organizations with audiences—the markets—through an increasingly positive UX. "Could" is the operative word, as big data gains power in shaping the UX through its application by news content producers through research and analysis. But it is no guarantee of success; in much the same fashion as Junior, a news organization must use the appropriate analytics and take productive action, focusing on a positive UX.

ELEMENTS OF A TRANSFORMATIVE UX

There are three elements that must be present for a news organization to positively transform the UX. These elements include: (1) a consumer-oriented worldview rather than the traditional journalistic view of the world, with a corresponding view of the news product as *content* rather than traditional journalism and audiences/viewers/readers as users; (2) an understanding of the new research and analytics paradigm, in which older tools are subsumed by an interactive approach that relies in large part on the constantly evolving digital analytics that are part and parcel of successful digitally based consumer organizations; and (3) a commitment to a continuous research process that empowers the individuals affiliated with the organization—those who use its products, consume its information, and interact with the organization through its content products—and includes them in a continuous product improvement process on the part of the news organization. Along with this come corresponding UX gains for the organization.

Consumer-oriented worldview. Research makes a difference in how people view the world. Big data make a difference. Analytical tools make a difference. Never before has research been more relevant, as big data and attendant methodologies offer the opportunity for news producers to get closer to their audiences. In fact, it not only offers the opportunity but, because it is a natural outgrowth of the 21st century digitization, it is a required part of a successful news/content operation going forward. News organizations rely on digital information at both ends of the product production process, from the gathering and shaping of information to the final content with which users interact. The big data research process forces organizations to move toward a consumer orientation merely through its ability to track the digital habits of audiences and largely know—based on data generated by user behaviors—what content strategies and implementation approaches work and what ones do not work.

Even the most relentlessly traditional news outlets are increasingly relying upon online tools and services to both shape their products and disseminate final packages to audiences. Integral to a digitized information product are tracking, storage, and analytical capabilities that demand organizations consider what users say and do while organizations are generating news content. Previously, the research process was tedious and episodic, offered to news producers at the tail end of a laborious process of ordering surveys or focus group sessions, planning and staging the research operation, gathering subjects who would represent the market segments under study, querying them about their behavior, analyzing the query results, putting together reports, and then disseminating the results of the process to the news producers.

But now information is increasingly digitized and news information sources have gone online; research has followed, with a universe of analytical tools and metrics make it relatively easy to view information about market behavior in real-time. In addition, a growing host of sophisticated and useful software applications provide organizations with the means to interact with audiences, offering the ability to track and analyze those interactions. News audiences, like all consumer markets, have a digital footprint that enables information producers to see which news production efforts attract an audience, and for how long. This research capability is impossible to ignore, as it is inherent in the very tools and information production processes that power the digital information age.

The ease of use and ubiquity of digital research toolkits strengthens the link between news organizations' two primary products – created and engineered – and the need to track audience behaviors and engage in dialogue with them. This ease of interaction encourages organizations to understand individuals in their markets in ways that were never possible before, and makes it almost impossible to ignore user preferences. It also brings to the news production process a revolution in attentiveness in the same way that baby monitors brought to parenting a more careful and baby-centered approach to caring for infants. When checking on a sleeping baby—L'il Darling, let's say—entailed an effort by mommy and daddy to turn off the television, walk over to the stairs, listen carefully, and decide whether to climb halfway toward the baby's room, the well-being of L'il Darling tended to be episodic—confined to television commercials or the breather between the main course and dessert. Parents had to schedule the time and make an extraordinary effort to research the well-being of L'il Darling. When it was an effort, such research ("L'il Darling, you still there? You okay sweetie?") was adapted to the many other activities of parents, such as eating, socializing, or watching television. Consequently, they checked in fewer times with L'il Darling; i.e. they did less research into the well-being of their child, compiling less information and compiling less of a mental database of the activities of L'il Darling.

But then came baby monitors, which grew in power and capability with each digital innovation, and pretty soon every hiccup and gurgle of L'il Darling was immediately available to parents, who were accompanied through every part of their lives by the digital presence of L'il Darling. On the road you have the L'il Darling-cam; in the yard, the L'il Darling Bluetooth and ear buds—you get the picture. Increasingly, powerful and ubiquitous digital monitoring changed parenting from "I'll-check-when-I-want-or-get-a-chance" to an "in-my-face-demanding-attention-can't-ignore" endeavor.

As goes baby monitors and parenting, so goes news production. The individuals who comprise the audience for news and information have become "L'il Darlings" in their own right, demanding attention as digital research and analytical capabilities force a worldview change upon the news industry. The industry is transitioning from the gauging of consumer preferences and reaction to the news product on a basis of "I'll-arrange-the-research-when-I-want-or-get-a-chance" to an "in-my-face-analytics-and-market-reactions-that-demand-attention." The result: a growth in market knowledge and measurement capability has brought pressure to *do* something 24x7 with the knowledge, the kind of pressure that once was as episodic as the research.

Research has traditionally been done at most news outlets about once a year, although a few larger news outlets have had their own marketing staffs or resources that supplied audience information more frequently. Each meeting with the editorial staff had been a special event.

This approach will become increasingly scarce among news operations embracing the digital era. As the online migration of news and information continues, the capability to know the behaviors – and even thinking – of users is growing dramatically. Once the information is out there, it is not easy to ignore. News producers now have the ability to know which individuals within the audience are most active, what stories they are clicking on, what they are viewing, what they're saying and thinking, with what intensity, and much more. The news channels that embrace the market knowledge that comes with this will greatly increase their chances of success in the new information marketplace. Research is now part of the fabric of digital operations.

The key to all of this is the interaction of the news producers with big data and its concomitant ability for organizations to provide its users with a positive and engaging experience (UX). Big data and the ongoing research-based analytics are forcing the following changes in worldview upon news producers:

News is no longer news; it is, instead, viewed as "content." Success in the coming years for those involved in the creation, dissemination, and management of news will come from thinking of news as *content* that flows from a continuing operational process that is big data-research focused on producing a positive UX. This stands existing definitions of news on its head, traditionally viewed as information in a news format shaped by members of a news production staff according to internal, journalistic standards. This approach, a staple of 20th century journalism education and news organizations, largely ignores the experiences of users in favor of a profession-centered view of market information needs.

The digital research and operations era of big data has shifted the locus of news content from what a limited number of news producers think audiences *need* to what individuals *want*. Because the UX continuously generates users' digital information preference and behavior data, forward-looking news operations will have contemporaneous access to research on actual user behavior, as opposed to periodically generated projections from the sampling of populations. This puts the UX in the center ring as individuals in the market pick and choose between a variety of sources; the content that they *want* and their preferences are continually tracked, collected, analyzed, and—for the growth-oriented news organization in the digital age—acted upon. As the focus and research paradigm shifts, so, too, does the nature of the information, from "news-that-I-think-you-need" to "content-your-UX-data-says-you-want," the result of a continuous UX feedback loop that is shaped by a digital research process. The assumption here is that letting users (viewers, readers, audience members) control—or, at the least, have a major impact—upon the distribution of news content enhances the value of the channel. There is, however, a significant number of news producers contend that such control lessens the value of the channel and results in content of less value to society.

Content, then, is information that is shaped purposively by a research process to attract and engage individuals in targeted markets, part of a progression that includes an expanding database accessible to news producers as they ready the next wave of *content*, rather than *news*. This is not a trivial distinction, as new research techniques force a two-way and interactive dynamic on the news process. Pre-digital news was one-way, controlled by gatekeepers who decided what information was necessary for an audience to consume in an analog world of limited accessibility to information. However, all has changed in the digital era (Carr, 2012).

The digital age has brought an explosion of outlets for information, an almost limitless availability of information on users to be used in understanding their behavior and, consequently, the potential to dramatically and strategically affect UX. Rather than readers and viewers, digital citizens have become users of the world around them, which includes information. Every user has a unique data trail that can be captured—hence the emphasis on users who generate digital data trails of behaviors that can be incorporated into continuing content strategies by user-oriented news organizations.

Think about the word "user." In the news industry, the thought of a reader or viewer as a "user" has largely been confined to editorial playpens: i.e., "News You Can Use" such as nightly news segments about how to beat the cold, newspaper feature stories about, say, selecting an appliance, heart attack-free snow shoveling, restaurant reviews, or beauty tips. But the digital revolution is transforming the news industry by the ease with which consumer habits and activities are documented and piled up in the form of big data. Digital news organizations have come to the point where, if they want people to "use" their news, the products of these organizations must be conceptualized as content to be shaped to the experiences of users. This occurs as part of a continuing process of inspecting the market through research, and then continually folding the results back into operational and marketing strategy.

The emphasis on UX has become all the rage these days and rightly so, especially in the technology and consumer merchandising sectors of the market, which have experienced dramatic growth in recent decades. Growth-oriented organizations, large and small, focus on the "users" of a product or service—something that a news organization with an interest in achieving above-average growth in the near future would do well to emulate. Questions to be asked include: What types of content do our users choose to experience? How do they think and feel about our content, services or organization> Do they feel connected enough to come back again, to "use" more, to choose us over other content sources?

If we take a look at the best practices of the firms that have been successful at understanding users, and then using that understanding as the foundation of creating and implementing successful relationships with individuals affiliated with the news sector, then we soon see that the most appropriate way to keep on top of this audience is through purposeful immersion in and analysis of the continuing collection of information regarding their behaviors and preferences—big data. Big data is an accumulation of user behavior relevant to an organization and its products or services.

The news organization that wants to succeed in the coming decade will focus on content that promotes a touching UX. The news business is like any other business that seeks growth, as it must take advantage of the technology of collecting and analyzing large datasets that point to the relationship of users and the coin of the realm. The product of the news organization is content. The news organization of the next decade will become normalized and follow in the footsteps of the technology and consumer merchandising sectors, in that a continuing research process based on big data will become "the currency of today (driving) almost every business process, from sales to marketing to HR to analytics. And, the ability to leverage it represents the future of business." (Datskovsky, 2013, p. 1) And, we might add, the foundation of a reinvigorated news business.

In this, the news business is catching up to the rest of the business world—better late than never. This paradigm shift from news to content, however, relies upon a conceptual foundation in which the UX is an asset to be developed for the organization through the shaping of content as part of a continuing research process. In order to properly shape content, however, research can no longer be the one-time reading of the preferences of an audience followed by a "what-do-we-feel-they-need-to-know" discussion. Rather, there must be a corresponding paradigm shift in the research and, consequently, marketing process.

Changing News Research and Analytics Paradigm. The successful news organization in the coming, even more digital and technology-driven decade must follow the advice of Master Yoda of *Star Wars* movie fame, who advised Luke Skywalker to become "one with the force"—a sure-fire path to success in his battle to defeat the Galactic Empire. For traditional news operations, the Galactic Empire with which they are doing battle is their own inertia, which can be overcome by becoming one with the research. These organizations, to succeed, must incorporate an understanding and cultivation of the UX into a revamped content production operation that, from beginning to end, involves research.

No longer is it adequate to create and implement a survey, discuss the results, and then give the consumer the 'same-old/same-old.' The key is now continuous gathering, collecting, and analyzing data that shapes an organization's strategies and product—content and related services—and becomes an integral part of the lives of the individuals who comprise its audience or market. Unlike the episodic research of the past, the new paradigm of big data and a corresponding positive UX requires the collection and maintenance of data so as to make sure that a pool of critical information is readily available; having the appropriate technology and access to be able to analyze that data for a variety of purposes related to an effective UX; and finally, the application of this to achieve growth.

The news industry has only scratched the surface of the methodologies and data sets available that will power its march into the digital age and use content to produce a positive UX. Rather than rely solely on traditional news research—episodic snapshots of the audience with analyses and results disseminated through a top-down series of insights and meetings— the typical news organization now can analyze an unimaginably large and exponentially growing pool of data, both structured and unstructured.

These analyses may be as much a part of content (news) operations using the many tools available for online, social, and interactive media as creating the content. However, this depends upon whether news organizations structure themselves so that continuous and instantaneous feedback is part of the content creation and management routine. The tools are available in the online era, with new types of analytics being generated to keep pace with the dramatic stride of innovations in social, mobile, and online applications. Critical elements for the news organization that will succeed in the coming decade include the following:

A commitment to a continuous research process. A research process integrated into news operations and used as the major input into content creation strategies empowers all affiliated individuals: the audience, those who use its products, consume its information, and interact with its services. The process makes them part of a product improvement process that was once largely internal to news organizations.

Digital research tools and analytics are designed to be used continually to obtain user feedback. The tools are a natural outgrowth of the dramatic changes that came about with the enthusiastic adoption by the technology and consumer merchandising industries. The goal of these new media and technologies is better understanding of existing and potential product users. These tools were a boon to organizations devoted to promoting affinity and loyalty among target markets, emphasizing increased and more frequent use of products, and more effective prospecting for new users. It has long been an axiom for growing consumer organizations that the more positive and passionate users are about services and products, the more frequently and the larger the amount they will consume or use. As a result, organizations outside the news business have worked the digital research process into their operating routines. Now, news organizations have a roadmap to integrating research and content operations.

The UX becomes the key to the direction of the content and the goal of integrated research processes and techniques. The emphasis of the content production organization is now on shaping content that will appeal to an audience and move the metrics, the statistical data that operators use to decide whether or not progress has been made toward increasing the affinity of the UX.

For example, a writer—a content creator—is assigned to a story about a controversy over taxes. The writer produces a story and it works its way through an editorial chain, to finally appear as part of the content of the digital publications of the employing or affiliated organization. Subsequently, an editor tracks the progress of various parts of the story, finding that only two percent of online visitors stopped on a portion of the story—the part that had also featured a video sidebar with a personal story, graphics, and an inviting headline. The editors are now in a position to benefit from research integrated into the operation of the content production area of the organization, having drawn the conclusion that certain manipulations of the story fare better than others, and that those manipulations should be applied to other iterations of the story—all based on the reactions of users as reported through the research analytics. This process continually repeats itself, as analytics show which content leads to the most comments, which videos produce more sign-ups for the organization's loyalty groups, which audio gets the most listeners and leads to click-through to an advertiser's products. The research process can be designed so as to enable any and all portions of the content production team to access analytics that allow them to better understand the contribution of content to a positive UX. The result is research that is oriented on understanding the meaning of content as it is offered to and by users. This changes the emphasis of news providers, pushing them to become more attuned to individual users. The difference between looking at news as news, or news as content: in the latter, the audience is factored in, and now the UX is the main area of battle, becoming the raison d'être for an integrated research process.

Many new tools are available to provide an immediate and insightful understanding of user reactions to news, regardless of content format. The result is a greater understanding of what a user is thinking, enjoys, and the types of individuals that discrete segments of the news/content stream (a single blurb, a column, a photo, video, or a piece of text) attract. Users, for example, expect to be able to comment and interact with content. Analytical tools now exist to track and extract trends from this user-generated content in real time (Hootsuite, Google Analytics, and Tailwind, to name just a few, with more popping up each day), providing news providers with the ability to gauge the success and direction of their news and entertainment strategies on the fly. This, in turn, may generate more popular and targeted material as content creators (news producers) are pushed to attune themselves to the market. The cycle begins again, as new and even larger collections of big data enable a content producer to understand the impact of targeting changes, material modifications, and the UX of the news. These new research tools, along with more traditional tools, may be looked at in the following ways:

Place research and analytics. This type of research measures where users are spending their time and, presumably, undergoing a more positive UX. Many of these analytics can also be used in assessing intensity of affect. This type of metric offers news teams the ability to understand where and with how much intensity users are interacting with an organization's products. To name just a few: tracking page views, audience presence, unique visitors, page views, amount of time on page or site, views of content within a site, or impressions.

Context. Another way to think of this category of tools is 'coming and going.' It enables researchers to understand more of the context in which the users of content surround their usage of the news. Do they visit one site or many, who are our biggest referral sites, what are the referral traffic patterns, the click-through rate, shares, and increases in in-bound and out-bound links, are just some of the questions that can be asked to provide context and a holistic picture of a user's online consumption patterns.

Engagement. It is not enough to understand that a user likes a product; how much he or she likes your products offers the key to successful future marketing and content creation. Likes, comments, tweets and retweets, replies, and brand mentions are among the hundreds of ways the digital world measures intensity of affect, and the metrics an organization uses depends upon the digital space it occupies (blogs, mobile applications, microsites, social media, etc.). The vast majority of social media applications have the ability to measure user affect and intensity; and there are a plethora of applications for web and blogging sites that do the same.

In the successful digital content (news) organization, the research emphasis will shift from the art and science of sampling, questionnaire design, and research logistics centered in a small group of professionals familiar with snapshot research methodologies to the ability of the content-shapers to analyze and understand how their content: video, audio, interactive, or text, etc.—has been embraced (or not) during a chosen time frame. News cycles are fast disappearing, as the collection and dissemination of news has become a 24-hour, seven-day-a-week operation through numerous digital channels, every part having the ability to be measured in terms of its success at increasing the positive experience of users, and the knowledge and understanding of how that content contributes to the UX. And research is an integral part of this new cycle-less news cycle.

As a result of engagement, the UX is intensified as the digital information sources—online, mobile, social, and interactive—feature more content attractive to users. Integrated research analytics promote engagement. For example, the School of Communication and Creative Arts at Liberty University produced video alumni profiles that provoked a sharp spike in hits to its social media channels, which in turn caused a spike in visits to the various web pages. In addition, the analytics told which profiles were of the most interest, which were drawing the most visitor reaction in the form of likes and comments, and continuous analytics suggested ways to shape the alumni profile content so as to maximize engagement. Just about every type of analytic can, in turn, be unpacked into metrics that suggest intensity and context. Reader/viewer/user behavior, for example, can be measured online and aggregated to provide engagement metrics; user behavior once in a content area can provide a gauge, too, especially if users remain on a page and consume certain types of content while ignoring others; or leave an interaction trail consisting of the nature, length and frequency of the comments left by users in a particular content area.

Snapshot Methodologies. The tools that news organizations have used for at least a half century and continue to use today are what may be termed episodic or "snapshot methodologies." Snapshot methodologies are comprised of the social scientific tools and techniques that have offered yeoman service in a variety of industries over the past half century. They include, but are not limited to, the design and implementation of appropriate research questions, sampling methodologies, statistical analysis and inference, focus groups, and a plethora of computer models and multivariate analyses. And, when used in combination with the exploding universe of digital research tools, can synergize the search for insight.

When used effectively, snapshot methodologies require effort and expertise. It takes knowledge of research approaches to design a valid and reliable survey, to relate the data to the market, and make projections that effectively guide news marketing and operations strategies. Which segments of the audience watch or do not watch, read or do not read, buy or do not buy a media product? Snapshot methodologies deliver a picture of a particular segment according to specified criteria at a certain point in time.

In the digital age, it is less important to take periodic snapshots, as online and mobile behavior leaves a digital footprint; many of the questions answered by snapshot methodologies, and much more, can now be answered in real-time by analytical dives into an organization's big data sets. But these methodologies can still be useful in gathering information on the individuals affiliated with the organizations, adding to individual profiles, or exploring a related topic that can later be integrated as a data set into the multiple data sets collected within the larger database of the organization. In addition, these research approaches, increasingly no longer the centerpiece of an organization's research effort, can still be critical in providing additional actionable information on affinity and loyalty groups and promotions, thereby assisting an organization in shaping the future direction of its big data and attendant analytics. Snapshot methodologies, too, are valuable in providing insightful additions to analyses of promotions, contests, affinity and loyalty programs, and content-based public relations campaigns.

Research Delivery. The days are gone when research moved at a relaxed pace through an organization. News organizations have long gathered data about readers and viewers in a variety of episodic ways. Survey research, for example, has been a favorite. And the industry has devoted, in the past, large amounts of resources to conducting periodic reader surveys. In addition, on the advertising side of the business, researchers have taken a look at where individuals shop, how far they travel for specified items, and, in the past decade, information regarding online and in-store shopping habits. Each study tends to occupy its own silo, with results relevant only to the data collected within a series; by design, it has rarely been connected to anything other than the actual behavioral events studied and with particular clients in mind. In that sense, the data are static and silo-bound.

Enter big data. Behaviors are connected through specific individuals, and anything left as a digital footprint by that individual is now fair game for analytics. And, as more behavior is tracked and added to the big data collection, more possibilities for knowing the preferences of an individual and opportunities to affect those behaviors and preferences are uncovered. For example, instead of the pre-determined demographics of, say, Nielsen, or the carefully constructed data categories of the typical readership survey, big data offers simultaneous sets of both structured and unstructured data that can be combined in a myriad of analytic and relational techniques and provide a picture of *actual*—rather than statistically projected—user behavior. The goal: get closer to the users and understand how content can be dynamically shaped to upgrade the UX of the affiliates of an organization.

FUTURE RESEARCH AND APPLICATION DIRECTIONS

Implementing a new approach to research in the coming years depends largely on the ability of news organizations to (1) develop a digital-based research approach and (2) integrate snapshot methodologies into this. This depends upon an organization acquiring the software—either through purchase, development, or a combination of both—to tap into the data stream, while at the same time putting in place processes and procedures that enable internal staff to view relevant metrics through real-time analyses. The effort, however, is worth it as news organizations can use research to provide a continuing stream of content adjustments that can be shaped into products more likely to provide a positive UX—which, in turn, provides a changed but equally valuable analytic opportunity that can be used to again shape the content, which in turn positively affects the UX of individuals in the market, which in turn—you get the picture.

So, where do we go from here? Growth-oriented news organizations have to complete the migration from the journalism of the past to the content creation and management of a user-oriented digital future. Both educators and practitioners should rethink their definitions of both journalism and research, and consider a toolbox of content strategies that are linked directly to a positive UX. Imagine, for academics, the excitement and challenge of generating a whole new set of methodologies linking existing research techniques to the methodologies that make effective use of big data. For practitioners, the excitement and challenge will comes from modifying operations to hold editorial staffers accountable for the effects of their content on users, and of having editorial staff assessments and performance reviews dependent, in large part, on user satisfaction and affinity to the organization.

CONCLUSION

Research based on the user experience (UX) is changing the face of news delivery, and will provide dramatically enhanced opportunities in the future. There are parallels to other industries. Just as in the consumer electronics, technology and consumer merchandizing sectors—where the theoretical and applied foundations of UX were developed and applied—the news industry is experiencing the same revolution in thinking and application. The success of the UX emphasis in technology brought about a continuing explosion of new and increasingly easier-to-use digital products. While the original emphasis of UX was on using traditional research (such as focus groups and surveys) to produce more user-friendly hardware and software, the pace of digital technology brought the industry new and better tools that soon allowed it to design and gauge user reaction to its hardware and software products in real time, to collect and make sense of previously unheard of amounts of data (big data), and bring together data from differing platforms and time periods in such a way as to generate continuing and more accurate insights. These, in turn, were applied to products—hardware and software—that led to more positive and intense UX...and more customers.

From a research point of view, it did not take long for the single-shot research project to go the way of the mainframe computer in the technology sector. The explosion of digital analytical tools enabled industry developers and marketers to develop more user-friendly and, consequently, more popular hardware and software—which dramatically expanded use of technology, popularizing it among consumers. A similar digitally driven revolution took place in the consumer merchandising industry, where the focus on the UX combined with growing real-time collections of consumer purchasing data led to a proliferation of big data sets and a dramatically expanded ability to affect consumers.

In the same way, an emphasis on the UX offers the key to accelerated growth for traditional news outlets. This holds the potential to reshape the face of news, opinion, and entertainment into "content," which also includes the vast and increasing amount of content generated by audiences themselves. To the consumer—or news audience—everything they read, hear, and view across platforms has become unified to their senses, all of it available to consume and thereby 'experience.' At the same time, organizations in the news category are experiencing a new age of accessibility of data. This allows them to look at a broad range of user behaviors and characteristics, and then slice and dice it as many ways as there are needs for specific insights to be pulled from the data.

Because of the continuing flow of data and the ability of the collected data sets—big data—to provide living repositories of actionable data on real behavior for insightful analysts, successful news organizations will cultivate the ability to mine the databases for answers as to the effectiveness of content strategies. Big data allows the news content producers to be involved in controlling and understanding insights into the news consumer, the user. These new ways of looking at the data also enables producers to set up a process in which they can gain insights on the fly into the UX, insights that were unavailable during previous research eras. Research has now evolved—and may even more so, as once-staid news organizations understand the power of using the big data research process to move closer to their markets—into an insightful strategic marketing tool that offers a greater chance of success for news organizations wishing to grow into the next decade. Organizational growth in the digital age depends upon the ability of a news organization to connect the dots between its knowledge of user on the one hand, and the ease and depth of insight of big data repositories of information about the actual habits of users on the other.

The result of the big data analysis process is to make content more personal for the audience of a news organization, increasing the potential for fashioning a more positive UX and a more loyal and frequent user. News outlets may look for growth in the next decade by borrowing from the best practices of other industries where the link between continuous research, big data, and a more complete and engaging UX has been successfully executed. The key to the best practices of leading players in the travel industry, for example, has been to "understand the ongoing requests of their customer base and identify patterns in consumer behavior to determine offerings they may want in the future" (Honigman, 2014, p. 1).

The result is not just more data, but more data critical to an understanding of the user and the growth path for news organizations to a more intense and positive UX. Social and interactive digital research tools provide immediate and actionable feedback on how audiences are engaged—or not—with content. This enables the content organization—newsrooms, blogs, social media, mobile, or websites—to asses in real time the synergy produced by cross-platform content; make adjustments across platforms and media on the fly; and create a more intense and lasting UX than had been possible in the pre-digital, episodic research era. As a consequence, big data research with its emphasis on the UX holds the promise of a new generation of news professionals more attuned than ever to the thinking of news and information consumers. Research is no longer a special event, but an increasingly more critical and integrated part of the content creation and management process.

REFERENCES

Attkisson, S. (2014). *Stonewalled: my search for truth against the forces of obstruction, intimidation, and harassment in Obama's Washington*. New York: Harper-Collins Publishers.

Bertolucci, J. (2013, August 26). Big data: A practical definition. *Informationweek*. Retrieved from http://www.informationweek.com/

Carr, J. (2012). No laughing matter: the power of cyberspace to subvert conventional media gatekeepers. *International Journal of Communication, 6*(21), 2825-2845. Retrieved from http://ijoc.org/index.php/ijoc/article/view/1317/826

Dadich, S. (2013). UX. *Wired, 21*(5). Retrieved from http://www.wired.com/

Datskovsky, G. (2013). Harnessing big data for competitive advantage. *Information & Management, 47*(2), 56.

Donsbach, W. (2013). Journalism as the new knowledge profession and consequences for journalism education. *Journalism, 15*(6), 661–677. doi:10.1177/1464884913491347

Goldberg, B. (2001). *Bias: A CBS insider exposes how the media distort the news*. Washington, DC: Regnery Publishing.

Honigman, B. (2014, May). How big data is transforming the travel industry. *ForbesBrandVoice*. Retrieved from http://www.forbes.com/sites/centurylink/2014/04/30/how-big-data-is-transforming-the-travel-industry/

Schiff, A. (2012, December). Big blue's "smart" marketing approach. *DM News, 34*(12), 12.

Siebert, F. S. (1956). *Four theories of the press: the authoritarian, libertarian, social responsibility, and soviet communist concepts of what the press should be and do*. Urbana, IL: University of Illinois Press.

Svilar, M., Chakraborty, A., & Kanioura, A. (2013). Big data analytics in marketing: From hype to real help: Finding valuable consumer insight in a stream of data. *OR/MS Today, 40*(5), 22.

Tien, J. (2013). Big data: Unleashing information. *Journal of Systems Science and Systems Engineering, 27*(2), 127–151. doi:10.1007/s11518-013-5219-4

ADDITIONAL READING

Anderson, S. (2011). *Seductive interaction design: creating playful, fun, and effective user experiences (voices that matter)*. Berkeley, CA: New Riders.

Bliss, J. (2007). *Chief customer officer: getting past lip service to passionate action*. San Francisco, CA: Jossey-Bass.

Buley, L. (2013). *The user experience team of one: A research and design survival guide.* Brooklyn, NY: Rosenfeld Media.

Davenport, T. (2014). *Big data at work: Dispelling the myths, uncovering the opportunities.* Cambridge, MA: Harvard Business Review Press.

Davenport, T., & Harris, J. (2007). *Competing on analytics: The new science of winning.* Cambridge, MA: Harvard Business School Publishing Corporation.

Eyal, N., & Hoover, R. (2014). *Hooked: How to build habit-forming products.* Seattle, WA: Nir Eyal.

Foreman, J. (2014). *Data smart: Using data science to transform information into insight.* Indianapolis, IN: John Wiley & Sons.

Freedman, L. (2013). *Strategy: A history.* New York, NY: Oxford University Press.

Goodman, E., Kuniavsky, M., & Moed, A. (2012). Observing the user experience, second edition: A practitioner's guide to user research. Waltham, MA: Elsevier.

Gothelf, J. (2013). *Lean UX: Applying lean principles to improve user experience.* Sebastopol, CA: O'Reilly Media.

Grantville, V. (2014). *Developing analytic talent: Becoming a data scientist.* Indianapolis, IN: John Wiley & Sons.

Hand, D. (2014). *The improbability principle: Why coincidences, miracles, and rare events happen every day.* New York, NY: Farrar, Straus and Giroux.

Hartson, R., & Pardha, P. (2012). *The UX book: Process and guidelines for ensuring a quality user experience.* Burlington, MA: Elsevier.

Hemann, C., & Burbary, K. (2013). *Digital marketing analytics: Making sense of consumer data in a digital world.* Indianapolis, IN: QUE.

Huber, P. (2011). *Data analysis: What can be learned from the past 50 years.* Indianapolis, IN: John Wiley & Sons. doi:10.1002/9781118018255

Jeffery, M. (2010). *Data-driven marketing: The 15 metrics everyone in marketing should know.* Hoboken, NJ: John Wiley & Sons.

Lund, A. (2011). *User experience management: Essential skills for leading effective UX teams.* Burlington, MA: Elsevier.

Manning, H., Bodine, K., & Bernoff, J. (2012). *Outside in: The power of putting customers at the center of your business.* Las Vegas, NV: Amazon Publishing.

Mayer-Schonberger, V. (2013). *Big data: A revolution that will transform how we live, work, and think.* New York, NY: Houghton Mifflin Harcourt.

Ng, W. (2013). *Content marketing: The future of marketing strategy and creating killer online content that sells.* Think Maverick.

Paharia, R. (2013). *Loyalty 3.0: How to revolutionize customer and employee engagement with big data and gamification*. New York, NY: McGraw Hill.

Provost, F., & Fawcett, T. (2013). *Data science for business: What you need to know about data mining and data-analytic thinking*. Sebastopol, CA: O'Reilly Media.

Ramos, A. (2013). *The big book of content marketing*. Etiquettes, USA.

Russel, M. (2011). *Mining the social web*. Indianapolis, IN: John Wiley & Sons.

Shron, M. (2014). *Thinking with data: How to turn information into insights*. Sebastopol, CA: O'Reilly Media.

Xu, G., Zong, Y., & Yang, Z. (2013). *Applied data mining*. Cleveland, OH: CRC Press.

KEY TERMS AND DEFINITIONS

Big Data: The continuing collection of structured and unstructured data sets into a repository from which actionable information is pulled regarding user preferences, habits, and behaviors, to be used for shaping affective content and product marketing strategies.

Consumer-Oriented Worldview: This is a new way of thinking about audiences for news organizations, which must make the switch to this worldview in order to effectively use big data and the User Experience to drive organizational growth. Audiences are no longer readers or viewers; instead, they are individuals who consume or use information products so as to maximize their personal utility and positive experiences.

Content Marketing: The delivery of content designed to promote a particular user experience, persuading or moving users in the direction of a more positive and intense link with the organization shaping the content.

Content: Information shaped into a usable product, leveraging all story channels for the consumption of a particular segment of the market.

Digital Analytics: The set of analysis techniques that allow content creators, producers, and managers to dive into the collected database and extract timely and usable insights regarding the effect of their content on users.

Digital Research: This is the analytical dives taken by researchers into the huge collection of big data. This is often done in real time on real behaviors, and can take place anywhere in the 24-hour 7-days-a-week continuous cycle during which data is collected.

Snapshot Research Methodologies: The plethora of research techniques and methodologies designed to project from a sample to a larger population. Before the development of big data, in which the actual actions, reactions, and behaviors of individuals affiliated with an organization and its products and services are tracked through their digital footprints, snapshot methodologies were the overwhelming methodologies of choice to paint a picture of a market. This includes surveys, sampling, focus groups, etc.

User Experience (UX): This is all of the perceptions, actions, and attitudes evoked in an individual as they interact with a product, service, or organization. The UX is shorthand for the holistic set of perceptions and emotions that come into play upon an individual's experiencing a product, digital or otherwise.

Compilation of References

Abedin, B., & Sohrabi, B. (2009). Graph theory application and web page ranking for website link structure improvement. *Behaviour & Information Technology*, *28*(1), 63–72. doi:10.1080/01449290701840948

Albarran, A. B. (2013). *The social media industries*. New York, NY: Routledge.

Allen, M. (1996). In time for campaign '96, a new political website. *The New York Times*. Retrieved March 12, 2012, from http://www.nytimes.com/1996/06/10/business/in-time-for-campaign-96-a-new-political-web-site.html

American Press Institute and Associated Press-NORC Center for Public Affairs Research. (2014). *The Personal News Cycle: How Americans choose to get their news*. American Press Institute, 17 Mar. 2014. Retrieved November 27, 2014, from http://www.americanpressinstitute.org/publications/reports/survey-research/personal-news-cycle/single-page/&gt

Anderson, C. W. (2011). Between creative and quantified audiences: Web metrics and changing patterns of newswork in local US newsrooms. *Journalism*, *12*(5), 550–566. doi:10.1177/1464884911402451

Anderson, C. W. (2013). Towards a sociology of computational and algorithmic journalism. *New Media & Society*, *15*, 1005–1021.

Aristotle, . (2007). *On rhetoric: A theory of civic discourse* (2nd ed.). (G. A. Kennedy, Trans.). New York, NY: Oxford University Press.

Arotariteia, D., & Mitrab, S. (2004). Web mining: A survey in the fuzzy framework. *Fuzzy Sets and Systems*, *148*(1), 5–19. doi:10.1016/j.fss.2004.03.003

Atkin, D. J., Jeffres, L. W., & Neuendorf, K. A. (1998). Understanding internet adoption as telecommunications behavior. *Journal of Broadcasting & Electronic Media*, *42*(4), 475–490. doi:10.1080/08838159809364463

Attkisson, S. (2014). *Stonewalled: my search for truth against the forces of obstruction, intimidation, and harassment in Obama's Washington*. New York: Harper-Collins Publishers.

Atuahene-Gima, K. (1996). Market orientation and innovation. *Journal of Business Research*, *35*(2), 93–103. doi:10.1016/0148-2963(95)00051-8

Au Yeung, C., & Jatowt, A. (2011). Studying how the past is remembered: Towards computational history through large scale text mining. In *Proceedings of the 20th ACM international conference on Information and knowledge management* (pp. 1231–1240). Glasgow: ACM. doi:10.1145/2063576.2063755

Baer, J. (2013). *YOUTILITY, Why smart marketing is about help not hype*. New York, NY: Portfolio/Penguin.

Bailey, R. W. (1996). *Human performance engineering: Designing high quality professional user interfaces for computer products, Applications, and Systems* (3rd ed.). Upper Saddle River, NJ: Prentice Hall.

Baran, S. J., & Davis, D. (2006). *Mass communication theory* (4th ed.). Belmont, CA: Thomson Wadsworth.

Bargas-Avila, J. A., & Hornbæk, K. (2011). Old wine in new bottles or novel challenges? A critical analysis of empirical studies of user experience. In *Proceedings of the CHI'11*. Vancouver, Canada: ACM.

Barnhurst, K. G., & Nerone, J. (2001). *The form of news*. New York: Guilford Press.

Barnhurst, K., & Nerone, J. (2001). *The form of news: A history*. New York: Guilford Press.

Barnouw, E. (Ed.). (1997). *Conglomerates and the media*. New York, NY: New Press.

Beam, R. A. (1995). How newspapers use readership research. *Newspaper Research Journal*, *16*(2), 28–38.

Beam, R. A. (1998). What it means to be a market-oriented newspaper. *Newspaper Research Journal*, *19*(3), 2–20.

Beam, R. A. (2001). Does it Pay to be a Market-Oriented Daily Newspaper? *Journalism & Mass Communication Quarterly*, *78*(3), 466–483. doi:10.1177/107769900107800305

Beam, R. A. (2003). Content differences between daily newspapers with strong and weak market orientations. *Journalism & Mass Communication Quarterly*, *80*(2), 368–390. doi:10.1177/107769900308000209

Bell, E. (2012, September 5). Journalism by numbers. *Columbia Journalism Review*. Retrieved from http://www.cjr.org/cover_story/journalism_by_numbers.php?page=all

Bertolucci, J. (2013, August 26). Big data: A practical definition. *Informationweek*. Retrieved from http://www.informationweek.com/

Binet, S., & Carter, S. (2014, June). Mythbuster: The vogue for real-time evaluation. Admap, pp. 2-3.

Bitzer, L. F. (1995). The Rhetorical Situation. In W. A. Covino & D. A. Jolliffe (Eds.), *Rhetoric: Concepts, definitions, boundaries* (pp. 300–310). Boston: Allyn and Bacon.

Bloomberg (2013, May 6). *The Berkshire Hathaway shareholders' meeting*. Retrieved May 8, 2013, from, http://www.bloomberg.com/slideshow/2013-05-06/the-berkshire-hathaway-shareholders-meeting.html#slide5

Boczkowski, P. J. (2004). The processes of adopting multimedia and interactivity in three online newsrooms. *Journal of Communication*, *54*(2), 197–213. doi:10.1111/j.1460-2466.2004.tb02624.x

Boczkowski, P. J. (2005). *Digitizing the news: Innovation in online newspapers*. Cambridge, MA: MIT Press.

Bolt, N., & Tulathimutte, T. (2010). *Remote research*. Brooklyn, New York: Rosenfeld Media.

boyd, d. m., & Ellison, N. B. (2007). Social network sites: Definition, history, and scholarship. *Journal of Computer-Mediated Communication 13*(1), article 11. Retrieved June 30, 2013, from, http://jcmc.indiana.edu/vol13/issue1/boyd.elison.html

Bradshaw, P. (2013, May 13). Ebook interactive: what do you think of it so far? *BBC News*. Retrieved June 19, 2014, from http://www.bbc.co.uk/blogs/collegeofjournalism/entries/e7addb23-3f6d-3cb7-9b5c-4cd8035d41cd

Brake, L. (2012). Half full and half empty. *Journal of Victorian Culture*, *17*(2), 222–229. doi:10.1080/13555502.2012.683149

Brandtzaeg, P. B. (2012). Social networking sites: Their users and social implications – A longitudinal study. *Journal of Computer-Mediated Communication*, *17*(4), 467–488. doi:10.1111/j.1083-6101.2012.01580.x

British Library. (n.d.). *Copyright at British library newspapers* [Text]. Retrieved June 16, 2014, from http://www.british-library.uk/reshelp/findhelprestype/news/copynews/index.html

Bruce, M., & Bessant, J. (2002). *Design in business: Strategic innovation through design*. Design Council.

Burke, K. (1950 [1962]). A rhetoric of motives. Berkley, CA: University of California Press.

Burnett, R., & Marshall, P. D. (2003). *Web theory*. London, UK: Routledge.

Business Wire. (1996, June). Washingtonpost.com launches on world wide web. Retrieved December 11, 2011, from http://www.thefreelibrary.com/washingtonpost.com+Launches+on+World+Wide+Web.-a018406746

Butts, C. T. (2008). Social network analysis: A methodological introduction. *Asian Journal of Social Psychology*, *11*(1), 13–41. doi:10.1111/j.1467-839X.2007.00241.x

Byrne, M. B., John, B. E., Wehrle, N. S., & Crow, D. C. (1999). The tangled web we wove: taxonomy of WWW use. In *Proceedings of ACM CHI 99 Conference on Human Factors in Computing Systems* (volume 1, pp. 544-551). New York: Addison Wesley. doi:10.1145/302979.303154

Carey, R. (2012). How to gracefully retire a brand name. *Search Engine Land*. Retrieved May 22, 2014, from http://searchengineland.com/how-to-gracefully-retire-a-brand-name-125611

Carr, J. (2012). No laughing matter: the power of cyberspace to subvert conventional media gatekeepers. *International Journal of Communication, 6*(21), 2825-2845. Retrieved from http://ijoc.org/index.php/ijoc/article/view/1317/826

Catledge, L. D., & Pitkow, J. E. (1995). Characterizing browsing strategies in the world-wide web. *Computer Networks and ISDN Systems*, *26*(6), 1065–1073. doi:10.1016/0169-7552(95)00043-7

Chaffey, D., & Patron, M. (2012). From web analytics to digital marketing optimization: Increasing the commercial value of digital analytics. *Journal of Direct. Data and Digital Marketing Practice*, *14*(1), 30–45. doi:10.1057/dddmp.2012.20

Chen, H., Chiang, R. H. L., & Storey, V. C. (2012). Business intelligence and analytics: From big data to big impact. *Management Information Systems Quarterly*, *36*(4), 1165–1188.

Chi, E. H., Pirolli, P., Chen, K., & Pitkow, J. (2001). Using information scent to model user information needs and actions and the Web. In *Proceedings of the SIGCHI Conference on Human Factors in Computing Systems* (CHI '01, pp. 490-497). New York, NY: ACM. doi:10.1145/365024.365325

Christensen, C. M. (1997). *The innovator's dilemma: when new technologies cause great firms to fail*. Boston: Harvard Business School Press.

Christians, C. G., Glasser, T., McQuail, D., Nordenstreng, K., & White, R. A. (2009). *Normative theories of the media: Journalism in democratic societies*. Urbana, IL: University of Illinois Press.

Chyi, I. H., & Lasora, D. (2006). The market relationship between online and print newspapers: The case of Austin, Texas. In X. Li (Ed.), *Internet news: The making of a mainstream medium* (pp. 177–192). Mahwah, NJ: Lawrence Erlbaum Associates.

Cohen, P. (2011, April 26). Technology advances: Humans supersize. *The New York Times*.

Cohen, S., & Yang, L. J. & Yu, C. (2011). Computational journalism: A call to arms database researchers. In *CIDR' 11* (pp. 148-151). Asilomar, CA. Retrieved from http://db.cs.duke.edu/papers/cidr11-CohenLi-EtAl-cjdb.pdf

Cohen, E. L. (2002). Online Journalism as Market-Driven Journalism. *Journal of Broadcasting & Electronic Media*, *46*(4), 532–548. doi:10.1207/s15506878jobem4604_3

Cohen, S., Hamilton, J. T., & Turner, F. (2011). Computational journalism. *Communications of the ACM*, *54*(10), 66–71. doi:10.1145/2001269.2001288

Colwell, B., & Taylor, M. A., & Razorfish. (2014). *The state of always-on marketing study*. Retrieved 2014, from http://www.alwayson.razorfish.com/#intro

Connolly-Ahern, C., Ahern, L. A., & Bortree, D. S. (2009). The Effectiveness of stratified constructed week sampling for content analysis of electronic news source archives: AP Newswire, Business Wire, and PR Newswire. *Journalism & Mass Communication Quarterly*, *86*(4), 802–883. doi:10.1177/107769900908600409

Conyard, R. (2014). *Planning and creating a digital strategy*. Retrieved from https://www.redant.com/digital-strategy-whitepaper/

Cooley, C. H. (1909, 1966). The significance of communication. In B. Berelson & M. Janowitz (Eds.), Reader in public opinion and communication (2nd ed.; pp. 147-155). New York: The Free Press.

Cooper, R. G. (2001). *Winning at new products: Accelerating the process from idea to launch* (3rd ed.). New York, NY: Basic Books.

Copyright term and the public domain in the United States. (2014, January). Retrieved June 16, 2014, from http://copyright.cornell.edu/resources/publicdomain.cfm

Corkery, M. (2009). Adobe buys Omniture: What were they thinking? *The Wall Street Journal*. Retrieved May 22, 2014, from http://blogs.wsj.com/deals/2009/09/16/adobe-buys-omniture-what-were- they-thinking/

Coull Newsletter. (n.d). *Long form -- The story audiences want.* Retrieved October 04, 2014, from http://coull.com/resources/long-form-story-audiences-want

Cypher, A. (1986). The structure of users' activities. In D. A. Norman & S. W. Draper (Eds.), *User Centered System Design* (pp. 243–263). Boca Raton, Florida: CPR Press.

D'Angelo, P., & Lombard, M. (2008). The power of the press: The effects of press frames in political campaign news on media perceptions. *Atlantic Journal of Communication*, *16*(1), 1–32. doi:10.1080/15456870701647391

Dadich, S. (2013). UX. *Wired, 21*(5). Retrieved from http://www.wired.com/

Daniel, A. (2010, November). *The Guardian reportage of the UK MP expenses scandal: A case study of computational journalism.* Paper presented at a meeting of the Communications Policy & Research Forum. Sydney, Australia.

Datskovsky, G. (2013). Harnessing big data for competitive advantage. *Information & Management*, *47*(2), 56.

Day, G. S. (1999). *Market driven strategy: processes for creating value*. New York, NY: The Free Press.

De Argaez, E. (2003). *Broadband usage USA*. Retrieved March 1, 2012, from http://www.internetworldstats.com/articles/art030.htm

Demers, J. (2013, May 8). *How social media is supporting a fundamental shift in journalism.* Retrieved from http://www.huffingtonpost.com/jayson-demers/how-Social-media-suppo_b_3239076.html

Denzin, N. K., & Lincoln, Y. S. (1994). *Handbook of qualitative research.* Thousand Oaks, CA: SAGE Publications, Inc.

Desrosiers, R. Interview by Gordon Murray. Phone interview. June 5, 2014.

Diebold, F. X. (2003). *Big data dynamic factor models for macroeconomic measurement and forecasting: a discussion of the papers by Lucrezia Reichlin and Mark W. Watson*. Cambridge, MA: Cambridge University Press.

Diebold, F. X. (2012). *A personal perspective on the origin(s) and development of 'big data': The phenomenon, the term, and the discipline*. Department of Economics, University of Pennsylvania.

Doctor, K. (2014, January 29). The newsonomics of why everyone seems to be starting a news site, *Nieman Lab.* Retrieved October 10, 2014, from http://www.niemanlab.org/2014/01/the-newsonomics-of-why-everyone-seems-to-be-starting-a-news-site/

Doig, S. (2014, May 13). Data driven journalism. *From Idea to Story: Planning the data journalism story.*

Donsbach, W. (2013). Journalism as the new knowledge profession and consequences for journalism education. *Journalism*, *15*(6), 661–677. doi:10.1177/1464884913491347

Duggan, M. (2013, September 19). *Cell phone activities 2013*. Pew Research Centers Internet American Life Project RSS.

Duggan, M., & Smith, A. (2013, December 31) *Social media update2013*. Retrieved from: http://www.pewinternet.org/files/2013/12/PIP_Social-Networking-2013.pdf

Dupre, E. (2013, November 1). Attitudinal and behavioral data: better together - Direct marketing news. *Dmnews.com*. Retrieved June 26, 2014, from http://www.dmnews.com/attitudinal-and-behavioral-data-better-together/article/317695/

DVorkin. L. (2012, February 23). Inside Forbes: How long-form journalism is finding its digital audience. *Forbes*. Retrieved November 14, 2014, from http://www.forbes.com/sites/lewisdvorkin/2012/02/23/inside-forbes-how-long-form-journalism-is-finding-its-digital-audience/

Edmonds, R., Guskin, E., & Rosensteil, T. (2012). Newspapers: By the numbers. The state of the news media 2012. *Pew Research Center's Project for Excellence in Journalism*. Retrieved March 1, 2012, from http://stateofthemedia.org/2012/newspapers-building-digital-revenues-proves-painfully-slow/newspapers-by-the-numbers/

Emerson, T., Ghosh, R., & Smith, E. (2012). Case study: Using the social share of voice to predict events that are about to happen. In *Practical text mining and statistical analysis for non-structured text data applications* (pp. 127–132). Waltham, MA: Academic Press. doi:10.1016/B978-0-12-386979-1.00007-4

Enda, J., & Mitchell, A. (2013). *Americans show signs of leaving a news outlet, citing less information.* The State of the News Media 2013, Pew Research Foundation. Retrieved September 18, 2014, from http://stateofthemedia.org/2013/special-reports-landing-page/citing-reduced-quality-many-americans-abandon-news-outlets/

European Commission. Directorate-General for Research and Development. (2014a). Standardization in the area of innovation and technological development, notably in the field of text and data mining: Report from the Expert Group. Luxembourg: European Union.

European Commission. Directorate-General for Research and Development. (2014b). The scope for special copyright arrangements for TDM (Section 3.5). In Standardization in the area of innovation and technological development, notably in the field of text and data mining: Report from the Expert Group (pp. 39–41). Luxembourg: European Union.

Fairfield, J., & Shtein, H. (2014). Big problems: Emerging issues in the ethics of data science and journalism. *Journal of Mass Media Ethics*, *29*(1), 38–51. doi:10.1080/08900523.2014.863126

Feldman, R., & Sanger, J. (2007). The text mining handbook. Cambridge University Press; Retrieved from http://www.roelsbeestenboel.nl/text.pdf

Fischer, M. C. (2014). The pay-per-visit debate: Is chasing viral traffic hurting journalism? *American Journalism Review*. Retrieved May 22, 2014, from http://ajr.org/2014/03/27/pay-per-visit- debate-chasing-viral-traffic-hurting-journalism/

Fleischner, M. H. (2013). *SEO made simple, Strategies for dominating the world's largest search engine* (3rd ed.). Lexington, KY: Fleischner.

Flew, F., Daniel, A., & Spurgeon, C. L. (2010). The promise of computational journalism. In McCallum, K. (Ed.) *Media, Democracy and Change: In Refereed Proceedings of the Australian and New Zealand Communications Association Annual Conference.* (ACT, pp. 1-19). Canberra, Australia. doi:10.1080/17512786.2011.616655

Foreign Broadcast Information Service (FBIS). (n.d.). [Text]. Retrieved June 17, 2014, from http://library.uoregon.edu/govdocs/fbis.html

Fox, J. (2014, April 16). A New Golden Age for Media? *The Atlantic*. Retrieved October 22, 2014, from http://www.theatlantic.com/magazine/archive/2014/05/start-the-presses/359810/

Franklin, T., Harrop, H., Kay, D., & van Harmlen, M. (2011). *Exploiting activity data in the academic environment.* http://www.activitydata.org/

Fuchs, C. (2014). *Social Media: A critical introduction*. Thousand Oaks, CA: Sage. doi:10.4135/9781446270066.n2

Gans, H. J. (1979). *Deciding what's news*. New York, NY: Pantheon Books.

Gans, H. J. (2004). *Democracy and the News. New York, NY.* USA: Oxford University Press.

Garrison, K. (2014, June 18). 5 key questions to ask before developing customer personas. *It's All About Revenue: The Marketing Blog*. Retrieved June 26, 2014, from http://blog.eloqua.com/5-key-questions-to-ask-before-developing-customer-personas/

Gartner. (2011, June 27). *Gartner Says Solving 'Big Data' Challenge Involves More Than Just Managing Volumes of Data*. Gartner.

Garton, L., Haythornthwaite, C., & Wellman, B. (1997, June). Studying online social networks. *Journal of Computer-Mediated Communication*, *3*(1). Retrieved from http://jcmc.indiana.edu/vol3/issue1/garton.html

Gerlitz, C., & Helmond, A. (2011, May). *The like economy: The social web in transition.* Conference Paper MiT7 Unstable Platforms - The promise and peril of transition. Paper presented at the MIT7 Unstable Platforms conference, Cambridge, MA (May 13–15).

German, K. (n.d.). Top 10 dot-com flops. *CNET*. Retrieved March 1, 2012, from http://www.cnet.com/1990-11136_1-6278387-html

Gibbs, W. J. (2008). Examining users on news provider web sites: A review of methodology. *Journal of Usability Studies*, *3*(3), 129–148.

Glaser, B. G. (1965). The constant comparative method of qualitative analysis. *Social Problems*, *12*(4), 436–445. doi:10.2307/798843

Glaser, B. G., & Strauss, A. (1967). *The discovery of grounded theory: Strategies for qualitative research.* London, England: Weidenfeld and Nicolson.

Goldberg, B. (2001). *Bias: A CBS insider exposes how the media distort the news*. Washington, DC: Regnery Publishing.

Goodman, I., Kuniavsky, M., & Moed, A. (2012). *Observing the user experience*. Burlington, Massachusetts: Morgan Kaufmann.

Google. (2014). *Google analytics*. Retrieved from http://google.com/analytics/

Gray, J., Chambers, L., & Bounegru, L. (2012). *Data Journalism Handbook*. Sebastopol, CA: O'Reilly Media, Inc.

Greene, B. (2014, October 22). 4 tips for successfully measuring your PR campaign. PR News Online. Retrieved October 22, 2014, from, http://www.prnewsonline.com/water-cooler/2014/10/22/4-tips-for-successfully-measuring-your-pr-campaign/

Greenhow, C., & Robelia, B. (2009, July). Old communication, new literacies: Social network sites as social learning resources. *Journal of Computer-Mediated Communication*, *14*(4), 1130–1161. doi:10.1111/j.1083-6101.2009.01484.x

Grueskin, B., Seave, A., & Graves, L. (2011). *The Story So Far: What We Know About the Business of Digital Journalism*. Columbia Journalism School, Tow Center for Digital Journalism. Retrieved October 10, 2014, from http://www.journalism.columbia.edu/news/448

Gumpert, G., & Cathcart, R. (Eds.). (1985). *INTER/MEDIA, Interpersonal Communication in a Media World* (3rd ed.). New York: Oxford University Press.

Habermas, J. (1989). *The structural transformation of the public sphere: An inquiry into a category of bourgeois society*. Cambridge, MA: MIT Press.

Haile, T. (2014, March 9). What you think you know about the web is wrong. *TIME.com*. Retrieved June 26 2014, from http://time.com/12933/what-you-think-you-know-about-the-web-is-wrong/

Hali, V. M., Wagh-Koppar, A., & Arora, S. (2013, November). *Humanising big data: Applying a qualitative analysis lens to big data*. Paper presented at ESOMAR. Qualitative, Valencia: Spain, pp. 2-3. Retrieved June 20, 2014, from http://www.warc.com

Hall, E. (2013). *Just enough research*. New York: A Book Apart.

Hansen, D. L., Shneiderman, B., & Smith, M. A. (2011). *Analyzing social media networks with NodeXL*. Burlington, MA: Elsevier.

Hartson, R., & Pyla, P. S. (2012). *The UX book: Process and guidelines for ensuring a quality user experience*. Waltham, MA: Morgan Kaufman.

Hartwig, E. (2013, November 22). How to lower your site's bounce rate. *Mashable*. Retrieved October 28, 2014, from http://mashable.com/2013/11/22/bounce-rate-metrics/

Haselmaier, J. (n.d.). *Think you know how to meet customer needs?* Retrieved October 25, 2014, from http://www.pragmaticmarketing.com//resources/think-you-know-how-to-meet-customer-needs?p=0

Hassenzahl, M., & Tractinsky, N. (2006). User experience – a research agenda. *Behaviour & Information Technology*, *25*(2), 91–97. doi:10.1080/01449290500330331

Heaney, M. T., & McClurg, S. D. (2009, September). Social networks and American politics. *American Politics Research*, *37*(5), 727–741. doi:10.1177/1532673X09337771

Heer, J., & Chi, E. H. (2002). Separating the swarm: Categorization methods for user sessions on the Web. In *Proceedings of the SIGCHI conference on Human factors in computing systems: Changing our world, changing ourselves* (CHI '02, pp. 243 – 250). New York, NY: ACM.

Heim, S. (2008). *The Resonant Interface: HCI Foundation for Interaction Design*. Boston, MA: Pearson Education.

Hoffmann, L. (2013). Looking back at big data. *Communications of the ACM*, *56*(4), 21–23. doi:10.1145/2436256.2436263

Hohmann, L. (2014, October 13). Disturbing mystery affecting your favorite news sites. *WND*. Retrieved October 14, 2014, from, http://www.wnd.com/2014/10/your-favorite-news-sites-shafted-by-amazon/

Holmlid, S., & Evenson, S. (2008). Bringing service design to service sciences, management and engineering. In B. Hefley & W. Murphy (Eds.), *Service science, management and engineering: Education for the 21st century* (pp. 341–345). Berlin: Springer Verlag. doi:10.1007/978-0-387-76578-5_50

Honigman, B. (2014, May). How big data is transforming the travel industry. *ForbesBrandVoice*. Retrieved from http://www.forbes.com/sites/centurylink/2014/04/30/how-big-data-is-transforming-the-travel-industry/

Horne, L. (2011). Sean parker: myspace could have been facebook. *P.C. Magazine*. Retrieved September 12, 2014, from http://www.pcmag.com/article2/0,2817,2387799,00.asp

Housewright, R., Schonfeld, R. C., & Wulfson, K. (2013). *Ithaka S+R U.S. faculty survey 2012*. Ithaka S+R.

Houston, B. (2010). The future of investigative journalism. *Daedalus*, *13*(2), 45–56. doi:10.1162/daed.2010.139.2.45

How Americans get their news - American Press Institute. (2014, March 17). American Press Institute RSS. Retrieved June 18, 2014, from http://www.americanpressinstitute.org/publications/reports/survey-research/how-americans-get-news/

Howard, A. (2012, November 26). Investigating data journalism. *Radar*.

Howard, B. (2008, November). Analyzing online social networks. *Communications of the ACM*, *51*(11), 14–16. doi:10.1145/1400214.1400220

Huffaker, D. (2010, October). Dimensions of leadership and social influence in online communities. *Human Communication Research*, *36*(4), 593–617. doi:10.1111/j.1468-2958.2010.01390.x

Hunsinger, J., & Senft, T. (Eds.). (2014). *The social media handbook*. New York, NY: Routledge.

IBM Corporation, (2010). *Social media analytics solutions: Social solutions powered by IBM Cognos Consumer Insight*. Retrieved from https://www-950.ibm.com/events/wwe/grp/grp004.nsf/f7002a8c9f4c84708525737f006be109/801ebdf1a1a2a8d1852579fb0052bbea/$FILE/Ed Burek's Presentation.pdf

IBM Corporation, (2013).*Big data at the speed of business*. Retrieved from http://www-01.ibm.com/software/data/bigdata/what-is-big-data.html

IBM Corporation, *Big data and analytics-overview-United States*. Retrieved from http://www.ibm.com/big-data/us/en/big-data-and-analytics/

ING Group, (2014). *2014 study on impact of social media on news: more crowd checking, less fact checking*. Retrieved from http://www.ing.com/Newsroom/All-news/NW/2014-Study-impact-of-Social-Media-on-News-more-crowdchecking-less-factchecking.htm

Internet penetration. (2011, June). Retrieved June 17, 2014, from http://www.oii.ox.ac.uk/vis/?id=4e3c0200

Isaacson, W. (2011). *Steve Jobs*. New York, NY: Simon & Schuster.

Ivory, M. Y., Sinha, R. R., & Hearst, M. A. (2001). Empirically validated web page design metrics. In *Proceedings of the SIGCHI Conference on Human Factors in Computing Systems* (CHI '01, pp. 53-60). New York, NY: ACM. doi:10.1145/365024.365035

Jarus, O. (2013, October 10). Clues to Lost Prehistoric Code Discovered in Mesopotamia. *LiveScience*.

Jenkins, H. (2008). *Convergence culture: Where old and new media collide* (revised ed.). New York, NY: New York University Press.

Jenkins, H., Ford, S., & Green, J. (2013). *Spreadable media: Creating value and meaning in a networked culture*. New York, NY: New York University Press.

Jenkinson, A. (1994). Beyond segmentation, Journal of Targeting, Measurement and Analysis for Marketing, 3(1) 60-72. Henry Stewart Publications, London

Jeong, O.-R., Oh, J., Kim, D.-J., Lyu, H., & Kim, W. (2014). Determining the titles of web pages using anchor text and link analysis. *Expert Systems with Applications*, *41*(9), 4322–4329. doi:10.1016/j.eswa.2013.12.033

Jinzhi, D. (2010, March 15). *The Google/China hacking case: How did the story flow through Chinese-language media*? Retrieved June 16, 2014, from http://www.niemanlab.org/2010/03/the-googlechina-hacking-case-how-did-the-story-flow-through-chinese-language-media/

Johnson, B. (2009). Experts puzzled over Adobe's surprise purchase of Omniture. *The Guardian*. Retrieved March 26, 2014, from http://www.theguardian.com/technology/2009/sep/16/adobe-mergers- acquisitions

Johnston, K., Tanner, N., Lalla, N., & Kawalski, D. (2013). Social capital: The benefit of Facebook 'friends.'. *Behaviour & Information Technology*, *32*(1), 24–36. doi:10.1080/0144929X.2010.550063

Jones, A. (2009). *Losing the News: The Future of News That Feeds Democracy*. New York: Oxford University Press.

Journalists killed in 2013. (n.d.). Retrieved June 24, 2014, from http://cpj.org/killed/2013/#

Katz, E. (1966). The two-step flow of communication. In W. Schramm (Ed.), *Mass communications* (pp. 346–370). Urbana, IL: University of Illinois Press.

Katz, E. (1971). Social interary of technical change. In W. Schramm & D. F. Roberts (Eds.), *The process and effects of mass communication* (revised edition, pp. 761–797). Urbana, IL: University of Illinois Press.

Kaushik, A. (2010). *Web analytics 2.0: The art of online accountability and science of customer centricity*. Indianapolis, IN: Wiley Publishing, Inc.

Kaye, K. (2014, October 27). A data lab rat in the city: Why trackers couldn't trap this city dweller. Retrieved October 27, 2014, from, http://adage.com/article/dataworks/data-trackers-trap-city-dweller/295562/

Kaye, J., & Quinn, S. (2010). *Funding Journalism in the Digital Age: Business Models, Strategies, Issues and Trends*. New York, NY: Peter Lang.

Keen, A. (2007). *The cult of the amateur: How blogs, MySpace, YouTube, and the rest of today's user-generated media are destroying our economy, our culture, and our values*. New York, NY: Doubleday.

Kerlinger, F. N. (1986). *Foundations of behavioral research* (3rd ed.). Orlando, FL: Holt, Rinehart and Winston, Inc.

Kiefer, G. Interview by Jan Leach. Phone interview. June 18, 2014.

Kinsley, M. (1996). *Welcome to Slate*. Retrieved August 25, 2010, from http://www.slate.com/articles/news_and_politics/readme/1996/06/welcome_to_slate.html

Kirchhoff, S. M. (2011). Advertising industry in the digital age (CRS Report R40908). *Congressional Research Service*.

Kiss, H. J., & Rosa-Garcia, A. (2013, July). On the mobilizing role of social media in revolutions: A game-theoretic approach. Discussion Papers; 2013/43. Institute of Economics, Centre for Economic and Regional Studies, Hungarian Academy of Sciences, Budapest. Available at SSRN: http://ssrn.com/abstract=2298662 or10.2139/ssrn.2298662

Klinenberg, E. (2007). *Fighting for air: The battle to control America's media*. New York, NY: Metropolitan Books.

Koh, J., Kim, Y.-G., Butler, B., & Bock, G.-W. (2007, February). Encouraging participation in virtual communities. *Communications of the ACM*, *50*(2), 69–73. doi:10.1145/1216016.1216023

Kohli, A. K., & Jaworski, B. J. (1990). Market orientation: The construct, research propositions, and managerial implications. *Journal of Marketing*, *54*(2), 1–18. doi:10.2307/1251866

Kovach, B., & Rosenstiel, T. (2007). *The elements of journalism: What newspeople should know and the public should expect*. New York, NY: Three Rivers Press.

Kunkel, T. (2001). Letters from the editor: The New Yorker's Harold Ross. New York: Modern Library.

Laney, D. (2012, January 14). *Deja VVVu: Others Claiming Gartner's Construct for Big Data*. Gartner Blog Network.

Lasorsa, D. L., Lewis, S. C., & Holton, A. E. (2011). Normalizing Twitter: Journalism practice in an emerging communication space. *Journalism Studies*, *13*(1), 19–36. doi:10.1080/1461670X.2011.571825

Lasswell, H. D. (1966). The structure and function of communication in society. In W. Schramm (Ed.), *Mass communications* (pp. 117–130). Urbana, IL: University of Illinois Press.

Law, E. L.-C., van Schaik, P., & Roto, V. (2013). Attitudes towards user experience (UX) measurement. *International Journal of Human-Computer Studies*, *72*(6), 526–541. doi:10.1016/j.ijhcs.2013.09.006

Lee, A. M., Lewis, S. C., & Powers, M. (2012). Audience clicks and news placement: A study of time-lagged influence in online journalism. *Communication Research*, *41*(4), 505–530. doi:10.1177/0093650212467031

Leetaru, K. (2011). *Data mining methods for the content analyst: An introduction to the computational analysis of content*. New York: Routledge.

Lefevre, A. S. (2014, May 23). *Thai media chafe under post-coup blackout*. Retrieved June 17, 2014, from http://www.reuters.com/article/2014/05/23/thailand-protest-media-idUSL3N0O80TZ20140523

Levy, D., & Newman, N. (2013). *Reuters Institute Digital News Report: 2013*. Reuters Institute for the Study of Journalism at the University of Oxford. Retrieved November 15, 2014, from https://reutersinstitute.politics.ox.ac.uk/publications/risj-digital-report/2013.html

Lewis, P. (1996). The New York Times Introduces a Web Site. *The New York Times*. Retrieved March 13, 2012, from http://www.nytimes.com/1996/01/22/business/the-new-york-times-introduces-a-web-site.html?scp=2&sq=The%20New%20York%20Times%20Introduces%20a%20New%20Web%20Site&st=cse

Lewis, P. H. (1996a, April 13). Yahoo. Gets a Big Welcome on Wall Street. *The New York Times*. Retrieved January 1, 2012, from http://www.nytimes.com/1996/04/13/business/yahoo-gets-big-welcome-on-wall-street.html?scp=2&sq=yahoo&st=nyt

Lewis, S. C., Zamith, R., & Hermida, A. (2013). Content Analysis in an Era of Big Data: A Hybrid Approach to Computational and Manual Methods. *Journal of Broadcasting & Electronic Media*, *57*(1), 34–52. doi:10.1080/08838151.2012.761702

Liang, T., & Lai, H. (2002). Discovering user interests from web browsing behavior: An application to internet news services. In *Proceedings of the 35th Annual Hawaii international Conference on System Sciences* (Hicss'02, pp. 2718 - 2727). Washington, DC, USA: IEEE Computer Society. doi:10.1109/HICSS.2002.994214

Lipovetsky, S., Magnan, S., & Zanetti-Polzi, A. (2011). Pricing models in marketing research. *Intelligent Information Management*, *3*(5), 167–174. doi:10.4236/iim.2011.35020

Lippman, W. (1922). *Public Opinion*. New York: Harcourt Brace.

Lipschultz, J. H. (2015). *Social media communication: Concepts, practices, data, law and ethics*. London, UK: Routledge.

Li, Q., Wang, T., Li, P., Liu, L., Gong, Q., & Chen, Y. (2014). The effect of news and public mood on stock movements. *Information Sciences*, *278*, 826–840. doi:10.1016/j.ins.2014.03.096

Locher, P., Overbeeke, K., & Wensveen, S. (2010). Aesthetic Interaction: A Framework. *Design Issues*, *26*(2), 70–79. doi:10.1162/DESI_a_00017

Lohr, S. (2013, February 1). The Origins of 'Big Data:' An Etymological Detective Story. *The New York Times*. Retrieved September 15, 2014, from http://bits.blogs.nytimes.com/2013/02/01/the-origins-of-big-data-an-etymological-detective-story/?_r=0

Los Angeles Times (1995). *Hi!* Retrieved January 15, 2011, from http://web.archive.org/web/19961221161651/http://www.latimes.com/HOME/HELP/WEBSITE/welcome.htm

Lowrey, W., & Woo, C. W. (2010). The news organization in uncertain times: Business or institution? *Journalism & Mass Communication Quarterly*, *87*(1), 41–61. doi:10.1177/107769901008700103

Luckerson, V. (2014, October 8). Fear, misinformation, and social media complicate ebola fight. *Time*. Retrieved October 17, 2014, from https://time.com/3479254/ebola-social-media/

Lyman, P., & Varian, H. (2000, January 1). About the project. *How Much Information?*

Lyons, D. A. (2010, November). Decade of Destruction. *Newsweek*. Retrieved February 24, 2012, from http://2010.newsweek.com/essay/a-decade-of-destruction.html

MacGregor, P. (2007). Tracking the online audience. *Journalism Studies*, *8*(2), 280–298. doi:10.1080/14616700601148879

Macnamara, J. (2014). *The 21st century media (r)evolution, Emergent communication practices* (2nd ed.). New York, NY: Peter Lang.

Main, R. S., & Baird, C. W. (1981). *Elements of microeconomics*. Eagan, MN: West Publishing Company.

Manjoo, F. (2009). The Internet of 1996 is almost unrecognizable compared with what we have today. *Slate*. Retrieved November 10, 2011, from http://www.slate.com/articles/technology/technology/2009/02/jurassic_web.html

Marketo. (2011). *Marketing metrics & analytics, The definitive guide*. San Mateo, CA: Marketo.

Marshall, T. (2008, July 21). *The changing newsroom*. Pew Research Centers Journalism Project RSS.

Matsa, K. E., & Mitchell, A. (2014, March 26). 8 key takeaways about social media and news. *Pew Research Center's Journalism Project*. Retrieved from http://www.journalism.org/2014/03/26/8-key-takeaways-about-social-media-and-news/

Mayfield, A. (2008). *What is social media?* Retrieved June 18, 2014, from http://www.icrossing.com/sites/default/files/what-is-social-media-uk.pdf

McBride, K. (2013, December 13). *Newtown's media blackout forces journalists to do their jobs*. Retrieved June 17, 2014, from http://www.poynter.org/latest-news/creating-a-framework-for-ethical-decision-making-among-journalists-and-those-who-care-about-democracy/233342/newtowns-media-blackout-forces-journalists-to-do-their-jobs/

McBurney, D. H. (2001). *Research methods* (5th ed.). Belmont, CA: Wadsworth.

McChesney, R. W., & Nichols, J. (2010). The death and life of American journalism: The media revolution that will begin the world again. Philadelphia, PA: 1st Nation Books.

McChesney, R. W. (1999). *Rich media, poor democracy: Communication politics in dubious times*. Urbana, IL: University of Illinois Press.

McChesney, R. W. (2004). *The problem of the media: U.S. communication politics in the twenty-first century*. New York, NY: Monthly Review Press.

McKenzie, C. T., Lowrey, W., Hays, H., Chung, J. Y., & Woo, C. W. (2011). Listening to news audiences: The impact of community structure and economic factors. *Mass Communication & Society*, *14*(3), 375–395. doi:10.1080/15205436.2010.491934

McManus, J. H. (1992). What kind of commodity is news? *Communication Research*, *19*(6), 787–805. doi:10.1177/009365092019006007

McManus, J. H. (1994). *Market-driven journalism: Let the citizen beware?* Thousand Oaks, CA: Sage Publications.

Meeker, M. (2014, May 28). *Internet trends*. Internet Trends 2014 Code Conference. Kleiner Perkins Caufield Byers.

Mehak, K. M., & Aggarwal, N. (2013). Web usage mining: An analysis. *Journal of Emerging Technologies in Web Intelligence, 5*(3), 240+. Retrieved June 20, 2014, from http://go.galegroup.com/ps/i.do?id=GALE%7CA350977892&v=2.1&u=ecl_main&it=r&p=AONE&sw=w&asid=36dcec8a9d7b5866c79a6f4f3bc6ede2

Meyer, P. (1987). *Ethical journalism: A guide for students, practitioners, and consumers*. New York, NY: Longman.

Milburn, M. A. (1991). *Persuasion and politics*. Belmont, CA: Wadsworth.

Miller, A. Interview by Jan Leach. Phone interview. June 19, 2014.

Miller, A. R. (1971). *The assault on privacy*. Ann Arbor, MI: University of Michigan Press.

Miller, M. (2011). *The ultimate web marketing guide*. Indianapolis, IN: Pearson Education, Inc.

Miner, G., Elder, J. E., Hill, T., Nisbet, R., Delen, D., & Fast, A. (2012). *Practical text mining and statistical analysis for non-structured text data applications (1 edition.)*. Waltham, MA: Academic Press.

Mishler, E. G. (1986). *Research interviewing: context and narrative*. Cambridge, MA: Harvard University Press.

Mitchell, A., & Page, D. (2014). Key indicators in media and news. Pew State of the News Media 2014, March 26, 2014, Retrieved October 16, 2014, from http://www.journalism.org/packages/state-of-the-news-media-2014/

Mohammad, S. M., Zhu, X., Kiritchenko, S., & Martin, J. (2015). Sentiment, emotion, purpose, and style in electoral tweets. *Information Processing & Management,* 51(4), 480-499. doi:10.1016/j.ipm.2014.09.003

Morris, R. J., & Truskowski, B. J. (2003). The evolution of storage systems. *IBM Systems Journal*, *42*(2), 205–217. doi:10.1147/sj.422.0205

Mui, Y. Q. (2014, June 4). Want to take economy's pulse? Try digging into Google, Twitter. *The Washington Post,* pp. A1, A5.

Murray, J. H. (2012). *Inventing the medium: Principles of interaction design as a cultural practice*. Cambridge, Massachusetts: The MIT Press.

Mussell, J. (2012). Nineteenth-century newspapers in the digital age. *Journal of Victorian Culture, 17*(2), 221–221. doi:10.1080/13555502.2012.683147

Mutter, A. (2014, July 16). The newspaper crisis, by the numbers. *Reflections of a Newsosaur.* Retrieved October 22, 2014, from http://newsosaur.blogspot.com/2014/07/the-newspaper-crisis-by-numbers.html

Napoli, P. (2011). *Audience evolution: New technologies and the transformation of media audiences*. New York, NY: Columbia University Press.

National Institute for Computer-Assisted Reporting. (n.d.). Investigative reporters & editors. Retrieved June 19, 2014, from http://www.ire.org/nicar/

Nelson, R. K. (n.d.). *Mining The Dispatch. Digital Scholarship Lab, University of Richmond.* Retrieved June 17, 2014, from http://dsl.richmond.edu/dispatch/pages/intro

Newspaper Association of America. (2014, April 18). Business model evolving, circulation revenue rising. Retrieved October 24, 2014, from http://www.naa.org/Trends-and-Numbers/Newspaper-Revenue/Newspaper-Media-Industry-Revenue-Profile-2013.aspx

Nielsen, J. (1993). *Usability engineering*. San Diego, CA: Academic Press.

Node, X. L. (2014). *The Social Media Research Foundation Graph Gallery*. http://nodexlgraphgallery.org/Pages/Graph.aspx?graphID=19466

Norman, D. A. (2002). *The Design of Everyday Things*. New York: Basic Books.

Nudd, T. (2014, October 24). Infographic: The ideal length of everything online, from tweets to YouTube. *AdWeek.* Retrieved October 25, 2014, from, http://www.adweek.com/adfreak/infographic-ideal-length-everything-online-tweets-youtube-videos-160972

Oplinger, D. Interview by Gordon Murray. Phone interview. June 11, 2014.

Parker, S., & Heapy, J. (2006). *The Journey to the interface: How public service design can connect users to reform*. London: Demos Magdalen House.

Paterson, C. (2008). Introduction: Why ethnography? In C. Paterson & D. Domingo (Eds.), *Making Online News* (Vol. 1). New York, NY: Peter Lang Publishing Inc.

Peary, B. D. M., Shaw, R., & Takeuchi, Y. (2012). Utilization of social media in the East Japan Earthquake and Tsunami and its effectiveness. *Journal of Natural Disaster Science, 34*(1), 3–18http://www.jsnds.org/contents/jnds/34_1_1.pdf. RetrievedJune192014. doi:10.2328/jnds.34.3

Peterson, I. (1996, September 23). Newspapers increasingly cooperate in the face of growing competition for ads. *The New York Times.* Retrieved October 12, 2011, from http://www.nytimes.com/1996/09/23/business/newspapers-increasingly-cooperate-in-the-face-of-growing-competition-for-ads.html

Pew Research Center for People and Press. (2012, September 27). *In changing news landscape, even television is vulnerable.* Retrieved from http://www.people-press.org/files/legacy-pdf/2012%20News%20Consumption%20Report.pdf

Pew Research Center's Journalism Project Staff. (2010). *How news happens: A study of the news ecosystem of one American city*. Washington, D.C.: Pew Research Journalism Project. Retrieved from http://www.journalism.org/2010/01/11/how-news-happens/

Pew Research Journalism Project. (2007, March 12). *Number of U.S. daily newspapers, 5-year increments*. Retrieved June 17, 2014, from http://www.journalism.org/numbers/number-of-u-s-daily-newspapers-5-year-increments/

Pinhanez, C. (2007). A services theory approach to online service applications. In Proceedings of IEEE Services Computing Conference, Application and Industry Track (SCC'07, pp. 395-402). Salt Lake City, Utah: IEEE Computer Society. doi:10.1109/SCC.2007.19

Pinhanez, C. (2008a). A service science perspective for interfaces of online service applications. In *Proceedings of the VIII Brazilian Symposium on Human Factors in Computing Systems* (IHC '08, pp. 11-20). Sociedade Brasileira de Computação, Porto Alegre, Brazil: ACM.

Pinhanez, C. (2008b). Service systems as customer-intensive systems and its implications for service science and engineering. In *Proceedings of the Proceedings of the 41st Annual Hawaii international Conference on System Sciences* (pp. 117-126).Washington, DC, USA: IEEE Computer Society.

Plotz, D. (2014, May 29). We are in a golden age for journalism. National Post. Retrieved [originally] October 23, 2014, from https://groups.yahoo.com/neo/groups/TYR/conversations/messages/61109 Retrieved January 30, 2015, from https://groups.yahoo.com/neo/groups/TYR/conversations/messages/61109

Pollak, S., Coesemans, R., Daelemans, W., & Lavrac, N. (2011). Detecting contrast patterns in newspaper articles by combining discourse analysis and text mining. *Pragmatics*, *21*(4), 647–683. http://elanguage.net/journals/pragmatics/article/view/3660 doi:10.1075/prag.21.4.07pol

Polsson, K. (2012). *Chronology of Personal Computers*. Retrieved March 1, 2012, from http://www.islandnet.com/~kpolsson/comphist/

Pompilio, N. (2009). A Porous Wall. *American Journalism Review*, *31*(3), 32–37.

Popescu, O., & Strapparava, C. (2014). Time corpora: Epochs, opinions and changes. *Knowledge-Based Systems*. 69, 3-13. doi:10.1016/j.knosys.2014.04.029

Portigal, S. (2013). *Interviewing users*. Brooklyn, NY: Rosenfeld Media.

Press, G. (2013, May9). A very short history of big data. *Forbes*.

Price, D. J. (1961). *Science since Babylon*. New Haven, CT: Yale University Press.

Quinn, S. (2005). Convergence's fundamental question. *Journalism Studies*, *6*(1), 29–38. doi:10.1080/1461670052000328186

Rafaeli, A., & Vilnai-Yavetz, I. (2004). Instrumentality, aesthetics and symbolism of physical artifacts as triggers of emotion. *Theoretical Issues in Ergonomics Science*, *5*(1), 91–112. doi:10.1080/1463922031000086735

Reporters without Borders. (n.d.). *World press freedom index*, 2014. Retrieved October 26, 2014, from http://en.rsf.org/

Reuters Institute for the Study of Journalism. (2013). Digital news report 2013 (Research Report). Retrieved June 21, 2014, from http://www.digitalnewsreport.org/

Rider, A. F. (1944). *The scholar and the future of the research library. A problem and its solution* [Advocating the use of micro-cards.]. Middleton, CT: Hadham Press.

Riepenhoff, J. Interview by Jan Leach. Email interview. June 24, 2014.

Riepenhoff, J. Interview by Jan Leach. Phone interview. June 19, 2014.

Riepenhoff, J., & Jones, T. (2011, Sept. 15). Secrecy 101. *The Columbus Dispatch*.

Rifkin, J. (2014, March 15). The rise of anti-capitalism. *The New York Times*, pp. 1-4.

Ritter, K. (2008). Study tracks news "fatigue" among younger readers. *Editor & Publisher*, (June 2).

Robles, E. (2015). How to identify disruptive new businesses. *Review of Business & Finance Studies*, *6*(1), 121–130. http://www.theibfr.com/ARCHIVE/RBFS-V6N1-2015.pdf Retrieved June 20, 2015

Rodrigues, E. M., Milic-Frayling, N., Smith, M., Shneiderman, B., & Hansen, D. (2011). *Group-In-A-Box layout for multi-faceted analysis of communities*. Retrieved June 7, 2013, from, http://hcil.cs.umd.edu/trs/2011-24/2011-24.pdf

Rogers, E. (2003). *Diffusion of innovations*. New York: Free Press.

Rohrer, C. (2014). *When to use which user-experience research methods*. Nielsen Norman Group, 12 Oct. 2014. Retrieved November 23, 2014, from http://www.nngroup.com/articles/which-ux-research-methods/

Rosenfeld, L. (2013). Seeing the elephant: Defragmenting user research. *A List Apart*. Retrieved July 24, 2014, from http://alistapart.com/article/seeing-the-elephant-defragmenting-user-research

Rosen, J. (1999). *What are journalists for?* New Haven: Yale University Press.

Roth, S. P., Tuch, A. N., Mekler, E. D., Bargas-Avila, J. A., & Opwis, K. (2013). Location matters, especially for non-salient features–An eye-tracking study on the effects of web object placement on different types of websites. *International Journal of Human-Computer Studies*, *71*(3), 228–235. doi:10.1016/j.ijhcs.2012.09.001

Rubin, A., & Babbie, E. (1993). *Research methods for social work* (2nd ed.). Pacific Grove, CA: Brooks/Cole Publishing Company.

Russell, J. G. (2012, March 19). *Copyright & the newspaper article*. Retrieved from http://www.legalgenealogist.com/blog/2012/03/19/copyright-the-newspaper-article/

Russo, T. C., & Koesten, J. (2005, July). Prestige, centrality, and learning: A social network analysis of an online class. *Communication Education*, *54*(3), 254–261. doi:10.1080/03634520500356394

Saldaña, J. (2009). *The coding manual for qualitative researchers*. Thousand Oaks, CA: Sage.

Salzman, M. (2013, January 18). *2013: The Year fatigue set in*. Retrieved from http://www.huffingtonpost.com/marian-salzman/fatigue_b_2471860.html

Sampson, S. E., & Froehle, C. M. (2006). Foundations and implications of a proposed unified services theory. *Production and Operations Management*, *15*(2), 329–343. doi:10.1111/j.1937-5956.2006.tb00248.x

Sasseen, J., Olmstead, K., & Mitchell, A. (2013). Digital: As mobile grows rapidly, the pressures on news intensify. The State of the News Media 2013, Pew Research Foundation. Retrieved October 21, 2014, from http://stateofthemedia.org/2013/digital-as-mobile-grows-rapidly-the-pressures-on-news-intensify/#the-second-screen-phenomenon

Schiff, A. (2012, December). Big blue's "smart" marketing approach. *DM News*, *34*(12), 12.

Schlesinger, P. (1978). *Putting 'reality' together*. Beverly Hills, CA: Sage.

Schmidt, A., Ivanova, A., & Schäfer, M. S. (2013). Media attention for climate change around the world: A comparative analysis of newspaper coverage in 27 countries. *Global Environmental Change*, *23*(5), 1233–1248. doi:10.1016/j.gloenvcha.2013.07.020

Schöch, C. (2013). Big? Smart? Clean? Messy? Data in the humanities. *Journal of Digital Humanities*, *2*(3). Retrieved from http://journalofdigitalhumanities.org/2-3/big-smart-clean-messy-data-in-the-humanities/

Schramm, W. (1972). Nature of communication between humans. In W. Schramm & D. F. Roberts (Eds.), *The process and effects of mass communication* (Revised ed., pp. 8–32). Urbana, IL: University of Illinois Press.

Schudson, M. (1978). *Discovering the news: A social history of American newspapers*. New York, NY: Basic Books.

Schulz, T., & Hartzog, P. (2011). Towards a critique of the social web. Retrieved June 18, 2014, from http://os-dir.com/ml/culture.media.idc/2007-11/msg00003.html

Schwadron, T. (1996). Welcome to the Los Angeles Time Web Site. *Los Angeles Times*. Retrieved December 11, 2011, from http://web.archive.org/web/19961223123414/http://www.latimes.com/HOME/HELP/WEBSITE/message.htm

Sela, S., Kuflik, T., & Mesch, G. S. (2012). Changes in the discourse of online hate blogs: The effect of Barack Obama's election in 2008. *First Monday*, *17*(11). doi:http://dl.acm.org/citation.cfm?doid=2063576.2063755

Senatore, M. (2014, February, 20). *Eight is not enough: increasing adoption of marketing automation platforms | sirius decisions*. Retrieved February 20, 2014, from https://www.siriusdecisions.com/Blog/2014/Feb/Eight-is-NOT-Enough-Increasing-Adoption-of-Marketing-Automation-Platforms.aspx

Service Design Network. (n.d.). *What is service design?* Retrieved September 21, 2014, from http://www.service-design-network.org/intro/

Severin, W. J., & Tankard, J. W. Jr. (2001). *Communication theories* (5th ed.). New York, NY: Longman.

Seymour, T., Frantsvog, D., & Kumar, S. (2011). History of search engines. *International Journal of Management and Information Systems, 15*(4), 47–58. http://www.cluteinstitute.com/ojs/index.php/IJMIS/issue/view/662 Retrieved June 18, 2014

Sharon, T. (2012). *It's our research*. Burlington, MA: Morgan Kaufmann.

Sharp, H., Rogers, Y., & Preece, J. (2012). *Interaction design: Beyond human-computer interaction*. Hoboken, New Jersey: John Wiley & Sons, Inc.

Shaules, J. (2007). *Deep culture: The hidden challenges of global living*. Buffalo, NY: Multilingual Matters LTD.

Shaw, J. (2014, March-April). Why big data is a big deal. *Harvard Magazine*. Retrieved from http://harvard-magazine.com/2014/03/why-big-data-is-a-big-deal

Shirky, C. (2008). Newspapers and thinking the unthinkable. *Edge.com*. Retrieved February 13, 2012, from http://edge.org/conversation/newspapers-and-thinking-the-unthinkable

Shron, M. (2014). Thinking with data. Sebastopol, CA: O'Reilly Media.

Sicular, S. (2013, March 27). Gartner's big data definition consists of three parts, not to be confused with three "V"s. *Forbes*.

Siebert, F. S. (1956). *Four theories of the press: the authoritarian, libertarian, social responsibility, and soviet communist concepts of what the press should be and do*. Urbana, IL: University of Illinois Press.

Siegel, D. A. (2013). Social networks and the mass media. *The American Political Science Review, 107*(4), 786–805. doi:10.1017/S0003055413000452

Silver, N. (2011, February 12). *The economics of blogging and The Huffington Post*. Retrieved from http://fivethirtyeight.blogs.nytimes.com/2011/02/12/the-economics-of-blogging-and-the-huffington-post/

Singer, J. (2005). The political j-blogger. *Journalism, 6*(2), 173–198. doi:10.1177/1464884905051009

Singer, J. (2008). Ethnography of newsroom convergence. In C. A. Paterson & D. Domingo (Eds.), *Making online news: The ethnography of new media production* (pp. 157–170). New York, NY: Peter Lang.

Skok, D. (2012, January 27). *Aggregation is deep in journalism's DNA*. Nieman Journalism Lab.

Smit, E., & van der Graaf, M. (2011). *Journal article mining: A research study into practices, policies, plans....and promises*. Amsterdam: BF Bronfonteyn.

Smith, M. A., & Ranie, L. Himelboim, & Shneiderman (2014). Mapping Twitter topic networks: From polarized crowds to community clusters. Washington, D.C.: Pew Research Center, Feb. 20, 2014.

Sonderman, J. (2011a). New generation of Web analytics applies 'big data' to newsroom decisions. *Poynter*. Retrieved March 27, 2014, from http://www.poynter.org/latest-news/top- stories/143389/new-generation-of-web-analytics-applies-big-data-to-newsroom-decisions-visual-revenue-jumptime/

Sonderman, J. (2011b). Newsbeat debuts as robust, real-time Web analytics tool for news publishers. *Poynter*. Retrieved March 27, 2014, from http://www.poynter.org/latest-news/top- stories/140998/newsbeat-debuts-as-robust-real-time-web-analytics-tool-for-news- publishers/

Statistics, O. Data & Demographics. (n.d.).The Columbus Dispatch. Retrieved June 25, 2014. http://www.dispatch.com/content/sections/news/databases.html?cmpid=tplnnv

Stats, I. W. Usage and Population Statistics. (2014). *United States of America: Internet usage and broadband usage report*. Retrieved September 14, 2014, from http://www.internetworldstats.com/am/us.htm

Sterne, J. (2010). *Social media metrics, How to measure and optimize your marketing investment*. Hoboken, NJ: John Wiley & Sons.

Stewart, D. R. (2013). *Social media and the law, A guidebook for communication students and professionals*. New York, NY: Routledge.

Stray, J. (2010, February 24). The Google/China hacking case: How many news outlets do the original reporting on a big story? Retrieved June 16, 2014, from http://www.niemanlab.org/2010/02/the-googlechina-hacking-case-how-many-news-outlets-do-the-original-reporting-on-a-big-story/

Sullivan, D. (2009, November 24). Under the hood: Google news & ranking stories. Retrieved June 16, 2014, from http://searchengineland.com/google-news-ranking-stories-30424

Svilar, M., Chakraborty, A., & Kanioura, A. (2013). Big data analytics in marketing: From hype to real help: Finding valuable consumer insight in a stream of data. *OR/MS Today, 40*(5), 22.

Tannenbaum, P. H. (1971). The indexing process of communication. In W. Schramm & D. F. Roberts (Eds.), *The process and effects of mass communication* (revised edition, pp. 313–325). Urbana, IL: University of Illinois Press.

Tanzer, M. (2014, May 15). Exclusive: New York Times internal report painted dire digital picture. BuzzFeed. Retrieved Nov. 1, 2014 from HYPERLINK "http://www.buzzfeed.com/mylestanzer/exclusive-times-internal-report-painted-dire-digital-picture" \l ".iiy184wX2" http://www.buzzfeed.com/mylestanzer/exclusive-times-internal-report-painted-dire-digital-picture#.iiy184wX2

Tapscott, D., & Williams, A. D. (2006). *Wikinomics: How mass collaboration changes everything*. New York, NY: Portfolio.

Taylor, S. J., & Bogdan, R. (1984). *Introduction to qualitative research methods: The search for meanings*. New York: John Wiley & Sons.

The world's newspapers. (2011, June). Retrieved June 16, 2014, from http://www.oii.ox.ac.uk/vis/?id=4e3c0222

Thomas, J. (2014, March 17). Little data vs. big data: nine types of data and how they should be used. *MarketingProfs*. Retrieved 26 June 2014, from http://www.marketingprofs.com/articles/2014/24670/little-data-vs-big-data-nine-types-of-data-and-how-they-should-be-used

Thuring, M., & Mahlke, S. (2007). Usability, aesthetics and emotions in human–technology interaction. *International Journal of Psychology, 42*(4), 253–264. doi:10.1080/00207590701396674

Tien, J. (2013). Big data: Unleashing information. *Journal of Systems Science and Systems Engineering, 27*(2), 127–151. doi:10.1007/s11518-013-5219-4

Tjomsland, I. A. (1980). Where do we go from here? Digest of Papers: The Gap between MSS Products and User Requirements. In *Proceedings of Fourth IEEE Symposium on Mass Storage Systems*. IEEE.

Tofel, R. J. (2012). *Why American newspapers gave away the future*. Venice, CA: Now and Then Reader.

Tracy, S. (2013). *Qualitative research methods: Collecting evidence, crafting analysis, communicating impact*. Malden, MA: Wiley-Blackwell.

Tubbs, S. T., & Moss, S. (1983). *Human Communication* (4th ed.). New York, NY: Random House.

Urbanski, A. (2014, January 1). 4 Modern Themes in Segmentation - Direct Marketing News. *Dmnews.com*. Retrieved 26 June 2014, from http://www.dmnews.com/4-modern-themes-in-segmentation/article/326267/

User Agreement. (1996, December). The Los Angeles Times. Retrieved March 3, 2012, from https://web.archive.org/web/19970217092615/http://www.latimes.com/HOME/HELP/WEBSITE/member_agreement.htm

Usher, N. (2013). Al Jazeera English Online: Understanding Web metrics and news production when a quantified audience is not a commodified audience. *Digital Journalism*, *1*(3), 335–351. doi:10.1080/21670811.2013.801690

Vaynerchuk, G. (2013). *Jab, jab, jab, right hook, How to tell your story in a noisy social world*. New York, NY: HarperCollins.

Vu, H. T. (2013). The online audience as gatekeeper: The influence of reader metrics on news editorial selection. *Journalism*, 1–17. published online October 28, 2013

Westley, B. H., & MacLean, M. S. Jr. (1957). A conceptual model for communications research. *The Journalism Quarterly*, *34*(1), 31–28. doi:10.1177/107769905703400103

What is Salon? (n.d.). *Salon.com*. Retrieved December 17, 2010, from http://web.archive.org/web/20000903031050/http://salon.com/12nov1995/bookfront/editorial.html

Wiggins, A. (2007). Data-Driven design: Using web analytics to validate heuristics. *Bulletin of the American Society for Information Science and Technology*, *33*(5), 20–24. doi:10.1002/bult.2007.1720330508

Winchel, B. (2014, October 20). 5 things to look for in social media analytics. *PR Daily*. Retrieved October 21, 2014, from, http://www.prdaily.com/Main/Articles/17473.aspx

Woodard, P. (2008). Hymns in North American newspapers 2000-2007. *Hymn: A Journal of Congregational Song*, *59*(3), 26–38.

Words appearing in newspapers controversially. (2013, April 4). Retrieved from http://www.economist.com/blogs/johnson/2013/04/illegal-immigrants

Worth, D. (2011, June 23). CERN experiments generating one petabyte of data every second. V3.co.UK. Retrieved June 8, 2014, from http://www.v3.co.uk/v3-uk/news/2081263/cern-experiments-generating-petabyte

Wright, A. (2011, May). Web science meets network science. *Communications of the ACM*, *54*(5), 23–23. doi:10.1145/1941487.1941497

Ziegler, D. (2014). *Ethics and social media: A collision course*. Retrieved from https://zperspectiveblog.wordpress.com/2014/05/29/ethics-and-social-media-a-collision-course/

Zikopoulos, P., Eaton, C., deRoos, D., Deutsch, T., & Lapis, G. (2010). *Understanding big data*. New York, N.Y.: McGraw Hill.

Zuckerberg, M. (2010). Building the social web together (blog post). Retrieved June 19, 2014, from https://www.facebook.com/notes/facebook/building-the-social-web-together/383404517130

Zwick, D., Bonsu, S. K., & Darmody, A. (2008). Putting consumers to work: `Co-creation` and new marketing govern-mentality. *Journal of Consumer Culture*, *8*(2), 163–196. doi:10.1177/1469540508090089

About the Contributors

William Gibbs, Ph.D., is an Associate Professor at Duquesne University. He teaches courses in digital media production, multimedia technology, user experience design, human-computer interaction, and interface design. His research interests include supporting cognition with digital interfaces, usability engineering, human-computer interaction, and interface design. Gibbs has authored a number of research articles and has conducted presentations at national and international conferences. He received a Ph.D. from The Pennsylvania State University.

Joseph McKendrick is an author, independent researcher and speaker exploring innovation, information technology trends and markets. He is a contributor to *Forbes,* and analyst for *Forbes* Insights, preparing research on topics such as cloud computing, digital transformation, enterprise mobility, and big data analytics. He is also a contributor to CBS interactive, authoring the ZDNet "Service Oriented" site. McKendrick is also a regular columnist on big data and analytics topics for *Database Trends and Applications*, published by Information Today, Inc. He has also been a featured speaker at The Stevens Institute of Technology's symposium on "Competitive Advantage in the Era of Big Data," as well as ITI's "Big Data Summit." McKendrick is a co-author of the SOA Manifesto, which outlines the values and guiding principles of service orientation in business and IT. He has also been contributing editor to IT industry publications including *Midrange Systems, Enterprise Systems*, and *E-Commerce World.* McKendrick served as communications manager of the Administrative Management Society (AMS), an international professional association dedicated to advancing knowledge within the IT and business management fields, as well as editor of *Management World*, its flagship publication. He holds a B.A. in journalism from Temple University.

* * *

Robert John Baron received his PhD in Rhetoric, Scientific, and Technical Communication from the University of Minnesota-Twin Cities in 2012. He is currently an Assistant Professor of Communication Austin Peay State University in Clarksville, TN. He teaches classes in rhetoric and persuasive theory, social media, video game studies, and media literacy. His research looks at the intersection of rhetorical theory and digital technology. His past research has examined a diverse array of topics including digital architecture in online games, the development of *ethos* through online collaboration, and presidential rhetoric. His current research interests include topics such as the rhetoric of social media, social media storytelling, video game studies, and classical and contemporary rhetorical theory.

Ronan S. Bernas is Professor at the Department of Psychology of Eastern Illinois University. He instructs the Advanced Statistics and Research Methods courses for the Graduate Programs in School Psychology and Clinical Psychology, as well as the Advanced Statistics and Research Methods/Experimental Design courses in the Undergraduate Program. He received his Ph.D. in Psychology (Committee on Human Development) from The University of Chicago. While at Chicago, he also received graduate training from the Committee on Research Methodology and Quantitative Psychology and was a research assistant at the Methodology Research Center of the National Opinion Research Center (NORC).

Gregg Bernstein received his MFA in Graphic Design from the Savannah College of Art and Design, where an interest in usable design led him to his current career in product research and development. He is now Research Manager at MailChimp and leads a team of both qualitative and quantitative researchers. Prior to his work at MailChimp, Mr. Bernstein taught design, branding, and typography at Georgia State University and worked as a designer in the music and advertising industries. Mr. Bernstein also writes and speaks on the topics of design and the user experience research process for industry publications and conferences.

Debora Cheney serves as Associate Director for Public Services at the University at Albany, SUNY Libraries. She served as he Larry and Ellen Foster Communications Librarian, Head, Libraries Initiatives to the World Campus/PSU Online, and Head, The News and Microforms Library at The Pennsylvania State University Libraries. As the Larry and Ellen Foster Librarian, she worked closely with the faculty and students in Penn State's communications majors, including journalism and media studies. As the former head, of the News and Microforms Library her work focused on the challenges large academic libraries face in providing access to news content for teaching and research and the role of libraries in providing access to content that is increasingly electronic and delivered via the Internet. She has co-authored articles on teaching students how to use libraries and information in *Portal* and *Journal of Academic Librarianship* and on how libraries can provide access to converging news forms in *College and Research Libraries* and presented papers related to news content use, marketing and promotion at Newspaper Section meetings of the International Federation of Library Association) IFLA conferences in New Delhi and Kuala Lumpur, at the ALA EBSS program in Washington D.C., at the Center for Research Libraries *Global Resources Forum on Electronic Media and the Preservation of News*, and the 2011 Charleston Conference.

Mike Dillon, Ph.D., is the Chair of the Department of Journalism and Media Arts at Duquesne University. He teaches in the areas of Journalism and Mass Media. He has authored or co-authored two books and numerous scholarly articles and book chapters. Prior to his academic career, Dillon was a newspaper reporter and won 15 awards for journalistic excellence in five separate reporting and writing categories. From 2000-2003, he was Associate Editor and Chief Writer of *Primo Magazine*, a national glossy. Dillon has profiled author Norman Mailer, pop legend Tony Bennett, and iconic football star Johnny Unitas. He continues to freelance and his essays have appeared in New York Newsday, the *San Francisco Chronicle*, the *Pittsburgh Post-Gazette* and the *Dallas Morning News*. Dillon oversees publication of the Duquesne-SPJ magazine *Off the Bluff*. He's received a Duquesne University Presidential Scholarship Award and a Creative Teaching Award.

Patrick Ferrucci received his Ph.D. in journalism from the University of Missouri's School of Journalism in 2013. He is an Assistant Professor in the Department of Journalism, College of Media, Communication and Information at the University of Colorado-Boulder. His research focuses on aspects of media sociology, specifically how economics and technology influence construction of news processes. His other research interests include depictions of race in sports journalism and journalism and popular culture. His work has appeared in *Journalism: Theory, Practice and Criticism*; *Electronic News*; *Journalism History* and several other peer-reviewed journals.

Kyle Gibson is a Distribution Associate at Streetwise Media, a local news and events company based in Boston that runs websites such as BostInno. He holds a Bachelor's Degree in Marketing from Emerson College and is an active contributor and researcher for papers and articles concerning web analytics, Big Data, and SEO.

Greg Gomer is one of the cofounders of Streetwise Media, a digital media and events company that owns and operates properties across the United States. In 2012 Streetwise was acquired by American City Business Journals, a subsidiary of Advance Publications which owns Conde Nast, Reddit and other media holdings. Prior to Streetwise, Greg worked at Fidelity Investments and is a graduate of Babson College with majors in entrepreneurship and information technology.

Jeremy Harris Lipschultz is Isaacson Professor at the UNO Social Media Lab for Research and Engagement, University of Nebraska at Omaha. Lipschultz is leading a team of interdisciplinary scholars in development of social media measurement best practices at the Barbara Weitz Community Engagement Center. Lipschultz served for a decade as director of the award-winning UNO School of Communication. He is author of Social Media Communication: Concepts, Practices, Data, Law and Ethics (2015). Lipschultz also is ethics chair for PRSA Nebraska, senior fellow Center for Collaboration Science and reviews editor Journalism & Mass Communication Educator. He blogs media for the Huffington Post, contributes to ChicagoNow and writes a "New Communication Technologies" annual book chapter for Communication and the Law.

Gordon Murray, Ph.D., is an award-winning former director, editor, videographer and writer for PBS television. He has produced broadcast programs and documentaries in the U.S., Europe, Middle East and Antarctica. He is an Associate Professor in the Kent State University School of Journalism and also teaches in the School of Digital Sciences. Murray was trained as an educational psychologist and has conducted experimental research on the effects of television and media on pre-adolescent artistic performance and creativity. He has been published widely in scholarly journals and has written popular articles for a variety of national magazines and websites. Murray is a pilot and his first book, *Lost in Oscar Hotel* chronicles his peculiar world-record flight of 36 hours and 6 minutes to Dayton Wright Brothers Airport in an antique airplane. His current research interests are in digital storytelling and the public understanding of science.

Judith Durgin Pilla, PhD, LSW, PMHCNS-BC is a professional qualitative researcher and a clinical nurse specialist in private practice. For over a decade she was Director of Qualitative Research for a global marketing research company, responsible for designing and conducting healthcare-related qualitative studies worldwide. She has adapted corporate marketing research methods for use by individual clinical researchers and to support interventions in patient care. Dr. Pilla obtained her Bachelor's Degree in Nursing from Thomas Jefferson University and her Master's and Doctor of Philosophy Degrees from Bryn Mawr College.

Louis Pilla, MSEd is a director of product strategy in the healthcare publishing division of a global information company, directing the overall strategy of websites serving the information needs of clinicians. During his career, he has served in editorial and product management capacities in management, technology, and healthcare publishing, including providing content for print journals, newsletters, books and websites. He holds a Bachelor's Degree in English and Master's Degree in Education from the University of Pennsylvania.

Stuart H. Schwartz, Ph.D., is Professor of Digital Media & Communication Arts at Liberty University in Lynchburg, Virginia. His major teaching areas include direct, mobile & interactive marketing, and social media strategies and effects. He is the winner of a 2012 Chancellor's Award for Teaching Excellence and is the author of the textbook, "The Savvy Social Media Guide: Succeed With Social Media...NOW!" He came to the school after a 30-year career, 25 as a senior executive with media and retail organizations. Companies where he headed divisions include Lee Enterprises, which owned daily newspaper, broadcast and specialty publications, and apparel merchandiser Steve Madden. He was also head of business development for a 150-store retail music chain. In addition, he has been a frequent contributor to American Thinker (americanthinker.com), the popular conservative political website, and guest on conservative talk radio, including The Dennis Miller Show and is a columnist for Beliefnet.com. He received a B.A. from University of Connecticut, M.A. in Corporate & Political Communication from Fairfield University, and the Ph.D. in Media & Communications from Temple University. In addition, he holds an M.A. from Liberty Baptist Theological Seminary.

Tricia Syed has more than 20 years of direct marketing, publishing, online and event experience. She is a seasoned marketing professional focused on user marketing strategy. Syed joined Penton as Senior Director, Marketing and Analytics. In 2013, she was promoted to Vice President, User Marketing & Marketing Analytics where she is responsible for user marketing, analytics, acquisition and engagement. Syed joined UBM's Everything Channel as Vice President, Online Marketing and Analytics where she was responsible for engaging Solution Providers through media, events and research, extending its database and creating innovative opportunities through audience analysis. Earlier, Syed was with TechTarget Inc. where she held several senior management positions in audience development, online and events, including Vice President of Audience Optimization. Prior, Syed was Marketing Manager at BizLand, Inc. Syed earned a BA from the University of Rochester and a MA from Northeastern University.

Edson C. Tandoc received his Ph.D. in journalism from the University of Missouri's School of Journalism in 2013. Since January of 2014, he has been an assistant professor of journalism in Nanyang Technological University's Division of Journalism and Publishing. His research focuses on the sociology of message construction. He has conducted studies on the construction of news and social media messages. His studies about influences on journalists have focused on the impact of journalistic roles and audience feedback on the various stages of the news gatekeeping process. His work has appeared in *Digital Journalism*, *Journalism Studies*, *New Media & Society* and several other peer-reviewed journals.

Laurissa Wolfram-Hvass received her PhD in English Rhetoric and Composition from Georgia State University in 2014. Her academic research focused on the User Experience (UX) research and design process and how UX research teams communicate findings within their organizations. Upon the completion of her dissertation, Dr. Wolfram-Hvass was hired as a researcher at MailChimp, an email marketing service provider. Dr. Wolfram-Hvass previously taught first year composition and technical communication at Georgia State University and was the layout and design editor for the *South Atlantic Review.*

Lady Dhyana Ziegler, DCJ, Ph.D. is the Garth C. Reeves Eminent Scholar Chair of Excellence in the School of Journalism and Graphic Communication at Florida A&M University. She holds a B.S. in Journalism from Baruch College, Masters in Radio and Television and Ph.D. in Academic Administration from Southern Illinois University, and an MLE Certificate from Harvard University. She's held several administrative positions and has worked in higher education for more than 25 years. Dr. Ziegler is a Governor's Appointee and current Chair of the Florida Virtual School Board of Trustees. She is the author of three books, book chapters, scholarly publications, and has presented at more than 100 national and international conferences. She is a Fulbright-Hays Scholar and has received numerous honors for her contributions including being knighted as a Dame in England. Her research interests are in the areas of big data, digital media, ethics, and communications technology.

Index

G

H

I

L

M

N

O

P

Q

R

S

T

U

V

W

Z

www.ingramcontent.com/pod-product-compliance
Lightning Source LLC
LaVergne TN
LVHW060422300926
849162LV00006B/1498